Messengers

Other books by Patricia Treece
A Man for Others
Nothing Short of a Miracle
The Sanctified Body

Messengers

After-Death Appearances
of Saints and Mystics

PATRICIA TREECE

Our Sunday Visitor Publishing Division
Our Sunday Visitor, Inc.
Huntington, Indiana 46750

Our Sunday Visitor Publishing Division
Our Sunday Visitor, Inc.
200 Noll Plaza
Huntington, IN 46750

International Standard Book Number: 0-87973-709-3
Library of Congress Catalog Card Number: 95-68834

Cover and jacket design by Monica Watts

PRINTED IN THE UNITED STATES OF AMERICA

709

This book is an act of Thanksgiving to
DIVINE MERCY
which hovers over every anecdote
in these pages

And an offering on behalf of my
children and godchildren:
Christopher, Katherine
Joscelyn, Gilien, Candice
Sabine, Elizabeth
Heather, Brina
& Julianna
Katherine Patricia

Upon them, as upon readers and writer, I ask
the blessing of St. Francis' good comrade St. Clare:
May Almighty God Bless Us
May He Look upon Us with the Eyes of His Mercy
May He Pour forth His Graces upon us Abundantly
And in Heaven, May He Place Us Among His Saints.

TABLE OF CONTENTS

ACKNOWLEDGMENTS

During many years of research on this book, I have received the help of innumerable archivists, members of religious orders, journalists, Postulators, personnel at shrines and other centers of devotion to particular saints, as well as individuals who believe they are alive, cured, or perhaps simply better people because God sent them a message carried by a dead saint.

Because I called on you so many times or asked for so much, I must mention several people by name: my deep gratitude to Mother Marie Lucile of the Lisieux (France) Carmel; Father Charles Fehrenbach, C.SS.R. of St. John Neumann's Shrine in Philadelphia; Father Joseph Pius Martin, O.F.M. Cap. of San Giovanni Rotondo (Italy); Sufi adherent, writer Susan Fine of Rochester, Michigan; Angela Boudreaux and Father Joseph Elworthy, C.SS.R. of the Seelos Center in New Orleans, and Dr. Yaffa Eliach, founding Director of the Center for Holocaust Studies and professor in the Department of Judaic Studies at Brooklyn College.

Trying to list all the others to whom I am indebted, I fear, will simply end in the embarrassment of leaving out one or more people who assisted me in important ways. If you helped in any way with this project, please be assured of my gratitude.

I also wish to thank those who read parts of the manuscript — or all of it — for style, clarity, or to verify accuracy. Included are many of you whose stories are in these pages, as well as Rolf Gompertz, Judith Hodgins, Cathy Schneir, and Katherine and Christopher Sariego. My editors, Jacquelyn M. Lindsey and Cathy A. Dee, also deserve a round of applause for all their hard work.

Finally, I thank the friends — living and dead — who have prayed for this book. If it is of value to anyone, I know whom to credit.

PROLOGUE

Turin, Italy   *The night of July 22, 1907*

Twenty-eight-year-old Sister Teresa Valse-Pantellini lies awake, coarse linen sheets clinging limply to her modest nightdress. Without losing her peace of spirit, through the tedious hours she struggles to breathe under the weight of the hot, humid air pressing on her TB-riddled lungs. Slowly the noises of the city die away until the only sounds in the dark infirmary sickroom are her raspy breathing and the occasional whine of a mosquito entering by the open, screenless window.

Very late, the infirmarian looks in. Cautioned against talking because it brings on hemorrhages, Teresa smiles and nods she is okay and needs nothing.

Closing the door, the infirmarian sighs as she pads down the hall on tired feet. She finds it hard to see someone die this young — even Sister Teresa who *longs* to be with God.

Alone again in the dark, do Teresa's eyes close for a moment? Later, she will not be sure. But they open when her dark sickroom is lit by a bright light. In it Teresa sees a man. She has never met John Bosco, the holy co-founder of her order,[1] who died when she was ten. But from the many photographs of Don Bosco[2] in circulation, she recognizes the saint at once.

Rather short, he appears the same athletically well-built priest who outran and outplayed several thousand slum boys until his lungs, too, gave out. There is also no mistaking Bosco's square, firm-jawed face with its handsome features lavishly topped with dark curls. Nor his irresistibly warm smile.

The only change, in fact, from his photographs, Teresa later explains, is that somehow — while unmistakably Don Bosco — he looks "younger" and "more beautiful" now that life's cares have been lifted from those powerful shoulders.

Looking at her with fatherly compassion, Bosco — who joked that someone should get him a bellows when his own lungs went[3] — steps out of the light and approaches the dying, tubercular sister.

"Wait, Don Bosco!" Boldly, Sister Teresa sits up in bed and puts out a cautioning hand. Seemingly unawed by the dead saint's arrival in her sickroom, she exclaims hurriedly, "I'm not the one asking for a cure. It's Sister Giovanna."

"The next room," she adds, pointing the way to God's messenger, as if he is some lost delivery boy.

Don Bosco stops. He grins at her; she later admits that. But we cannot expect any more from a woman whose secret motto is "to pass unnoticed." In fact, behaving just like the authentic saint she is reputed to be, Sister Teresa makes public *nothing* about what she and her dead visitor say to each other.

We don't even know how *long* they communicate. What is known is that at some point Don Bosco strolls out Sister Teresa's door and into the next room of the infirmary. The sick woman lying there, half-awake and miserable in the hot night, is Sister Giovanna Lenci. Seriously ill for years, she has been a resident of the infirmary much longer than Teresa. But unlike Teresa, Giovanna dreams not of heaven, but of health.

In fact, she is just finishing her third consecutive novena,[4] asking Don Bosco's prayers for her recovery. As the dead priest is about to be named "Venerable" — that is, one determined by his Church to have practiced virtue at heroic levels — the sister has hopes God will work a miracle in the saint's honor. After all, once a Catholic is named "Venerable," the road to beatification and canonization rests on God speaking through miracles. Giovanna wants to be one of Bosco's.

The saint does not stay with her long. As he leaves, the nun springs out of bed with a leap of joy and rouses the house with her cries, "I've seen Don Bosco and I'm cured!" Puzzled medical men later verify the instantaneous return to health.

Does it last? It does indeed. It will be over thirty productive years before Sister Giovanna sees heaven.

That this miracle of God has been visibly hand-carried, so to speak, by a dead saint is corroborated when Sister Teresa — whose good sense and rectitude they know — confesses she saw Don Bosco, too. Of course, when she admits — does the infirmarian groan? — that, longing for paradise, she forestalled any attempt to cure *her*, belief in Teresa's good sense wavers in some. Not even every nun is *that* otherworldly. And then, some chuckle, Teresa's cure would have provided such a bang-up double miracle to add to their celebration when — only two days after Bosco's Turin visit — his "Venerable" title becomes official.

Has Teresa extracted from her dead visitor precisely when her longing for heaven will be satisfied? Probably. For just over a month later, the sister in the late stages of tuberculosis sets her watch ahead for 7:00 A.M. without winding it. Asked to send a message about her condition to her family, she answers, "Let's wait 'til tomorrow."

At precisely 7:00 A.M. the next day, September 3, 1907, Teresa dies peacefully, letting slip that Don Bosco — accompanying Jesus and His mother — is there again waiting for her. This time the visitors are seen only by Sister Teresa. But those around her bed see something of their glory in her luminous face.

The Master of the Universe plays love games with his saints. In this case God has snuck up on Teresa Valse-Pantellini even as the quiet nun believed she held off a miracle cure.

Obviously God knew in advance what Teresa's response would be. But Don Bosco was sent to her as well as to Sister Giovanna anyway.

Think about it a moment. Knowing her motto, Teresa undoubtedly revealed she saw Don Bosco in July only to buttress Sister Giovanna's claim. But by Bosco's admitted visit to Teresa — which, you note, is so nicely validated as neither "a hallucination" nor "fever dream" by Sister Giovanna's cure and testimony — the Cause of Teresa Valse-Pantellini for official sainthood, introduced in 1926, got an incalculable boost. Put simply, by sending a dead saint to chat with her, heaven called attention to Teresa, thereby nicely forestalling the young nun's desire to "pass unnoticed"!

ENDNOTES

1 The Daughters of Mary Help of Christians (commonly called the Salesian Sisters).

2 Don is the Italian title for a priest.

3 He died of emphysema caused by returning to work too soon after almost dying of some lung complaint — probably bronchitis — in those preantibiotic days.

4 Prayer for some particular request said for nine days. Novenas (from the Latin word for nine) take many forms and may be addressed to God directly or request the prayers of a saint.

1 ❧ It's Going On All the Time

S aint John Bosco appeared to two nuns after his death in two different rooms of an infirmary in 1907. Saints are also making after-
death appearances *now* — that is, in whatever year you pick up this
book. Nor are such appearances something new. Witnesses who spied on
St. Francis of Assisi during prayer more than once saw dead saints — among
them Peter, Paul, and John — speaking to him.[1] After-death appearances of
the holy in western tradition go back, in fact, to the beginning of Christianity and beyond into Judaism. It was, after all, two dead, holy, Jewish men
who appeared to Jesus on the Mount of Transfiguration.

All spiritual traditions make a place for important appearances of the
dead. Several chapters of this book will look at after-death appearances by
non-Christian friends of God to people in their traditions. If nothing else,
this will show the idea of the dead returning to do God's work is not some
weird Catholic notion, but a universal belief.

As for Christianity, as Paul says in the Bible, it is nothing — a gyp and a
fraud — if Jesus Christ did not rise from the dead in His scourged, crucified
body and appear to His disciples. No one has made more visits to the human family after his earthly life than the Savior. These, too, are always
occurring.

I think of the little girl from Prestonville, Kentucky mentioned in *Exten-
sion Magazine*[2] the summer I write this. Diagnosed with liver cancer and
given six months to live, Mary Ann chatted with Father Joseph Muench,
who visited the little Protestant in the hospital before she became a member
of his St. Martha's Catholic parish. Asked by Father if she prayed, the six-
year-old replied, "If I didn't pray everyday, I wouldn't make it." Then she
added, "I like it best when Jesus comes into the room, sits on the bed, and
tells me what to say." Was the kid hallucinating? I don't know. But maybe
Jesus did tell her "what to say," for the article reports her terminal cancer is
inexplicably gone.

Lakota tribe member Harry Blue Feather won the 1992 Lumen Christi award for his evangelization work as a catechist. In the 1930s, Harry was a rough, tough, young guy "in trouble all the time." His life changed after Jesus appeared to him, bound and wearing the crown of thorns.

These folks aren't sophisticated enough for you? Distinguished novelist Reynolds Price teaches at Duke University, where he graduated *summa cum laude*. The former Rhodes scholar, fighting a life-and-death battle with a spinal tumor in 1984, had a mystical experience in which he found himself somehow at Lake Kinnereth in Israel with Jesus. Jesus forgave his sins and when Price asked, "Am I also cured?" the Savior said, "That too." Against all odds, Reynolds Price survived.

Yes, Jesus Christ is still personally appearing — to all kinds of people — to change destinies. But, just as long ago in Galilee the Master sent others out to preach, teach, and heal in His name, the Lord still sends His closest friends as His messengers. This book is about them: The people called saints.

What do I mean by "saint"? I mean the people like John Bosco who reach the heights of human development. "Whole" men and women[3] whose lives as much as their lips can say, with the writer of Romans: "... whether we live or die, we are the Lord's."

Of course all in heaven, whether they achieved the purity during life to walk right in or entered following some after-death work, are legitimately called saints. But heaven is not a democracy where all souls are equal. To explain let me borrow an illustration given St. Therese of Lisieux as a little girl. Told people in heaven have different degrees of glory and joy, tender-hearted Therese felt bad. Her wise older sister got two glasses, one big, one tiny. Into each she poured water to the rim.

"See," she said, "they each have all they can hold."

In this book we are going to look at the big-glass folks, those who hold the maximum love and goodness. We will do this for the simple reason that when God uses human messengers, it seems to be His good pleasure to entrust the spectacular cures, the radical conversions, and the most beautiful gifts to their hands.

A second distinction: This book is only about *purposeful* apparitions, never sightings — even if they involve saints — originating, it appears, in psychic sensitivity. Hand a relic to someone sensitive in this way, and they might sense or even see the saint. The dead, in such an instance, are not messengers nor even present as we normally understand the idea. Instead the viewer somehow tunes in the past. St. Maximilian Kolbe, who did not have the gift himself, theorized the past is "out there" and that with the right technology one might see Jesus as he walked the dusty roads of Galilee. Maybe, but if that happens it won't be an after-death appearance!

Let twentieth-century Catholic Caryll Houselander illustrate. A mystic who had genuine supernatural experiences, the Englishwoman was also a natural psychic[4] who could hold a piece of folded paper, handwriting hidden, and give accurate information about the writer. Perhaps because of her great sensitivity to others' sufferings, Caryll once had an experience of the type I mean. Glancing as she passed into an upstairs room of the English country house where she was visiting, the writer-therapist-artist glimpsed a little girl leaning against a doll house. Face ashen, darkly-circled eyes shut in concentration, the child's spindly body sighed with exhaustion as she struggled to pull off her boots. Mentioning the youngster downstairs, Caryll learned she'd seen a child found dead from undetected diabetes years earlier in that room. This was not a "haunted nursery," nor was the child a messenger of God, for she took no note of her observer. Caryll had somehow simply tuned into the past.

Another distinction may be useful. This is the gulf between a *purposeful* visit by either a saint or a non-holy person, and the traditional ghost. The slain, the slayer, the mad, the lovelorn, the crazed suicide — with a few gentler spirits, the gallery of so-called ghosts is filled with troubled souls attached to sites where they played a morbid role. Pathetic figures generally, the ghost is a self-centered phenomenon. Real or imaginary, the spectre signals human unwillingness to break away from past misfortune — some would say sin — and move on. Thus you understand why saints do not "haunt" places: remorse, despair, the desire for revenge and/or refusal to forgive; unrenounced, unrequited (thus possessive) love — all the traditional emotions associated with ghosts are long jettisoned by the holy. At death the saint, unfettered by such chains, simply flies to God. So do not consider dead saints as ghosts, please!

One other word before we begin. Whenever a Catholic writes about saints, the question always comes up: what about apparitions of the Virgin Mary? Having studied many reports, I believe that, after Jesus, no one gets around like His mother. The visits of the woman the Bible quotes as saying prophetically, "all generations will call me blessed" are extremely frequent in the nineteenth and twentieth centuries, both to groups and to individuals. The topic can fill a book of its own.[5] So expect in these pages only an occasional reference to Jesus' mother. Fortunately I can sum up her appearances for you. Today, as at Cana, her message is, "Do as my Son tells you."

To appreciate the after-death appearances of saints — which are both the same and yet differ strikingly from other after-death appearances — we need to look first at after-death appearances in general. Occurring to those who describe themselves as "not religious" or "rationalists," as well as to people of all creeds, they are as likely to be experienced by those who would never think of such things as those who do. Mostly, people keep mum about such an experience. But one woman I barely know (she worked in my pediatrician's office), learned I take after-death appearances seriously. She eagerly shared with me how her dead father appeared in a dream one night to warn her that her mother would die suddenly — and soon.

"Of all my children, you understand this the least," he worried aloud. This totally unexpected dream, says my informant, made the shock of her mother's sudden death bearable.

I can also add two experiences of people I do know, thus whose stability and honesty I can vouch for. Lutheran professional woman and homemaker Eva Engholm — a true mystic — was one of my mentors and closest friends until her early death a few years ago. Eva was left a young widow with four children when her businessman husband died in the crash of a commercial airliner near San Diego. A down-to-earth woman who loved cooking and gardening, Eva confided in me how much it helped her cope when her dead husband appeared to her, consoling, "It was my time. Don't feel bad."

Designer Nancy Parker of Pasadena, the talented, vivacious wife of my husband's lifelong friend, was once worried to the point of being physically ill over a teenage daughter's serious troubles. Having returned to school, one noontime Nancy was perched on her bed trying to tackle some home-work. As she fought to keep her mind off her child, Nancy looked up, and there was her dead dad standing at the end of the bed. He gave his dis-traught daughter the strength to go on by assuring her everything would turn out okay — which it did.[6] Raised a Methodist, Nancy had followed Christian Science for ten years, but at the time her father brought the mes-sage of hope, she had dropped away completely from any formal church affiliations.

Not everyone agrees with the politics of Jesuit peace-activist Daniel Berrigan. But his honesty has never been questioned. In his autobiogra-phy,[7] Berrigan reports that his troubled father appeared after death to Dan's niece in Minnesota, who was due to make her first communion. Her dead grandpa came only to ask the little girl for prayers, but the sudden sight of him so unnerved her that she screamed and fainted. The child's mother, who came running at the scream, attested again to the incident on her own deathbed.

In the late 1870s Father Arnold Damen, another Jesuit, founded Holy Family Church in Chicago. Those who visit the old church, which stands on Roosevelt Road near the University of Illinois' Circle Campus, sometimes notice two unusual statues in the chancel area of the high altar — altar boys facing each other. Father Arnold had them put there after he was summoned one snowy night by two boys who took him to their dying mother so she could receive the last rites.[8] The woman welcomed the priest but wondered who sent him. When he told her, she told *him* that her sons — altar boys at Holy Family long ago — were both dead.

Are such things rare? In one sense, yes. With millions of people in the world, the full experience of *seeing the dead* is not something that happens to most of us. It certainly never has to me. On the other hand, many of those with whom I share deeply have had or know someone who has had — if not such a dramatic experience — at least something of a lesser degree. Feeling the unseen *presence* of a beloved dead person, for instance, is fairly common.

If you think — dramatic or otherwise — all this has to be imaginary, Episcopalian priest-author Morton T. Kelsey cautions that those "who believe we live confined in a completely rational and understandable world where nothing unusual ever happens … simply haven't lived very deeply." Kelsey, who has done a lot of counseling, speaks of the "amazing experiences" people tell when, masks down, they speak from "the depth of their being."[9]

In many after-death appearances, like some of those mentioned, the dead help people deal with a loved one's death or bring help for the dying. Even more common, is for those who are dying or will die soon to see dead loved ones. To again mention something I have personal knowledge of, I recall a charming German-Swiss lady, mother of my onetime college exchange-student roommate, and later my hostess in Zurich. A few days before the unexpected death of Mrs. Koch, she confided in my roommate's older sister, Elizabeth, that in "a dream of light and beauty" she had seen her own mother "coming and wanting to take her with her." Mrs. Koch said to Elizabeth that she felt eager for the reunion, but told her mother "to wait a little, until she had arranged all her affairs." A few days later, having made some last arrangements, Mrs. Koch was found dead of a heart attack. My nominally-Protestant former roommate is solidly earthbound and not "religious" but she told me how much her mother's experience comforted her.

French Catholic philosopher Jacques Maritain, who taught at Princeton University, will be known to most readers as not only a confirmed Christian but a man of intellectual acumen, not associated with anything bogus or superstitious in spirituality. Jacques Maritain's sister-in-law Vera lived for many years with Maritain and his wife, running their house for them. After Vera was diagnosed with cancer, Maritain reports her "dream or vision" on April 10, 1959. In it her father approached her, "radiant with youth and with light." When she asked him, he said he had not come to take her "yet." That December, Vera died quietly at the Maritains' home, her last intelligible word "papa."

Well-authenticated also are occasions where the dead "visit" the living before it is known the visitor is, in fact, dead. A later chapter will be devoted to such incidents among recent saints. But to show that this happens in the wider sphere, let me turn to Rabbi Herbert Weiner of Temple Sharey Tefilo-Israel in South Orange, New Jersey. The rabbi tells in his book *9 1/2 Mystics* of personally studying with a Kabbalist (an expert in Jewish mysticism) named Setzer.

Setzer, who lived on East Broadway in lower Manhattan, described himself as "a rationalist" but told his student he had to accept the following anyway because he *experienced* it. Quoting Setzer:

> I had two sisters. One of them … became seriously ill. One day I was sitting alone in my room and suddenly … I am a rationalist, but still, it happened … I saw something dressed in black and it was my sister. She came close to me and kissed me, then suddenly dropped away. Then I heard a voice close by, whispering clearly in my ear, "Your sister died, your sister died." The whole next day I heard music, beautiful music … so loud and clear that I was sure it was a radio or something which the neighbors also heard, but I found out that they didn't. Then I got a telegram telling me that my sister had died. I figured out the time and hour, and it was the exact moment when I heard the whispering.

Such experiences draw on the reality Catholics like myself call the Communion of Saints. Don't be misled by the word "saint." The reality is much more inclusive, referring to the supportive interconnectedness of not just the holy or even Christians, but of all those on earth and beyond who do not opt out of friendship with God — "beyond" including the blessed in heaven and those still undergoing growth and purification after death in preparation for heaven, a state we Catholics call purgatory.

When trying to explain this interconnectedness as it operates on earth,

I'm reminded of an experience of a woman named Anne S. Watson.[10] Watson tells of a woman named Helen Hayden "who carried such a burden of (neurotic) guilt she seemed almost to apologize for being alive." Diagnosed with cancer, Helen lay in the hospital one morning waiting to be taken into surgery, while in another city Anne and a prayer partner knelt in a church by the altar rail. As they prayed, they received an image of Helen "desperately trying to lift an enormous stone from her chest." So they used imaging to see Jesus help her. (Note this was not a vision but an exercise of their imagination, a meditation technique taught by St. Ignatius Loyola among others.) By imagination, they saw the Savior smile down at Helen, lifting the stone off her chest while saying, "This is too heavy for you; let me take it."

Helen at that time actually felt "utterly squashed," too depressed to even pray. When a hospital chaplain came in with communion, Helen protested with her usual outlook, "But I'm not worthy to receive it."

The chaplain sat down on her bed. Taking Helen's hand, he explained that "the worst sin is to believe you are the worst sinner." He urged her to accept forgiveness, "not to be freed of responsibility" for her actions but to stop dragging this unhealthy guilt with her.

"Suddenly," Helen later told Anne, "I felt as if a great stone had been lifted from my chest." As she received the communion, she knew that she was a member of the "blessed company of all faithful people."

Or, as Catholic Cindy Cavnar puts it, "we are never alone and our prayers and sacrifices for one another do bear fruit." Anne Watson didn't have to be in the same city when she prayed for Helen Hayden, for distance is no barrier to our connection in the Communion of Saints. Neither, this book will offer ample evidence, is time or state of being. Ironically, since Christianity rests on Christ's return after death, some Christians deny there can be contact between the living and the dead, citing the story of Lazarus (Luke 16:19-31). Read the story if you have such concerns. I think you'll see two things: 1) The abyss which cannot be crossed is not between life and death but between two conditions after death: those who are with God, like Lazarus, and those, like the dead rich man, "in torment" (probably purgatory since he cares about his five living brothers, whereas those in the state we call hell care for no one. 2) Asked by the dead rich man to send Lazarus back from heaven to warn the rich man's brothers to change their ways, Abraham replies, "If they do not listen to Moses and the prophets, they will not be persuaded even if one should rise from the dead." That is an evaluation of the state of soul of five particular people, who have hardened their hearts against God and others. Abraham does not say "no one" would benefit from a visit by the dead. Or that the dead are not permitted to return. Christ who tells the parable will soon be both "risen from the dead" and visiting his living followers. As the Savior and His saints down the centuries demonstrate, if we are deep enough in God, as Cavnar says, "we are at one another's disposal — both in life and in death."

In this great interconnectedness of all people of good will, the veil between this life and the next, *for those with eyes to see*, can be very thin. And rent sometimes on deathbeds. I think of the dying mystical poet William Blake who — with shining face and brightened eyes — "burst out singing of the things he saw in Heaven."[11]

Then there is the testimony of a child. Daisy Dryden was the daughter of Reverend David Anderson Dryden, a Methodist Episcopal minister who became head of the women's department of Santa Clara College, today known as Pacific University.

Daisy was one of those children who have great faith. When she was only five, her mother was so ill it was thought she would die. Finding her father weeping, Daisy told him not to worry: she would ask the Lord and he would surely make her mother well. From that hour the mother began to recover, causing Reverend Dryden to remark he could hardly claim to be a Christian when he saw the faith of his child.

When Daisy was around ten, she herself became ill with typhoid. Recovering nicely, one day she told her father, who was struck by her expression of pleasure and amazement, that she saw Jesus and that He said she was going to heaven. Her condition suddenly deteriorating, during the last three peace-filled days of her life, Daisy saw clearly into the next world.[12]

Before Daisy's death, which occurred on the day and hour she foretold, a visitor remarked, "Well, Daisy, you will soon be over the dark river." After the visitor left, the dying girl commented to her father, "It is all a mistake; there is no river; there is no curtain; there is not even a line that separates this life from the other life."

If for most of us the veil between this life and the hereafter does not lift so readily, for certain people (not all) who live close to God that veil is often breached during their earthly existence. Mystic visionary Adrienne von Speyr, for one, was told during a supernatural visitation when young that she would "live in both worlds at once." Her confessor, theologian Hans Urs von Balthasar, testified that the Swiss physician, wife of a University of Basel professor, frequently interacted with the dead — saints and others — until her death at age sixty-five in 1967.

Readers familiar with Franciscan stigmatic Padre Pio, who died in 1968, know he was visited by Jesus, the Virgin Mary, and various saints. Legions of dead who still had spiritual work to do also came to ask his prayers[13] — the Italian priest remarking in all seriousness that there were more (invisible) dead than living at his crowded daily mass.

The ordinary dead — as distinguished from the holy — are at times permitted or sent by God to reach out to those with whom they have a connection, almost always loved ones. Besides examples previously mentioned, such as my friend Eva's husband, there are even first-person testimonies of Holocaust survivors where after-death appearances of family members, usually in dreams, helped children and grandchildren survive death camps.[14]

Catholics are among those who believe growth into wholeness continues after death for non-saints who don't (in the full knowledge possible for many *only* after death) utterly reject God. While not specifically a Catholic doctrine, there seems evidence that, in rare instances, individuals who "didn't get it right" in life are sometimes allowed to return — after such a growth period — to patch up a mess. Witness the experience of Kat Carrol, who as of 1993, had been teaching interpersonal communications at the college level for ten years. She writes:[15]

> My mother was a gentle, loving woman who lived a submissive life in a dysfunctional marriage. Unfortunately, she allowed her kind, passive approach ... to affect the way she dealt with health issues. After two decades of medical treatments, which included several surgeries and countless numbers of drug therapies, my mother found herself physically addicted to prescription drugs, as well as pain shots she received almost daily in the emergency room of our local hospital. She was thoroughly convinced that she was helplessly and hopelessly ill.

With several "major body organs" failing, her doctors decided her problems were psychosomatic. They refused to give her any more pain shots and withdrew from her case. In pain and despair one day from being denied help in the emergency room, the desperate woman drove home and shot herself in the heart. It was her daughter's nineteenth birthday. Kat writes:

> ... Sixteen years later ... I was (still) not healed of my *own* wounds over my mother's death. I could feel the hole in my heart....

To release the pain, Kat was in the middle of a meditation on forgiveness when she says:

> I felt a gentle presence surround me, carefully lift me, and place me in what I perceived to be a "cradle of light." A permeating wave of energy moved through my body and my entire heart space began to swell and pulsate. I felt unconditionally loved and whole. I wept with gratitude, for I knew this light was an infinite part of my connection to God. With my inner eye, I looked up to thank the presence who had led me there, and I found myself gazing into the smiling face of my mother.

While by far the greatest majority of after-death visitations of non-saints are like this one, to someone known and loved while alive, some souls — I postulate those who have moved farther from ego concerns during life — appear to those with whom they have slighter ties.

An outstanding example — because it happened to a woman many of us regard as a saint and took place in broad daylight — is an experience of English writer-artist-and therapist Caryll Houselander during the tense days in 1939 before World War II. Wide awake, Caryll saw her dead family doctor plop down next to her on a London bus. Chatting matter-of-factly about the family's health, he referred to things *only* this doctor knew. Then he spoke of the coming conflict and what it would bring before hopping off with the remark "I won't vanish; people have enough to contend with." His appearance, Caryll said, made it possible for her to face the war.

Saints may be involved in all the types of after-death appearances sketched so far in this chapter. Thus, although this is probably rarer than with non-saints, they at times appear to family members. Dead St. Maria Goretti, for example, saved her niece from lightning. And St. Therese of Lisieux appeared to various family members. Much more often than the non-holy, saints appear, like the doctor to Caryll, to those with whom they were not intimate but had some earthly connection. St. Maximilian Kolbe, for instance, apparently appeared during this decade to Francis Gajowniczek, a former Polish army Sergeant. Father Kolbe died in 1941 in Auschwitz, voluntarily taking the place of Gajowniczek when the father of two cried out for his wife and children as he was randomly marked for execution.

Like Kolbe laying down his life for an almost total stranger, in loving

God to the degree they do saints are connected to *all* people. Thus looking at the overall phenomena of after-death appearances, one finds a spectrum ranging from the self-absorbed dead (like those who come solely to request prayers for themselves) to the unselfish dead caring for loved ones (like the boys God permitted to get a priest for their dying mother), all the way to the dead saint — the individual at the acme of human development — who loves *all* in and for God. Like angels, dead saints are spiritually equipped to serve as pure, loving messengers to whomever God sends them. So in addition to the appearances mentioned above, saints may appear to: 1) people they never knew; 2) people who never heard of them; or, 3) those from whom they are separated by the widest barriers of culture, centuries, and — of course — death.

Thus Benedictine Sister Geralyn Spaulding told me about a friend of hers (no name because he shuns publicity). This young member of the Benedictine community in Pecos, New Mexico, saw dead St. Frances of Rome who offered advice on what the monastery should do regarding a certain difficulty. Although he is an American male celibate and St. Frances was an Italian wife and mother most of her life, the dead woman and the young man she visited *are* linked by the fact that, in her final earthly years, widowed Frances became a Benedictine. Still, she has been dead since March 9, 1440 — more than five hundred fifty years!

About here I expect a number of people to say, hey, wait a minute: how do we know this isn't a book about people's hallucinations of dead saints? After all, people's minds are capable of strange things, like the person reported in my daily paper as saying she was comforted by a living rock star during what she calls a near-death experience. Such bizarre incidents are fodder for those who insist after-death appearances and near-death experiences are purely interior events, defense mechanisms triggered in the brain in time of severe stress.

Guidance in such visions — say, where a saint appears to a combat soldier and instructs "Move!" just before the shell hits where he was standing — would come, in this view, from the hallucinator's unconscious intuitions and wisdom. Physical cures, like that of Sister Giovanna in the prologue, would be explained as the immune system's response to the hope stimulated by the hallucination.

Let's agree that some people *have* hallucinated a dead saint's appearance. This "event," creating expectation of a miracle, could then jolt the immune system as if by a massive electrical shock and set up biochemical responses that could indeed lead to "impossible" cures. If this is the way it works, we can only hope lots of people with terminal illnesses become hallucinators!

However, while I wish to follow ration as long as it can sustain the burden of evidence, there are a few problems with the theory that after-death appearances are all in the head. First after-death experiences differ from near-death experiences. Speaking of near-death experiences on American television, British professor Dr. Susan Blackmore spoke of the lack of oxygen and/or mind chemicals called endorphins producing visions and out-of-body experiences. But unlike near-death experiences, after-death appearances almost never occur when someone is suffering from lack of oxygen. As for the presence or absence of endorphins (secreted by the brain in certain emotional states) after-death experiences occur to people in the whole gamut of moods from the most banal to the most dramatic.

And there are other problems when one considers individual cases: take the two women in separate rooms in the infirmary. If they hallucinated, each did it without knowing the other was so engaged, and they didn't even do it at the same time but consecutively. Consider also the very young child with cancer, which takes a sudden turn for the better, who begins asking for someone the family has never heard of. Later the family discovers a friend has been asking for the prayers of a dead holy person by the unknown name.

OSV file photo

Then there is the recent Montana case involving Blessed Katharine Drexel (1858-1955). Withholding names because these people don't want to be harrassed, let me just sum it up by saying a non-Catholic young mother was with her very ill baby, born with an "incurable" syndrome, in the hospital late one evening when a nun came into the room, introducing herself as "Sister Kate." The nun reassured the mother about the child, made the sign of the cross on the baby's fore-

Blessed Katharine Drexel

head, then vanished. No one around the hospital had seen or knew of a nun in that particular habit. When the young mother confided in her Catholic mother-in-law over the phone about the eerie experience, they were both awed to learn that the mother-in-law was invoking the prayers of Mother Katharine, a dead American heiress turned nun who used her fortune to aid those least apt to get a piece of the American dream — African and Native Americans. Until her death at age ninety-six, Mother Drexel wore the type of religious costume — now outdated for most nuns — sported by this "Sister Kate."

I could go on. But hopefully you see that the hallucination theory leaves a lot of loose ends that can all be accounted for if dead saints do simply appear when and where God wills.

Since my research has convinced me this is fact, the remainder of the book in your hands consists of what those who experienced them believe genuine after-death appearances of saints who come — like St. Frances of Rome and St. John Bosco — to help the living. To offer you the utmost in immediacy, I limit myself, with the occasional exception, to saints from the nineteenth and twentieth centuries.

Included will be a number of instances where dead saints have appeared to living ones. What these incidents offer, besides their intrinsic interest, is the greatest possible proof that this is an authentic event.

To be frank, lots of nuts — not all of them in mental hospitals by any means — think they have been visited by supernatural visitors. As I write this I have before me an article from a respected magazine in which artist Howard Finster claims his art grows out of visits "from the dead and from extraterrestrial life forms." Whatever you make of Finster, think for a moment of all the articles in those checkout stand newspapers full of outrageous claims. A researcher on the track of those who claim visits by dead saints must tread warily.

It certainly helps if a *bona fide* saint, before death, leaves a testimony that she saw a dead saint because: 1) I know from her well-plumbed life before she was given the honor of official sainthood that she wasn't crazy. 2) I know she understood and valued truth so she was not a spoofer like those people who, for fun, created the famous photo of the Loch Ness monster, nor a con artist who stages after-death appearances for money and power.[16] 3) I know she knew enough theology to distinguish the dead from angels. There *are* faiths, such as Hinduism, that believe the dead become angels. But as a Christian, I go by the teachings of the Bible and tradition that an angel is a spiritual being created by God. To help someone out an angel may *pose* as a person,[17] but *always as a stranger or new acquaintance*, never as someone who is now dead. 4) I know she had enough humility to seek wise guidance as to whether this was, indeed, a real event, an imaginary one, or an illusion created by forces of darkness. Even saints can imagine something, one reason the Catholic Church will publicly canonize someone for heroic virtue, but never insist anyone believe in that saint's visions. And just about all the world's spiritual traditions join Christians in recognizing that "dark apparitions" do take place. Both St. Frances de Sales and Blessed Marie of the Incarnation (Madame Acarie) were involved with a young woman called Nicole Tavernier, who had many visions of Jesus. It was only as she became more and more self-enamored ("Look at me, how special I am since Jesus Himself delights in my company") that the saints saw clearly that while her visions and other gifts were real, they were not from God. "Jesus" was a dark spirit, playing on Nicole's egocentricity to incite her to the pride that turns one away from God in self-absorption.[18] 5) Finally, I know the saint has both the perspective and guidance not to go off half-cocked with interpretation of any visit.

Pause, if that last criteria sounds unimportant, to consider how many cults, spiritual movements, and religions are rooted in a claimed visit by a spiritual being — whether perceived as outer space aliens, angels, or the dead. Islam, which began with appearances of an angel to Mohammed, many people will exempt from this criticism as one of the world's great faiths that has produced authentically holy people. But even exempting Islam, if you envision the world spiritual scene minus all groups that began this way, our human family would be free of many of its more bizarre theologies. Such "visits" then, judged by the aftereffects, may have more to do with forces of division than God.

If a Catholic saint appears to a non-saint, while we cannot use the five helps to authenticity listed above, the fact that the "visitor" is a saint still provides more help at verification than if the visitor is non-holy. This is because if an individual claims to have seen a saint, the dead saint's Postulator (if the Cause for beatification or canonization is still underway) will be interested in this claim — not with wide-eyed wonder or publicity in mind, but with a critical eye. Whether it is just seeing a dead saint or being healed while seeing a dead saint that is claimed, the claimant will be discreetly or forthrightly scrutinized. The more claimed, the more scrutiny.

Even after a saint is canonized, those associated with them continue to be concerned that claims are truthful. Knowing the topic of this book, Father Charles Fehrenbach of the Shrine of St. John Neumann in Philadelphia, for example, has been keeping an eye out for people who believe long-dead St. John Neumann has appeared to them. But while Father Fehrenbach passes on some information as worth an interview, he mentions other claims he "thinks we should pass on." Similarly you will note in the chapter on soldiers who claimed they were saved by appearances of St. Therese of Lisieux on the battlefield that the nuns receiving those testimonies requested corroborating material *on the credibility of the individual making the claim.* In their archives testimonies from those competent to make judgments about honesty and stability rest alongside the testimony by the witnesses. Does that make you feel more assured in reading them? It did me.

Of course every now and then I simply have to hope a saint's shrine is making this kind of effort to weed out the untrue. Fortunately when an after-death appearance is really God-sent, there are aftereffects which speak for its authenticity. Called "the fruits of the apparition," especially where the claimant's honesty and stability are established, one or more of these is a powerful confidence booster that something supernatural may really be happening here. These possible fruits are:

1. Physical healing from serious, even terminal, illness.
2. Emotional healing, often with visible radical personality improvement, particularly in behavior toward others.
3. Spiritual growth from egotism into greater other-centeredness. (Padre Pio, for example, judged by his directors one who authentically saw the dead, thought ever less about himself and more of God, urgently desiring that God, not Padre Pio, be known and loved, no matter what sacrifices this demanded. Contrast Padre Pio's humble gratitude for God's favors with Nicole Tavernier.)
4. Rescue in a life-threatening situation either from natural peril such as fire or flood, man-made peril such as enemy troops, or self-destruction.
5. New direction in life, particularly regarding vocation.
6. New acceptance — even joy — in carrying some burden, (including illness and/or facing one's own or others' deaths).
7. Resolution of spiritual questions or difficulties.

Having said all this, do you expect me to insist that no one has ever been fooled in this area? If so, think again. Even the nuns who amassed the many hundreds of testimonies on after-death appearances of St. Therese, Carmelites proficient at sniffing out the phony or sick might have been fooled now and then, in theory anyway. If some testimony in this book puts your hackles up, dismiss it. I have certainly dismissed from these pages incidents that smelled funny to me. My belief is there are enough instances in this book that even if you judge that one (or even several) got by the saint who experienced it, his counselors discernment of it, the saint's postulator (who went over that saint's life with a fine tooth comb), later guardians of his earthly affairs (like Father Fehrenbach), and/or my journalist's nose for the phony, the sheer bulk of the testimonies *left* will compel you to take the idea of after-death appearances of the holy seriously.

ENDNOTES

[1] Francis himself is said to have appeared after death — for instance, centuries ago to Conrad of Offida whom he is said to have sent on an important errand to the saint's at-that-time still-living companion, Brother Leo. Recently a psychoanalyst in Detroit, during a personal crisis, encountered "someone looking exactly like St. Francis" who spoke to him in Latin. He believes it *was* Francis.

[2] June 1994.

[3] For more on how an individual reaches this point see my book *The Sanctified Body*.

[4] Something apparently inherited like another person's ear for music.

[5] Fortunately there are good books about visits of Mary, such as John J. Delaney's *A Woman Clothed With the Sun*, Doubleday Image, 1961.

[6] Nancy's daughter (who was not living at home at the time) was visited more than once by a certain "Christian Science practitioner" who was an enormous help to her. Later it was found no such practitioner exists.

[7] *To Dwell in Peace*, Harper & Row, 1987.

[8] Jean Glockler, Holy Family Preservation Society's Administrative Director, who verified the origin of the statues, cites parish archive material that was collected into a book in 1923 by Brother J. Mulkerins.

[9] I quote from his article "The Transfiguration and Religious Experience," in the September 1994 issue of *The Pecos Benedictine Bulletin*.

[10] In her letter printed in the Winter 1992-3 *Bulletin of The Institute of Noetic Sciences*.

[11] According to a letter by his friend, George Richmond.

[12] That Daisy's mind was not simply losing touch with reality is clear from testimonies that show both her intellectual and sensory faculties were sharpened. In addition she told people things she should not have known. For example, Daisy was visited by a woman who had lost children long before Daisy was born or the Dryden family lived in the town, children about whom the woman never spoke. Yet the dying child volunteered she saw this boy and girl, now grown, in heaven. To another mother, she described a dead child she also had never seen down to the mole "she used to have on her neck; but she doesn't have it now."

[13] An entire book by one of his fellow Franciscans, *The Holy Souls: "Viva Padre Pio,"* by Father Alessio Parente, O.F.M. Cap., "Padre Pio of Pietrelcina Editions," Our Lady of Grace Friary, 1988, reports on this phenomena.

[14] See these in *Hasidic Tales of the Holocaust* by survivor Yaffa Eliach.

[15] In the Winter 1992-3 *Bulletin of the Institute of Noetic Sciences*.

[16] See *The Psychic Mafia*, Dell, 1976, by reformed con artist M. Lamar Keene, who has written what *Publisher's Weekly* called "an eye opener" on this topic.

[17] See the book of Tobit in the Bible for an example.

[18] For material on Nicole Tavernier, I am indebted to Dom Antoine Marie of Abbaye Saint-Joseph de Clairval in France who cites the following sources: *Works* of St. Frances de Sales, Vol. 18, p. 325; Abbe Trochu's *Life of Saint Francis de Sales*, Vol. I, p. 672; and J.B. Boucher's *Life of Blessed Mary of the Incarnation*, p. 190.

2 ❧ How Do the Dead Come Back?

How do dead saints appear to the living? Appearances take many forms: A slim hand reaching out of dazzling light, a person who strides into the room, a figure briefly glimpsed when half-asleep, a stylized tableau, even disembodied voices, or appearances in dreams — where the telltale aftereffects follow, all may legitimately be called after-death appearances. And so may even odder things. For instance, since her death, hundreds of individuals believe St. Therese of Lisieux has made her presence known by the scent of flowers — usually roses.

As for the condition of the recipient of an apparition, appearances may be: 1) to a person fully awake and going about normal activity; 2) to a person in various altered states of consciousness, from those semi-conscious states which immediately precede and follow sleep, to the deep relaxation of profound prayer, on into ecstasy and rapture; 3) or, lastly, to a person who is fully asleep. You note I do not mention someone attending a seance or otherwise "summoning up" the dead. Trying to call up a dead saint is a waste of time. Saints are God's servants and respond to only one call — God's.[1]

That dream appearances *are* included in these pages may make some readers shake their heads. Yet dream appearances by spiritual messengers are accepted in most spiritual traditions. Among the Greeks in the classical, pre-Christian era, for instance, devout individuals used to spend the night in certain healing shrines when ill, hoping for the gods to appear to them in a dream and heal them. At times healings did take place.

Among so-called primitive peoples, healers, such as the African shaman Dorcas studied by anthropologist Adrian K. Boshier, report being commissioned for their work through dreams. Dorcas' shaman grandfather appeared repeatedly in her dreams cajoling and scolding until she accepted her calling. Both Judaic and Christian scriptures, too, are rich in numinous, guiding dreams (not often specifically after-death appearances, however).

Of course, important dreams arising from one's own unconscious change lives dramatically. Jung and other recent thinkers[2] address the question of when a dream ceases to be from the personal unconscious, coming instead from God, by proposing the depths of the mind open out into numinous realities ("the kingdom of Heaven is within you"). While I don't pretend to know the workings of God, it could be from these regions that God's messengers enter dreams.

Without ranking them in any way, here are forms of after-death appearances I've come across, including a couple too nebulous to play a role in this book. For each, adequately detailed examples will be given, mingling the holy and non-holy for, again, I am not saying only saints make these appearances. Although admittedly in my years of research I've never found certain modes associated with non-saints, such as the with-apparently-good-reason named odor of *sanctity*!

1. Seeing when one is fully awake something that seems perfectly "real" such as Caryll Houselander's experience on the bus. Caryll also "spoke of meeting St. Jude on a Chelsea street." When she was six (this is many years before she became a Catholic) Adrienne von Speyr met St. Ignatius Loyola on the streets of her hometown, La Chaux-de-Fonds, Switzerland, the saint taking the little Protestant child by the hand. He was "small, appeared poor, and limped a bit," Adrienne said.

2. Seeing the dead in some obviously otherworldly, but still visual form. This could be a tableau, such as the one by the gable wall of a small, rural parish church in Knock, Ireland, where Sts. John the Evangelist and Joseph appeared with angels, accompanying the Virgin Mary and Jesus (seen as the Lamb of God) on August 21, 1879. Over a dozen witnesses agreed the figures were "full and round as if they had a body and life," but they did not speak and no one felt impelled to speak to them. When a seventy-five-year-old woman tried to kiss the feet of Mary, she found nothing in her embrace but the wall. This type of appearance can include movement. For in-

courtesy Sheed & Ward

Caryll Houselander when young

stance, early one morning in November 1917, fifteen-year-old Adrienne von Speyr saw in a golden light above her bed the Virgin Mary accompanied by angels and saints, among whom she recognized her old friend St. Ignatius. While Adrienne reported "the whole thing had the character of a picture," she also noted that the angels changed places and the golden light faded, letting the features of the Virgin Mary become more prominent.[3]

To mention two other forms this type of appearance can take, saints have appeared in an effulgence of light so great it is almost blinding, or they may appear in a kind of mental vision that only one or some of a number present see. For example, on July 17, 1918, sixteen-year-old Caryll Houselander was sent out by her mother to buy potatoes for dinner. Hurrying along a London street, she suddenly saw "wiping out the sky" what she later learned was a Russian-style ikon of Christ as a crucified King, his face filled with grief and "ineffable love." That night or the next, on the same corner, Caryll saw newspapers on sale revealing the assassination of Czar Nicholas II (who I, for one, believe was a saintly man). The face in the newspaper was the same as the crucified Christ the King of her vision. Speaking of her visions of this type, Caryll explains, "What do I mean by saying that I 'saw'? Frankly, in the ordinary way I did not *see* anything at all; at least I did not see … with my eyes. I saw … *with my mind* … in a way that is unforgettable, though in fact it was something suddenly *known*, rather than seen. But it was known not as one knows something through learning about it, but simply by *seeing* it" … 'alive' and 'unforgettable.' " Theologians who distinguish among various types of visions call this mental vision one of the *least* apt to be hallucinatory.

3. Seeing the dead in a dream, like the pediatrician's assistant in the first chapter who dreamed of her dead father. Some canonization miracles involve dying people who saw dead saints in dreams and woke cured.

4. Seeing the dead while one is in a strongly altered state of consciousness that onlookers can verify. Such apparitions are often called visions. Mystic stigmatic Therese Neumann of Bavaria often went into medically-verifiable ecstasy and saw various saints or the Lord. During this time, Therese was observed out of touch with the reality around her, while caught up in another reality that usually included the full range of sensory perceptions — sight, hearing, touch, etc. Those present at such moments themselves saw nothing of what she experienced.

5. Not only seeing but touching. Caryll Houselander's dead doctor nudged her in the ribs when he sat down next to her on the bus. Similarly St.

Catherine Laboure rested her hands in the lap of the Blessed Virgin Mary during the two-hour-long conversation they had on June 6, 1830.

6. Touch also has occurred alone, sometimes followed by cures. A woman dying of cancer who was making a novena to St. Therese of Lisieux for a miracle awoke to feel a hand on her shoulder. That was her sole mystical experience; but the huge tumor was gone.

7. The odor of sanctity. Certain saints' visits, such as those of St. Therese or Padre Pio, are often associated with numinous odors. For instance, those with a woman expected to die after an automobile accident smelled a strong, unusual odor which could not be accounted for just before she unexpectedly came out of the coma. They had been asking the prayers of Padre Pio. Of course, if the only indication a dead saint is present is the odor of sanctity, there must be no possible natural source for the perfume and the visit must be followed by some strong "fruit," such as a cure.

8. Hearing a voice only (which again obviously must be authenticated by what follows, such as a cure, rescue, etc.). The sound may be heard exteriorly or purely interiorly. Padre Pio when alive, as I mentioned, used to be visited by many dead people who needed prayer to help them with their after-death growth so they could attain the development necessary for heaven. One time during World War II, the friary had been locked up for the night with the door held in place with its two big iron bars. Yet in the downstairs entrance hall a group was heard shouting "Viva Padre Pio!" The Superior, Padre Raffaele, sent Brother Gerardo, the porter, down to investigate. But there was no one there and the bars were intact. The next morning Padre Raffaele asked Padre Pio what was going on. The saint explained that a bunch of dead soldiers had come to thank him for his prayers.

9. A feeling. Of course, this is very hard to verify if it relates to the invisible presence of a dead saint and, for that reason, I rarely write of such things. But an example that may or may not mean *presence* is the priest's testimony in the *Bulletin* of St. John Neumann's shrine. Tracing his vocation to his visit to the saint's tomb as a youngster, the priest says "I *felt* him urging me on to the priesthood." Note this has been recalled for years as something significant, but for a researcher it is still nebulous.

10. A knowing or sense of presence. This occurs in varying degrees, from slightly more than a feeling to something that is kinesthetic. Thus, at the lowest level, because it is very ambiguous as to whether the speaker means he has faith or actually feels a sort of presence, a Japanese actor pilgrimaging to places associated with a Buddhist saint says "walking in

the company of the (holy) Daishi I was never lonely, nor did I worry about death." Episcopal priest Carl E. Buffington, Jr. made a special pal of Chris Wright, a young hemophiliac who got AIDS from a tainted transfusion. Chris died in Houston's Hermann Hospital as Rev. Buffington, there with the family, massaged his feet. The next morning Buffington and Chris' father, Weldon Wright, were driving when the car was filled with a joy that "was persistent and overpowering." The Episcopal priest suddenly pictured Chris celebrating and worshiping God. Embarrassed to be so joy-filled, he glanced at Weldon and saw he was filled with this joy, too. "We were graced with a 'knowing,' " writes Buffington in 1992, "that Chris was better than okay."[4] Again, even at this level it is uncertain whether this was the "presence" of the dead boy or some other spiritual touch. During the WWII bombing blitz of London, among the extra jobs Caryll Houselander took on to help others was volunteer work in a London hospital. There one night in the fall of 1940, while Luftwaffe planes spewed death on the city, a friend's dead child gave Caryll the courage to keep up the spirits of patients too ill to move to bomb shelters. Caryll had been terrified of the screaming bombs until she says she "became acutely and *unquestionably* conscious of the personality of a little child of three at my side — the child of a friend whom I never knew, but of whom I had heard constantly from this friend, and to whom I had often prayed." Caryll said that while she did not *see* the child, she felt her presence accompanying her through hospital halls the way one feels the presence of someone beside one in a pitch black tunnel — a tactile-kinesthetic sensation. A couple days after the bombing attack, Caryll received a letter from the dead child's father, who lived outside London but had heard the deafening barrage. He wrote to say he had prayed to his child, Mary, to stay with Caryll through that terrible night.

11. No presence in any way, even feeling, but signs of an extraordinary nature. Mark Hoyle of Swansea, Massachusetts, is another hemophiliac teenager who died of AIDS in 1986. His father, Jay, in May, 1988, was standing at his son's grave "desperately sad." He said aloud, "Mark if you can hear me, send a bird to land on your headstone." A bird appeared from nowhere and lit on the stone. "Send another." Immediately a second bird flitted to the tombstone. The dad asked for a third. It, too, came and perched on the headstone. "That's enough," Jay Hoyle said. During the next forty minutes not another bird came anywhere near.[5] In another instance where presence may have been indicated by a sign, a father and mother in May, 1981, sat by the hospital crib of their unconscious thirteen-month-old

child Darren, who had bacterial meningitis. As the dad was asking the prayers of dead Padre Pio, he later wrote Pio's friary, "all of a sudden my head was lifted towards the ceiling by a strange force under my chin. I saw what seemed like a little blue light no bigger than a flash light bulb come down from the ceiling very slow(ly).... (Coming) down to the no-vena leaflet[6] in my hand, it shot in a ball of light from the leaflet into Darren's back." Immediately the child's eyes opened and for the first time in a week he spoke. In a week he was home.

12. Appearances in or out of dreams where the dead leave something mate-rial behind them. For instance, Mrs. A.D. Allard of Providence, Rhode Island, told a strange experience to a priest named O.A. Boyer. In May, 1934, Mrs. Allard had some kind of attack, losing consciousness. The doctor told her family she was dying. A second doctor, called in, agreed there was no hope. That she was given what were called in 1934 "the last sacraments" testifies to these assessments. Three years earlier a local, French-Canadian Catholic mystic had given Mrs. Allard's ill daughter Clara, twenty-three, a red relic ribbon when praying for her. Clara was cured, but died fifteen months later of something else in a Rhode Island hospital, at which time the ribbon, which she always wore, was lost. Now as Mrs. Allard lay unconscious and dying, she dreamed her dead daugh-ter came to her. The girl had the red ribbon, which she tied around her mother's head, telling her to keep it on for six hours. Mrs. Allard awoke. The ribbon was on her head. She got up — well — and went to assist her own mother on *her* death bed. Of course someone could have secretly tied a second ribbon on the dying woman and she, feeling this, evoked the dream. Make of it what you will, the strange event is corroborated by witnesses who believed it supernatural. Padre Pio and other saints left and carried away things during lifetime bilocations. With that to steady the mind, let me note that Mrs. Allard's experience is not as far as these things can go. While it is not a type of after-death experience precisely, the dead have apparently, on rare occasions, left behind even more tan-gible physical souvenirs. At one time there was in Rome quite a collec-tion of such "physical evidence." Believing much of the material ques-tionable, a priest made a complete investigation of each item. Only a few met his research standard. Among these I mention just two: On Novem-ber 1, 1731, the dead abbot of Mantova, Father Panzini, appeared to Mother Chiara Isabella Fornari, prioress of the Clarisse Sisters of Todi, Italy. There is no record (maybe they were saints!) of what he told Mother Chiara, but he left the imprint of his left hand and a crude cross burned into the wood

of her worktable. In 1798, a Madame Leleux appeared to her son twenty-seven years after her death, begging him to change his ways. She touched his sleeve and left on it the scorch mark of her hand. Whatever anyone thinks of this melodramatic gesture, the son changed completely, living the rest of his life "in a holy manner" and even founding a religious order. The table, sleeve, and a few other items some consider "proof" of after-death appearances may be seen in the annex of the Sacro Cuore del Suffragio Church on the Lungotevere Prati in Rome. Something in the twentieth century of the same ilk — although it has to do with a visit by an angel of darkness, not the holy dead — is verified by the nuns who were in charge of the Convent of Les Feuillants in Poitiers, France, in the 1920s. These Mothers of the Society of the Sacred Heart were with the simple Spanish lay sister Josefa Menendez during some of her visionary experiences. On the day before Easter in 1922, Josefa had a horrific vision of hell.[7] As she came out of it, "suddenly she clutched at her chest and cried: 'Who is burning me?' There was no light or flame anywhere near, and her religious habit was apparently untouched. With a rapid movement, she tore open the front of her dress, and at once the cell … filled with the acrid smell and fetid fumes of smoke, and her inner garment was seen to be on fire." Josefa herself was badly burned near her heart. On ten separate occasions the holy young nun saw the devil vomit flames on her. Each time she was set afire, leaving scars she carried to her grave and scorched garments, some of which were kept by the sisters as evidence of what they saw. As to whether Josefa Menendez was some sort of conjurer trying to make a name for herself, those familiar with her life know she sought obscurity and died in it. The women of her order, some of the best-educated in the Church, believe her virtue — and her visions — authentic.

And finally, having given you a dozen forms that after-death appearances may take, let me immediately add that these modes may be mixed like the experience of Bavarian visionary Therese Neumann, who heard a voice that said it would help her sit up as she saw an effulgent light from which came an arm. The hand took hold of Therese and pulled her up in her sick bed. She was healed.

Regarding apparitions where a saint simply walks into a room, people ask, "Is that a real body?" Or assume a saint appearing in a dream is unequivocally nonmaterial. As always reality is messier. People dreaming have had a tactile sensation of someone pulling a tumor out of their body, for instance, and wakened, screaming with pain, healed. With such things going on, I can only quote my betters. St. Paul, whose own mission began when the risen Christ appeared to him, wrote "there are heavenly bodies and earthly bodies." When teenage St. Dominic Savio appeared after his death to his mentor St. John Bosco, reaching out to detain his spiritual son, Bosco grasped only air.

"Are you bodily here?" he asked.

Dominic answered, "This is how it is. If in God's Providence, someone dead has to appear to someone alive, he's seen in his normal bodily appearance and distinguishing characteristics. He cannot be bodily touched, however, since he is pure spirit. He ... (will only be) reunited with his (physical) body at the resurrection."

Catholic theologians state that because one is a saint does not mean every opinion, even those quoted from a dead saint, is either correct or covers all aspects of a truth. For one thing, reducing supernatural realities (the dead appear to communicate wordlessly heart to heart) to language is tricky; for another, even saints do not always grasp everything said to them, and can innocently make mistakes. In this case, Dominic has not explained situations (or Bosco did not retain what he said) where a dead individual appears and, touched, is apparently just as much warm flesh as anyone alive. Christian mystical theologians add that such a warm body, too, just like one that proves only "air" when grasped, is not the original body.

With two exceptions,[8] saints even in warm, fleshly bodies, theologians continue, are actually in a temporary body that replicates — but is not — the body that lies in the grave or has already returned to ashes or dust.

This is not solely a Catholic idea. I think of Hindu spiritual master Sri Yukteswar paying an after-death visit to his spiritual son, Paramahansa Yogananda. When the holy Yogananda asked, "But is it you, master, the same lion of God? Are you wearing a body like the one I buried ...?" his mentor assured him that this was a created body "made from cosmic atoms" exactly like, but not actually, the body Yogananda had buried.

In the testimonies of individuals who believe they have experienced visits by dead saints acting as God's messengers, besides the various aftereffects (see chapter one), these witnesses display something called *ineffability* — that is, the teller's absolute conviction that this experience is utterly true, *totally real*, completely authentic. Thus they will underline, as Caryll

Houselander did in speaking of the presence of the dead child during the Blitz, that the dead individual was *unquestionably* present. Or humbly admit, like Padre Pio, that the more he tries at times to consider that his visions may not be real, the more struck he is by their reality.

Mystical theologians, who find this an important component of genuine spiritual experiences, say it comes from suddenly knowing something, no longer just intellectually, but experientially.

Unfortunately the fact that I can swear that something is absolutely true may prove nothing to you; after all, I could be sincerely wrong. All that can be said is those who believe they have been visited by a dead person often declare themselves willing to die rather than term the experience a fantasy, hallucination, or other product of their own mind.

For example, in 1917, three children ages seven to ten claimed they were visited, first by an angel, then by the Virgin Mary at Fatima, Portugal, a California-like region of rolling oak-sprinkled hills. These were simple peasant children whose world was a couple villages of white-washed homes and the fields where they herded sheep. Never had they been spoken to by anyone "important." An embarrassment in the village to their two sets of parents — only one of the four adults believed them, while the ten-year-old's mother beat her child repeatedly for "those dreadful lies you're telling" — the threesome's anxiety escalated to terror when they were kidnapped by the angry administrator of the area, determined to stamp out "senseless superstition."

Each child, after a period spent together in the common cell of an adult jail, was separately interrogated by this ferocious, looming figure, who snarled down from his adult height that the only hope of avoiding immediate death by being boiled in oil was to admit their talk of apparitions of angels and the Virgin Mary was a lie. Each terrified child, even shown a dreadful, leering "executioner" who rubbed his hands and gleefully assured the interrogator that the oil was "plenty hot," though fainting with terror, refused. "Kill me," each sobbed, "but I saw her."

Besides the sense that this is "so real I must die rather than deny it," a final characteristic of genuine apparitions is that such experiences do not dim in the memory. Accounts given fifty years later by Lucia Abobora (b. 1907), the sole surviving Fatima child, are as vivid as those given in 1917.

It is said the Virgin Mary still appears to Lucia, now a Carmelite nun. If she isn't a hallucinator (a position we who have studied Fatima find untenable),[9] the peasant who never dreamed she'd end up a nun is just one more case of a destiny changed by God's messengers.

ENDNOTES

[1] The reason that seance transcripts are so incredibly banal, boring, and sans "soul food," I theorize, is that, to use the St. John Vianney's, the Cure d'Ars, term, only the lowest souls (that is, the most spiritually undeveloped) are "close enough" to this dimension to be summoned up. Of course as *The Psychic Mafia* shows (see footnote 16 on page 30), most "call-ups" are phony. Sent to investigate, both Protestant (see footnote 11, page 298, on minister John G. Lake) and Catholic saints have also found, on occasion, dark spirits posing as the sought-for dead.

[2] See, for instance, Morton T. Kelsey's *Dreams: A Way to Listen to God*, Paulist Press, 1978.

[3] That this was not a dream was made clear by aftereffects. Among them: the young student, who would become a physician like her father, was left with a small wound under her left breast, a physical sign, she knew, of her mysterious connection to God.

[4] In the May/June issue of *Acts 29*, the magazine of the Episcopal Renewal ministries.

[5] This anecdote is taken from an interview by Tricia Hempel with Hoyle in *Our Sunday Visitor* (May 13, 1990).

[6] See footnote four on page 13 in the prologue.

[7] Hell, to Catholics, is the state of being in which an individual has rejected God definitively, even in the after-death clarity that offers (for some people, for the first time) full knowledge of the goodness and love of God. For there to be free will — so that we are not robots forced to love God — there must exist this possibility to reject him totally. Hell, the state of absence of God, of utter self-absorption and total hatred of good, can only be entered by one's own choice. God does not "send" anyone there.

[8] Chief of these to Christians is Christ. Christianity rests on Christ's rising, not in spirit, but in that scourged, crucified body. It is in this glorified but fully human body, Christians believe, that he still appears to individuals as he appeared to the first, fear-filled disciples huddled in a locked room in Galilee. To show them he was not appearing in spirit but in his *physical* body, he asked for and ate a piece of fish.

Jews agree a body can join spirit to pass from this dimension to the next (although they don't believe that Jesus' earthly body was resurrected) because of Elias, also called Elijah, the prophet who did not undergo death but was simply "snatched up" into heaven. Catholicism has no formal doctrine on the mysterious "ascension" of Elias. But Catholics do believe — Protestants do not — that what Scripture says happened with Elias,

God definitely did for Mary, "assuming"the woman chosen by God to be the mother of His son bodily into heaven either before or after her death.

9 At Fatima, for instance, the children's claims were buttressed by miracles, from cures to a spectacular "dance of the sun" seen on a day named ahead of time by the Virgin Mary. This particular miracle was witnessed by many in a huge crowd and by those alone in their homes miles away. Another major corroboration are prophecies given by Mary: to mention only some dealing with world political events, in 1917, while WWI was still underway, she predicted the much wider conflagration of WWII, the rise of Communism in Russia, its spread over many parts of the world, and its fall.

3 ❧ THERESE AT WAR

P arents, wives, and sweethearts of able-bodied young men look glum.
Only forty-four years ago — in the 1870 Franco-Prussian conflict
— German sabers cut down the flower of France's manhood. Now
France and Germany are at war again.

Soon, it appears, the Germans will again take Paris. When that happened
in the earlier war, the Virgin Mary appeared at Pontmain, promising "My
Son will show mercy." An unexpected peace between the two nations followed.

This time the Virgin will not show herself publicly in France. And the
new conflict will be much worse. Over four times as long, it will engulf so
many nations it becomes the first "world" war — hell on earth to many. A
so-called "lost generation," by the war's end these individuals will be shorn
of all faith in supernatural realities. But the same war will bring others
closer to God. They see His hand everywhere. To many of them, bands of
angels and human "angels of mercy" — live and dead — are at work, as
God's messengers, on bloody battlefields and in pain-wracked hospital
wards.

Among the human angels of mercy between 1914 and 1918, none is
more prominent than a young dead woman. Only twenty-four at her death
just seventeen years before 1914, this Sister Therese was a Carmelite nun
in the provincial town of Lisieux. In her after-death appearances she often
is recognized, or that it was indeed she verified, by the pictures[1] of her in
wide circulation.

Judging by the letters of thanks and petition pouring into the Lisieux
Carmel as 1914 starts, Sister Therese is already known all over the world
for favors like the one in 1910 to the old fellow in the Lisieux Home for the
Aged. His tongue eaten away by gangrene, Ferdinand Aubry listened as the
Home's doctor patiently explained that, sadly, the human body cannot re-
grow the missing parts of a tongue. An ignorant old man who obviously
lacked proper respect for medical knowledge, Aubry obstinately turned to

the dead Carmelite who had already obtained his cure from gangrene. He told *her* he needed a new, *whole* tongue. And she went to the Father and got one for him. The flabbergasted physician himself formally attested to that, attaching a photo of Ferdinand Aubry's restored appendage to the declaration.

No wonder that four years and hundreds of such favors later, wives and mothers press tiny relics or medals of the dead nun on men departing for the front and/or urge soldiers to "put yourself under Sister Therese's protection."

Devout young men — there are some still in 1914 France — accept with alacrity. Another type grimaces and squirms, accepting the medal or relic only as a sop to some teary-eyed woman. Let the women and old men weep, they think. Their new uniforms sharply creased and boots still shiny, this breed of young men is impatient for action and glory.

Let us follow some of these strong young men, the devout and the less devout — Paul-Henri Joly, Joseph Martin, Roger Lefebvre, Auguste Cousinard and nameless others — into bloody battles and rat-and-rain filled, disease-breeding trenches. We go with them through their letters or more formal documents.

When the individual is not named, it is not because their reports are unsigned but because, in a more spiritually-modest age, out of humility or with other qualms, the individual has asked the nuns at Lisieux in whose archives I worked to make public only his initials. Such accounts, too, I assure you, come with corroborating statements and/or attestations of good character.

Was it a strain to fill this chapter?

Hardly. I can share with you only the barest sampling of the World War I work done by the messenger of God's mercy today known as *Saint* Therese of Lisieux. Yet this was no Joan of Arc, but a quiet, cloistered nun who had no visions, healed no sick, and passed without a ripple through her world. After living quietly, barely out of her teens, she died quietly. If people knew about her, it was because as she was being eaten up by tuberculosis, she had written a couple of notebooks about her very unsensational inner life at the request of two of her blood sisters.[2] The focus of that life had been a gospel-based reliance on God's boundless love and mercy and her burning desire to respond with love and surrender. That Therese of the Child Jesus then should be noticed at all, let alone that it was she to whom millions were turning as a great intercessor, beloved of the Father, is as flabbergasting as Ferdinand Aubry's tongue!

But on to the testimonies. To include more incidents, character references and other attestations of veracity that accompany these reports are omitted. If you believe that mentally-balanced young men of good character and sincere devotion to the truth may still hallucinate in extreme situations, what good are such documents? Conversely, if you believe that by divers — and sometimes unusual — means God responds to the prayers of people in crisis, then to you what others call a "hallucination" may well be "of God."

Speaking of God, some of you will have problems with God sending a warning to one soldier so he can save his life by killing another, or with the fact that a praying soldier may still *die*. I can only remind you that we all die and, from God's view, that may be as much gain as loss. Therese, for instance, lived only twenty-four years and found greater work and happiness after death. As to why one man is tagged to die young and another live long, that lies in realms I cannot chart, but I can affirm my own belief that the one who dies is as much in God's love and mercy as the one who lives.

Let us now flip our mental calendars back to October, 1917. The Second Company of the Sixth Regiment of Sharpshooters from Tlemcen, Algeria, a group often used as scouts, is in possession of one sector of the woods of Courrieres and Bezonvaux, facing the enemy lines. This is a perilous position as the Sharpshooters are sixty meters (more than two hundred feet) in advance of their own main line.

Taking up this position on October 3, for the next eleven days, one Sergeant Diez notes, they are "exposed daily to intense bombardments and to poison gas attacks." That Diez himself has been spared to this point he attributes to the intercession of the Servant of God, Sister Therese.

At the moment the squad the Sergeant commands has a highly important assignment. They are guarding the opening of the communications trench that leads over those sixty meters back to the French lines.

Surprise German attacks under cover of darkness on other squads in these woods have been frequent. Diez remarks to his lieutenant that they should expect to be woken up one of these days themselves by such an attack.

Now let me turn (translating from his French) to the Sergeant's own account:

> On October 14, about three thirty in the morning, I was at my
> habitual place, (at the head of the communications trench he and

his men are guarding) when I was dazzled suddenly by a great silvery light. To my stupefaction, before my eyes I saw Sister Therese (looking) like an angel. She went from left to right, holding in her hand a very short saber. I felt no choice. I had to follow her and found myself facing a swamp which served as a kind of natural defense for us and was situated behind our lines. (Watching her) I rubbed my eyes, I pinched myself, and I said to myself, "You're not sleeping. What does this mean?" I went back and took up my former position only to see with astonishment, the vision repeated.

Then I understood that this was a warning from Heaven. At that, I didn't lose a minute; I made a rapid inspection all around my post and I pulled the pins of my grenades[3] to be ready for a sudden attack.

After this, I checked my watch and saw it was 4 o'clock, just the time when the Germans usually made their surprise attacks. I didn't say anything to my men — except to keep a good watch and be on the alert.

It wasn't two minutes later that I was surveying the side of the swamp when I saw a creeping shadow, then two, then three (approaching) Indian file. At first I thought it was the arrival of the patrol which was to relieve my men and so I called out to them in Arabic "Who goes there?" For answer I heard the bursting of a grenade, which, happily, fell outside the parapet of the trench. "Here's the Boches," I cried.

(I ordered) "Fire, gunners!" and immediately I threw three grenades. Then I saw a German advancing on me. Without hesitation, with my automatic pistol, I killed him cleanly and he fell at my feet.

From then on, it was a heavy exchange of grenades and nearly hand to hand combat. I didn't lose courage, I kept ordering my men, "Fire!" even though I was soon wounded. Then the enemy fire stopped. Not being able to do more (due to the wounds), I sat down on the side of the parapet. Everything was calm again. I was relieved by my superior officer who arrived to reinforce us, then evacuated to the aid station with four of my wounded men.

I didn't forget to thank my Protectress whose celestial warning had saved us....

The sergeant was hale and hearty, and had pinched himself and rubbed his eyes to be sure he was awake at the time he believes he saw Therese.

Another soldier was in a military hospital, with pneumonia, about to become one of many WWI soldiers who died of disease from long days and nights in sodden, rat-infested trenches. Knowing his condition kept worsening in these pre-antibiotic days when pneumonia even in the young was often fatal, the soldier asked to see a priest to receive the last rites. Told there was no priest around, the very ill young man turned to God and Sister Therese, asking for the grace to "suffer patiently." Taking up his testimony:

> The following day (Jan. 6, 1917) my fever went still higher. I was suffocating little by little (as his lungs filled up)…. In a crisis … my body stiffening and trembling … at moments I couldn't breath at all. But I didn't lose consciousness. I recall very well that a Red Cross nurse took my pulse and then, turning away from (my bed), said to her buddies who were playing cards in the hall, "He's dying."
>
> But all at once, I perceived in front of my bed a great light: at first I thought it was my feebleness that was giving me vision trouble, but when the night had completely come, I saw the same light and then the little sister Therese with a halo. I experienced a happiness that I could never express. I don't hesitate to say that this night was the most painful of my life due to the great (physical) sufferings I endured, yet at the same time it was also the happiest time of my life.

Having written this shortly after his unexpected recovery, the soldier fulfilled a promise to come to Carmel and share more details of his extraordinary night. Leaving out some repetitious material about his pneumonia, his fuller report continues, as the Mother Superior took it down on April 10, 1917:

> After the bitter crisis of which he spoke in his letter, he found he could sit up in his bed, aided he felt by an invisible hand for, by himself, he was absolutely incapable of making such an effort. He saw above the bed a great brightness, then that disappeared and Sister Therese showed herself to him. She had a halo but he only saw her within a mysterious penumbra, which still did not keep

him from perfectly recognizing her (from the image he had been given by a fellow soldier). He experienced a joy beyond telling.

Vehemently he insisted that he would gladly suffer again — even if it should be for years — as he suffered that night to pass again a night like that one.

"But did you see Sister Therese all night then?" the Mother Superior asked.

"Yes, from ten hours in the evening to five hours in the morning, and she instructed me the entire time. We conversed together. I had doubts on the truths of religion and she made me understand everything; it was as if she taught me catechism. She said to me that this life is nothing, that there is a better and that anything that one has to endure on earth is nothing in comparison to the happiness with which we will be recompensed. As I was very chagrined at how I had fallen away from God, she consoled me, assuring me that if I had repented and had confidence (in God) the good God would forget everything, and I could still be pleasing to Him. She brought to mind several saints who had been sinners before they became holy ... Everything (she said) was as if the words were imprinted on the very depths of my heart. I felt a courage to suffer no matter what in this life, as long as I could serve the good God and go with Him to Heaven. And this courage has not left me. I'm returning to the front Friday and I'll be in the front lines but that doesn't make me at all afraid. If I die I'll go to Heaven, Sister Therese promised me.

Carmelites are not credulous. The Mother Superior suggested that perhaps all this took place in a dream. Certainly anyone who has ever been very sick with a high fever knows what strange "fever dreams" one can have. But the soldier insisted that during his night with Therese he was sitting up in his bed, just as completely awake as now talking to the Mother Superior. Then he confided that he had wished very much to die that night. But Therese had replied "No," with a shake of her head.

Fever dream or a visit by a messenger of God, in the morning the young soldier was out of danger, fever fallen and drowning lungs drained so he could breath freely once more — in a word, "convalescent" rather than "dying" as the nurse had pronounced.

Body saved, spirit had been remade too. Before leaving the Carmel, the soldier remarked that if anyone mocked religion, he now knew how to respond.

Not that it mattered to him what others thought. He understood, he said, that if he told his fellow soldiers about his experience, they wouldn't believe him. But "when you've had this kind of experience yourself," he added, "I assure you, one believes and would never forget it if one lived to be a hundred!"

There are many other "change of heart" reports. Take macho Auguste Cousinard, who hadn't darkened the door of a church since his first communion. His wife begged him to prepare his soul for war by going to confession. Not he! He would have been ashamed before the world, he said later (though he squirmingly accepted a relic). That stance lasted until he was pinned down under artillery fire in a trench at Gotha (near Reims), began to think about his wife and children, and called out to Therese. In his words: "Hardly had I completed this prayer than I saw a cloud open up and the visage of the saint appear against a blue sky. I thought I was hallucinating. I rubbed my eyes, several times … (but) the face became ever clearer and more resplendent.… How beautiful her eyes were as she appeared to look up to heaven in prayer!"

After this visible prayer of the dead nun for him, Cousinard not only left the trench alive: he no longer cared what other macho-types think of men who go to confession. Putting what he told the Carmelites personally into an official written testimony, Cousinard adds he will be proud to have his name made public.

I think also of the sub-lieutenant who didn't believe in God until a sweet voice three times said, "Get out of there!" in ever more urgent tones. He left his position just seconds before a shell wiped it off the map. His loved ones had been praying for Therese's intercession and she had not only saved his life but opened the eyes of his soul, he said, on November 30, 1919, when he left his Cross of the Legion of Honor at Carmel in thanksgiving.

Paul-Henri Joly, a soldier of the 229th Infantry Regiment, described as "a very serious fellow," wrote from Abbeville on September 14, 1916. The war had gone on now two full years, Joly from its beginning carrying on his person "with the most profound respect" a precious relic of Therese. He has had "some bad moments" so far, he writes, but "always my little saint shows up to save me."

That he means this literally is clear in the long letter, picked up as he begins to speak of the fighting in the Somme where Germany lost 500,000 men and the Allies, 600,000:[4]

> Among the dangers I've run, above all I have to mention this
> July 30th and the days following. We were then in the Somme,

ordered to reinforce the first line of troops. I was serving as liaison and we were under terrible bombardments during four long days as we successfully repulsed enemy attacks.

One evening, August 2, we were cowering — a whole half platoon — around a tumble down cottage which was being blown to pieces under the rain of machine-gun fire.

Fellow soldier and Christian Brother Jean-Baptiste Vidal gives more detail:

The Germans (were) bombard(ing) us with an unbelievable violence and the roof timbers of our shelter were going to pieces. We were all squatting in the dust covered with phosphorescent sulphur; one could have said our clothes were on fire.

Things were so bad that Vidal says, "I encouraged my poor comrades to make an act of contrition, then we said the rosary together." Returning to Joly's account:

… praying in our peril, which was ever mounting, … my buddies were saying the rosary. As for me, while praying to the Virgin, I invoked Sister Therese, calling her with confidence to our help. Suddenly, about eleven o'clock, while the battle raged on, I saw her standing at the foot of a machine gun which was there. She looked at me and blessed us all. Then she said to me, smiling, "Don't fear anything. I've come here to protect you."

Terribly moved, I called to my companions, "I see Sister Therese. She's (over) there! We are saved!" And, in fact, not a single one of us was hit and we soon emerged from that dreadful situation healthy and safe.

Something else in Jean-Baptiste Vidal's corroborationg report cannot be omitted. The Christian brother writes that while the men said their acts of contrition and rosary:

Paul Joly was calling out in a loud voice invocations to Sister Therese when around eleven o'clock in the middle of the din of shells, I heard him cry out, "I see Sister Therese; we are saved!"

Writing books, I've run into the phenomenon of those who seek notoriety by claiming association with dead heroes or saints. So for those of you, like me, whose cynical bent makes them wonder if soldiers sometimes made this stuff up after the fact, note that Joly does not confide *after the battle* that he saw Therese. There he is, calling out *aloud* to her in front of the whole half platoon as hell rages around them! Truly no spiritual shrinking violet, when he sees her he bellows that out, too! Some people may still claim he hallucinated, but no one can claim he made this up after the battle. And those who believe his testimony can point to an impressive fact: after he claims Therese blessed all the men, not a single one was lost or even hurt in a situation where troops who had been in combat for two years estimated the situation called for acts of contrition in preparation for death.

Joly made it home alive, writing the sisters at the end of the four terrible years, "she is always with me."

Another soldier sends a report "from the front" on September 10, 1916. His perilous job at dreadful Verdun was to carry messages by bicycle without protective escort. That on May 22, as the French took the fort of Souville from the Germans, he found himself under enemy bombardment. It was tough going between shell holes and debris from destroyed buildings until he got to the main road to Verdun. Hope that conditions would be better on the main artery died at once. An easy artillery target, this road was under such heavy machine gun fire that, "enveloped in an ocean of lead and fire," as he puts it, the bicyclist felt himself lost and wailed "Come here, Sister Therese!"

Immediately, he says, she appeared "all luminous and aureoled." She held up an arm and the enemy fire stopped instantly. The grateful cyclist continues, "not a single shell was fired until I had entered (the town of) Verdun."

Those on the home front also felt they had helpful "visits." A Paris doctor and his wife, the Freysselinards, have left their long, written testimony about what happened on July 7, 1918. They had two sons in the war and the oldest, a lieutenant, had been missing in action for forty-three days. Like parents immemorial in such a position, they were, as the mother puts it, "in mortal anguish," but the wife clung to hopes for help through Sister Therese.

That morning about 9:00 A.M., her husband was in the corridor that led from their living quarters to his consultation rooms. He smelled a very agreeable odor there, a mix, it appeared, of roses and violets. But there were no flowers around. Still he attached no importance to this. It was not an olfactory hallucination (if such is possible!) because his wife, discovering her husband sniffing around the hallway, verified the reality of the unseen "bouquet."

An hour later, Madame Freysselinard was in their dining room when she was struck by a wave of fragrance. This seemed to be violets. Again, no flowers were around. She called her husband and they searched among the things there for some natural explanation, but found none. A man of science, Doctor Freysselinard was getting disturbed. As for his wife, welling up in her was a growing conviction that Sister Therese was announcing good news regarding their missing son.

"Would you believe in the perfumes of Sister Therese as symbols of her protection of us, if we get good news about our son?" she asked her physician husband.

"Yes, I would," he replied without hesitation.

The following morning the mail brought a letter from the missing son. A prisoner, he was still safe and sound. *He* later told his parents a long, hairy story about his experience on March 13, 1915, near Beausejour (in Champagne), where at only eighteen he won the Cross of the Legion of Honor for his valor. That blood-soaked morning sixty men were cut down all around him in one of those "over the top" attacks on the German trenches. He alone was left alive. Pinned down in a shell crater only twenty meters from the enemy, he did not cease, he later told his parents, to invoke Sister Therese's help from eleven in the morning until six in the evening. Only then, in the early dark of that time of year, did he manage to slip away and rejoin the French forces.

He is one of dozens who did not *see* Therese but was as persuaded he owed his life to her protection as those who did. Another to represent this huge group is the gunner, Paul Dugast. When he stumbled in combat while rushing for ammunition on December 28, 1914. Dugast's big weapon — a piece of field artillery known as a "75," weighing four thousand pounds — rolled over his legs. His buddies shouted "Miracle!" when they picked him up and saw he still had two legs without a scratch on either. The elated gunner shouted, too: "It's my little Therese I owe!" and immediately wrote on the big gun in large white letters: "Battery of St. Therese of the Child Jesus." For the rest of the war — three more bloody years — the French gunner kept that inscription on his artillery piece. If the rain washed it off, he put it back as soon as possible. He never saw her physically either, but insisted that it was she who saw him safely home through times like the thirty-two days of continual combat in unrelenting rain when he never left his gun site night or day until evacuated by orders of his major.

Another French family felt that both those at home and their man at the front *saw* Therese in dreams. The wife's testimony written May 31, 1916, from Bourg-Saint-Andeol in the Ardeche area:

> My baby was three years old when he came down with whooping cough (this was May, 1915). I confided him to Sister Therese of the Child Jesus and I began a novena. Now the last night (of the novena) I had particularly asked the saint to watch over my son during his sleep. In the morning, when he woke up he said to me he had a dream. He said "I saw a beautiful lady, dressed like a nun; she was sitting near my bed smiling at me." When I showed him the image of Therese, my little angel at once recognized her as "the beautiful lady." And, moreover, his illness was aborted immediately.
>
> By a coincidence which is, at the least strange, my husband who was in service at the same date and therefore far away, unaware of all this, on the same night also had a mysterious dream. He saw himself in great danger of losing his life, when at his side a young Sister appeared with angelic features and the dress of a Carmelite nun. She stopped her horse which was ready to dash away and raised her hand in a gesture of protection. This dream turned out to be a prophetic sign. I attribute to the humble saint my dear (husband)'s return (alive) from Verdun and his having been protected when he took part in the artillery struggle at the Argonne.[5]

This is all very pious and nice about the husband's dream. But it becomes much more intriguing by a detail the husband adds. After getting home safe and sound, he authored what the Carmelites call "a philosophical book" on the war. A lawyer — therefore by profession one engaged in looking at events critically with an eye for "evidence" — the ex-soldier wrote that sometime after his unusual dream he arrived at Verdun, which was to be one of the horrific battle sites of the war where French casualties were 540,000 and German, 430,000.[6] At once he recognized certain prominent landmarks, such as the old fortress, not because he had been to Verdun before, but because *he had seen them in the mysterious dream.* Later he ran into a picture of this Sister Therese so many people were talking about and recognized the nun of his dream. You make of it what you will, of course, but this family had no doubt: God had somehow used the dead nun to shepherd the husband safely home.

This lawyer-soldier was a rational man. I cannot make the same claim for Roger Lefebvre, a twenty-nine-year-old roofer from Saint-Aubin-du-Thenney in the Eure. But see what you think ... In spite of being the father of a family, Lefebvre was off to war in its first month (August, 1914) as a soldier in the 224th Infantry. He carried a little relic of the saint and said he "invoked her at least twenty times a day."

September 17 at La Neuville near Reims, about four-thirty in the afternoon on a battlefield where enemy shells seemed to be falling as thick and fast as raindrops, Lefebvre was hit six times. His head was wounded, as was his face, and thigh. Several veins in his neck were cut and a terrible gash rent one foot. Collapsing, he lost consciousness.

He came to in the freshness of the evening to find himself bathed in his own blood, which continued to flow from his open wounds. He felt weak to the point of death. He cried out "with ardent faith" to the one whose relic he carried and whose protection he was constantly invoking: "My Sister Therese, come help me!" At once he saw right by him the "little saint," as so many of these soldiers call Therese. She appeared beautiful and compassionate and held in one hand a large crucifix. With the other she grasped the dying soldier's right arm and lifted him to his feet. Then she smiled at him and disappeared.

A hallucination by a man whose mind is naturally fuzzy as he slowly bleeds to death?

Maybe.

But the blood had stopped flowing "as if a celestial hand had bandaged the wounds." And he who had been weak to the point of death a moment earlier now "no longer felt the least suffering." He *ran* to the first aid post, which was four hundred meters (a quarter mile) off the battlefield.

Although he had to have more than one operation on the dreadful wound in his foot, he never suffered after seeing Therese. To the fellow Carmelites of Therese, when he visited Lisieux, completely hale, on February 4, 1915, he confided "my heart still leaps when I think about it."

He was heading back to the front with aplomb, he told the mother superior, telling everyone what had happened and certain that "Sister Therese, who protected me once, will protect me always."

Perhaps because of such perfect faith in the intercessory power of one of His saints, God just couldn't let him down. At any rate, there is more to the military history of Roger Lefebvre, who on December 15, 1915, was returned to the front lines, this time with the 24th Infantry. Still alive and uninjured, he was back in Lisieux (he visited Therese's tomb on every leave) in May, 1916. On this visit he told his dead friend that he had only one fear, that of being taken prisoner. He asked her for death over captivity. Then rethinking this request, he modified it: If he had to be taken captive, let her see that he was severely wounded so he would have a good chance to be repatriated.

This prayer is why I make no claim for the clear thinking of Roger Lefebvre! Be careful what you pray for, they say. In His mysterious wisdom and perhaps sometimes shaking His head — God answers some pretty dumb prayers. Just a month after this one, on June 1, 1916, Roger Lefebvre found himself surrounded by Germans, the French badly outnumbered. Something seemed to command him to resist, he reported later, although surrender seemed the way to go. So ignoring the enemy's offer to let them throw down their arms, he and several buddies went on fighting. He later wrote:

> After no more than a minute, two of us were dead and I had taken a bullet in the right shoulder. But I threw two more grenades with my left hand. Then I was hit again in the right side and the left shoulder and I fell on my back, unable to move. Soon my last comrade went down while the captain, refusing to surrender, was killed at point blank range. A German soldier aimed at my cheek to finish me off, but an officer stopped his arm. I stayed thus for three days, stretched out, unable to move but it was clear that my holy Protectress did not abandon me. I lay in a narrow trench down which the enemy was advancing, taking ground. Past me marched hundreds of German soldiers in solid ranks but not a single one walked on me. All of them, on the contrary, at risk of being killed, stepped up on the edge of the sloping (trench wall) in order not to touch me.
>
> However I was at the end of my strength and suffering so much that the third day I asked Sister Therese to free me from my pains by letting me die. At that very instant, without my being able to explain how, because by myself I couldn't move at all, I found myself suddenly upright in the trench and able to walk.
>
> (He set out to seek help and) I ran into some Germans and one of them gave me some coffee to drink, rather than giving it to a wounded German, who wasn't very happy about that but the officer who was giving me the drink told him that I was more badly wounded than he and he only got water. Then they sent me on to an aid station. Since the bombardment by our artillery continued without let up as we tried to regain the ground we had lost, when I got to the post, a German military chaplain there had me get down,

courtesy the January, 1993, *Review Therese de Lisieux*

holy card from the author's collection

Above, a typical statue of St. Therese as she appeared to some WWI soldiers, such as Roger Lefebvre. At left, a holy card representation of the saint.

with a warning which deeply touched me, into a nearby shell crater. Eventually they took me to the rear to a hospital because I was
so severely wounded and I was operated on at once. After that they
transported me to a hospital in Stuttgart where I found some good
nuns who took care of me very well.

I stayed in Germany until December 15 when I was repatriated
via Switzerland as a severely wounded, although I was almost completely recovered. It was there that I knew the soldier Latus (he
tells of teaching this comrade to seek the intercession of Therese
and how Latus, very ill with tuberculosis, was suddenly cured and
mentions another very sick soldier for whom he prayed that he
either be cured or die happy and how Therese, he believes — before Lefebvre knew of the death — came via the lovely odors which
often signal her favors, to report that the soldier died happy).

After this perfume-signaled "appearance," Lefebvre began to make novenas to her for himself, for he could not use his right hand, plus following
an operation on the elbow of the same arm, abscesses kept forming.

Nine faith-testing novenas later, nothing. But Lefebvre did not give up
and after novena number ten, the abscesses were cured and he regained the
use of his right hand. From then on, he had no more suffering.

Home for good, he returned various times, wife and children in tow, to
Lisieux, where the Carmelite nuns noted with pleasure that he was able to
return, in spite of a stiff elbow, to his physically demanding prewar job as a
roofer.

Another soldier's special relationship with Sister Therese preceded the
war by several years. He put himself under her care when he marched to
war with the Sixth Company of the 150th Infantry regiment. And he felt she
"often" protected him on the battlefield. Then, having almost made it unscathed to war's end, on July 15, 1918, at Bois-le-Roi (some kilometers
from Reims) during a great Allied offensive drive, he was "mortally wounded
in the chest." Picked up by compassionate Germans, he was evacuated with
them as they kept retreating until he finally arrived, in skeletal state, he
says, at a German camp in Laudan and was sent from there to a hospital at
Germersheim.

Finding himself in moral and physical distress over the "hopeless" prognosis of the doctors, it was natural to him to turn to his longtime spiritual
friend.

In spite of the doctors' prediction, he suddenly overflowed with joy and confidence when he heard Therese tell him, "You shall see your parents and your dear France again!"

He returned home alive and well and was studying for the priesthood when he wrote the nuns.

But what about the hundreds of thousands of soldiers who died? Near-death-experience studies indicate God does not let any one die alone. To some are sent angels. For instance, in a May, 1994, television special on angels, a medical doctor who was stabbed more than thirteen times and left to die, reports angelic beings surrounded him with love and light until he was discovered and restored from clinical death. Many other testimonies imply that God often sends to the dying person loved ones who have gone before them. To some WWI soldiers it *appears* God sent Therese.

But until He sends one of those dead soldiers to me bearing "testimony" (which might create its own questions, especially regarding whether *I* hallucinate) I put this possibility before you simply as conjecture. For instance, Auguste Cousinard died some months after Therese appeared to him and changed his stance toward confession. After the former macho soldier's death, his wife was cured through Therese's intercession. Did Therese "come for" Cousinard?

On Therese and the dying you recall Roger Lefebvre, who believed he received sensory evidence that Therese saw that a comrade died happy. There are also two other suggestive events. First, from military chaplain Father Chevalier of the 24th Infantry Regiment is a detailed account of the death of a corporal, Robert Pochet, at which Chevalier assisted. Pochet believed Therese was helping him die. And when he asked her to lessen his suffering, the chaplain observed his pain lesssened. Was this a coincidence?

Or was Therese there? The busy chaplain took the time to write the nuns in belief that *somehow* Therese helped Pochet. But he does not report the dying man *saw* her.

There is also this incident:

Carmelite nuns have personal friends just like everyone else. A family that included a married sister and a single one were "well known" at the Lisieux Carmel. The two sisters put one's strange experience in writing for the nuns so it could become part of the official data being accumulated on Therese.

Among the two women's friends was another family with a twenty-one-year-old son. "A true apostle" in his work for an organization called Catholic Youth, the young man went to war[7] and the sisters joined his family in calling upon Sister Therese to watch over him.

Everyone waited for news from the new soldier, but none came.

Just after eleven in the morning on August 24, 1914 — so the war had barely broken out — the unmarried sister was in her room when she suddenly saw a mysterious spectacle, distinctly, but as if at some little distance. Their soldier friend was in the arms of Sister Therese. Celestially beautiful and smiling, with one hand the little saint supported the young man; with the other, she presented to him a palm. Both of them were looking upwards, with expressions that were radiant and triumphant.

The brief vision was deeply moving. At its end, the viewer ran to tell her sister, adding that she was certain their young friend was dead or going to die. The sister who claimed to have just seen Therese was believed because, as her sibling later wrote, she was known to be neither given to flights of imagination nor a seeker of "spiritual experiences."

And most importantly, the vision proved prophetic: Two weeks later, on September 7, the young man was killed at La Fere Champenoise, struck by a bullet in his forehead, after he had just been cited for heroism and promoted to sergeant on the battlefield.

Why did Therese appear this way? Perhaps because by her "visit" to a family friend, as the sister writes, the devastated father found comfort and even a sort of sorrowful pride in what the vision said about his boy, his only child.

Did God only use Therese to help the French? Since they turned in droves to this descendant of French military men, obviously God could use Therese mightily in France. German soldiers undoubtedly didn't as often ask the prayers of an "enemy" nun. And if they did, they could hardly send a letter to her French Carmel. Nor were French wartime publications — even by Carmelites — going to headline Therese's miracles for the other side's soldiers! If Therese appeared to any Germans on the battlefield then, it was out of the public eye. But there is some evidence that, as you would expect, when German military men asked for her help, she responded.

For instance, before the war the father of Bavarian mystic Therese Neumann obtained some relics of Sister Therese for his family. When the devout Catholic tailor was drafted, his wife and children asked Therese to bring Ferdinand Neumann safely home. The Bavarian soldier did not see the saint but he came home alive and well.

Moreover, on March 14, 1980, an elderly Sister of Divine Providence in Alsace wrote Carmel regarding various favors to her family. Among these is a "miracle" in favor of her uncle Joseph Mathis de Housch, a WWI non-commissioned officer in the Germany Army. On the battlefield, Mathis saw every one of his men fall. Shot in the lungs himself, he fell to his knees invoking Sister Therese and somehow survived. Nine years after the war, he died a saintly death looking at an image of Therese, his last words of her.

Better known is the Carmelite's works as God's messenger for German civilians and other non-French during the war. I've chuckled over one German cure. Therese made an after-death appearance *immediately* after a mother superior stood over the dying individual — a young nun — and taunted that, since they were at war, French Therese probably wouldn't help a German!

Because it is so brief, a letter the Carmel received in 1919 can close this limited sampling of Therese's work during WWI. Let it stand for the appearances Therese made on non-French battlefields. Carmillo Cessi writes October 20, 1919, from Bassanello in Italy.[8]

> I'm carrying out the sacred duty of a grateful soul. For a long time my family has had great devotion to Sister Therese of the Child Jesus; but when war came, our confidence and our supplications (for her prayers) redoubled. My wife and my children never quit praying for her intercession and I felt myself protected on thousands of different occasions, above all at Mt. Frikoptel, at Mezli, and particularly at Mont Noir. At this last I believed I would fall on the battlefield but at the moment of most greatest peril, I heard the voice of "Little Therese." She told me that she was watching over me and that I had nothing to fear. This sort of thing one doesn't forget.
>
> Being now returned to my loved ones, I want to give great witness to my gratitude to the saint of miracles.

He closes with his permission to publish "these humble lines" with his signature. "The saint of miracles," he calls her. Doesn't sound exaggerated to me.

Endnotes

[1] Besides drawings, this was primarily a composite photograph, the work of one of her blood sisters, Celine, a Carmelite and amateur photographer. Frustrated that no photograph was "right" in all her sister's features, Celine

snipped the nose from one, the mouth from another, etc. to get what her fellow nuns agreed was "Therese." Unfortunately, this led to charges that the Carmel was distorting photos to make Therese "lovelier." This has been done with other saints at times. But to a man, the soldiers she appeared to found Therese "beautiful." Today the original photos are available from Carmel. From them it is clear that Therese no more needed retouching in body than in soul.

2 Now known worldwide as *The Story of a Soul,* her autobiography has sold millions of copies and appeared in all the world's major languages.

3 According to an interview by A.J. Daly with Master Sergeant Soister of the U.S. Marine Corps Weapons Training Battalion, these must be the type that have both a safety lock and the pin, which once pulled will permit the grenade to explode. Diez obviously has pulled only the safety lock!

4 According to Peter Young, head of the Royal Military Academy (Sandhurst)'s Military History Department.

5 A huge battle area of the 1918 period as the Allies pressed against the Germans' Siegfried Defense Line. There were many casualties on both sides, including Americans.

6 See footnote four above.

7 Some reader may wonder that an "apostle" was not a pacifist, but in WWI for good Catholics going to war when called was part of "rendering to Ceasar...." This does not mean the Church favored war. Pope Pius X tried desperately to stop WWI and died, grief-stricken, ten days after it began. It is said, and true or no, illustrates his attitude, that when he was asked by the Austro-Hungarian monarchy's representative to bless their armies, the saint-pope replied, "I bless peace, not war."

8 Italy was first on the side of the Germans, then switched sides and fought against them.

4 ❧ ALL THE WAY FROM HEAVEN

On July 5, 1969, a Syrian Melkite rite Catholic from Brooklyn named Margaret (at their request, these are not their real names) married a widower with a half-grown daughter. Eddie, a Maronite-rite Catholic born November 2, 1919, in Beirut, Lebanon, had been in the United States twenty years, since arriving as a seaman. Four years after their marriage Margaret became pregnant. This was great news but, at the same time, Eddie became ill. His stomach bothering him more and more, X-rays finally diagnosed an ulcer.

On March 24, 1974, as her stepdaughter started college, Margaret gave birth to a girl, joy mingled with a bit of anxiety since the infant had a heart murmur (several years later re-diagnosed as a more severe defect, but successfully corrected). As she lay in her hospital bed recuperating from a Cesarean delivery, Margaret was more worried over Eddie. In spite of treatment for his ulcer, his usual healthy color from working an outdoor job was gone. Week by week he got paler and felt worse. Picking up her bedside phone, she called for the results of his new X-rays. As she feared, the news was not good: Eddie's condition had only grown more serious.

During the next six months, although he followed the doctor's orders, Eddie continued to get sicker. When baby Katie was six months old, a third set of X-rays revealed that Eddie — now a very sickly color from losing blood internally — was "much worse."

"You'd better see a surgeon," the couple was told.

On September 17 at the Methodist Hospital in Brooklyn the surgeon operated. As Eddie was coming out of the anesthesia, the grave-faced physician's words to the patient's wife made it, Margaret still recalls with emotion, "the worst day of my life."

There was no ulcer.

Instead a five-pound tumor had been removed, along with a full three-quarters of Eddie's stomach. Worse, Dr. A., the surgeon, told Margaret with regret, this was no benign tumor, but "cancer in a very advanced stage."

Although he tried to encourage her to have faith in God, medically-speaking the surgeon could give his patient's wife no hope of Eddie's recovery. His doctors would try a ten-week course of strong chemotherapy, but without any real hope. Due to the misdiagnosis, things had simply gone too far.

Eddie, an outgoing man who has a positive attitude toward life, took the news much better than she did, Margaret recalls. He wasted no energy on anger over the misdiagnosis, nor did he become depressed. Accepting his situation, he said, "if it's not my time, I won't go," and was able to smile and joke with the hospital staff.

Margaret was devastated. At only three weeks old, she had lost her mother. Her father had died before her marriage and her stepmother soon after. Now she was about to lose her husband. And their little Katie, just as Margaret never knew her mother, would never know her dad.

Back when she was only fourteen, Margaret had been a patient in St. Anthony's Hospital, run by the Franciscan Sisters of the Poor. The teenager became friends with one of the nuns she believed a holy person. Now Margaret shot off a letter to this Sister Fidentiana, desperately begging prayers for Eddie.

courtesy the Franciscan Sisters of the Poor

Mother Frances Schervier

Sister Fidentiana wrote back an encouraging letter: the foundress of the Franciscan Sisters of the Poor, Mother Frances Schervier (pronounced SHURE VER) had been beatified that April. "Let's ask her prayers," she suggested, enclosing a novena booklet. Also in the nun's letter was a little touch relic of the tenderhearted Frances — who died during emergency surgery at only fifty-seven in 1876.

Margaret began the novena and tucked the relic in her husband's shirt pocket, telling him to keep it with him at all times.

The Brooklyn housewife knew nothing of Blessed Frances. But she was to learn that this frail, nineteenth-century nun, fiercely protective of the poor and needy, had "done it all." A sampling: Mother Frances took in thirty prostitutes who wanted to turn their lives around despite flak from "good people" over a nun associating with "fallen women." In an epidemic she bent consolingly over dozens of smallpox victims, nursing them devotedly with complete disregard for her own rotten health that made her a likely victim. Amazingly, she survived unscathed. Often she companioned the condemned, whom she did not send off with pious blessings, but accompanied all the way to the end — serene, indomitable — staying close enough that the axe severing her spiritual charges' heads more than once spattered her brown habit with their blood. Along the way the daughter of well-to-do Germans reluctantly founded a religious order, collected a Cross of Merit from the King of Prussia for her nursing work on bloody battlefields (her nuns did the same in the United States' Civil War), built hospitals and homes for her beloved poor and, as the Vice-Postulator of her Cause wrote, "mothered all alike" — including Protestants and Jews — "without distinction and without letup."

Margaret learned Mother Frances had been twice to the United States where her sisters, sent as missionaries, in only five years had spread out from their first assignment under the bishop of Cincinnati into Kentucky, Indiana, Illinois, and New Jersey. Maybe she had even passed through Brooklyn!

Eddie had never heard of Mother Schervier either. But he is from a devout family in Beirut, where a sister is a nun. As a child he experienced what he believes a dramatic rescue by his guardian angel: as he began to slip into a deep trench, invisible hands grasped him under his armpits, hauling him back to the gasps of astonished onlookers. He knew what God can do.

Not a reader, he never read nor joined Margaret in using the novena booklet, nor did he look at the relic she transferred each day to the pocket of his next shirt.

But he assured his wife "I'm praying to that nun from the Bronx." By which he meant Blessed Frances, who was actually from an area that at one point belonged to France — her town then called Aix-la-Chapelle — and today, as part of Germany, is known as Aachen. Eddie referred to Blessed

Frances as "the nun from the Bronx" because he has no memory for names but he knew her order has a hospital and home for the aged there — a place named for Frances.

The ten weeks of daily chemotherapy was tough. Eddie says in an understatement "it made me very tired. I didn't have the energy to walk." Yet Margaret points out her husband still insisted on climbing on the treatment table himself to spare the nurses' backs the strain of lifting him.

In his formal testimony he writes: "I finished the treatments on December 5. On Saturday, December 7, I was too tired to get out of bed and I had severe chills. I was due back at work on Monday the 9th, but my wife begged me to wait till January hoping I would have my strength (back).…"

That Sunday, December 8 (for Catholics the Feast of the Immaculate Conception), Eddie managed to drag himself to a special mass for the sick of their parish. He stood the whole time in the back of the church because it "was all old ladies" going up to be blessed and that made him feel out of place. Without receiving a blessing, he returned home "completely exhausted." Margaret pleaded with him again not to try to work the next day. But with the quiet heroism of the world's working men with families to support, he intended to try. His testimony continues:

> That night I went to bed about 10 P.M. My wife turned out the light. I turned on my right side. The room was pitch dark. I saw a nun kneeling next to me, her elbow resting on the bed. There was a white arch [see picture] around her face with a black veil. I lifted myself up to get a closer look at her eyes. The closer I got the deeper her eyes went. I saw her habit was brown. Her stockings and shoes were black. Her shoes had laces with a rounded toe and her foot was small. She told me to relax. She had a round metal box in her hand. She opened it and took a small host (the body of Christ by Catholic belief), rectangular shaped with a green cross in the center. She told me to open my mouth and placed the host on my tongue. Then she asked me where I had my operation. I unbuttoned my pajama and pointed to my stomach. She took another host and made the sign of the cross on my stomach. I felt it on my skin (later he says this sensation was of being touched with something sharp as she blessed his flesh with the rim of the wafer.) She said, "You're cured" and disappeared. I went into deep sleep. The next morning I woke up feeling well. I put in a full day's work with no tiredness and have since felt very well.

To this written testimony he can add a few more details: as she rested her arm on his bed, his visitor knelt on one knee with the other leg stretched out behind her. When she put the host on his tongue he felt it but it disappeared — absorbed mystically, somehow, as in certain saint's communions? — without his swallowing. The sick man saw the nun's clothing very clearly, but her body was somewhat hazy, the flesh slightly blurred. The eyes, for instance, which drew him in "deeper and deeper," he can fix at no particular color.

Perhaps because he went into such a deep sleep, when the alarm went off at 5:30 the next morning, although excited to feel well, Eddie did not immediately recall the nun's visit. He rushed off to work to Margaret's final plea, "Please if you don't feel well, come home early."

Through all ten weeks of her husband's radiation Margaret had been fervently asking Mother Frances to beg God for "a sign that Eddie would be cured." On the previous day, knowing he was determined to try to work the next day, she had prayed especially hard for a sign — above all, for the sake of their six-month-old baby.

Still when Eddie left for work his wife was sadly sure — after all, he'd been exhausted just standing up in church the day before — he'd never finish his workday. Not in the physically demanding job of a truck driver who lifts heavy loads in and out of his truck and does a lot of walking beside.

That particular day, as it turned out, Eddie did even more walking than usual, covering the whole length of the pier at Port Elizabeth in New Jersey. Yet he felt equal to everything.

When he came home after a full day's work they discussed with joy how well he felt — he wasn't even tired. Margaret recalls, "I was so happy I told him how hard I'd had been praying for a sign."

That triggered his memory.

"You know I saw a nun," he replied.

"What do you mean you saw a nun!" Margaret exclaimed.

Then he told her about the sister who had knelt by their bed the past night. When he described the nun's clothing, Margaret ran for the novena booklet. She placed the picture of Mother Frances before him.

"That's her exactly!" he said of the brown-robed Franciscan nun whose order's headwear has white around the face with a black veil.

"Maybe you saw her picture on the relic?" Mary Ann suggested.

Eddie shook his head. "No, you put it in my pocket and I never took it out. I just prayed to her."

Later it was realized that in his careful description of Mother Frances and her clothing, Eddie also detailed the stockings and shoes *which do not show in the novena picture*. And one of the nuns, Sister Rose Margaret, confirmed "yes, Mother Frances did have a small foot."

Dr. A., Eddie's surgeon, is a Syrian Orthodox believer. When he began his professional career he was moved by a portrait of Mother Frances and asked the saint to help him succeed in his practice. Margaret says gratefully the surgeon tried to give his patients hope, reminding her and Eddie that whatever the situation, humanly speaking, regarding the cancer they should remember Christ said faith moves mountains.

Now they came back to this "believing" doctor — Eddie alive and bursting with good health — for a six months' check up. Her husband's surgeon said to Margaret of Eddie being even alive, let alone well, six months after surgery bared his desperate condition, "that's a miracle!"

The sisters were interested too — to a point. Because it costs money for doctor's fees to pursue the detailed medical investigation by specialists that can lead to an officially-designated miracle, money they believe better spent on the poor, the sisters are opting not to pursue canonization for Blessed Frances. "That's how she'd want it," they feel. And Eddie's cure might not make it as a canonization miracle because for some people — not Dr. A., who saw his interior — the radiation treatments could get credit for the cure.

Assume for a second that radiation did cure Eddie, against all medical expectations when others in his condition died whether they had radiation or not. God's role is in no way negated. Blessed Frances announced a cure; she did not go into how God was bringing it about. Those who believe "radiation" is not the best reply to "what cured Eddie?" point to something significant: Eddie went to bed on December 8 in sad shape and woke up December 9 — a dead nun having dropped in on him during the night — a new man.

The recipient of a miracle (official or not), as he sees it, Eddie asked God to let him see Blessed Frances one more time. On July 13, 1975, that prayer was answered. The saint came to his bedroom again. This time the red-cross emblem on her brown robe stood out more, perhaps in deference to those nuns who worried that he had not noticed it before. But she did not touch or speak to him. He saw her in a static type of vision, sitting in a chair next to a table on which were three books.

In her own life Mother Frances, whose frailty never kept her from arduous work for the sick, was miraculously cured of asthma at Lourdes, the French healing shrine inaugurated by appearances of Jesus' Mother to St.

Bernadette Soubirous. From the time of her asthma cure, Mother Frances placed her congregation under the protection of the Blessed Virgin Mary. Perhaps that is why when Frances came, apparently wanting, saint-like, to get the spotlight off herself, it focused on the one who brought *her* miracle. At any rate, Blessed Frances disappeared and Eddie saw in her place the Mother of Jesus, radiant with a heavenly crown, in garments of white and blue. Mary blessed the Lebanese-born truck driver. Then she, too, disappeared.

Twenty years have passed. Eddie is now seventy-five and retired. From the night of Blessed Frances' first appearance, he has been able to eat anything he wants. At first, with only a quarter-stomach left, he could only take in small quantities at one time, but gradually his stomach expanded until even quantity was no longer a problem.

When he became anemic again some years ago, doctors, suspicious of malignancy, immediately ran a new gastrointestinal test series. The tests showed some intestinal bleeding — but in a perfectly normal, cancer-free intestinal tract. Turns out Eddie was having a problem common among those who take aspirin for arthritis, one solved by simply laying off aspirin.

Margaret was not surprised. As she says, when a saint comes all the way from heaven to say, "you're cured," you can count on it.

5 ❧ "CHEER UP, LADY!"

Vacationing in St. Louis when she was sixteen, Mary Wilson, a Presbyterian born in 1846, attended her first mass at St. Louis University, a Jesuit-run institution there. Miss Wilson was swept away spiritually and, after a series of instructions, was received into the Catholic church on May 2, 1862. Not a tolerant century, her Protestant family immediately disowned the young woman, just as Catholics would have done had matters been reversed. Four years later Mary joined the Society of the Sacred Heart, the order founded by St. Madeleine Sophie Barat. Her health poor, the young convert's superiors wanted to spare her harsh climates and snowy winters. They sent her briefly to a convent north of New Orleans, then to their Academy of the Sacred Heart (still operating today) at Grand Couteau in southern Louisiana, where the climate is optimum.

On the evening before she graduated, so to speak, from postulant (the first phase of becoming a nun) to novice, Mary collapsed with terrible pains in her side, vomiting blood. Had guilt over her family's rejection caused her body to prevent her taking an even more definitive step away from them? Possibly. In a similar situation, Venerable Francis Libermann had developed epilepsy. Whatever the cause, it appeared Mary Wilson was not long for the world. A Jesuit from the local college was hastily summoned. Hurrying over, he gave Mary the final rites. As it turns out he could have strolled. To the surprise of all, the dying twenty-year-old lingered, neither dead nor alive, for the next month.

Since, however precariously, she clung to life, the sisters decided to make a novena to Jesuit Blessed John Berchmans. Why they picked Berchmans I don't know. But in choosing him, they were asking the prayers of a young man born in Flanders in 1599 — that is, two hundred sixty-five years earlier — who had studied there, then in Rome in order to be ordained a Jesuit priest. Known for cheerful humility, holiness, and trying to do little things as perfectly as possible for God's sake, Berchmans never reached his goal. Still a Jesuit novice he died on August 13, 1621, at twenty, the same age that Mary lay dying at in 1866, two hundred forty-five years later.

Death, it is wisely said, is the final healing. As the novena progressed it seemed it would help Mary out of her sufferings by helping her die. For during the last three days of the nine-day prayer, her limbs grew cold while her tongue swelled and bled until she could hardly talk. Again she received the last rites.

Somehow she managed to communicate that she was asking Blessed Berchmans "for a little relief and health. Otherwise, that he give me patience to the end. I am resigned." Left alone at one point, she lay a holy card[1] of Berchmans across her mouth, whispering, "If you can work miracles, I wish you would do something for me."

"Open your mouth," came a young man's voice.

She obeyed and felt a finger on her swollen, bloody tongue. The same voice continued, "You'll get the desired (novice's) dress. Be faithful. Have confidence. Fear not."

Opening her eyes, Mary Wilson saw a luminous figure by her bedside. "Is it Blessed Berchmans?" she croaked.

"Yes," he answered. "I come by the order of God. Your sufferings are over."

Later that same day when her Superior came in, Mary astounded her by speaking clearly. The astonished Mother Martinez was afraid this improvement was the somewhat common respite before a dying person's final moments. So she ordered Mary to stay in bed. The postulant obeyed. But when a sister came to redo her bed that evening, the patient could stand it no longer: With a chair for a partner, Mary danced merrily round the infirmary.

When physician Edward Millard made his daily call the next morning, it was Mary Wilson who opened the door. He almost fainted, the account says, and was teased by Mother Martinez that they better get him a chair before he keeled over.

Recognizing the magnitude of what had taken place, formal documents were drawn up with depositions from all the witnesses. Mary Wilson, of course, had to write her testimony, too. Perhaps because she had been so ill she was very concerned about whether her report was totally accurate. Berchmans reappeared at this point to the healthy young woman and assured her she had everything right. He also told her that just as he had died before he completed his novice period, so would she.

The documents, which included not only medical records but the depositions of thirteen people who had been involved, were sent by the Archbishop of New Orleans to Rome where the miracle, accepted as genuine, was used for the canonization of John Berchmans in 1888.

As for Mary Wilson, after some months of a healthy, happy, fervent novitiate, on the Eve of the Feast of the Assumption (August 14) she suffered a stroke. At her death three days later, observers believed, although they saw nothing, that Blessed John Berchmans came a third time to assist her.

Today on the Academy's second floor a shrine open to the public marks the spot where a young man dead almost three hundred years brought God's healing to a young American woman in a nation that didn't exist when he left this life.

This chapter is a sampling of cases like Mary's where people with serious ailments were cured, they believe, through the prayer intercession of a dead saint — who actually showed up to announce the cure or trigger it with a compassionate touch or word. Some of these people believe the healing brought them through the saint was imposed from without by God's "fiat"; others would say the sight of the dead saint, in God's design, set off the body's inner healing powers in a sudden mega-explosion. But all cured credit God as the source.

For greater immediacy, after three to represent the nineteenth century, all cures are from the twentieth. Moreover, the first nineteenth-century cure — that of Mary Wilson — does double duty: It also stands for hundreds of dead saints *who died longer ago than the past hundred and seventy-five years*, the limits of this book, but who are still appearing as God's messengers.

Maria Marazzi was born in the middle of the nineteenth century in Castel Gandolfo, the little Italian town where Catholic popes retreat from Rome's summer heat. Gazing at their newborn, Maria's parents noted with concern a wen on the baby's right eyebrow. This proved so large as the child grew that she could not see out of that eye. Surgery for such things was so crude at the time that the little girl's mother could not bear to subject Maria to that possible remedy. So the child lived, essentially one-eyed, until she was five. Then her mother took Maria on a pilgrimage to the tomb of a dead priest. Father Gaspar del Bufalo was a man used by God in astounding ways during his lifetime, whether preaching on a crowded plaza while straightening out souls individually in the confessional of the plaza church at the same time (bilocation at its highest form), converting armed thugs sent to kill him, or drinking poison without harm. That until his death in

1837 he worked miracles and healed the sick — both the physically and mentally ill — goes almost without saying.

Now as the disfigured little girl peered with her one usable eye at the marble tomb, into her half-range of vision came a priest dressed in a rose-colored chasuble.[2] Walking up to the child, he suddenly bent to touch the grotesque wen with his right hand. Dizzily, little Maria suddenly saw the world out of two eyes. But there was no priest there. He had vanished — apparently carrying the wen with him. For it, too, was gone.

Ecstatically the mother and child returned to Castel Gandolfo, where the parish priest, who had known Father Gaspar personally, interrogated the little girl about the appearance of the priest who had touched her. Ingenuously the child — who had never seen Gaspar — described him feature by feature.

Another healing visit by this wonderworker took place in 1861, also at Father Gaspar's tomb in Albano (the body has since been moved to Rome). Clementina Masini was a local woman who had an absolutely terrible physical problem: chronic suppurating peritonitis aggravated by a purulent cyst, which perforated the wall of her abdomen and her intestines. Yuk! The doctors of the day did not even have an antibiotic to offer her and could only tell her sadly that her situation was "incurable."

Like so many who receive this verdict, Clementina Masini turned to God. She witnessed:

> I went to the tomb of the Venerable (Gaspar) and from the heart I recommended myself to him. Night and day I prayed without losing faith. During the night of January 21 (1861) while I was lying in my bed, Venerable Father Gaspar del Bufalo appeared to me.
>
> I begged "my holy advocate, obtain this grace from God for me." He responded "Cheer up lady. Don't be anxious. Tomorrow morning you'll get up with nothing wrong."
>
> After saying this he lifted the baton he held in his hand and touched the part of my body where the cyst had its mouth. Then he disappeared. After he was gone I said some Our Fathers and Hail Marys in honor of the Venerable. After a little bit, I fell asleep. I got up the next morning about five o'clock cured of all illness.

Clementina Masini went right back to a normal life, which in her case included hard physical labor. The illness never returned.

Sezze, Italy   *1934*

About seventy-five years after Clementina's cure in the area where a century earlier Father Gaspar broke up gangs of Mafia-type "bandits," Ursula Bono, a widow from the town of Sezze, lies bedridden. Before her malignant abdominal tumor got this bad, she has travelled to Rome, consulting cancer specialists there. Her hope at that time is for an operation to remove the tumor. But the doctors refuse — with admirable honesty — to take the widow's money for surgery since, as they tell her, "yours is a hopeless case."

Unable to retain any nourishment for some time, Bono is now too weak and wasted to get out of bed. Without hope of a natural cure for their mother, her two daughters — nuns in a group called the Sister Adorers of the Precious Blood — think of a beatified saint, a spiritual friend of theirs, who needs God to speak on his behalf through miracles[3] of canonization calibre. At her daughters' recommendation Ursula Bono has been asking the intercession of this Blessed Gaspar del Bufalo.

On the night of the 23rd or 24th of May, the bedridden, emaciated widow is alone when a priest strides into her room.

"Oh Father Francisco," she says gratefully to her parish priest.

"No, it's not Father Francisco," the priest replies in quite a different voice than she expects. "I'm the Blessed Gaspar."

Ursula Bono bursts into tears. Between her sobs she begs her visitor to either help her get well or help her die "because I can't live any more like this."

"Courage!" encourages the dead saint, placing his hand comfortingly on Ursula's forehead. "In a short time you'll be healed," he promises the terminal patient.

St. Gaspar del Bufalo

Then without walking out, he disappears.

Does she sleep at once the sleep of a child whose terror is over? Or does the widowed cancer victim weep, laugh, and praise God for joy all night? Such things are missing from the rather clinical report. But it does tell us that the next morning the nuns' dying mother was completely cured except for the kind of weakness associated with fasts of many days. Two or three days of eating normally — which she could do now with grateful gusto — and her strength returned too. Her doctor's verdict after his careful palpitation and tests revealed the big tumor completely gone: "This is a true miracle!" Specialists in this type of cancer (whose religion — or lack thereof — is never an issue, by the way) who were asked by the Congregation for the Causes of Saints to examine both Mrs. Bono and all her medical records agreed with the local doctor. The healing is one of the official miracles for Gaspar's 1954 canonization.

Abbot Paul (born Francis Luyckx), a Belgian Benedictine, died in Flanders in 1896. When he was not long in the Benedictine order, he later confided to a friend:

> … I was so ill [of TB], that my life was despaired of. I have been cured miraculously and I have but one lung. Our Savior appeared to me, accompanied by the Blessed Virgin, Saint Joseph and Saint Benedict. Our Lady held my hand, while Our Savior placed his right hand on my head and said: "Be cured; henceforth you will live for the consolation of many others. I grant you everything that you shall ask of me for others."

Known in the following years as a "wonder worker" who obtained many miracles, including cures, for those who came for his help, Father Paul is still being asked for his prayers, as I can attest having stood by his grave which was relocated in 1970 from a cemetery to inside the Benedictine church in the small city of Dendermonde to accommodate those who come in all weathers to seek his help. According to the testimony supplied by a convent's Mother Superior to Edward von Speybrouck (a friend and early biographer of Father Paul) in January, 1900, only four years after Father Paul's death, the little girl of impoverished farmers living at Waas had a fall "which inflicted a frightful wound on her head." The child fainted from the loss of so much blood and a doctor, summoned to treat her, said the wound would prove fatal.

Brought out of her faint, she could only scream with pain and babble a few incoherent words. Then a neighbor gave the anguished mother a small piece of Father Paul's monastic clothing. Some would insist the neighbor was superstitious when she advised the screaming child's mother to place it on the wounded head while they all solicited the dead Benedictine's prayers. But the mother did as her neighbor advised.

After they asked Father Paul's help, the child stopped her screams and seemed to slip into a restful sleep for about a quarter of an hour. Then she suddenly sat up saying that a "holy monk" had come "and cured me."

"I don't have any more pain," she exulted.

Half a century later, in 1951, attorney Francesco Belsani of Naples had some kind of illness that appeared to be influenza. After twenty days of fever he was put on penicillin and given another drug to make him sweat. If anything he got worse. With a temperature of one hundred four degrees, he suffered so many violent coughing spells, accompanied by fierce hiccups, lasting an hour at a time, that his heart was eventually affected.

Finally doctors discovered this was not just a flu: Belsani had a cancerous growth near the right lung. Unfortunately by this time, the lawyer was too weak to withstand an operation. During the night of August 23, the sick man entered a crisis where the fever, the coughing, and the hiccupping brought him to the realization he was "in immediate danger of death."

Choking and his damaged heart pounding furiously, he turned to a tenderhearted Pope who died of grief in 1914 as his spiritual children prepared to slaughter each other in WWI. This was Pius X — the first Pope to be beatified in centuries. Belsani was devoted to Pius — even had his picture hung over his bed. Now he begged the saint's intercession fervently.

To his amazement Pius X appeared at his bedside. The dead Pope clapped his hands as if giving an order and told the suffering man that tomorrow he would be well.

As the early hours of the new day began, without any medical intervention or explanation, Belsani was perfectly cured of cough, hiccups, fever — and the tumor. The cure became an official miracle when it was accepted by the investigating arm of the Congregation for the Causes of Saints as one of St. Pius X's formal canonization miracles.

A nun also believes her miracle was delivered by the same dead Pope. Daughter of Charity Sister Maria Luisa of Palermo came down in 1952 with meningoencephalomyelitis. That means she had meningitis which went into encephalitis (inflammation of the brain), with the additional complication of myelitis (inflammation of the spinal cord). Her hands and legs were paralyzed, her vision clouded, and there was little hope for her life. Her fellow Daughters of Charity began a novena to Blessed Pius X. They prayed their hearts out for nine days and the only result was: not dead, but no improvement.

Nuns who work with the poor and sick know how to hang in there. The Daughters prayed another nine days with the special intention of restoring Sister Maria Luisa's health.

She got worse.

The indomitable nuns were on their third novena and Sister Maria Luisa was continuing to deteriorate. But her faith in Pius' help remained firm. She not only had a framed picture of the white-haired, gentle-faced priest over her bed, she tied an image of him around her neck, a kind of improvised locket photo. Pius X was Sister Maria Luisa's spiritual hero and she was positive he was going to help her by his prayers.

They say that kind of faith moves God to respond. At any rate on June 18, 1952, still paralyzed and half-blind, Sister Maria Luisa suddenly saw the Eucharist, the flat, white wafer of flour and water that Catholics believe — from His promise of the Last Supper — is the Body of Christ. This Eucharist wasn't in the hand of a priest who had come to give her communion. It was a large Eucharist suspended in midair above a chest near her hospital bed. She reports:

> It filled the room with a brilliant light. With indescribable joy I tried to move but couldn't. Then I saw a figure dressed in white moving slowly toward my bed, and I heard a voice which said to me, "Rise, my child, and walk!"

Popes, of course, wear only white. He did not announce he was Pius X, but Sister Maria Luisa had no doubt. She was paralyzed, but her hero, in the presence of God in His effulgent *Shekinah* light and Eucharist, was telling her to get up. What's paralysis in a moment like that? Get up — how, she admits she has no idea — she did . Dressing herself, she raced down to the nun's chapel where her appearance stupefied the community which, seconds later, erupted in cries of joy and thanksgiving. This healing, too, was approved as a formal miracle.

Not every pope is holy, by any means. Think of the Borgias and other political popes whose relatives thrust them into the office. But in recent times Catholics have been blessed with pope after pope who truly live as "other Christs." Of no one is this truer than of Pope John XXIII, the rotund, peasant-born Italian who called the Second Vatican Council.

John died soon after that historic event began. Three years later, in 1966, another nun was dying in Naples. Although she was still a young woman, Sister Caterina Capitani's troubles went back to years of internal bleeding from ulcers. As a radical remedy, three-quarters of her stomach and her spleen were removed in 1965. In May, 1966 the quarter of a stomach she had left developed a peptic ulcer complicated by a fistula, that is, an open, running sore, which broke through her abdomen emitting everything she ate.

Her pulse weak, breathing labored, temperature high, and the fistula making it impossible for her to be nourished normally, Sister Caterina was close to death.

She received the last rites and, at her request, was left alone in her hospital room to pray. Saying her rosary, she suddenly felt a hand on her ravaged stomach while a man's voice said her name.

The sudden touch and voice frightened her, as she had heard no one enter. Nervously she rolled over and saw Pope John "smiling and indescribably beautiful" at her side.

"Don't be afraid," he reportedly told her. "It's all over. You're well."

They spoke together for about ten minutes, undoubtedly saying much that will remain forever a secret. But it is known that the dead Pope told the nun the fistula would close up and she'd be able to eat anything she wanted.

When he left, the ecstatic sister found her pain, temperature, and all other symptoms gone too. And so was the fistula. A tiny black dot pinpointed where it had been, as if to aid her in showing future medical men who would want to judge the miracle. (A fistula can close, but not instantaneously in medical knowledge.) Joyously she got out of bed at once, calling for something to eat. Within forty-eight hours nourishment restored her strength to the point that she actually left the hospital and went back to her demanding work as a nurse. When last examined, the young nursing sister was in perfect health with none of the digestive problems that ought to exist in her case. Of course because the study of Pope John XXIII's widely-acclaimed holiness is not concluded, I cannot offer this cure as "proven" or even officially acknowledged, but only as an "alleged" event on which the Postulator of the pope's Cause will not comment.

There is a tradition among Jews as well as Catholics that saintly people often have digestive difficulties. This may explain why there are so many miracles involving ulcers, stomach cancer, etc. Here's another:

In 1913 a member of Mother Cabrini's Missionary Sisters of the Sacred Heart, twenty-four-year-old Sister Delfina Graziola's chronic digestive problems got much worse. For the next seven years — on top of her original problems, which often made her vomit after eating — she had the pain of serious gallbladder trouble. Mother Cabrini died in 1917 and Sister Delfina, who had loved her spiritual mother, continued to decline. In my book *Nothing Short of a Miracle* I have detailed her four operations between 1921 and 1925 — none of which solved the problems. Doctors at Columbus Hospital in Seattle (a hospital founded by Mother Cabrini) knew the problem: Delfina's body kept forming fibrous adhesions — badly scarred tissue — around her pylorus, gall bladder, duodenum, and colon. This scar tissue obstructed the passage of food.

In 1925, she refused a fifth operation, a decision the doctors accepted because they felt her case was "hopeless," to quote just her surgeon, Milton D. Sturgis.

Sent to a house of rest and relieved of all duties, Sister Delfina continued to decline. By December, 1925, the emaciated nun lay dying. It was the Bishop of Alaska, who saw himself as a miracle recipient (see page 85), who recommended that the nuns and the children in their care ask Mother Cabrini to intercede with Jesus for the young nun's cure. Prayers aplenty were said; still, "realistically," there was no question of anything but helping Sister Delfina die. Then Mother Cabrini appeared to her in a dream between the night of December 13th and 14th.

Luminous and laughing happily, her beloved Mother Cabrini, who seemed to be in the nun's community room with Delfina, said, "I'll send you with Mother Carmela," pointing to a third nun.

Sister Delfina awoke. She was in more pain than ever, pain so atrocious she could barely croak out a word or two, but she felt the numinous quality of this dream: Mother Carmela was in charge of heavy physical work. Oblique though it was, Delfina believed this message meant she was going to be able to work again.

Just a "wish dream," most of us would say. But, it had that ineffable quality to Delfina, who said to herself: "It's certain I'm not going to die."

It is said those with no faith are often healed the moment they pray, while those with great faith are sometimes given the chance to stretch that virtue to heroic limits. The next three days Delfina suffered atrociously but she clung to what she believed was a promise from Mother Cabrini. Quoting a few paragraphs from *Nothing Short of a Miracle*:

> On the sixteenth the dying nun still had enough faith in the dream message to whisper to the community Superior, "Mother, our Mother Foundress is fulfilling the Bishop of Alaska's request for a miracle."
>
> The Mother Superior … later testified "Yet even as she said this to me her condition was so atrocious that she was writhing in agony. And her voice was so feeble … that I paid no attention. She saw that I hadn't understood, so she made an effort and said (it) another time.…
>
> Hearing this from her and seeing that she was suffering immensely, I thought she was delirious and her death must be very near.

Yet while this same Superior, Mother Tranquila, rushed off to phone Mother Cabrini's other Seattle establishments so they could all unite in prayers for Sister Delfina's "happy death," a cure was beginning. But only Delfina, God, and Mother Cabrini knew it. The next morning, her solicitous Superior saw that Delfina received "the blessing for the hour of death." Afterwards, when she was brought coffee just to moisten her dry mouth — even one swallow would make her vomit — Delfina surreptitiously drank a few sips with no ill effect. The pain was ebbing, too. Next she called for and drank orange juice. Then it was grapes and sugared almonds. By evening, pain replaced by hunger, the dying woman was enjoying a full supper.

Was it just a brief respite of the kind those surgeries had once brought? Not exactly. This was the end of 1925. Sister Delfina lived until 1967, dying at age seventy-seven.

St. Jeanne Antide Thouret, who died in 1826, appeared to a child hospitalized with a bone tumor which threatened her life. During the night of the fourth day of a novena begging the saint's intercession, young Philomena Pantanella of Arpino (near Naples) awoke. A nun, bending over her, appeared to be doing the impossible: she was non-surgically plucking out the tumor. Obviously, this was a hallucination or dream of the critically-ill child. Yet as Philomena "saw" the tumor pulled from her body, she experienced pain so great it made her scream. Her parents, sleeping in the same room, jumped up and ran to her. Their child's momentary pain was gone. So was the tumor. And so was St. Jeanne. This was one of three official miracles accepted for the French saint's beatification in 1926.

The following year in Naples, a holy physician, apparently in good health, told his friend he was going to die and a few hours later did just that. During his lifetime gentle, kindly Dr. Giuseppe Moscati's favorite patients were those too poor to pay for his help. While accepting modest fees at times to maintain their dignity, he was known to tuck money under poor patient's pillows when no one was looking. Like spiritual giants of all cultures, this twentieth-century physician understood that physical health is intimately bound up with psycho-spiritual health. He felt he was saving souls by caring for bodies and at the same time he counseled his patients on the importance of having their spiritual life in order to stay healthy — counsel often accepted, not because of the doctor's undisputed brilliance, but because of his kindness. It is interesting that the forty-six-year-old Moscati, who knew his life was to be short, did not die the way most people do. Instead, like some of the great Hindu and Tibetan masters, apparently feeling ill he retired to his room April 12, 1927, at three o'clock, sat down in his chair, crossed his arms, and simply left his body.

Beatified in 1975 and canonized in 1987, he has appeared to various sufferers as a harbinger of graces and cures. In 1954, for instance, Costantino Nazzaro was a mess. Addison's disease had not only made him weak and turned his skin brown, it had atrophied most of his body. In his misery, Nazzaro often asked the selfless, dead physician to pray for him. Then one night Dr. Moscati came to him in a dream. The dead doctor placed his hands, which had comforted so many patients during his lifetime, on the diseased body. Then he gave a verbal prescription: "Return to living peacefully and don't take any more medicine."

A funny dream? Maybe. But Costantino Nazzaro woke up feeling awfully well. Doctors confirmed he was completely healed — and this cure, too, became an official miracle before Giuseppe's Moscati's beatification.

St. Charbel Makhlouf (1828-1898) is the first canonized saint of the Maronite rite.[4] In his lifetime he was one of those thousands of quiet monks who pass through the world in great sanctity without being noticed beyond their own monastery or, possibly, the immediate locality. This is no tragedy, for it isn't God's purpose to hold up every saint as an example through beatification and canonization. Some feel the greatest saints — the ones who, as Hasidic Jews put it, "hold the world together" — pass among us completely unknown. But God decided otherwise with Charbel (also sometimes spelled Sharbel). After his Christmas Eve death in rural Lebanon, so many strange phenomena took place — inexplicable light hovering over the grave site, the unembalmed body found floating completely incorrupt on a sea of water and mud in the burial cave, a mysterious oil with apparent healing properties that oozed for years from the lifelike corpse, and "miracle cures," that it became obvious God was saying, "Hey there! Take some notice of this friend of mine!"

Among the miracles, let me mention two where believers claim they saw the saint. One day in 1937, Alexander Thomas Oubeid was walking through the Lebanese countryside near his village of Baabdat with a relative. Carelessly the other man let a cypress tree branch swing back into Oubeid's face. The retina of one of Oubeid's eyes was torn. In spite of treatment at several hospitals, including American Hospital in Beirut, the retina did not heal. Oubeid could see from that eye only if he was lying down. By 1942 even that much vision was gone. The complete blindness might have been bearable — after all, he had another eye — but he also suffered intermittent pain in the injured area and the misery of migraine headaches.

When it became public knowledge that tremendous healings were taking place at a holy, old monk's tomb, Oubeid's wife made a pilgrimage there. Her husband stayed home. But he made four novenas seeking guidance as to whether he should go to the trouble and extra pain of a trip to the monastery. Nothing he saw as a sign to seek Charbel's intercession occurred. Then he was given a piece of cotton saturated by the strange, bloody sweat the saint's incorrupt corpse exuded. He put this on his eye. He slept and dreamed a monk said to him, "If you don't come to me, you won't be content."

That Oubeid felt was the sign. He pilgrimaged to Charbel's grave and, like the ancient Greeks seeking healing (see page 31), he spent the entire night in the monastery church. The next day he returned home, his condition unchanged. Except for one thing: Now he somehow experienced great faith in God. Still he only got worse. Due to blocked tear ducts, a large swelling bulged out below the injured eye. The pain became so bad he could neither sleep nor continue his work as an ironsmith. He could only lie around, moaning and suffering with pain. Finally one night he was so exhausted he slept. Again he dreamed.

This time he was back at the monastery delivering some iron but a man threw a piece of it, which hit his bad eye. The pain caused Oubeid to scream and awaken. This is commonplace: we are in some physical distress and fit a dream around it.

He slept once more and dreamed again that he was at the monastery. This time he was drilling through a wall and some of the dust got in his sore eye, paining him badly. He did not wake up this time though. Instead in the dream he went to the monastery well and washed his eye. Then he sat down outside the church.

An old, emaciated monk came along.

"What's wrong?" he asked Oubeid.

The ironsmith explained how the dust had aggravated his injury. The monk fetched some medicine with which to treat the eye.

"You'll be healed," he told Oubeid, "but only after you've suffered severely from the swelling caused by that blocked tear duct." Then he put the medicine in the injured eye.

Immediately he disappeared and Oubeid searched the area fruitlessly.

"Did he go away because I did bad work?" the dreamer asked himself. Wondering, he went to look at the wall he was drilling. On it in Syrian letters he saw the words *The Servant of God Charbel*.

Trembling, he awoke and immediately was aware of the swelling, bulging painfully beneath the blocked tear duct. Moved by the numinous dream, he picked up a picture of Charbel and kissed it. Then he drew it across the painful, blind eye.

With that simple motion, Oubeid says, its sight returned, after thirteen years.

Doctors may have pursed their lips at tales of dead monks appearing in dreams, but they did know Oubeid was blind — their records were clear on that and on their inability to help — and now here he was before them with vision. After inquiry by two physicians and seven professors from related fields — a full investigation — the cure met all criteria for a miracle and was so proclaimed at the Servant of God's beatification in 1965.

Twelve years later in 1977, reporter Joe Alex Morris, Jr. of *The Los Angeles Times* described a quest for healings through St. Charbel that followed on the heels of his canonization. In the city of Beirut, Morris wrote with dismay of people in a religious frenzy, weeping mothers practically forcing crippled children to walk only to have them fall. The reporter saw others grubbing in the earth for what they called "miraculous incense," actually, Morris suggested, rock impregnated with soap from a defunct factory. Hawkers worked the crowd, selling everything from the "incense" to St. Charbel medals and calendars. Meanwhile in the war-torn country, Christian militia patrolled the site with guns, using this massing of Christians in a Moslem area of the city to establish a new political beachhead. Reading Morris' article, most *Times'* readers must have concluded that if God exists he would surely have nothing to do with so much blatant credulity, downright cruelty, and cynical exploitation. Yet Morris mentions that in one night three miracles were reported at the site. They followed, he said, the event which started the whole circus. Writes the *L.A. Times* reporter:

> One evening last week Charbel[5] is said to have appeared before a blind child who was praying to him (for his help). The saint reportedly told the child to get incense, to light it and to pray, and that his sight would be restored.
>
> As the story goes, the boy told the saint that he had no money to buy incense, and Charbel told him to go to a place next to the church of the "Sabteeya," as the Seventh-Day Adventists are called here, and to dig there. The boy got his mother and they went to the place, where they dug up a soft stone that smelled like incense and burned like incense.
>
> The boy regained his sight.

ENDNOTES

[1] Usually a pocket-size picture of a saint with a prayer for their intercession on the back.

[2] The outermost garment, shaped roughly like a poncho, worn by a priest saying mass. The colors vary with the season, rose being rare.

[3] The seven criteria given in more detail in my book *Nothing Short of a Miracle* include that a cure be instantaneous, complete, permanent, and not explainable by any medical treatment given or other natural means.

[4] The Catholic Church has a number of rites, many very ancient, with their own liturgical language and customs. The so-called Latin rite of the West dominates, however, in much of the world.

[5] Morris spells it Sharbel.

6 ✑ "I WILL COME DOWN"

Just before TB sent Saint Therese of Lisieux to bed for good, her blood sister Marie, also a Carmelite, came across her little sister forcing her disease-racked body to pace back and forth in the cloister garden.

"Why are you doing that?" Marie cried in exasperation at Therese's obvious exhaustion.

The infirmarian told her to take some exercise, Therese responded. She didn't mind, Therese assured Marie, because "I'm walking for a missionary." She figured, she explained to her sister, that somewhere far from France one of them was exhausted. To lessen his weariness, she was offering God hers.

Marie probably was not surprised. All the Martin family knew how much their youngest member loved the missions. Soon she would beg them not to buy flowers for her coffin, but send that money — where else? — "to the missions."

Only illness prevented Therese herself from sailing off to Vietnam, where she had volunteered to join the understaffed Saigon Carmel. Shortly before she died, someone chuckled, "those Saigon nuns are probably still expecting you." With all mail traveling by boat, undoubtedly they were. But Therese only remarked offhandedly, "Oh well, I'll be with them very soon."

Paired with two missionary priests as their spiritual backup by her prioress before her illness, Therese had ingenuously turned many of her most monotonous chores — doing laundry or sweeping spider-infested stairs — into prayers for these two men or missionaries in general.

In her last letters to them she promises she'll "return" and "come down," after her death, urging they believe "your little sister will keep her promises." Did the missionaries think these pious platitudes? If so, they misunderstood. Therese staked her whole life on a belief in supranatural realities that would let her work for God even in places far from France " 'til the end of time." Not from megalomania. But because, with a loved child's certainty, she trusted heroically that her "immense desires" "to make God loved everywhere" came from God whose work it would be, therefore, to see them fulfilled.

Can one go too far? Trust God too much? Therese thought not. And God's response to that trust — her greatest claim to fame, when you think about it — indicates she was not as naive as those claims to come back might imply. Therese was barely dead and her unassuming little autobiography (written in obedience to others, not on her initiative) barely in circulation when reports of miracles linked to her began to arrive in the Carmel letter-box from places like Madagascar, the East Indies, and China. Soon that mailbox was receiving fifty letters a day, then hundreds. The nuns remembered then that Therese had said another older Carmelite blood sister — her "second mother," Pauline, called Agnes of Jesus in Carmel — "would find consolation through the letter box" and "be kept so busy with me she'll scarcely suffer (grief) at all."

How busy was Agnes of Jesus (and the other Carmelites?) Consider, for only one indication of many that could be given, that in the first twenty-eight years following Therese's death in 1897 — that is, just up to her canonization — more than thirty million pictures and seventeen million relics were sent out by the Lisieux Carmel of about twenty nuns in answer to requests from all over the world.

Only thirty years after her death as an unknown, cloistered sister who never put a foot out of Europe, God had used Therese to work so many miracles — including many involving after-death appearances — *in the missions* alone that the Pope, by

OSV file photo

Saint Therese of Lisieux

a 1927 Pontifical Decree, made the young nun equal patron, with the great Jesuit missionary St. Francis Xavier, of all missions and missionaries. I like to ponder that as an example of the many things in this world that make sense only when we take supernatural realities into account.

Almost seventy years after the Pope's recognition of her after-death missionary work, one still finds Therese beloved in countries far from her native France. I note the far-eastern monk in his saffron robe, who brought a pilgrimage to Lisieux — yes, of Buddhists — in 1973 out of reverence for Therese's "universal love."

As you read these lines, there are statues of St. Therese in most Catholic Eskimo homes. They are there, three-dimensional photos, so to speak, because she is loved for the many proofs of her friendship across snowy wastes and eye-stretching tundras.

That friendship began five years *before* Therese was made an official saint. In 1917 a Jesuit born in France in 1858 (so fifteen years older than Therese) was named the first Catholic Bishop of Alaska. By then the entire Catholic world knew God was pouring out favors in missionary lands through Sister Therese. This no doubt explains why when one morning as the new Bishop, Joseph R. Crimont, ate breakfast and a prune pit slipped into his throat, she came immediately to mind. Choking to death, he called on Sister Therese for help, promising — was he a prophet, too? — to make her patroness of all the Alaska missions, if she would save his life.

When she came to his rescue, Crimont kept his promise.[1] He encouraged others to ask her prayers. When they received cures or other favors, the Bishop himself sometimes fired off the reports to Lisieux. And as soon as her holiness was officially recognized by the Church, he put up a statue of Therese at St. Mary's Mission chapel in Akulurak.

(Statues, by the way, for those who wonder, are a visual prayer aid growing out of a universal human desire: When you love someone you like to have their likeness where it can remind you of them. Museums are full of busts the rich had sculpted of their loved ones; we Catholics do likewise for our saints. Seeing such statues reminds us of those who love us in God and are willing to pray on behalf of anyone — non-Catholic, too — who asks.)

St. Mary's Mission Chapel also served Eskimo children who, leaving their villages to receive an education, boarded at a Catholic school in Akulurak. To one of them Therese appeared two years before Bishop Crimont's death. Chronicled in *The Alaskan Shepherd* (publication of the current bishops of northern Alaska), 1992 September-October issue, here is the eyewitness account of Sister Lucy Daly, O.S.U., who was thirty-seven at the time:

> ... On the feast of St. Therese, October 1st, there was always much celebration ... (including a Mass with) usually twenty-five altar boys. After Mass all — pupils and people of the village — were invited to go up the river on the large mission boat to pick berries ... on the tundra ...
>
> In 1943, the day before the feast ... one of our little girls (in the school), Christine, had a nosebleed. This was not unusual among the Eskimos, but our Sister Superior thought that, because there was a sheet of ice on the river and it was already cold, Christine had better not go up the river, especially since the Eskimos at that time were susceptible to tuberculosis. Christine did not have the disease, but was susceptible to it.
>
> The warmest place in our cold building was in bed so our Superior told Christine she should stay in bed while the other girls went up the river. This was hard for poor Christine, but she understood. She was eight years old, spoke very little English, had not yet made her first Communion, and was my pupil in second grade.
>
> After returning from berry-picking, the girls went to the dormitory.... As soon as they entered the dormitory, Christine very excitedly called them to her bed. The girls began to talk with great excitement in Eskimo, which I did not understand.
>
> Then the girls began to tell me what Christine had said: that St. Therese had talked to her for a long time and told her that, in honor of the feast, she would bring her to heaven that evening. St. Therese had surely communicated in Eskimo, because Christine knew very little English.
>
> I certainly did not believe the story and neither did our Superior, Mother Mary Louise Ronnenbaum. When she told it to Father Segundo Llorente, S.J., he replied, "All Eskimos have visions of one kind or another."
>
> Since I had charge of the dormitory at that time, I brought up Christine's evening meal. She was very happy and talked enthusiastically, though I did not understand her dialect, having been in Akulurak only two years. When I returned for the tray, she seemed unconscious, with the pallor of death on her face.

I rushed to Mother Superior with word that Christine seemed to be dying. She and Father were both shocked.

That was at 7:00 P.M. Five minutes before midnight, after five hours of suffering, Christine slipped peacefully into the next life. Sister Lucy ends her account by mentioning that, far from sad, the other Eskimo pupils, including the eight-year-old's sister and brother, were filled with joy that "Christine is in heaven."

In 1934, of course, Therese was already official co-patroness of the missions. Let me now back up to give a 'round the world sampling of those early favors that led to this honor. July 20, 1909, is the date on one letter received at Therese's Carmel from China. A missionary priest writes that a native non-Christian woman dreamed of "a radiant and mysterious being who showed her heaven" without saying a word. Probably because the "being" looked like a European, the woman rushed to the missionary and described all this in great detail, including the garb of the celestial being. The missionary was struck that what he was hearing from a Chinese non-Christian, who should know nothing of the details of nun's dress (almost every group of nuns has distinctive garb), was a description of the clothing of the cloistered Carmelites. Digging around, he found a picture of Sister Therese, who in 1909 had been dead only twelve years and was neither beatified nor canonized. He showed the picture to his visitor and she exclaimed at once, "Yes! That's it! That's exactly it! I recognize her!" Immediately the excited woman arranged both to begin studying Christianity and to put her two children in the missionary's school. The report does not say if she came from another faith tradition or was one of many in every culture who ignore spiritual realities. All that is known is that God called her in this way and she responded.

In Dahomey, Africa, Therese was also at work before official recognition by the Church. In 1915, a young black tradesman in Calvai, who was studying to become a Christian, was severely bitten by a normally tame dog. Adrien Metamehou Quenum was toting his collection of fetishes — rather uneasily, having been threatened that they would take their revenge — determined to "give them up" to Bishop Francis Steinmetz. Although Metamehou (who went by his middle name) was "built like a Hercules," the wound was not quickly history. Whether because he was the victim of a shamanistic curse or his body responded to the thought that he was, something like blood poisoning set in and he began to wither away with ceaseless fever.

One of the missionary priests, Father R.P. Barril, meeting him at the hospital at Godomey in August of that year, decided to interest Sister Therese in Metamehou's case. He gave the young tradesman one of those seventeen million relics of Therese and encouraged him to confidently ask her prayers.

A few days later the sufferer — uncured but still joyful, he insisted, in his new faith — visited Father Barril. The priest had a large picture of Sister Therese on his wall. Metamehou went up to it and, speaking aloud, asked her to obtain his cure.

That was August 29th. When night came, Metamehou — as every night now — tried in vain to sleep. Finally toward four in the morning he fell into a heavy slumber. But this was no ordinary sleep, for the sick man dreamed he saw Jesus Christ, at whose side was the young saint whose prayers he had begged that day. Jesus presented her, radiant and beautiful, to the sick African and she put her hand on his head. "I'm the little Sister Therese of the Child Jesus," she told him, "sent to cure you. I've prayed for you and you are delivered from your trouble." Speaking his language and using a figure of speech very understandable in his culture, she explained that she had a lot of credit with God she could draw on to help him. She also told Metamehou, "The good God has made me powerful, because, out of love for Him, I knew how to make myself very small."

"Soon," she predicted matter of factly, "He's going to glorify me and do still bigger things." Metamehou, of course, was not yet even baptized, only studying to become a Christian. His mind did not turn to things like beatification, canonization, or, rarest of all, someone being named a universal patron of the Church. But when he repeated her words to Barril and other priests (the Bishop and three of his clergy sign the deposition sent to Carmel) their minds did. In their deposition they affirm that Therese is not only "known, loved and invoked" in Dahomey, but that they are praying "to hasten" her beatification.

Far more important than things like beatifications to young Metamehou was another fact: When Therese's dream visit ended, he woke up filled with joy and perfectly healthy. Was this a case of a mind substituting, as more powerful, one "fetish" — devotion to Jesus and Therese — for an older one? Some nonbelievers may look at it that way. But Metamehou felt he had freed himself from a religion that controls by fear, for something that brought him healing and love.

Baptized that September 8th, he already had "in every room of his house," according to the priests who took down his story (he could only sign with his "X"), " ...a portrait of Sister Therese." The joy of his encounter with the dead French Carmelite even drew into her Faith Metamehou's mother and "entire family" — the very people who had heaped curses on his head when he went to "turn in" his fetishes.

From Tunisia came another cure testimony. This was the case of an eleven-year-old girl, who in September, 1911, was gravely ill with typhoid fever — a great killer in that era — complicated by deadly peritonitis. The family's doctor had called in other medical men but — remember, this is before antibiotics — they could only echo she was "beyond human remedy," or "lost" as one put it melodramatically.

The doctor tried to prepare the child's father that she could not make it through the night. As he struggled to deal with the coming loss of his child, a woman the written signed testimony identifies only as Madame B. placed a picture of Sister Therese of the Child Jesus near the dying child who, delirious, had recognized no one for two days.

The sick girl at once said, "Sister Therese turned her head toward me and smiled at me." Weeping and praying by her daughter's bedside, the mother paid no attention. Who would? The child was delirious.

Then the girl began to look fixedly at a point in the room as if someone were there. Her face expressed astonishment succeeded by joy. After several seconds like this, she spoke again to her mother. This time she said, "Mama, don't cry anymore. Sister Therese has come to cure me. I've seen her; she came near me with angels around her. I was surprised at first but then I felt so happy. I smelled the roses. And I still smell them now."

More delirium? Who can say? But something definitely was happening in the girl's dying body. When the doctor arrived for his next visit, most likely (the report does not say, but remember he has prepared the father for the child's death) expecting to find a dead body, he exclaimed to the parents; "What have you done? It's a miracle to find this child in this state!"

As for the perfume of roses the child claimed to smell, strange as it may seem, it does not appear to have been an olfactory hallucination. At least a number of people who came to visit the "little miracle child" before she was allowed out of bed sniffed, following a belief of the times, "Roses in here! You'll give the child a headache!" From the strength of the odor, they failed to observe there were no roses in the bedroom, nor in the entire house.

Recovery was quick and permanent. When the formal testimony of this cure, written by "a close friend of the family" (probably the self-effacing Madame B), accompanied by written attestation as to the report's accuracy by the child's father, was submitted to Carmel on April 3, 1913, the only aftereffects of the girl's "fatal condition" were gratitude toward God and "tenderness without limits" toward the dead messenger of her cure.

A cure that took place in Khandwa, India to a woman born Catherine Augert (on October 26, 1888 at Fontcouverte in Savoy, France) was considered so remarkable that the local head of the Church, Bishop Coppel of Nagpour, made a formal inquiry into it and sent a complete account to the Carmelites. In her late twenties in 1915, Catherine was a missionary of the Sisters of St. Joseph, renamed Sister Emma.[2] Besides mentioning Sister Emma's qualities that indicate good mental health, the Bishop's report states explicitly that she does not have any "sign of eccentricity or nervous symptoms," a formal way of saying that whatever happened to her should not be attributed to her being a nut!

We also have the briefer first-person testimony of Sister Emma herself, which she sent to her brother Joseph, a missionary priest stationed in Fribourg, Switzerland. He contributes his attestation, too. All in all these detailed sources give rather more information than most of us want about Sister Emma's innards.

Reduced to the basics this is the story: Ever since arriving in 1911 in the portions of India under British administration, Sister Emma's "stomach troubles" — already evident before she left Europe — only grew worse. Various British military doctors — majors and colonels all named in the Bishop's report — treated her in the several different places where she was assigned over the next four years for what they diagnosed, by its symptoms — in those days before X-rays and barium — as a very bad stomach ulcer. Typical of the treatments — which all failed — was having her eat nothing whatsoever for eight days except for a few spoons of water. This to give the ulcer a chance to heal by eliminating further irritation from digestive acids or from the food itself. By 1915 in spite of all that medicine could do, the young nun's digestive apparatus could tolerate only eggs beaten in milk. Then she had to give up the eggs. That April she was in terrible pain and her doctors concluded the ulcer was "incurable." Her order did not give up. They called in a new doctor.

Same verdict.

Things were so bad Sister Emma was hoping to die.

Then on the seventeenth of that month, she was inspired to try a novena for the prayers of Sister Therese, whom she admired as a model Christian. She also had one of those millions of relics people were requesting from Therese's Carmel and, having begun the novena, laid the tiny object on her chest. With new confidence she fell into a light, intermittent sleep.

Neither dead to the world nor awake, she saw in a sort of dream Sister Therese who, smiling, took her hand and asked "What do you want me to do for you?"

Sister Emma immediately requested good health adding, with a confidence reminiscent of Therese's own, that she "knew" Therese could obtain this for her.

She awoke immediately and understood she was completely well.

Nuns tend more to the skeptical than the credulous. When Sister Emma bounced in and announced her cure the next morning, her Superior says she simply "attached no importance to her declaration." But when the nuns sat down to eat and Sister Emma sat down, too, and — spurning her usual diet of several drops of milk — ate with gusto *everything* served, even meat, the Superior's own spoon dangled in astonishment, as did those of the other sisters present.

A meal like this ought to have killed Emma or at least had her in agony after the first bite or two. Instead there were no ill effects whatsoever.

Even the skeptical Superior had to agree with the Bishop's verdict that Sister Therese had hand-carried a miracle to British India.

In the South Malabar region of East India in 1913, another nun had a visit. She was Sister Marie Cornelia of the Sacred Heart. A native of the area, she entered, as a novice, the Carmelite Convent of Saint Joseph at Ambazhakad on the Malabar coast, only to become tubercular. After three years' attempts to cure her, on February 7, 1913, her doctor threw in the towel and said the nuns should call a priest to prepare Sister Cornelia for death. Two days later, death imminent, the chaplain of the nuns, Father Anthony Kachapully, gave her the last sacraments in the presence of the nuns and two other priests, who later signed his report as witnesses.

Sister Cornelia almost at once lost consciousness, but suddenly was heard to speak in a low voice, as if with someone invisible, her face showing now joy, now sorrow, as the conversation progressed. Trying to gauge her level of unconsciousness, someone brought pictures of St. Therese and the Virgin near her face. Unexpectedly she reached out at once, grabbing and kissing them with great reverence. About an hour later, her face became sad and, at the same time, she lost even her former level of awareness of what was going on around her, the pictures falling from her hands while she rested immobile a long time, apparently in some sort of deep trance state.

Rather than lapsing further into unconsciousness and dying, however, she eventually returned to normal awareness. To her Superior's question, the report says, she replied: "The Virgin Mary and Sister Therese appeared to her and told her not to be afraid because she was not going to die of this malady. They said she would get worse this day and the next but that Sister Therese would always be with her to sustain her until her cure which would take place suddenly."

Some deathbed hallucination! Except that while she did get worse, she didn't die (and remember, she was already dying, so "worse" should have only meant one thing). *And* those who were there say they felt "a supernatural presence" in the room, which they credited with sustaining the dying nun even though whoever was there remained invisible to everyone present.

On February 11, Sister Cornelia fell again into that mysterious state in which she claimed to have seen Therese and the Mother of Jesus. This time there were several priests, including a Carmelite father, joining the sisters as witnesses.

As the church bell of the parish church tolled the hour Catholics of the day knew as the Angelus, the deathly-ill nun again returned to complete consciousness. Questioned by Father Kachapully, she said that Mary, this time with the Child Jesus, had appeared to her again, accompanied by Sister Therese. Sister Therese had repeated that Cornelia's illness was going to end this very evening.

And "in effect she was cured," the priest continues, "with no more symptoms whatsoever of tuberculosis." The doctor, he adds, "affirmed that he attributed the cure to supernatural intervention."

In Calavi, Dahomey, where she cured the young tradesman, Therese also paid a visit to a missionary nun who was a widow with four children. Her oldest son had just drowned and she asked Sister Therese, whom she addressed — thinking of her spiritual maturity, not her chronological age — as "little mother" to obtain the strength necessary to bear her grief. On the night between the fourteenth and the fifteenth of October, 1916, the nun was awake around 4:00 A.M., her heart racked with sorrow, when she saw Sister Therese by her bed.

"You'll be consoled," she said simply, "if you unite your pain to the pains of the holy Virgin (who lost her son) and your tears to those of Jesus when he wept over the tomb of (his dead friend) Lazarus."

That was the whole visit. No long chummy chat like that with the soldier (see chapter three). But as God who sent his saint obviously knew, it was enough: no sooner had the sister followed Therese's advice than peace filled her soul to such an extent that she later commented "resignation" was not the right word; what she felt, she said, could only be called "supernatural joy."

In 1919, some nuns in Korea had a garden too far from their convent to be watched at night. Whatever they grew, vegetables or fruits, vanished almost every night, picked by intruders. Don't ask me why the sisters didn't take turns sleeping in the garden with a shotgun ready to fire in the air. Maybe nuns don't do that sort of thing in Korea. Or maybe they refrained because even mock violence isn't the way to show Jesus to the world. All I know is the Superior testified she felt there was nothing she could do until in desperation she asked dead Therese to "stand guard." She even planted medals of the dead nun at either end of their field. You may find this very silly, even superstitious. I won't contradict you, although we can take these — she is a Mother Superior, after all! — as symbolic, not magical, gestures. And maybe Sister Therese did start patrolling the place, for all thefts abruptly ceased.

The Carmelites also heard from Father R. P. Seraphin, the Superior of a Catholic missionary effort in what is now Ethiopia. He dated his testimony April 4, 1919, sending it from the Church of Notre Dame in Addis-Abba. In December, 1918, he writes, he came down with the pernicious flu that killed twenty million of the world's people in the year 1918-19. When he felt himself definitely near the end, he decided to receive extreme unction, a once-in-a-lifetime event at the time.

He placed a relic and picture of Sister Therese on his bed's bolster, hoping in his weak condition — whether through thinking of Therese's life or invoking her help, he does not say — to muster up some devotion so he "could make a good end." But while thinking only of how to die well, he heard an interior voice reproach, "Why are you thinking of abandoning the mission this way? Why not have compassion on the Apostolic Vicar? Better to ask for a cure." (The Apostolic Vicar was the priest who would have the difficult job of replacing the missionary.)

A man after my own heart, Father Seraphin was cautious about this voice. After all, he was very sick and could be prey to something like a "fever dream." So he made a mental pact with Sister Therese. If it wasn't an imaginary voice, but really the saint, she should see that he was much better by Friday (this was Tuesday). If that did not occur, he would take the last sacraments.

To his astonishment by that very evening, his condition had improved dramatically. On the second day there was no longer any danger of death whatsoever. Relapses are common in influenza. But when Father Seraphim wrote three-and-a-half months later, he had not experienced a moment of ill health since the voice reproached "It'd be better to ask for your cure...."

A similar experience took place at Lokandu in the Belgian Congo in the fall of 1919. The same terrible influenza hitting a missionary who had worn himself out during the war years when even the colonies of the combatants were involved in the struggle.[3] In June, 1919, with the war over, this Father Mulder had been told to return to Europe to recoup his strength. He stayed at his post because the new young missionary sent out to help him did not yet grasp either the native language nor the Africans' customs.

By July, Father Mulder later wrote, he was "exhausted, at the end of my strength." Taken ill with the dread disease, he began vomiting, then experiencing bloody urine, a very bad sign. Thinking always of the mission rather than himself, and with no doctor in this remote outpost, he turned to Therese "asking her prayers out of pity for the poor mission." Two days after his appeal to Therese, he was better. Not well, but well enough by July 15 to travel to his regional missionary Superior, with whom he was in touch by radio.

Arriving there, Father Mulder learned that a doctor was at Kindu, some sixty-two kilometers from Lokandu. This medical help was summoned, arrived, and prescribed a dozen injections of arsenic. Did this help or sabotage the recovery? All we know is that on August 2, after returning to Lokandu, the missionary had one of the relapses, so common and so often fatal, of the deadly virus. This time he had bloody urine, then couldn't urinate at all, while he vomited, was racked with "an agonizing cough," and experienced all the miseries associated with a very high fever. "The doctor and everyone else," he writes, "judged me lost."

But Father Mulder was a fighter. He mobilized his young assistant to get the entire parish together daily for a novena asking Sister Therese of the Child Jesus' prayers "that I might recover if it was useful for the good of the mission." Using imagery to represent mysterious realities, he had them place a picture of Therese by the tabernacle so she could "plead my cause."

Another of her pictures, he relates, he had where he could see it, lest he forget in his misery to keep supplicating her prayers.

Translating his French precisely here:

> On the second day of the novena, on August 4, at six o'clock in the evening, while my faithful flock prayed in the church and I united myself to their efforts, the image of Sister Therese that I had where I could see it grew in size and appeared as if alive; then I heard a voice say to me very distinctly with a sweet tone: "No, my father, you won't die yet; it's necessary that you continue to work...."

Embarrassed or not, he reports honestly that he couldn't control himself at that point: he began to weep.

However, there was no change in his condition at all: Every deadly symptom persisted. But he seems to have had that sense of ineffability in regard to his experience that makes doubt impossible. For when the next morning the Provincial of his religious order, who was now there, proposed he receive the last sacraments, Father Mulder refused, confiding "the heavenly promise" he had received. Typically, the Provincial was skeptical but he agreed to let Mulder wait a bit. The novena continued and on its last day, Mulder notes joyously that the Provincial had "a happy surprise" when he saw his head man at Lokandu "out of danger."

By August 24, Mulder writes he was able to attend Mass. There he could not contain himself. Probably still too weak to be speaking, he got up and, "with a voice half cut by sobs and tears" because he felt he was not worthy of the grace, a humility that indicates to me, he was one of those "pure as crystal" priests after Therese's own heart, he told his flock "the secret of my cure," — that is, about the visit of the dead nun he calls "the dear little BIG saint."

In the last portion of his long testimony, Father Mulder notes he has talked about his cure to three doctors, two of whom have been practicing tropical medicine for more than fifteen years. All three, he says, are in accord that "they have never seen a cure where there was bloody urine and then urinary failure for five days."

As for the doctor who personally treated him, that physician urged Mulder, when he inexplicably recovered, to leave *at once* for Europe to avoid another relapse. But "today," the recovered priest boasts in his testimony, "six months after my cure, I'm still here and I'm working as if I'd never been sick."

The New World missions were not bypassed, either — by Therese or influenza. Besides Alaska, reports came from the vastness of Canada as well. To give just one, a Father R.P. Van den Bossche sent a testimony from Yorkton in Saskatchewan. Some Ruthenian sisters had come from Europe to staff a school there and as 1919 ended and January 1920 came up on the calendar, one sister was also fighting influenza. This was probably not the lethal type the two priests had suffered. At least there was no danger of death for this sister until the disease went into into pneumonia. Then things deteriorated fast.

As one of his colleagues was summoned in the night to give the missionary teacher the final rites, Father Van den Bossche, who was in his bed, said to himself, "it's Sister Cecilia dying."

But immediately interiorly he heard the words, "She shall be saved."

After being prepared for death, the next morning Sister Cecilia was so much better the doctor "didn't recognize her." Everyone at this mission was delighted when some days later she reappeared —well — at Mass.

Note this missionary had no proof that Sister Therese, who had obtained many favors for him in the past, had spoken to him: but he believed it was she at the time and, for him, the inexplicable cure was the seal of an after-death appearance. To others, of course, the nun simply got lucky and cheated what had appeared certain death.

Blessed Arnold Janssen (1837-1909) is the German-born (in Westphalia) founder of three missionary groups — an international group of priests and brothers, an order of nuns, and a women's contemplative branch to provide the spiritual power behind the other enterprises. Saints come in all kinds of personalities. Janssen, a mathematician and expert in the natural sciences, had the rather cool and reserved personality associated with not only mathematics, but those born in the Prussian part of Germany. Even his own secretary acknowledged "it was only after his death that we recognized what a great saint we had in our midst." His personality is the only clue I find to one of St. Therese's strangest after-death appearances, for in the miracle that was accepted for Janssen's beatification — that is, attributed to *his,* not her, prayers — she apparently played stand-in for this saint. Quoting the authenticated account furnished by his order:

It was during the severe winter 1928-29. As a result of frostbite Missionary Brother Kostka (born Joseph Wasel at Allrath on March 23, 1863) began to suffer from a serious leg ailment. At the time Brother Kostka was living at St. Wendel Mission Seminary. Both feet became numb. Both legs were badly swollen up to and above the knee. Blisters and boils began to form. Although the bandages were changed daily no improvement occurred. Brother Kostka relates that one day he heard a noise behind him. He turned around and saw the figure of a Sister, who looked like the picture of St. Therese of Lisieux. She smiled at him and, pointing to the picture of Father Arnold Janssen, said "You could pray to your founder (for his intercession with God) and ask that your legs be healed." Then the figure waited a short while, as if to assure herself that he had understood her. Then it disappeared.

Looking at the picture, Brother Kostka now prayed for the cure of his leg ailment for about ten minutes. Next he heard a voice saying to him verbatim, "Now go into the water. Your leg will get well. Moreover you will never again have any trouble."

When Brother Infirmarian Juventius came to the room a half hour later and heard what Brother (Kostka) had experienced, he immediately removed the bandages and to his great astonishment observed that both legs had a normal appearance; in place of the previous boils only smooth scars were visible. No trace of the swelling remained. Standing and walking did not cause the least pain. Brother Kostka could immediately take a bath.

As patroness of the world's Catholic missions, St. Therese has some claim to appearing *for* a missionary *to* a missionary. But it still raises a chuckle that, even dead, Blessed Arnold was too reserved to come himself.

As we near the year 2000, much has changed in what we now call "the third world." African-born missionary priests out of bulging seminaries are bringing Christ back to "post-Christian" European societies that once sent missionaries to them. But one thing has not changed: devotion to St. Therese of Lisieux around the world is stronger than ever. I think of Matta el Masquin, for instance, an Egyptian Orthodox Coptic Christian studying to become a pharmacist. When he experienced God's call, the young, twentieth-century student abandoned his studies and went into the desert of upper Egypt as a hermit, following in the footsteps of St. Macarius, who went into the same desert around 335 A.D. and became one of the fathers of Coptic monasticism. In 1964, Therese's autobiography became available in Arabic. In his Egyptian hermitage Matta el Masquin read the book and was profoundly moved. So moved, that it is from her teachings that he's created the "base" and "fundamental rule" for himself and others in a new monastic experiment called Wadi Natroun.

The only constant is that nothing is constant, the Greek philosopher Heraclitus insisted. Obviously he didn't know St. Therese.

ENDNOTES

[1] The bond between this missionary Bishop and the dead saint held to his death in 1945, when Crimont had himself buried at a shrine to St. Therese, twenty-three miles north of Juneau.

[2] Members of many religious orders have traditionally taken a new name upon entering the community to symbolize beginning a radically new life. This practice is less common today when the continuity of lives is more emphasized.

[3] See the novel *The African Queen* by C. S. Forester for a fictional example of how civilians were affected.

7 ✒ A Smile
From Heaven

I t is late at night [as a man alighting from a Paris taxi].... follows a bellboy through the whirling door into the lobby of one of the big Paris hotels ... before World War II.

... He is a businessman, and an important one.... A Frenchman ... he walks through the lobby like a man ... used to stopping at the best hotels.

... Suddenly aware that someone is looking at him, he turns around. It is a woman, and to his astonishment she is dressed in the habit of a nun.

If he knew anything about the habits worn by the different religious orders, he would recognize the while cloak and brown robe as belonging to the Discalced Carmelites. But ... a man in his position ... is far too important and too busy to ... [think about] religious orders ... although he occasionally goes to Mass as a matter of form.

The most surprising thing of all is that the nun ... is smiling at him. She is a young sister, with a bright intelligent French face: and her smile is a smile of frank, undisguised friendship. The traveler instinctively brings his hand to his hat, then turns away ... assuring himself that he does not know any nuns. As he is signing the register, he ... [glances back]. The nun is gone.

Putting down the pen, he asks the clerk, "Who was that nun that just passed by?"

"I beg your pardon, monsieur ...?"

"That nun — who was she anyway? The one that just went by and smiled at me."

The clerk arched his eyebrows.

"You are mistaken, monsieur. A nun, in a hotel, at this time of night! Nun don't go wandering around town, smiling at men."

"I know they don't. That's why I would like you to explain the fact that one came up and smiled at me just now, here in this lobby."

The clerk shrugs: "Monsieur, you are the only person that has come in or gone out in the last half hour."

Not long after, the traveler ... was no longer an important French industrialist, and he did know something about religious habits. In fact, he was wearing one.... He had become a Trappist in a southern French abbey ... fasting, praying, reading, keeping silence with his tongue in order that the depths of his mind and heart might be free to seek God....

The thing that needs to be stressed about this story is that it is true. That lay brother is living today in the abbey of Aiguebelle, and the reason he is there is to be traced ultimately to the fact that one night he walked into a Paris hotel and saw a nun smiling at him, though the clerk told him no nun was there.

A few days later he saw a picture of the very same nun in the house of some friends. They told him that her name was St. Therese of the Child Jesus.... And before long his beard had grown ... his head was shaved ... and he was ... [in] a brown robe....

No one has ever reported a clearer example of how God uses dead saints to guide ordinary people — that is, we who are not holy — than this true account from *The Waters of Siloe* by Trappist writer and contemplative Thomas Merton (1915-1968).

Of course, many dead saints appear to people whose lives need no dramatic turnaround. In these cases, guidance takes such forms as comfort, consolation, or encouragement. I think of a family friend, George Pitts, who lives close to the Lord. George and his wife, Mary Ann, were close to Los Angeles Jesuit Father John Dugan, who occasionally said mass at their home. Father Dugan will be remembered by many who attended Catholic Charismatic conferences in Anaheim during the 1980s as the priest in the light blue stole who came down the aisles, arms upraised, dancing for joy like David before the ark, without ever for a second losing complete dignity. All grace and spirit, Father Dugan seemed more of heaven than of earth.

The Jesuit died June 1, 1991, a time when George was suffering career disappointments, Mary Ann was fighting what would prove to be fatal breast cancer, and the couple were unable to move to Florida to be near their college-age sons, because a dreadful economy coupled with deterioration of their neighborhood made it impossible to sell their immaculate home. During this difficult period, no more than eight weeks after Father Dugan's death, George saw him in a dream.

The dead priest, dressed in a beautiful, off-white robe, was "utterly glorious," says his friend. "Obviously he was in heaven as his face was radiant, his whole being glorified and full of joy."

"I'll be praying for you," he said.

"Oh you don't have to do that," George said typically, not wanting, he says, to trouble his dead friend. But later, as things got worse and Mary Ann died, George found comfort in that promise.

Similarly, a neighbor of mine, whose daughter was suddenly wondering if she should call off her imminent wedding in 1994, dreamed of one of our dead parish priests, whose transparent goodness had impressed many of us. My neighbor felt warmly cared for and safe as Father Ben Murphy put his arms around her and said, "Everything will be fine." Which it was, even though the wedding was indeed called off.

As I have said elsewhere, guiding visions to the non-holy — involving saints or other special messengers of God — are part of human spirituality, whether one speaks of Eskimo or American Plains Indian shamanistic traditions, mainline Hinduism, Pentecostal Protestantism, Hasidic Jews, or Japanese Shingon Buddhists.[1] In Catholic tradition they go back to the beginning of Christianity, when apostles like Peter and Paul had such experiences long before they were holy. Year after year, age after age, down the centuries witnesses leave first-person accounts. One example[2] of the many guiding visions that involve God's messengers who are not quite saints can also represent the entire period of God's work, through non-holy and holy, between the apostolic era of Peter and Paul and the last roughly one hundred seventy years covered by this book:

Born in 1645 at the French town of Paray-le-Monial, Marie de Reclesnes de Lyonne grew into a noted beauty sought in marriage by many noble and distinguished men. A bit stuck on herself, one day a humiliation in front of the whole town did her a world of good. Parading down the main street dressed to the teeth as usual, Marie fell afoul of the stampede of a market-bound herd of snorting pigs. Frantically clutching one pig's tail in terror of falling and being trampled, expensive hat broken, hair and clothes dirtied and askew, Marie bobbed up and down like a Punch and Judy figure as the huge porkers lunged this way and that. Those who moments before were bowing to and fawning on the promenading beauty in her silks and satins let her bob. How could they help while shrieking with laughter?

Much later Marie learned to laugh herself at the incident. But disillusionment as to the steadfastness of worldly admiration seared her soul as she stumbled home — filthy and smelling richly of pig — in her broken satin heels and dangling finery. Softening her hard shell of pride, the incident readied her for the influence of St. Claude de la Colombiere.

The otherworldly priest still took it easy with the slightly less proud beauty when they became friends, making few demands she change her sumptuous lifestyle lest she bolt from spirituality altogether. Perhaps Father Claude suspected her secret — which was that she, who apparently lived for finery, jewels, and dancing, was pushing away in horror a call to the cloister heard in her depths.

Even the saint might not have pried it out, had not Marie wakened one morning to see in her room a dead nobleman of Charolais, one of her long-time suitors, who had been killed in some quarrel not long before. They spoke at length, the French lord praising God's goodness and holiness.

Marie emerged from her room physically aged a decade. Her famous looks were no more. Spiritually she held out a bit longer, but she ended up — ecstatically happy — in the cloister as a comrade of St. Margaret Mary Alacoque, the saint to whom Jesus was appearing to reveal a symbol of His love for humanity, the image known as the Sacred Heart. To Margaret Mary, Jesus confided his plans for Marie — plans, we can see today, involved sending a dead nobleman to pay her a visit. Why didn't the Savior go himself? I asked myself that question and concluded that if one of her good-hearted, but basically worldly admirers appearing from the next life aged her by ten years, a vision of the Lord himself in all his purity probably would have killed her. And I can relate to that, can't you?

And now to guiding appearances involving nineteenth and twentieth century saints.

A later chapter will be devoted to the visits by French educator St. Madeleine Sophie Barat to simple Spanish visionary Josefa Menendez. But here is the place to note that Josefa's mother, Lucia Menendez, also had a visit from the foundress of the Society of the Sacred Heart. It came about in 1907 in Madrid, when one of the Menendez family's four daughters died in childhood. Both Lucia and her husband took their child's death so hard it seemed it would be their end, too. One came down with typhoid, the other with a lung illness. Josefa, the oldest daughter, struggled to support the family as a seamstress while also running the household and nursing her parents.

Some teaching nuns came to the rescue. Besides tactfully providing means by which Josefa could earn more money, they also proposed the devout

Menendez family join them in a novena to their foundress, Mother Barat. Its purpose: the healing of the parents, particularly the mother, who lacked the psychological and spiritual strength to go on and seemed certain to die.

In the middle of this novena, Lucia Menendez called her girls to her bedside and said, "Don't cry anymore. Mother Barat has just been here to visit me. She told me I'm not going to die because you still need me." The saint did not leave behind an instantaneous cure. But Sophie's encouragement turned the tide in the mother's battered spirit. And since spirit and body are somehow one, by the next day she was completely out of danger — and lived many more years.

Because she received a miracle cure through an after-death visitation by a saint, it may encourage someone to know Lucia was a good wife and mother, but definitely not a holy woman. In fact, lacking in gratitude after this miracle, she impeded her oldest daughter's vocation to Mother Barat's order not just once but a number of times, caught up in her own needs, rather than thinking of what was good for Josefa. Lucky for her — and the rest of us — God doesn't only love the holy or big-hearted!

An exceptionally talented star reporter, magazine writer, and Hollywood screenwriter, Eddie Doherty was a household name in the United States around the middle of the twentieth century. The hard-boiled, susceptible-to-women, Irish-Catholic was married three times. First wife, Marie, died in the great flu epidemic of 1918-19. The second Mrs. Doherty, Mildred — a newswoman herself — fell to her death in 1939 hiking alone in a southern California canyon. Both Catholic Marie and non-church-going Mildred were close to God. Then in 1940 Eddie met and later married Catherine de Hueck, a Russian Catholic servant of the poor and apostle of racial justice in places like Harlem. Catherine — along with the one-time tough-reporter himself — some believe will become a formal candidate for beatification. Before I tell about a saint's after-death experience involving Catherine, I want to cheat and throw in a non-saint appearance involving Eddie, which took place in 1951 in Rome after his third marriage.

In the rain on the porch of St. Susanna's Church, as he kept vigil alone through the last hours of the night, Eddie was visited in succession by both of his dead wives during what he calls a visionary "tour of my past." Admitting that he did not understand how it happened, like a good reporter — such a relief after so many maddeningly reticent saints — Eddie details his dialogue with Marie and then Mildred in an account which takes up more than two chapters in his book *A Cricket in My Heart*. Both wive's appearances seem, from the dialogue Doherty reports, to have increased Eddie's understanding of the joys of heaven, lessened old griefs, and prepared him spiritually (he was about sixty) for the rest of his life — another twenty years — during which he would embrace celibacy with Catherine, be ordained, and die with the reputation of a holy priest.

Could he simply have dreamed the experience? The cynical reporter who had seen it all asked himself that question and concluded he didn't know what had happened to him, but he was sure of one thing: It definitely wasn't a dream.

But it is an experience in which Eddie's third wife, Catherine de Hueck Doherty, was on the sidelines, so to speak, that I should be telling. As it takes up a whole chapter in Catherine's book *Not Without Parables*, regretfully I condense it, too.

To understand its origins in Catherine's likely holiness — something the Russian one-time baroness' account leaves out — let me note that Catherine and Eddie founded Madonna House in Combermere, Ontario, Canada, in the 1940s. It was the newest of Catherine's apostolic outreaches that began in the early 1930s, when the formerly-penniless refugee from the Bolsheviks gave up a new, well-earned, luxurious lifestyle to live in a slum for Christ's sake. Combermere, her first foundation outside a major city, became, as it still is, a center for retreats, as well as a residence and/or spiritual community for people who sought a lifestyle that proclaimed the gospel.

Catherine died at about ninety on December 14,

courtesy Madonna House Archives

Catherine de Hueck Doherty and Eddie Doherty

1985, leaving a spiritual legacy that, her mostly lay followers (they now live in twenty-five locations) say is *incarnational,* that is, rooted in simple day to day tasks, *all-embracing*, that is, reaching out to every sphere so that nothing is ungraced except sin, and *rooted in the Cross* of Christ, which plunges one into the pain of the world as a carrier of God's healing, transforming mercy.

This is the spirituality Catherine was living when a local Ontario farmer came up to her one day as she worked in the community garden. His wife, very ill with cancer and being cared for at home by a daughter, needed someone who could come daily to give her a shot of morphine. The nurse doing this was no longer available, he said, and he could find no other. He had heard Catherine did some nursing. Would she take on this daily job? Especially, he wondered, would she — a Catholic — do it for a family of "Protestant Orangemen,"[3] as he put it.

She would — gladly. Daily the farmer picked up the lay evangelist and drove her up an old, rutted lumbermen's road to his lovely, remote farm. On the first visit Catherine read the doctor's notes left for the previous nurse. The cancer was located in the wife's intestines and alimentary canal, too far gone to do anything except ease pain with what Catherine said was "the highest dosage of morphine I have ever seen prescribed for a patient."

Daily Catherine climbed the farmhouse stairs to the bedroom, gave the shot, tried to make the woman comfortable, visited a bit, and "consoled her the best I could." This went on most of the summer — about two-and-a-half months. Then the husband failed to show up for a few days. Catherine assumed that the first nurse, a niece, had been able to come back.

Then again one day the farmer, George, came looking for Catherine. Agitated, George said, "Ma'am, I want you to phone them Sisters. My woman wants them back. I'll pay for the call."

Catherine was flabbergasted. He seemed to mean nuns. No nuns could drop in on such a remote farm. None were even in the area. She asked George to explain. Quoting Catherine's account:

> He had been milking, he said, and had been late with his chores. It was past seven o'clock when he finally got to the house for supper. He found his daughter Ella in the kitchen quite perturbed. She said she had gone upstairs and found her mother looking fairly well from what she could see through the door — but it seemed her mother was talking to two nuns! They had their backs to Ella. She

would have gone in, she said, but Mom looked so happy that she didn't want to intrude.

George joined his daughter in waiting uneasily for the nuns — strange and fearsome creatures, indeed, to Orangemen — to come downstairs. Father and daughter agreed they had not seen or heard any car arrive. They concluded the Catholic nurse (Catherine) must somehow have dropped them off. Hours passed and no one came down the stairs. Neither father nor daughter felt able to go up and deal with something so out of their experience. Eventually each went to bed (due to his wife's pain George, like his daughter, was sleeping downstairs now), still without anyone having descended the stairs.

The next day George talked to his wife whose face, he told Catherine, was shining.

> She said that from the time those nuns had come to see her, all her pains had left her. She felt especially good when the young one had held her hand. She said they didn't talk much.... The older one remained in the rocking chair. The young nun simply sat on her bed and held her hand. She was a powerfully good person. She took the pain away.

Because of her illness, the wife had only been able to take a few sips of water or suck on ice. Now she wanted strong tea with cream — and it stayed down. Although moving her pain-wracked and bedsore-ulcerated body even slightly caused agony, now she wanted a bath and a fresh nightie — and could be comfortably moved to have them.

The next couple of days continued this peacefully. Then the pain returned and the wife sent her husband to Catherine with the urgent request those sisters visit again.

George described the pair to Catherine. The older of the two, his wife said, was the most beautiful woman she'd ever seen. The young one had a round face, dark eyes, and a soft voice. They wore rough brown robes with black "aprons" tied up high, white around the necks, and sandals on bare feet. Catherine says she became physically dizzy when it hit her that St. Therese had apparently sat on the woman's bed while the mother of Jesus sat in the rocking chair. This made sense in a supernatural way: These two were Catherine's patron saints for nursing. When she made a house call she always asked Our Lady of the Visitation (one of Mary's titles, based on the helpful visit she made to her cousin Elizabeth) to go with her and she always asked St. Therese to stay on as night-nurse when she left.

Catherine says she tried hard to convince George that she couldn't phone those nuns, at the same time trying not to sound as if anything too unusual had happened.

She asked him what he thought about "the mother of our Lord." Did he think she would be powerful enough to help people?

George did.

That gave Catherine the opening to offer him a medal with a picture of Mary on it, telling him that Mary was better than any nun and it would be nice for his wife to have this.

To her pleased surprise, he took it.

Two weeks later he was back. He had given his wife the medal. Oddly enough, the Protestant farm wife did not seem distressed at this odd substitute for the requested visit. She put it on her nightdress. Then she slept. In the middle of the night, she called George. Her pain was once again gone. She could even sit up a little.

Theirs had been a happy marriage. Now she wanted her husband to hold her while they reminisced about their years together and thanked God for them. They kissed and with her head on his shoulder, she quietly, painlessly died.

There is a half-humorous, half-sad postscript. George was lonely after his wife's death and took to spending evenings at a local hangout, where he soon told the story. People began coming to Catherine thinking she could give them some kind of token that would heal them — which, of course, she couldn't. Their requests and the talk going around led to suspicion about Madonna House by the local priest, who rightfully didn't want people in his jurisdiction gulled with superstitious nonsense. Finally Catherine had to tell him the whole story. Did he report it from the pulpit to buttress his flock's faith?

He did not.

The mid-twentieth century was the height of rationalism. The social gospel alone respectable in much of mainstream Protestantism, that branches' avant garde theologians were preparing to proclaim that Jesus' miracles "weren't meant to be taken literally because things like that can't really happen." Catholics, eager, even sometimes desperate, to be accepted into the mainstream Protestant culture of the United States and English-speaking Canada, were also starting to keep quiet about miracles, laying the foundations for the same anti-miracle preaching to erupt in their church, a couple of decades after its Protestant appearance. This priest was not so atypical then, when far from using the story as a God-given aid to spreading the gospel, he opted to say nothing and actually hope the talk would peter out. One wonders if, in another dimension, the Virgin Mary and St. Therese looked at each other and shook their heads.

Therese also made appearances at times to give information about her own Cause and, it seems, saw that a Bishop carried an interest in God's works through her back to the Philippines.

The first of these two instances requires a little background: When a saint's Cause reaches a certain point, the body must be exhumed, identified, and then reburied in some place, such as inside a church, where it cannot readily be dug up and made off with. If this sounds weird, consider it was common in the early Church for cities to fight over — and, yes, kidnap — the relics (remains of a saint), which is why we end up with the rather grisly state of affairs of one city having the head of a saint, another the heart, while some lesser place "makes do" with a toe bone! Later (helping bring on the Protestent Reformation and the Counter Reformation), selling relics — often fakes, of course — flourished in spite of condemnation by the Church. If you think people today would never try to filch a relic, never try to sell one, and never dream of offering a spurious object as a holy one, you will not understand exhumation but the rest of us do.

The official exhumation of Therese's body was scheduled for September 6, 1910, in the Lisieux cemetery, the remains then to be reburied in the church of the Lisieux Carmel. With so many miracles involving Therese, there was talk that her body would certainly be found incorrupt, as has occurred in the twentieth century with a number of saints. That she had said during her lifetime, when someone commented on this possibility, that they would find only "a little skeleton," and another time remarked she would prefer to be reduced to ashes, was taken not as prophecy, but saintly humility that God would surely override.

During the night between the fifth and sixth, God sent Therese on an after-death visit on just this question — but not to Lisieux.

It was the Prioress of the Carmel in Gallipoli, Italy, Mother Carmela, who had no idea this exhumation was even going to take place, who saw her. Therese's "countenance ... very beautiful and shining, her garments glitter[ing] with … light as of transparent silver," in Mother Carmela's description, the dead saint came to tell the Gallipoli Prioress "only my bones will be found."

This announcement helped ease the disappointment when that indeed proved the case. There could be no accusation that the three biological sisters of Therese in the Lisieux Carmel engineered this apparition, as would undoubtedly have been said had she appeared to a Carmelite in Lisieux.

In life, Therese said another time she would not want to be incorrupt, because she wanted in everything not to be extraordinary. But perhaps God, while honoring this wish, just had to do a little something for the occasion. At any rate, the palm branch buried in her coffin was found fresh and green, as if it just been cut, while a number of people who turned out to watch her coffin carried from the cemetery back to her Carmel received miracle cures, including a disabled World War I veteran.

Without any commentary, the Lisieux Carmel included the following testimony in an early English-language compilation of Therese's "favors." Signed by Cardinal Bourne, Archbishop of Westminister, England, one must assume he is the "stranger" of the August 14, 1912, testimony, given here in its entirety:

> On the 12th December, 1911, there took place at Lisieux the closing Session of the informative process for the beatification of Sister Therese. Monsignor Lemonnier, Bishop of Bayeux and Lisieux, wished to give especial solemnity to this final Session. He held it in presence of numerous priests in the chapel of the Grand Seminaire, and gave orders for a solemn Benediction on the same day in the Chapel of the Carmel of Lisieux.
>
> Canon Domin, Chaplain of the Benedictines of Lisieux, who gave Sister Therese her first Communion gave the Benediction. He was assisted by Canon Faucon, from whom the Servant of God received last absolution.
>
> The Bishop had authorised the celebrant to recite the prayer for the beatification of the Servant of God. It was recited after the *Adoremus* and followed by a hymn composed for the occasion.
>
> On the night which preceded this feast, that is to say the night of the 11th to the 12th December, a stranger to the Diocese of Bayeux, who has never been favoured with a similar grace, and who was ignorant of what was going to take place next day, saw in a mysterious dream, a young Carmelite whom he recognised at once from

her portraits to be Sister Therese. She was smiling, and whilst he contemplated her with rapture, she said to him: "Tomorrow there will be a feast in my honour at Bayeux; I will let fall a torrent of roses." [Her poetic language refers to special favors to the living that did take place on each notable day of her Cause. See chapter 23 for examples.]

Then he felt urged to recite the prayer "O God Who didst inflame with Thy Spirit of love the soul of thy Servant, Therese, grant that we also may love Thee and may make Thee much loved" and also the one asking for the Beatification of the Servant of God. Then Sister Therese disappeared, but he continued several days to feel her presence, and it excited in him very great fervour.

Therese was canonized on May 17, 1925. Her Cause had moved with unheard-of speed due to the outpouring of miracles with which God signaled His interest in its success (once heroic virtue is determined by the investigation, it waits upon miracles, which are God's vote in the saint-making process). That September 30th, Lisieux celebrated the first Feast of *Saint* Therese of the Child Jesus. Eager to participate, more than forty abbots, bishops, and cardinals descended on the small city. Among them was Bishop M'Closkey of the Philippines, who confided to Philadelphia's Cardinal Dougherty a strange experience.

Dropping in at the Carmel in Lisieux, the Bishop entered the public Hall of Relics, where various items pertaining to the new saint were on display. To his strong surprise, a Carmelite nun joined him and explained the exhibits.

He was so surprised because in that era, once Carmelite nuns crossed the cloister threshold, they sacrificed the freedom to go outside the Carmel the same way they gave up meat, dressing as they liked, and other good things. Unless she entered as an extern sister,[4] a Carmelite generally planned to "go outside" her walled enclosure only in a hearse. Later in the day, Bishop M'Closkey had an opportunity to speak with Mother Agnes, the blood sister of the saint, who was now Prioress. Through the visitors' parlor grill, which both kept the public out of the cloister and let the nuns sacrifice touching their loved ones, the Bishop questioned the Prioress about the nun who had showed him the exhibits. In turn, *she* questioned him, knowing that none of her flock had been outside what Carmelites call "the enclosure." Finally, hearing his description, Mother Agnes reported to the Bishop her conclusion: "the one who explained the souvenirs was none other than St. Therese of the Child Jesus herself!"

Abbot Paul of Moll, a Flemish Benedictine monk, was buried in 1896, the year before Therese. Called "the singer of divine love" because he constantly preached and taught on the fathomless love of God, this seventy-two-year-old priest had all the charisms Therese hadn't been called to in her life: He healed the sick, worked miracles, read hearts and minds, bilocated, levitated, was luminous at times, and — when *his* coffin was exhumed in 1899, and again in 1960 at the Benedictine abbey of Dendermonde in Belgium — his holy body was found incorrupt.

Before his death, when Father Paul was at the Dendermonde Abbey, a working woman from another region twice saw him praying in her town's church. He'd be there, then immediately disappear. Boldly the woman wrote and asked the Benedictine priest if it was indeed he that she had seen. He replied it was. As he was a known bilocator, that is no big deal. However, this same woman later witnessed:

> Since the death of Father Paul, I have seen him three times at prayer in our church. From afar I greeted him, nodding my head, and he responded in the same manner. Some moments afterwards I saw him leave the church and go away. I followed him; but the more I advanced, the more the distance that separated me from him increased, until at last he disappeared from my view.

In the case just reported — one of those hundreds of testimonies in my files where someone is maddenly reticent, usually from the spiritual modesty very much in vogue at the turn of the century when this testimony was written — we get the bare facts that she saw the dead saint, but are left clueless as to the spiritual meaning. God does not let dead saints appear to people for no reason, but what this witness got from the experience is by now buried with her. Fortunately Father Paul has appeared to other people since his death with clearer benefits (see pages 73 and 170).

In the opening pages of this book, I mentioned that St. Maximilian Kolbe, the martyr of charity at Auschwitz, appeared in recent years to Francis Gajowniczek, the man he died for in 1941 in the concentration camp. About 1988, Gajowniczek, who travelled around the world for years speaking without fee about the man who laid down his life for him, was in an accident and pronounced dead. Before he revived, the elderly Pole found himself on the road to heaven, but saw Father Kolbe, who told him it was not yet his time.

Father Kolbe also appeared to a dying woman in Trinidad, according to a testimony sent from a hospice there to an American group of the saint's Conventual Franciscan order in Libertyville, Illinois. I condense the testimony from the Winter, 1994, newsletter of the Shrine of St. Maximilian Kolbe.

A native of Trinidad, the ninth of ten children, married a man who beat her. She left him, after having three children, and married a kind man who was good to her and her children. Years passed and she got breast cancer, which in spite of treatment proved impossible to cure. A compassionate Catholic woman cared for her each day while the husband worked. This woman knew that both the sick woman and her husband had prior marriages which had never been annulled. She wanted to help the dying woman get all this straightened out so she could once more receive the sacraments and succeeded.

I mention the above because it *may* mean — coupled with the sick woman's later complete lack of recognition of his name — that at the time Kolbe was officially proclaimed a saint in 1982 with worldwide publicity, due to her marital situation, the woman may have been one of the billions who pay no attention to whom the Catholic Church canonizes. She *may* then never have heard of St. Maximilian Kolbe.

As death neared and she needed more care, the dying woman was brought to a hospice for the sick run by a Catholic charismatic community. It was then she began telling the nursing staff that a strange man was walking around her bed. He said he had come to take her to "the banquet" (of heaven). He also told her to have the hospice staff gather around her bed and pray for her husband and children.

The staff did this willingly, but were still curious to know if they were deal-

Father Maximilian Kolbe

ing with a hallucination. So they counseled the dying woman to ask the man his name if she saw him again. She did and reported his name was "Maximilian."

Because these details are "skimpy," this is one of those cases I was going to throw away. I present it to you for one reason: Whatever was going on that to me as an American investigator is not adequately detailed as to names of the staff, dates this took place, etc., was compelling enough to the hospice staff that they went to their Bishop. And whatever they told him seemed meaningful enough that he came over and dedicated that hospice to St. Maximilian.

Another group of Franciscans, those who lived with Padre Pio in San Giovanni Rotondo, Italy, received a testimony that is of interest because the after-death appearance involves only the sense of touch. The writer of the testimony asks to remain anonymous, but the story's veracity is vouched for by Father Joseph Pius Martin of San Giovanni Rotondo, a man who would rather be drawn and quartered than offer any "made-up" or "enhanced" material. Nor need he since so many testimonies on Padre Pio's favors are arriving in San Giovanni that it can be called the Lisieux of the present day. The anonymous writer reports:

> On July 3, 1984 my mother died suddenly. I was crushed and broken and never having suffered grief before I thought I would surely die in despair..... I asked God each night to call me home. On the night of July 20 of that year I prayed to Padre Pio (this sounds idolatrous but it isn't; such "prayers" always ask the saint's prayers to God the same way one phones a friend to pray for one) using the little prayer leaflet. I was sitting up in bed at the time. After finishing the prayer I eased my way gently under the covers. I had just settled myself into a lying position when in the silence of the night my two hands were taken gently and held by two very large hands. At once I stiffened ... but (realized) ... that someone wanted to comfort me....

The mourner kept wondering during the next days whose hands had offered that comforting touch. Could it have been Padre Pio? Then one morning this individual picked up the day's mail and found a publication with a cover photo of Padre Pio's hands. "I think," the writer continues, "Padre

Pio was saying, 'Yes, it was me.' " What is believed a saint's visit didn't wipe out all grief, as it sometimes dones; the writer adds that it wasn't until All Souls' Day, several months later, that the weight completely lifted. So the after-death touch eased, but did not eliminate, the natural grieving process.

Another priest I personally know to be eminently dedicated to the truth is the Jesuit paster of Sacred Heart Church in Hsinchu, Taiwan. Over roughly half-a-century, Jesuit John Baptist Palm has taken many hundreds of written and taped testimonies about Rose Ferron, the Woonsocket, Rhode Island stigmatic. Rose's Cause is not favored by her local Bishop, who never knew her, but many people are directly petitioning the Congregation for the Causes of Saints to investigate her possible heroic sanctity based on the favors, cures, and after-death appearances by which they believe God is speaking on her behalf. I don't know if Rose is a saint. But I do know Father Palm is a great lover of God and I don't believe he has made up the several thousand pages of material he has shared with me over the years. So I'm going to stick my neck out and offer two testimonies here that both involve Father Palm.

When he left for China in 1948 to become a missionary there, Father Palm knew it was *forever*, since Jesuit missionaries didn't get home leave. But the Jesuit is a very devout man who puts the things of God ahead of even those he loves. Before departing from the United States, on his way to Baltimore, Maryland in June, to say good-bye to his family, he made a private pilgrimage to Rhode Island to meet the family of Rose Ferron and visit her grave. After a brief visit which increased his certainty that Rose was a genuine saint, Father Palm says, "I said good-bye forever to the mother of little Rose." Two other Ferron daughters drove him to his train. He told them "good-bye forever" too. He writes:

> On their return when their mother asked them why they seemed so sad, they answered, "We'll never see Father Palm again." Mother Ferron said "He will return before he goes to China. They said, "No! He said he would not come back forever!" "Yes, he will return...."

Much later Father Palm would learn from the daughters how their mother comforted them by explaining she had had what she referred to as "a dream."

In it Rose told her the young priest would return to Woonsocket and when he did, her mother should give him the crucifix that Rose died holding in her hand.

Meantime Father Palm recalls:

> On the 3-4 hour train ride to New York I kept smelling the sweet fragrance of rose powder and at the same time kept hearing, at each turn of the wheels ... the insistent *you must return! you must return*!

Since he had only a limited time to spend with his family before leaving, he thought, to never see them again, the last thing the Jesuit wanted to do was make another trip to Woonsocket, Rhode Island. But the "voice" was so insistent that finally he cried, "Okay, I surrender. I'll go back." And he somehow fit it in. He writes:

> When I did return, Mother Ferron placed this crucifix lovingly and slowly in my hands, pressed her two hands against mine, and said "Little Rose told me to give you this crucifix, that it would do more good in China than here."

This time when he left Mrs. Ferron again told her daughters the priest would return, "but I'll be gone." Due to the Communist takeover in China, Father Palm's life took an unexpected course and he did return to Woonsocket in 1959, Mrs. Ferron having died in 1956.

Who can insist Rose really returned after death to give her mother advice and prophecies? I can tell you only that I have read many testimonies by those who knew her that Rose's mother, too, was considered a holy woman. Holy women don't lie. Of course, the holy may be mistaken or deceived. At any rate, the aftereffects of this, that is, what Rose Ferron's crucifix accomplished in China, fill a large book written by this Jesuit missionary. In it I have read testimony after testimony by foreign and Chinese Jesuits, as well as by Chinese lay people, of cures, conversions, and other favors — most of them involving the so-called odor of sanctity similar to that Father Palm experienced on the train — that took place whether Father Palm had the crucifix, or someone else had it and he was not even in the same city.

A second incident involving Father Palm and, it appears, Rose Ferron, grew out of the years 1941-44 when Father Palm was stationed at Our Lady of Lourdes Catholic Church in Bethesda. Not yet an ecumenical era, the

1940s were a time when people schemed, sweated, and prayed to get a Protestant to turn Catholic, or a Catholic to turn Protestant. It may not edify you but it is not odd then that one of Palm's parishioners was determined her non-Catholic husband, Evan Scholl (who ran Scholl Cafeteria in Washington D.C.), was going to become a Catholic. For fourteen years the woman fasted and prayed just for this. Young Father Palm, who years down the road would discover ecumenism, tried to help by arguing with Scholl about religion. That did about as much good as arguing usually does. In short, Evan wasn't buying. Then in 1948 the priest came by the Scholl home to say "good-bye forever." In his enthusiasm for Rose Ferron, he told the couple about her. Boldfacedly he said he would ask Rose's prayers for Evan's conversion and advised the wife to do this too.

Weeks later in Nanking a letter arrived from Bethesda. Right after Father Palm left, Evan Scholl was enveloped in a cloud of fragrance as if from masses of fresh roses. The odor was not heavy or cloying. Instead it filled him with a very cool and refreshed feeling. Accompanying the odor, repeated like a mantra, was the message "you must become a Catholic."

A fairly trivial incident. But Evan was absolutely, one-hundred-percent sure (remember the quality of ineffability) that this was supernatural. He demanded to be baptized that very day. Of course, that wasn't possible. He had to study all the teachings of the Catholic Church and make sure he could assent to them, a matter usually of many months. But he never wavered in his sudden resolve. He became a fervent Catholic who, Palm says, "lived to bring others into the Church" where he had discovered so much spiritual wealth and who gave so much of his time and money to help others he was eventually knighted by the Pope for his charities.

And speaking of his charities, it was in search of money for a good cause that Rose Ferron, Evan Scholl believed, paid him a second visit.

Again Father Palm was involved. Having been expelled by the Communist regime from mainland China, the priest was working in Taiwan — as he still is — when his Bishop sent him back to the States in 1959 to give talks in churches to raise money for the Jesuit order's Far-Eastern seminarians. While home, Palm also had permission to contact his personal friends and family for money to build what is today Sacred Heart Church in Taiwan. Father Palm visited the Scholls in Florida and asked if they would help. Generous though he was, Evan had to tell the visitor that times were tough. He didn't see how he could contribute to this appeal too.

At that point, the host took a swim in the ocean, only to have a large sea nettle wrap itself around him, poisoning him in many places. Taken to the hospital, Evan heard the same voice he remembered from his earlier, never-forgotten experience. This time it was saying, "You must help Father Palm to build his church!" There were two aftereffects: Evan Scholl received a complete physical healing on the spot and Father Palm received twenty-five thousand dollars toward the church — five from Scholl and the rest from four friends the businessman persuaded to match his gift.

At the end of Evan Scholl's life, after a funeral attended by many priests, religious, and bishops, including Scholl's good friend, retired Cardinal O'Boyle, the Cardinal wrote a letter to the Bishop of Providence asking him to consider looking into the case of Rose Ferron, who played such an important role in the life of Evan Scholl, a man who in turn touched so many others.

ENDNOTES

[1] Some smaller groups of Buddhists distrust such visions and warn "if you see the Buddha, kill him," meaning don't put any stock in them. More Buddhists welcome them, it appears.

[2] I thank the Abbey of St. Joseph de Clairval at Flavigny-sur-Ozerain for making this anecdote known to me.

[3] Orangemen were a group founded in Northern Ireland in 1795 to work against Catholics, particularly Catholic Emancipation, and to promote Protestantism and an Ireland under British rule.

[4] Every Carmel had one or two of these "extern" sisters, whose vocation was to "go out" on behalf of the community when this was needed. It would have been easy, by the description, to rule out that the Bishop had seen an extern sister. They also, of course, did not stand around outside the enclosure but left only for definite errands.

8 ✍ SAINTS NEED GUIDANCE, TOO

People striving for holiness need guidance, too. So it is no surprise to find in most spiritual traditions some variant on the theme of super-natural guides for those who yearn to live completely for God. It may be a figure appearing in dreams, like the unidentified being who once told the three wise men of some long-vanished faith not to return to King Herod. Shamans, like medicine man Black Elk (see chapter 24), may learn from "spirits" who come as animal figures. Angels are known in many groups as God's messengers.

And so are the dead. Incidents of the holy dead guiding Hasidic saints, Hindu saints, and, possibly, entire shamanistic peoples are found in this book. And, of course, in Christianity such events go back to the long-dead Moses and Elias pointing out Christ's glory to three awed apostles, and continue in the early Church when Paul is unhorsed by Christ Himself on the road to Damascus.

As Paul's experience reminds us, in Christianity it is the Lord who most often comes to guide His special friends — especially among Protestant groups lacking a tradition of saints — with the next most frequent visitor His mother, who appears to Orthodox Christians, Catholics, and Protestants, too. Their own and others' guardian angels often are seen by saints. And, of course, angels may accompany an appearance by dead saints. But it is saints appearing to saints that is our topic.

To indicate this sort of thing, too, is not limited to the nineteenth and twentieth centuries, here is a quick mention of this type of appearance to a handful of Catholicism's best-known saints from earlier eras: St. Ambrose (340-397), one of four Catholic Doctors of the Church, St. Augustine's mentor, and the man most responsible for establishing Christianity in the west, was consoled by after-death appearances of his dead brother, St. Satyrus. The father of monasticism, St. Benedict (circa 547), visited still-read Flemish Benedictine mystic, St. Gertrude the Great (c. 1256-c. 1302). A boy of great purity, received by St. Francis (1181-1226) into his order, once spied on Francis, seeing and hearing the world's favorite saint talking with Christ, the Virgin Mary, St. John the Evangelist, St. John the Baptist, and "a great throng of angels." Francis' companion, Brother Masseo, praying near him in a church, was joyously assured by Francis himself that Saints Peter and Paul had just brought him a message from God, promising the Franciscans the holy poverty Francis longed for as a priceless treasure.

Many more instances of visits Francis received are known to anyone familiar with this saint. And, as mentioned before, God sent Francis back after his death to encourage various spiritual sons individually and also, like St. Therese at Gallipoli, to reveal things about himself for the edification of his spiritual followers down the centuries. It is also said the saint appeared to two friars to send them to a dying sultan, whom Francis had promised years earlier that Franciscans would receive as a Christian on his deathbed. Is that true? I don't know. But it is said.

In the autobiography she wrote under obedience to Superiors, St. Teresa of Avila (1515-1582) admits dead St. Peter Alcantara appeared three times to advise her on the reform she was undertaking of the Carmelite order. She writes:

> His appearance caused me no fear — indeed, it made me very happy, for he always appeared as a glorified body, full of great bliss, and it gave me the greatest joy to see him.…

In 1601, now dead herself, Teresa appeared to a Madame Acarie (1566-1618) in France and told her she was to bring the reformed Carmelite order[1] from Teresa's native Spain to France, a command that remained engraved on the soul of Barbe Acarie as she struggled to found Discalced Carmelites in Paris, joined them after she was widowed, and achieved such holiness that today she is known as Blessed Marie of the Incarnation.

Having established that saints have been sent to future saints throughout Christian history, let's jump to the nineteenth and twentieth centuries, starting with an appearance by this chapter's earliest nineteenth-century saint (by which I do not mean born after 1800 but that spiritual maturity may be placed after this year).

Anyone who thinks God only sends His saints for the purpose of encouraging and consoling has never read the life of Venerable Cajetan Errico. As a young priest, Cajetan made a yearly retreat at a college of Redemptorists, an order founded by St. Alphonse Ligouri, who died in 1787. In 1818, praying on one of these retreats, Errico got the idea to found a congregation similar to the Redemptorists. The modest priest dismissed the thought as presumptuous and a temptation to pride.

But on Errico's next year's retreat, St. Alphonse himself appeared to command him, in God's name, to found a congregation of missionaries. He even told him what to name them. Then the dead priest told the living one that God would enable him to build a church dedicated to Our Lady of Sorrows in his hometown of Secondilliano, where Errico was a parish priest. That the church actually was built would sign Errico he should proceed to found the new order.

A wise person, Cajetan Errico did not rush out to follow those instructions. Aware that he could be slipping a mental cog or that this might be a vision from dark spirits, he sought counsel from various religious leaders, including his spiritual director, who knew him like a book. Their consensus: Wait and pray. If this is the real stuff, you'll get more confirmation.

So he waited. And confirmation kept coming in the form of more visits from St. Alphonse who, on the last of several appearances, was insistent: Do as God wants *now*!

But Cajetan sagely continued to balance what the dead saint ordered with what his living spiritual advisers and church Superiors said. At last they meshed when he received permission in 1827 to build the church.

After that everything should have been easy. But this is real life. When he broke the good news to his townsfolk and began collecting money for the church, all hell broke loose. He was accused of extorting money from the poor. He was accused of diverting monies to enrich his family, in order to marry his sisters above their station. He was reported to the church authorities as out to supplant the town's main parish church with a church where Cajetan would reign supreme. He was accused of hurting local businesses because he bought up and demolished houses on the site for the new church. And on the side, so to speak, for "being so dumb" as to give uninvited talks about God inside taverns and other places where preachers aren't exactly clamored for, he was tied to a tree and beaten with clubs. Surprisingly, none of this killed him.

Did his friends and family stick by him? Well, sometimes. At times his timid confessor said, "Right on." Then let the criticism reach a fever pitch and he would suddenly say "Stop! Don't do this." Cajetan's mother and sisters were more consistent: They never supported him. Instead they nagged at him to give up this nonsense because it was an embarrassment to them.

"Take a pastorate somewhere else," they begged, anxious to get him out of their hair. You can't choose your relatives, of course. Unfortunately his friends, too, suggested he back off, and called St. Alphonse's visits "your bad dreams." As for his enemies....

But that old ineffability factor was at work. Cajetan Errico had taken a long time to be convinced, dead saint's orders or no. Once convinced, he commented "as soon as we know the will of God, we must fulfill it, even if we die."

So he kept going. And one day St. Alphonse appeared again with the Virgin Mary. They provided a little comfort. But it is not too much to say it was in suffering and struggle that the church was built. But built it was, and the Missionaries of the Sacred Heart founded. In spite of Cajetan Errico's understandable early death — he certainly had enough stress — the order can be found today as far away from Secondilliano as Linwood, New Jersey.

Could the visits of St. Alphonse have been imaginary, swirling into Cajetan's consciousness from a secret hankering to become important by building churches and founding orders? Perhaps. But it is a mark in his favor that the Church's investigation on Cajetan Errico has progressed to the point where "a life of heroic virtue worthy of veneration" (hence the title Venerable) has been established. Heroically virtuous people can imagine things. But considering how much doubt he had about his visions and how many people were counseling him, I think it improbable that Cajetan imagined St. Alphonse — whose appearance, after all, caused him, humanly speaking, nothing but trouble.

St. Clement Hofbauer (1751-1820) was the son of a very poor, very pious, half-Slovak, half-German family (the surname was changed from its Slavonic equivalent Dvorak) living in the Austria of Maria Theresa and her son Joseph II. Apprenticed to a baker, the ninth of the Hofbauer's twelve children longed to be a priest. An enterprising fellow, after his apprenticeship he got himself employed at a monastery bakery, where the abbot permitted him to attend the Latin classes. But the abbot soon died and it was back to a Vienna bakery. Saving his money, the young baker managed two pilgrimages to Rome. On the second, he received permission to become a religious hermit there, living near Tivoli. Then God made it clear that he was not to be a hermit, but work actively in the world. And this time, valuable lessons no doubt having been learned in those years of struggles, God smoothed the way. Clement was financed in his studies for the priesthood in Rome by two women whom he had met on a trip home to Vienna when, after serving the mass they attended, he good-naturedly ran out into a downpour to grab them a carriage. Not only was he ordained in Rome, he joined the Redemptorist order founded by St. Alphonse there. Then he returned to Vienna.

The rest of this life is so extraordinary I can only hit a few highlights. Soon exiled from Vienna to Warsaw by Catholic Joseph II's well-meant laws against religious orders, Hofbauer's holiness made him known there as a preacher, confessor, convert-maker, and true father to the poor. Once begging in a tavern for the orphanage he opened for Warsaw's homeless children, he was called over by a card player, who coolly spit in Hofbauer's face.

"Now that you've given to me personally, how about something for my poor children," the saint said with equal coolness. The anti-cleric not only red-facedly dug into his pocket, he became a follower of the dynamic saint.

After twenty year's work, Hofbauer was imprisoned by another anticlerical decree, this time Napoleon's suppression of religious orders. In prison, Father Clement's influence only grew, crowds gathering outside the prison to listen to his hymns. Released but ordered to leave Warsaw, he was imprisoned again on the Austrian frontier, but finally made it back to Vienna where he worked his last years, a magnet there, too, to all interested in the spiritual life.

At the 1815 Congress of Vienna, it is he who is credited, along with one of his spiritual sons, Prince Ludwig of Bavaria, with defeating attempts to sever the German Catholic Church from the pope, as the English Church had been severed by Henry VIII. One statesman remarked he could name only three people with real energy: Napoleon, Goethe, and Clement Hofbauer.

"The apostle of Vienna," as he was called, needed every ounce. His role as a spiritual mentor to people like Prince Ludwig kept him in his confessional for stretches as long as eighteen hours. At the same time, he was at the center of Vienna's intellectual life. Besides promoting good literature, he founded a Catholic college in the city. And in a day when bigotry was the rule, he was known for his charity toward the German Protestants. Due to his kind of holiness, the saint's twelve years there left Vienna at his death a city where Catholicism was a vital spiritual force. And he had done it in spite of the fact that the laws originally exiling him from Vienna were still on the books. The king had simply refused to permit his chancellor to enforce them against one all believed a saint.

Hofbauer died with the prophecy that "scarcely shall I have breathed my last" than the Redemptorists would once more have a legal right to exist. This at once occurred.

Such a man can hardly be expected to sit quietly after death. Indeed God sent him to various friends and people he had protected or mentored. Appearances include one in 1822 to Father Zacharie Werner, who had been "one of his most intimate collaborators."

> Father Zacharie had just finished his evening prayers in his room when suddenly his cell was illuminated by a great light that surpassed the radiance of the sun. In the midst of this light he suddenly saw Clement....
>
> He heard him say "Zacharie, come. Come. Come soon." Then the figure disappeared. Zacharie Werner testified ... that he was not dreaming or hallucinating.

He answered the call, dying just a few weeks later.

Two other appearances were to a Sister Sebastiana, who belonged to the Sisters of St. Ursula religious order. The first time he came to Sister Sebastiana he told her that she was to become a saint. Embarrassed and bewildered because she was a very humble person, the nun could not answer at first. Finally she croaked, "I'm not worthy." What Clement answered she does not tell us. In fact, she goes blank here about the rest of their conversation, except for one item: She admits that Clement assured her he would be present to assist her when she died.

When the day came that Sister Sebastiana lay dying, she exclaimed to the other nuns around her bed that Clement had kept his promise. And, quite unusual for such deathbed visions, suddenly the other nuns, too, saw Clement Hofbauer for a few minutes. He disappeared just as Sister Sebastiana died.

(Had she become a saint? She isn't canonized, that's for sure. But then almost every faith recognizes those "hidden souls" who keep the world from splintering, their holiness known only to God.)

In saints' after-death appearances to saints, a kind of spiritual compatibility can often be seen. This definitely seems the case in an 1869 apparition of Blessed Anna Maria Taigi. Anna Maria was an impoverished housewife during her lifetime, with a difficult husband and seven children, a woman who worked part-time to stretch her man's meager paycheck while carrying on all the time-consuming, early-nineteenth-century household chores. Pretty, she had been vain until Jesus began appearing to her. Then her life took a sharp turn God-ward. She died in 1837, revered as a holy mystic with great prophetic gifts and healing charisms. A member of a spiritual support group affiliated with the Trinitarian fathers, the Rome housewife's incorrupt body lies in a glass casket in one of the churches served by those priests.

Maria del Pinto was another Italian mystic, who — like Anna Maria — felt called to all sorts of sacrifices in the hope that Christ could use those gifts of love to help other suffering souls move closer to light and truth. Such people (please don't confuse them with masochists who *like* to suffer[2]) are wary of praying for relief when suffering comes their way, figuring God will weave some beneficial design into whatever happens, whether it was His direct will or only permitted by Him. So when Maria del Pinto was reduced to a near-skeleton by an infection of her womb and its lining, she never prayed to be healed. Urged to pray for her life when the doctors' verdict became "hopeless," she still refused. Finally she accepted making a novena to the Holy Spirit to ask if God *wanted* her to pray for healing. Maria later wrote:

> During the course of the novena, I seemed to see Our Lady Immaculate, shining with light, receiving a petition from the hands of a gracious old lady who was kneeling in front of her.
>
> "Beg for your cure, my daughter," said the Blessed Virgin; "you shall be perfectly cured of this disease. There will be plenty of other opportunities for you to suffer."

So finally Maria del Pinto began asking God to cure her. And now she had a second visit: Again the Virgin Mary was accompanied by the gracious old lady. "Behold your deliverer," said Jesus' mother, pointing to the old lady. Maria del Pinto understood that this person's prayers were to be responsible for her cure. Somehow it was also made clear to del Pinto that the gracious old lady was Anna Maria Taigi, then dead for thirty years. Anna Maria had a handkerchief in her hands, reports del Pinto, "as if to wipe away the tears that I shed in abundance because of the intensity of the pain."

While that makes sense, it should also be noted that during Anna Maria's lifetime, in one of Jesus' visits He gave her the power to heal by touching someone with her hand. To keep notice from this gift, she always went to ill people with something in her hand, such as cotton soaked in oil. Carrying the handkerchief then was a further visual clue of the identify of this saint.

Del Pinto writes that no sooner had the Virgin Mary pointed to Anna Maria then:

> … I felt a wrenching that made me cry out loud. People came to my assistance, but I was cured. I arose without difficulty to make a pilgrimage of thanks.

The "Miraculous Medal,"[3] often worn on a chain around the neck, is named "miraculous" because of the thousands of cures, rescues, and favors claimed by those for whom it is a visible reminder — like the cross or star of David others wear — to keep close to God. Its wearers are usually familiar with St. Catherine Laboure (1806-1876), since it was the Blessed Virgin Mary's appearances to Catherine that led to the making and distribution of millions of the medals. I'm not going to detail *those* apparitions, but want to go back much earlier in the life of St. Catherine when, as an eighteen year old whose mother was dead, she was keeping house for her father, a prosperous French farmer. At this time Catherine dreamed she was attending …

> … the Mass of an old priest, who was a stranger to her. At the end of Mass he turned and beckoned to her, but she fled in fright. Then, in her dream, Catherine went to visit a sick neighbor, only to encounter the same venerable priest.
>
> As she turned to flee from him a second time, he called after her "You do well to visit the sick, my child. You flee from me now, but one day you will be glad to come to me. God has plans for you; do not forget it."

Four years later, her father having refused his permission for her to become a nun, Catherine was cutting a rather hopeless figure at the fashionable finishing school run by a sister-in-law, who had rescued her from waitressing in a brother's cafe. On an outing with the schoolgirls, Catherine saw a portrait of St. Vincent de Paul (1580-1660), who had been dead over one hundred sixty-five years, and instantly recognized the old priest of her dream. Based on the interior understanding accompanying this moment,

Catherine — who had known for years she was to become a nun — now felt God specifically desired she be a Daughter of Charity, the order St. Vincent founded to minister primarily to the sick and the poor. Daughter of Charity she did become and lived a humble life in service to the aged poor for forty years after her visions[4] of Mary, visions no one linked to her since only one or two of her Superiors knew and they honored Catherine's desire to live and die unknown.

Young and beautiful, intelligent and charming, she who would one day be known as *Saint* Gemma Galgani (1878-1903) had lain in bed for about a year in 1899 suffering from kidney nephritis, paralysis, and deafness. Even her lovely hair had all fallen out. Worse was her spiritual turmoil: She who from childhood had always been so devout now wrestled with every spiritual temptation.

Then she was given a book, the life of a Passionist student for the priesthood, who had died before he could be ordained only thirty-seven years earlier. Perhaps someone thought the story of Gabriel of the Sorrowful Mother (Passionist priests, like Carmelite nuns, take such names) would comfort her for her own broken dream of becoming a nun.

Gemma read the book and felt a strong spiritual rapport with Gabriel. That night Gabriel Possenti (1838-1862), who would be canonized in 1920, appeared to bedridden Gemma.

"Go ahead," he instructed her, "and make your vow to be a nun, but add nothing further."

"Why not?" she countered, for she wanted desperately to know which religious order might even yet receive her if her health returned.

Gabriel, who in his pre-Passionist days had been nicknamed "the ladies' man" for his charm and good-looks, only smiled.

"My sister!" he said warmly a few moments later. Dressed in the traditional black Passionist cassock with its heart-shaped badge on the breast, Gabriel unpinned this distinctive sign of the Passionists and wordlessly offered it to Gemma to kiss. A few moments later he was gone.

Only later would his cautionary remark regarding her vocation make sense; for Gemma Galgani, saint, mystic, and stigmatic, would continue to knock in vain at the doors of religious orders:

"Too singular!"

"Apt to have a bad influence."

"Could prove divisive."

Those were some of the remarks accompanying the refusals. Although the investigation after her death that proved her sanctity would conclude the pharmacist's beautiful young daughter had practiced poverty, chastity, and obedience *to an heroic degree*, Gemma would wear a nun's dress only in death. Then the Passionists (whom she had not known at the time of St. Gabriel Possenti's visit) would see that the young woman was dressed for her burial in the garb of one of their nuns, fulfilling Gabriel's gentle hint "My sister!"

At the time of that first after-death appearance of Gabriel to Gemma, he said nothing about her health. But shortly thereafter the dead seminarian appeared again, chiding her for neglecting the novena for the prayers of Blessed (today Saint) Margaret Mary Alacoque for healing. This novena both a holy priest (later a bishop) and nuns who had taught her were urging Gemma make, while Gemma — because she remained indifferent — kept forgetting. Let her be cured or not, as God willed, was her attitude. Now here was Gabriel, insisting God wanted to heal Gemma, and wanted to do it by utilizing the nine-day's prayer asking the intercession of Margaret Mary. To see Gemma followed through, the cheerful, dead Passionist returned each evening to say the novena prayers with her. As the nine days drew to a close, Jesus Christ appeared to Gemma, who was instantaneously and totally healed. (While everyone cheered her cure, Gemma was more delighted that Jesus had said to her, "I choose you for my daughter.")

Although Jesus and His mother appeared to Gemma Galgani more frequently than did Gabriel, the visionary was to see the young Passionist a number of other times during her brief life. Her Church, of course, in canonizing her makes only two assertions: She is with God, who worked miracles in her honor at the behest of her prayers after her death, and she practiced heroic virtue during her life. As to whether the visits Gemma received were in her head or "real," as with all saints, the same Church makes no judgment.

But let me offer a few thoughts. That it was Gabriel Possenti — an individual who lived and died quietly, and who was neither beatified nor canonized during Gemma's lifetime — whom Gemma said she saw, I find interesting. One would be more apt to imagine an individual hallucinating visits by a recognized saint, not an obscure candidate for Church honors. Bright and literate, Gemma had read many saints' lives and she was often ill. If she hallucinated a saint after reading about him when not well, this should have happened more than once. Yet Gemma never claimed any supernatural visits by saints (she did see Jesus, His mother, and angels) except one — Gabriel Possenti. He, she said, appeared to her at intervals after that first visit, the rest of her brief life. Before her death at age twenty-five, she predicted the date of her dead friend's future beatification, tieing its occurrence to other events, all of which took place after her death in the order and time foretold. How did she know? She said Gabriel told her.

Even canonized, St. Gemma — with her visions, ecstatic levitations, and stigmata — is regarded by most people as a "flaky" sort. St. Francesca Xavier Cabrini (1850-1917), on the other hand, is the quintessential well-balanced, equal-to-everything missionary — a "perfect" woman saint. Beloved teacher, foundress of an order of down-to-earth nurses, teachers, caretakers, and administrators, herself a master businesswoman, who built hospitals, orphanages, schools, and other practical expressions of divine love all over the United States and other parts of the world, Mother Cabrini, on the surface, couldn't be less like Gemma. And yet, while she was much quieter about them, Francesca Cabrini, I believe, had as many dead visitors as St. Gemma.

From the time Francesca was a tiny child, the little curly-haired blonde Italian dreamed of becoming a missionary to China, even giving up "goodies" forever when someone teased "missionaries don't eat sweets." As with so many saints, doors seemed to slam shut as she tried to follow the vocation to which she heard God's call. To become a nun, she finally had to found her own order. (No one called *her* "singular"; she was just found too frail for the life of a missionary.)

Throughout her life, Mother Cabrini was "shown (things) mystically in ... un-

courtesy Cabrini Archives, Cabrini College, Radnor, PA

Mother Francesca Xavier Cabrini

usual dreams," the nun who was her secretary puts it, with understatement, in the biography[5] she wrote of Cabrini. These "dreams" were actually much more than the modest saint and her followers imply by that low-key word. Sister Frances Cairo testified to that. For a brief time, she shared a room with Mother Cabrini, but when Sister Frances woke one night to see the room flooded by a mysterious bright light and said aloud, "Mother do you see it?" her bed was moved out the next day. Whoever was appearing to Mother Cabrini — whether God Himself, who often comes as warm, sweet, so-called *Shekinah* light, or one of the saints in an effulgence of glory, the very reticent Cabrini did not want it talked about.

While she still yearned for China, she was asked to commit her fledgling order to undertake work among Italian immigrants in the United States. What to do? Like all saints, she sought wise advice, trying not to get her own way but to discern the will of God, since she wanted to do that will more than she wanted any dream, however cherished or holy, of her own.

Now during this particular time of interior struggle, worried because the Bishop of New York had made her such a vague proposal, the saint wrote him from Rome, asking for the precise conditions he had in mind for her and her spiritual daughters (who numbered one hundred forty-five at that date). At the same time in Rome, Monsignor Scalabrini, a saint himself, was pressuring her not to wait for the reply, but tell him immediately whether or not her nuns were going to the United States to work with the men's order he had founded. At this point ...

> ... Mother (Cabrini) had recourse to the Venerable Antonia Belloni of Codogno (the Cause of whose beatification was pending at the time) in order that, through her intercession, she might obtain the desired answer (to Cabrini's letter). After ten days ... the Venerable Antonia appeared in a dream in which she handed Mother a letter from New York that answered all her questions. In this dream Mother Cabini also saw her own mother coming towards her. She asked her why she was hesitating and why she bore the name of "Missionary" if she was afraid of going to the foreign missions.

I omit the rest of the dream in which Mary and other saints appeared without speaking and in which Jesus showed up last of all, reassuring Francesca — whose motto was "I can do all things through Christ who strengthens me" — that He would be with her.

Let me also quote the interesting aftereffect of this dream.

> At the Vatican the next morning, Mother met Monsignor Scalabrini, who asked her if she had any news. With a smile, she told him that she had had a very vivid dream. The prelate smiled, in turn, and walked away. Mother then entered St. Peter's and remained there for an hour in prayer. When she returned home … she was surprised to see a carriage in front of the house. She was still more surprised to see Monsignor Scalabrini, who approached her and said, "Oh, you and your dreams! Here is a letter from America; now you can set out for New York."

While most of Mother Cabrini's other *known* (I've noted her extreme reticence) visits from the next world were by Jesus and/or Mary, it is certain other holy dead, too, came to her during those hours while her comrades slept, and she received the guidance that let her run, with almost as much efficiency as love, what amounted to a missionary empire, with branches in North, Central, and South America, as well as in many European countries (but never China!).

For instance, she herself confided to her sisters that on one occasion when "she needed immediate help" she prayed to one of the dead sisters, who had been very holy, to go to God and obtain the favor. Night came and Mother Cabrini heard a light knock on her door. Then the unlocked door opened and in walked the dead sister. She comforted her former boss, assuring Mother Cabrini that the problem of the moment would be solved happily. While she was there she also told her foundress where to find some important lost documents. The dead visitor's prophecy as to things turning out well proved as correct as her directions to the missing papers.

With Blessed Faustina Kowalska (1905-1938) we return to the type of saint who arouses suspicion because her holy work is not tangible, like Mother Cabrini's, but mystical. That is, it does not build hospitals and orphanages, but instead a new spiritual understanding or directive. Which is not to mean Faustina did not, as an uneducated, lay nun in pre-WWII Poland, do plenty of cooking, baking, gardening, and other plain old work in her convent. Merely that her claim to fame is purely mystical, rather than bolstered by material works. With all saints — contemplative or active — one does well to remember, however, the Hasidic saying that if one were holy enough the simplest gesture could redeem the world. Faustina's special mission was to spread the word about the immense Mercy of God. To her, then, it is somehow fitting that dead souls came, as they did to Padre Pio, to request her prayers. Again like Padre Pio and Adrienne von Speyr, Sister Faustina also bilocated, invisibly, at times to the bedsides of the dying to assist them with her prayers. Often Faustina saw Mary but Jesus was the humble nun's most frequent visitor. The mutual love between Savior and this Polish peasant incited demons to attack her, as they did a similar saint, Josefa Menendez, but without leaving on Faustina's body the physical evidence of their visits one finds in Josefa's case.

Saints were also sent to Faustina Kowalska.

On July 30, 1935, Sister Faustina, in fervent prayer, reproached St. Ignatius, the patron of her congregation, whose feast day it was, for not coming to her aid in carrying out a very difficult project God was asking of her. Quoting from her diary:

> Then I saw Saint Ignatius at the left side of the altar, with a large book in his hand. And he spoke these words to me, "My daughter, I am not indifferent to your project.[6] This rule can be adapted and it can be adapted to this Congregation." And gesturing with his hand toward the big book, he disappeared. I rejoiced greatly at the fact of how much the saints think of us and of how closely we are united with them. Oh the goodness of God! How beautiful is the supernatural world, that already here on earth we commune with the saints! All day long I could feel the presence of this dear Patron Saint.

Again quoting Sister Faustina's own account:

> I want to write down a dream that I had about Saint Therese of the Child Jesus. I was still a novice at the time and was going through some difficulties which I did not know how to overcome. They were interior difficulties connected with exterior ones. I made novenas to various saints but the situation grew more and more difficult. The sufferings it caused me were so great that I did not know how to go on living, but suddenly the thought occurred to me that I should pray to Saint Therese … (and) I started a novena….
>
> On the fifth day of the novena, I dreamed of Saint Therese but it was as if she were still living on earth. She hid from me the fact

that she was a saint and began to comfort me, saying that I should not be worried about this matter, but should trust more in God. She said, "I suffered greatly too," but I did not believe her and said, "It seems to me that you have not suffered at all." But Saint Therese answered me in a convincing manner that she had suffered very much indeed and said to me, "Sister, know that in three days the difficulty will come to a happy conclusion." When I was not very willing to believe her, she revealed to me that she was a saint. At that moment, a great joy filled my soul, and I said to her, "You are a saint?" "Yes," she answered, "I am a saint. Trust that this matter will be resolved in three days." And I said, "Dear sweet Therese, tell me, shall I go to heaven?" And she answered, "Yes, you will go to heaven, Sister." "And will I be a saint?" To which she replied, "Yes, you will be a saint." "But, little Therese, shall I be a saint as you are, raised to the altar?" And she answered, "Yes, you will be a saint just as I am, but you must trust in the Lord Jesus." [Faustina then asks the state of soul of various relatives. Some are fine, Therese responds; others need "much prayer."]

In her diary Faustina concludes:

This was a dream. And as the proverb goes, dreams are phantoms: God is faith. Nevertheless three days later the difficulty was solved very easily, just as she had said. And everything in this affair turned out exactly as she said it would. It was a dream, but it had its significance.

Although Faustina was dismissed as a nut during one period after her death, her Cause was opened, and successful: She is now "on the altars" as a beatified saint. Those who want to read more of the diary of this sister who died a year before WWII, but seemed to know a lot about it — its terrible extent, duration, and its special horrors in Poland — can readily do so, as the diary is available in English as *Divine Mercy in My Soul*.

Therese (in German pronounced THER EZ) Neumann, the Bavarian mystic and stigmatic, had similar foreknowledge of events, the ability to bilocate, and is also known to the world for living many years on what the world called "nothing," and she corrected to "I don't live on nothing; I live on the Savior," meaning the Eucharistic wafer that Catholics believe, as Christ said, is His Body.[7]

Thick books have been written about Therese and her visions, most principally again of Jesus. In a later chapter I will detail some of Therese Neumann's cures from various ailments that were accompanied by visits from St. Therese of Lisieux. During those cures, Therese of Lisieux also gave Therese Neumann much spiritual guidance, directives preparing her for her unusual apostolate that began the year following her return to good health. But Therese Neumann saw non-canonized holy dead too. Here one instance:

When Adolf Hitler's Nazis seized power in Germany, all Jews (whether by religion, culture, or ethnic heritage) were at terrible risk. A Jew didn't have to do anything — just be a Jew. Another group who got into trouble — but at least they did something — were serious Christians, including German Catholic priests and lay Catholics who fought the Nazis, not out of personal hatred, but out of hatred for evil doctrines that advocated eliminating from the earth whole segments of our human family: Jews, gypsies, Slavic races, the retarded, the handicapped — in short, all those not the perfect Aryans fantasized in one little dark-haired Bavarian's twisted brain. Among those beaten to death, hounded to death, or executed by the Nazis were a number of Therese Neumann's closest male friends, including newspaperman Fritz Gerlich and two brothers, both priests, Adalbert and Karl Vogl. I have spoken to Albert Vogl, nephew of the Vogls, who fled for his own life due to his anti-Nazi stance. Albert recalls Therese telling him about his uncles. The dead priest brothers had appeared to Therese, she said, chuckling delightedly that the two balding men, one a Catholic editor hounded to death and the other formally executed for his anti-Nazi work, came "in their prime," each sporting a full head of hair!

Therese Neumann also saw various dead members of her devout family and their guardian angels. She was present at the death of her saintly sister, Ottilie, and saw the guardian angels of Ottilie, of a deceased brother and sister, and of their mother come to fetch the dying holy woman. Moments later the Savior, as Therese always called Jesus, appeared, Ottilie with him in glory. Interestingly, in that same vision, Therese also saw her strong-minded father, who had died earlier in the same year, still at his spiritual work in purgatory. Later that year she saw him, too, in heaven.

I mention this saint seeing dead family members because I have noted a number of saints in my research who claimed to see their very good or holy mothers who were dead. (This does not mean that only people with good mothers become saints; Adrienne von Speyr, for instance, was rejected from birth by her mother.) Saints who said they saw their dead mothers include

St. John Bosco in the late nineteenth century and St. Frances Cabrini around the turn of the next century. In the twentieth century, I think of Catherine de Hueck Doherty (1896-1985). Catherine's parents — her half-Polish, half-Russian, Catholic father and her mother of English and French descent, both bred and raised in Czarist Russia — were extraordinary people. When Catherine's father Theodore de Kolyschkine died, it was found this great bear of a man had helped two hundred fifty young people through college, while financing a host of other secret charities. Emma Thompson Kolyschkine, Catherine's mother, a gifted pianist, rejected a concert career in favor of a menial job as a telephone operator so she could teach the catechism to workers, who would accept it from one of themselves. Tiny and seemingly fragile, she even toiled as a domestic on farms, helping the aged with their crops and the young with their lessons. She survived the Russian Revolution and spent hard years in exile, including living through the Nazis' occupation of Brussels, keeping herself and others fed, while her daughter was off in the United States and Canada, carrying on Emma and Theodore's ingrained outreach to the poor and needy. Finally Emma died, her son telling a close associate of Catherine's "my mother was a saint."

In October, 1976, Catherine de Kolyschkine de Hueck Doherty was eighty years old[8] and very concerned about her health, as her doctor had just told her she had a severely diseased heart. At that apparently appropriate time she dreamed her mother came to her. But Emma's visit was not to ready her for death or take her to the next life. Instead Emma told her daughter that God still had lots of things for Catherine to do. Laughing, Catherine told her confidant, Father Emile Briere, that they weren't even the things she herself had in mind: No, her mother said God wanted Catherine to write.

Shortly after that, doctors at the Mayo Clinic unexpectedly found Catherine's heart fine and she went on to a new, active, five-year period that included writing four books in a year!

Another person who had this sort of experience frequently was Blessed Andre Bessette (1845-1937) the indomitable if frail little French-Canadian Holy Cross Brother in Montreal, to whom God gave one of the most incredible gifts of healing of the twentieth century. Blessed Andre's widowed mother lived a life of incredible hardship, yet never lost her trust in God even when her impoverished family had to be split up, kids sent to this and that relative who could handle an extra mouth or two; Andre said, "I never saw my mother when she was not smiling — and what a lovely smile! Since her death she often smiles at me. She comes and, without speaking, looks lovingly at me." Andre said he did not feel the need to pray for his mother (Catholics pray to assist souls doing their spiritual work in purgatory) but he *often* asked her to pray for him.

As writer Michael H. Brown points out in *The Bridge to Heaven*, the final twenty years of the twentieth century are awash in people claiming to be seers and visionaries.

I mention one of these people, the subject of Brown's book, in spite of the fact that I do not normally write of mystics or visionaries who are still living and thus have not stood the test of time or after-death Church investigation. I write of her only because the site of this visionary's apparitions of Mary — Betania, Venezuela — is unique among currently active Marian apparition sites in being fully approved by its local bishop, Pio Bello Ricardo. And Bishop Ricardo says of Maria Esperanza Medrano de Bianchini: "It seems to me that Maria Bianchini is a very, very good person, a very good Christian. She has a great prayerful spirit. I would like for my own self the spirit of prayer that she has and the union with God that she has and her constant contact with God. For her there is nothing strange about her spending a whole night in prayer...."

A cynic pointed out that those who come to Betania — whether hoping to see the mother of Jesus or the "visionary" — often leave donations that go into diocesan coffers, a good reason for a Bishop to favor such events. However, the testimonies of so many people from all walks of life — especially of well-authenticated cures of terminal illness — indicate "goings on" beyond what con artists can pull off. And Brown buttressed the Bishop's opinion of Maria Esperanza by finding the sixty-six-year-old visionary met the test of St. Ignatius Loyola, who had no interest in someone's levitations but wanted to know "how does he treat his wife and children?" A devoted wife, mother of seven married children, and a grandmother, Maria Esperanza is profoundly loved, Brown says, by all her family. Some of the phenomena attributed to her, however, are about as bizarre as such things can get. So with the caution that no one should be called a saint until dead and the Church's investigation has established heroic virtue, here is a sampling of Maria Esperanza's guiding visions:

Born on November 22, 1928, when she was only five years old the brown-eyed little girl saw "a smiling woman rise from the Orinoco River with a rose in her hand," which she threw to the child. Later Maria Esperanza came to believe it was St. Therese of Lisieux letting her know via this beautiful red flower of God's love and special plans for her. A couple years later, Maria Esperanza asked St. Therese to "teach me to feel her presence." Her request, the visionary claims, was granted so that Therese became the special friend the child talked everything over with, from childhood's wants to a very mature hope that some day there might be a hospital for all those who have nowhere to go — an idea that Therese let Maria feel would in time come to fruition. Above all, even when playing, Maria Esperanza says "I felt her presence."

After what she terms "a very happy childhood" as a deeply loved child, who still endured much suffering from heart and respiratory ailments, Maria Esperanza entered a convent in her mid-twenties. Around the middle of the 1950s, one day just as Mass ended, the would-be nun saw St. Therese again. "Work out your salvation as a wife and mother," God's messenger directed, throwing her another rose. This time, where the rose landed in her right hand, it pricked and blood began to flow, the start of periodic stigmata.

St. John Bosco visited Maria Esperanza, too, to counsel her that she would meet her husband-to-be on November 1, 1955. At that date, living with some nuns in Rome, she met Geo Bianchini Gianni, who worked for Catholic Action. (Interestingly, they met in front of Rome's Church of the Sacred Heart built by Don Bosco.)

From childhood Maria Esperanza had also seen Jesus — who once came to cure her when she was near death — and Mary. In the fall of 1956, Mary told Maria Esperanza she would be married that December 8. The marriage took place that day and the couple returned to Venezuela, where over the years of their happy marriage they produced six daughters and one son.

In one of her visions before her marriage, Esperanza had been told about Betania. In 1974, Maria and Geo found and bought the picturesque hillside ranch located about an hour and a half from Caracas on the Tuy River.

In Italy once again in February, 1976, Maria Esperanza was directed by Mary to be back in Venezuela by March 25, the Feast of the Annunciation to Catholics. "You shall see me on the land you purchased," she promised. On that day Mary appeared at Betania, calling herself "Mary, Reconciler of Peoples and Nations."

Enough. I think the reader can see that, if we have an honest report — and her Bishop's discernment is that we do — then here is a life guided by God's messengers.

ENDNOTES

[1] Since St. Teresa's reform, there exist two Carmelite orders: The original and her newer group who are known as Discalced (literally, shoeless) Carmelites.

2 Such individuals — sometimes called victim souls — have to be very carefully sorted out by experienced spiritual mentors from masochists. The true reparatory sufferer agrees with one of their number, Therese Neumann, that "suffering is something one cannot want." Yet Therese also said, "when the day of suffering (sent by God) comes, I say 'Savior, it's all right with me.' "

3 The medal commemorates God's creating Mary free from original sin, in order to make her a fitting vessel to bear Jesus. (If original sin is a new idea, think of it as the innate human tendency to make bad choices and "screw up.")

4 These apparitions, like those much later at Fatima, were accompanied by some correct prophesies regarding future political and ecclesial events.

5 *Mother Frances Xavier Cabrini* by Mother Saverio De Maria.

6 I have changed the translation here from the Polish to "project" rather than "cause" as the latter may be confusing since it generally relates to one's investigation for beatification. Also for reasons of clarity, in the same quote, I have changed "spiritual world" to "supernatural world."

7 See a chapter on her inedia in my book, *The Sanctified Body*.

8 There is some confusion as to her birthdate, but this is probably correct.

9 ✣ THERESE, HER SISTERS, AND A FEW FRIENDS

No dead saint in the twentieth century has been seen by more people aspiring to holiness than St. Therese of Lisieux. So it may be of interest that Therese herself received three known after-death visitations from holy people. The first, when as a very ill ten-year-old she was cured instantaneously by a "visit" of the Virgin Mary, who smiled at her, is outside the area of this book.

The second instance was a numinous dream after Therese, by special dispensation, entered the Lisieux Carmel at the age of fifteen. The aged foundress of this Carmel, Mother Genevieve, who at age eighty-three was sixty-eight years Therese's senior, confirmed the young girl's sense of God's call to serve Him in peace and joy with total confidence in His goodness. When Mother Genevieve died, Therese captured a tear that lay on the dead woman's cheek with a scrap of linen and kept it as a precious relic in the locket that held her own vows. A few nights later, the youngest Carmelite dreamed about the aged one. In this dream Mother Genevieve, still on her sickbed, was making her will. She had something to give each nun until she came to Therese. Then, with apparently nothing left, she raised herself in the bed and said three times "To you, I leave my heart."

The third instance, also in the form of a dream, came as a great consolation during a period when Therese was in spiritual turmoil. From her autobiography, *Story of a Soul*:

> I dreamt I was in the corridor, walking alone with Reverend Mother. Suddenly without knowing how they had got there, I saw three Carmelite nuns, wearing their mantles and long veils. I knew they were from heaven. "How happy I should be," I thought, "to see the face of one of them." As if my wish had been heard, the tallest of them walked towards me. I knelt. She lifted her veil or

rather covered us both with it. Instantly I recognised the Venerable Mother Anne of Jesus, the foundress of Carmel in France. Her face had a beauty not of this earth; no ray of light shone from it, and yet, in spite of the thick veil which covered us both, I saw her face lit by a gentle glow.

She caressed me and, moved by her love, I ventured to say: "I implore you, Mother, to tell me if God is going to leave me on earth for long. Will He come for me soon?" She gave me a tender smile: "Yes, soon ... soon. I promise you." I went on: "Tell me also, Mother, if God is pleased with me. Does He want anything from me beyond my poor little deeds and longings?" As I spoke, her face shone with a new splendour and her gaze grew even more tender. She said: "God asks nothing more from you. He is pleased, very pleased." She took my head between her hands and I cannot give you any idea of the sweetness of her love for me. I was aflame with joy, but I thought of my sisters and wanted to ask some favours for them. But I woke up.

Therese — bless her! — adds to this account at least some of its after-effects:

> When I woke ... I knew that heaven exists and that souls dwell there who love me and look upon me as their child. The realisation of this never left me, and it was all the sweeter because until then I had been quite indifferent to the Venerable Mother Anne of Jesus. I never thought of her.... But now I know and really understand that she is far from indifferent about me. This knowledge deepens my love both for her and for all the blessed ones in heaven.

In her turn, Therese after death returned to give spiritual direction — including occasionally a gentle scolding — to those aspiring to sanctity. Those seeking the heights of wholeness included some among her own Lisieux Carmelites. A later chapter details how God used Therese to raise the Carmel as a whole to a higher level of love for God and each other, but that involves nuns across the gamut from holy to "difficult." Spotlighted here is Therese as a God-sent guide to that elite group whose lives set a direct course to heaven, represented primarily by interventions in the lives of her four blood sisters — all nuns.

Like Therese, the four other Martin daughters did not enter convents to become "good little nuns," but saints. Three of them living in the Lisieux Carmel, the family's "ugly duckling," Leonie — not strong enough for the taxing physical demands of Carmelite life — found her path in a cloistered convent of Visitation nuns in the larger city of Caen. Undoubtedly, Therese carried God-given favors to her sisters, which will forever be unknown, particularly in the years after the investigative tribunal finished its questioning about such things, but here a sampling (in the sisters' birth order).

Marie, the oldest child of the Martin family and Therese's godmother, as Carmelite nun Marie of the Sacred Heart shared a large-visioned way of thinking with her littlest sister that made them, in a sense, kindred souls. Marie early grasped the depths of sanctity hidden in her youngest sister's quiet life. Original and frank, Marie's disdain for much that passes for "pious" masked her own holiness; but Therese saw and reverenced in her a heart given totally to God. The day after Therese's death, Marie later testified under oath before the tribunal investigating Therese's possible holiness, "after I did a charitable act, I felt her soul approach mine with an expression of joy that I can't [adequately] express."

In her private notes, Marie wrote:

> The dominant grace, since my dear little sister went to Heaven, is that I sense her near me. I know that she is not dead, that she has only put off for a time her garment of flesh, but that her life is not extinguished, rather she is in the fullness of life.

Marie goes on to say that she feels Therese explaining to her the path Marie should follow to become a saint and details her dead sister's recommendations at length.

God guides Marie without miracles or apparitions for most of the remaining forty-two years of her life, since Therese's sisters want to follow her in living heroically by faith, rather than in the easy euphoria of Therese's "consolations." Still perhaps a dozen times at the very moment where Marie — suspicious of "phenomena" anyway — would least expect such manifestations, showers of perfumes mysteriously envelop her. Like the very first grace the day after Therese's death, these signs of her dead sister's presence always sanction some act of charity or humility of Marie's, as if applauding, "That's it! You're on the right track!"

Interior graces, with only the smallest manifestation of Therese's presence, continue, too. For instance, on July 5, 1889, during the year after Therese's death, Marie writes:

I was praying my little Therese to help me prepare well to receive the good God [in communion], when I was invaded by a feeling of faith so strong, so penetrating, that I wondered how I was going to be able to take the steps necessary to receive communion. If I had seen with my own eyes Our Lord, I could not have had more faith. When I received the communion wafer, I seemed to hear an interior voice which said to me: "Here is your Creator, your God, your Father and your Savior!" But that can't express well what I experienced then....

This and similar events caused this thirteen-years-older sister, who had helped rear Therese (then four) after their mother's early death, to now

OSV file photo; inset courtesy the Lisieux Carmel

The four Martin sisters with their prioress, Mother Mary Gonzague.
Standing from left: Celine and Pauline. Seated are Mother Gonzague,
Marie, and Therese. Inset: Leonie.

humbly ask Therese to mother her in God, instructing Marie in His ways and helping her practice virtue.

The last eleven years of Marie's life, the independence-loving, free spirit was confined to bed or wheelchair with crippling rheumatism. If Therese did not come to cure her, Marie wrote to Leonie, "It's surely because there are some great graces hidden in all this." And Therese did show up a couple times. Marie writes, again to Leonie:

> It was the night of January 29 [1939] that I was suffering a lot from rheumatism in my knees and my devoted nurse, who sleeps in a cell near mine in order to be able to look out for me, saw that I could feel my legs and knees all twisted — which happens sometimes. Being unable to help me after trying a lot, she said to me: "I'm going to ask our saint to come to your rescue." Then she left sad but confident. Just a few moments later, I felt as if someone was very gently straightening out my legs without any trouble, and I had no doubt of a supernatural intervention. The prayer of my nurse had been heard and my little Therese truly came to my aid. I had no more suffering and was able to sleep the entire night.

On a second occasion, Marie had a piercing pain in her shoulder, found herself as if paralyzed and unable to re-cover herself when her blankets slipped off. The account has the fuzziness of the true saint's efforts to down-play such things. Thus it is not said that Therese was seen, but simply that she "descended" and, with her sisterly hand, pulled up Marie's covers and soothed her sufferings. But Marie *must* have seen her dead sister or been positive of her presence, for the account[1] from Lisieux says that after thanking her, the rheumatic said to Therese, "Go back to Heaven now."

Pauline — known in Carmel as Mother Agnes of Jesus — the second child of the Martins, was born the year after Marie and these two were always close. Pauline said, when questioned after Marie's quiet death at age eighty on January 19, 1940, that she felt neither Marie's nor Therese's "presence," but was certain of assistance nevertheless.

Pauline's winning, loving ways ("she sowed joy all her life," one source says) and her motherly style of leadership make her probably the closest to Therese of the sisters in personality. It was sixteen-year-old Pauline of whom their mother Zelie exclaimed as she lay dying "I know you'll become a nun — and a saint."[2]

As the prioress of Carmel for many years after Therese's death, saintly, capable Pauline, or Mother Agnes — so as not to lead her spiritual daughters into misplacing their energy from the quest for virtue to that for wonders — was very reticent about anything Therese did for her personally. We know from her under-oath testimony that she, to whom four-year-old Therese had spontaneously turned when Zelie died with the cry, "Pauline, you will be my mother now," was not ignored by her dead "child." Pauline admits to the tribunal that at least ten times in the first decade or so after her little sister's death she has experienced "visits" from Therese through the odor of sanctity alone (who knows what she may have experienced in other ways). But the bare fact is *all* we know. Not a single detail escaped those humble lips.

Diminutive Pauline, whom Therese always addressed as "petite mere," lived to be ninety, dying in 1951. In her old age, she did feel free to mention a humorous event she called a dream. Therese had come to her looking just as in life and said with a smile, "You're getting old, my little mother."

Eager to take off for heaven, Pauline said she replied to Therese, "Nothing could give me more pleasure than to hear that!"

Leonie became a Visitation nun only after Therese's death, having previously flunked out first at the Poor Clares and then twice at the Visitation cloister, physically and emotionally unable to take the demands of either lifestyle. As Therese lay dying, she promised she would see Leonie's dream fulfilled. Not long after Therese's death, the Caen Visitation got new leaders who were less severe in their demands: Thirty-six-year-old Leonie was permitted a fourth try and succeeded at last.

The rest of her life Leonie relied greatly on her dead little sister and often promised favors in Therese's name to those asking Leonie's prayers. It was noted that during WWI, for instance, soldiers' families she promised "Therese will bring them back" were not disappointed, even in one family where several sons fought four years in the front lines.

As with all her sisters, Therese's help was not so obvious that the Visitation nun lost the merit of living most of the time by "pure faith." But now and then a gesture reminded Leonie that Therese was looking out for her. Leonie testified during the official investigation of Therese:

> Around 1900 one evening in winter, feeling a lot of ennui and revulsion, I was praying in slipshod fashion.... Suddenly a luminous form which dazzled me appeared on our Book of Hours. I wasn't afraid, quite the contrary. After an instant, I realized that this luminous form was a hand. I believe firmly that it was my little

Therese; I was perfectly consoled and experienced a delicious peace. This has never happened again. But on September 30, the anniversary of Therese's death, I've felt, two or three times [during the day], the odor of roses; this has happened four or five years; other years it hasn't.

Not long after giving this testimony under oath, in 1912, Leonie writes her three Carmelite sisters about one of those visits:

On the thirtieth of September, Therese visited me in the evening by sweet, penetrating odors of roses. They only lasted several instants, long enough that, in my joy, I was able to say "O my beloved little sister, you're here near me, I'm sure." Since [then] I feel myself more fervent [so that] this "little nothing" wants to become a saint too.

During her last years, Leonie was healed of pneumonia when someone at her bedside called on Therese, but her convalescence was long and painful. Several times in this difficult period the official account of her life from her Visitation convent[3] says "a supernatural presence — that of her Therese — comforted her."

When Leonie died in 1941 at age seventy-eight, Cardinal Suhard of Paris spoke of her as one of the hidden saints who keep our world going. It was to her entire family's prayers and Therese's guidance that Leonie gave the credit for her change from a mentally-slow, allergy-wracked, physically-frail, psychologically-damaged (a housekeeper secretly terrorized her in childhood[4]), melancholy person weighted down with a sense of inferiority into a woman buoyant with the joy that all her lacks and miseries were only so many more claims on God's mercy. To the minds of many, one of Therese's miracles, Leonie is a candidate for beatification.

Celine Martin — known in Carmel as Sister Genevieve of the Holy Face — was only four years older than Therese and the two youngest of this family were inseparable.

In October, 1897, only two weeks after her death, Therese came to this artistically-gifted,[5] independent-minded sister who had been depressed by certain spiritual difficulties for a long time. Fully awake — in fact, making the Way of the Cross (a holistic meditation on Jesus' Passion) outdoors in the Carmel cloister — Celine saw "a kind of flame coming from the depths of the sky." At the same moment she realized interiorly, "It's Therese." She told the tribunal she could not put into words "the interior grace I received then," claiming "it is beyond my powers of expression." But years after seeing this "living flame" in the daytime sky, she insists it "was one of the greatest graces I have ever received." All sorts of groundless worries that had kept her occupied simply disappeared, questions were resolved, and she found herself securely on higher spiritual ground.

Then the following March, as Celine completed a retreat, she affectionately reproached Therese that her dead sister hadn't helped her, only to suddenly feel invaded by an intimate sweetness that fired her with divine love.

On various occasions Celine experienced the presence of Therese through the odor of sanctity. While often giving the "well done!" to acts of humility or charity, the perfumes also marked special occasions. Celine experienced these odors, for instance, on February 5, 1912, an anniversary of the day she entered Carmel — which was also the day that the diocese's investigation of Therese's sanctity was sent to Rome — and again on March 17, 1915, the anniversary of Celine's taking the veil and the opening of Rome's part of the Theresian investigation. Sometimes Therese spoke to her. For example, on the Feast of the Transfiguration (August 6, 1939), Celine complained that she hadn't the strength to go on, only to hear Therese comforting her that she had nothing to fear, that she would always have the strength found in having no strength...." (See additional instances of both speech and perfume visits to Celine in chapter 14.)

On the morning their oldest sister, Marie, died in 1940, Celine was inundated with those mysterious perfumes, which lasted for eight days and made her understand, she said, how precious the death of His true friends is to God. Were the perfumes an indication, as they can be, of the divine presence? Or did they signal the presence of Therese or Marie? Or both sisters? Take your pick.

Celine herself would die on February 25, 1959, just two months short of her ninety-first birthday, with the same reputation of holiness as her sisters, parents, and other relatives. Her death replicated Therese's in many ways, such as its heavy suffering followed by something like ecstasy in the final moments. Did Celine's ecstatic gaze see Therese? Or the "good God" she longed for even more?

After little Therese lost her mother, her father, Louis Martin, moved his family from Alençon to Lisieux at the urging of his late wife Zelie's younger brother Isidore Guerin and his wife Celine (Fournet). The Guerins proved second parents to the five living (four siblings had died) Martin girls. Leonie and Celine even lived with them full-time when Louis Martin — who later died at the Guerin home — was incapacitated (and for a time institutionalized) due to a mysterious affliction similar to Alzheimer's.

Some of the last weakly-scrawled or gasped-out verbal messages of the dying Therese were to tell Aunt Celine and Uncle Isidore how much she loved them and to promise her help once she reached heaven.

Neither were hard to love. Isidore's crustiness was readily seen through by his nieces — and all of Lisieux — who revered the well-to-do, Catholic philanthropist's heart of gold that sometimes single-handedly kept the Carmel financially afloat in its leaner years. As for Celine Fournet Guerin, the Martin girls' aunt by marriage was one of those "born-nice" people whose kindness and love of God only deepened with the years. Two years after Therese's death, her Aunt Celine — then in her fifties, with one daughter married and the younger in Carmel — experienced a rapid decline in health. To a daughter after a sleepless night, she confided:

> I would suffer a lot, but my little Therese watches over me tenderly. All night, I felt her near my bed. Several times, she caressed me, which gave me an extraordinary sense of courage.

Accepting death as sweetly as she had lived, Celine Fournet Guerin died smiling on February 13, 1900. The priest who brought her the last sacraments marvelled that in twenty-five years of ministering to the dying he had never encountered such "angelic piety."

Marie Guerin, the second of Isidore and Celine Guerin's two daughters, grew up with all the advantages of affluence (a distant relative of Celine Guerin's, dying childless, left the Guerins a lot of money) and the greater riches of parents who were fine human beings and loved her dearly. Like the Martin girls, Therese's cousin and same-age playmate wanted to become a nun and a saint. But wracked by a sense of inadequacy (perhaps she inadvisedly compared herself to Therese's spiritual genius?), Marie lived in self-torture for years after Therese, at only fifteen and a half, entered Carmel by special dispensation. Things got to the point that Marie's scruples about her "unworthiness" kept her from receiving the Eucharist she longed for.

First by letters, then by on-the-spot direction after Marie — taking the name Sister Marie of the Eucharist — entered Carmel in August, 1895, Therese crossed swords with Marie's fears. Therese chided her cousin for considering the Eucharist a reward for the good, and proposed she see it instead as nourishment for Marie's spiritual journey.

Therese was dead by fall, 1897. But the dead saint did not leave Marie to fight her battles alone. For instance, in 1898 Marie's spiritual life took a whole new direction the day after she asked Therese to "take me in hand again and help me walk the way of pure love." Without seeing Therese or sensing her presence, while at prayer Marie suddenly saw clearly *how* to move toward her goal. She attributed to Therese her life-changing insight. In a letter written around this time, she writes: "It is certain that since the death of our little saint, I don't feel the same any longer and others notice too."

Completely cured of scruples, Marie Guerin turned around and "cured" a married cousin of the same malady, writing letters that are so joyfully confident in God's parental forbearance and love they could pass for writings of Therese herself.

In her mid-thirties, Marie of the Eucharist, too, became tubercular. Near the end of her life, she wrote to her family that Therese was for her "a veritable Guardian Angel, guiding her every moment and proving her love" for Marie "by all sorts of little delicate attentions which could only come from Heaven." To our frustration, Marie leaves unspecified what forms the dead saint's guidance and little attentions took.

Instinctively repulsed at the thought of death, Marie turned that over to Therese, too, as her disease proved incurable. To Marie's astonishment and joy, all her fear and repugnance vanished. Sister Agnes of Jesus wrote to Leonie in Caen that their cousin Marie "died the death of a saint. It was absolutely celestial." Marie of the Eucharist's serenity, in fact, so struck even non-relatives who witnessed her last days and death that nine years later, one witness, Mother Isabelle of the Sacred Heart, remarked, "When one has seen Sister Marie of the Eucharist die, one can no longer fear death."

That Therese played a major role, all were sure. But if any form of after-death appearances were involved, this again is hidden from view — perhaps a good reminder that all the appearances of Therese together add up to only a minuscule part of the works God has done through her.

Besides helping her relatives, Therese has guided many men and women — as so many chapters of this book detail — who want to give themselves completely to God, such as the three visionaries mentioned in the last chapter: Blessed Faustina Kowalska of Poland, Maria Esperanza of Venezuela, and Therese Neumann of Bavaria.

Therese has also appeared to one of the Catholic Church's candidates for official sainthood from the Malabar Syrian rite in India, Sister Alphonsa. Born Anna Muttathupandatu, when quite young this God-intoxicated girl had a dream in which "a young Carmelite" told her God was calling her to become a nun. Anna even burned herself — hoping to be less attractive — to get out of the marriage her family was arranging. After several close matrimonial calls, in her late teens she was allowed to become a Franciscan Clarist nun (not the same order as the Poor Clares, but called by their name in the Malabar part of India).

Sister Alphonsa had a lot of health problems. One day St. Therese appeared to her to talk about them. One of those "good news, bad news" conversations, God's messenger promised the young Indian nun would get no more contagious diseases, but said she would have other types of ailments until her death. Usually sent to heal people, Therese in this case confirmed a very unusual vocation. The invalid sister died in 1946 at only thirty-five.

Does Therese still show up to guide people striving for holiness? It appears so. In the Lisieux Archives I noted the letter from a Father Andre whose last name I withhold. He writes of how he saw Therese in 1979 while praying the rosary. She said nothing, according to his account, but definitely communicated, for he was "filled with joy."

ENDNOTES

[1] I am working from the biography *Marie* published by the Carmel and authored by priest-Theresian authority Pere Stephane-Joseph Piat, O.F.M. As far as I know, it has never been translated into English.

[2] Pauline was alone near her mother's bed. Zelie took her second child's hands, kissed them with respect and said: "O my Pauline. You are my treasure. I know very well you'll be a nun, that you'll become a saint. I'm not worthy to have a daughter like you — you are my glory and my happiness." Pauline shared this for what it shows about Zelie, but added "I felt rather embarrassed ... because I knew how far I was from meriting [the remarks]."

[3] Published by the Lisieux Carmel however.

[4] This abuse was uncovered by Marie twenty days after their mother's holy sister, a Visitation nun with a special love for Leonie, died, promising help for the difficult child from heaven.

[5] Her painting of the Holy Face of Jesus based on the Shroud of Turin is considered a "masterpiece," which won an international religious art prize in 1909, was acclaimed by St. Pius X and, "in vulgarized form," has circulated throughout the world in millions of copies. Celine's photos of Therese and the other Carmelites have given the world priceless information on the saint's life.

10 ❧ THE ALL-AMERICAN SAINT

N o saint has a more All-American background than Barney Casey (1870-1957) member of the nine Casey brothers' baseball team, streetcar conductor, and kindhearted, part-time prison guard, who befriended one of Jesse James' sidekicks. All this, of course, before the Irish-descent farm-boy, who entered life in a Wisconsin log cabin, evolved into Father Solanus Casey, holy Capuchin (they're the Franciscans with the pointy hoods) healer of souls and bodies.[1]

Until his death, the reed-thin, white-bearded priest with the innocent blue eyes of a young child was known at his posts in New York, Indiana, or Michigan as *the* man to see when you needed serious prayer. His trust in God so great that he urged "thank God ahead of time," Solanus inspired belief that, "live or die, God is doing what's best for me." Thousands of cures and favors — inexplicable by human standards — took place during his lifetime. And continue after his death.

Formal recognition of the simple Capuchin's sanctity took place on July 11, 1995, when his Church titled him "Venerable," worthy of veneration, for his heroic virtues. The Father Solanus Guild[2] was founded by grateful friends to promote this official recognition which will probably lead to beatification and perhaps canonization. Each quarterly issue of the Guild's publication contains letters from people who've asked the former porter and soup-kitchen worker's prayers and not been disappointed. I quote one individual from New York:

> Four and a half years ago I had a heart attack at the age of 43. After two unsuccessful angiographies, my doctor told me I needed open heart surgery. I went into shock. A friend of mine heard about my plight and sent me the prayer and relic of Father Solanus. At the time I was skeptical about someone's intercession with the Lord for others. A few weeks later my husband found a very reputable surgeon who saw me and told me that I did not need major surgery.

Angioplasty would solve all my problems. I remember the night before my surgery I prayed so hard and asked Father Solanus to help me. After the procedure was a success, I was brought to recovery. That night I had the strangest dream-vision. I remember opening my eyes in the middle of the night and seeing this man in dark clothes [the Capuchin habit is dark brown] sitting next to my bed facing me. He seemed to be keeping some kind of vigil over me. In an instant I was completely awake and the person had disappeared.

Writing four and a half years after the angioplasty to give public thanks for Father Solanus' perhaps even literally "watching over" her, this witness says her life is ninety-nine percent back to normal.

Capuchin Brother Richard Merling is stationed at the Detroit monastery where Solanus lived for many years. Headquarters of the Guild and site of the church where Father Solanus' remains rest since the official exhumation in 1987, the monastery opens its doors to a constant flow of visitors. From them Brother Richard hears many stories about Father Solanus, including instances where people believe they've seen the holy friar.

Brother Richard spoke of the Fort Wayne, Indiana, woman who knew nothing about Father Solanus, but was worried sick about her husband, who was seriously ill in the hospital. Someone suggested she make the twenty-five-mile trip down to St. Felix Capuchin monastery in Huntington, Indiana, to ask for prayers and enroll her husband in the Seraphic Mass Association of the Capuchins.

courtesy the Father Solanus Guild

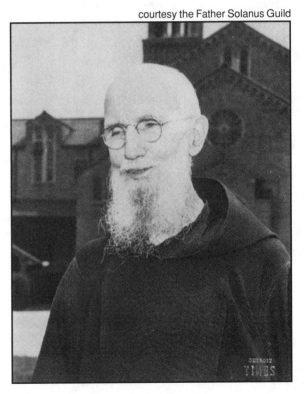

Venerable Solanus Casey

She made the drive and went first into the chapel to pray. After awhile an elderly friar with a long, white beard came up to her.

"My husband's sick," she nervously blurted out. "Will you pray for him?"

"Yes, yes. Don't worry. He'll be all right," the aged Capuchin assured her.

Feeling better she went over to the office. As she talked to the staff she mentioned that she had been in the chapel and "this elderly friar assured me my husband will be fine."

"Elderly friar?"

"Yes, the one with the long, white beard."

"Really! Can you describe him a little more?"

"Sure, he was — well, actually he looked just like this friar in the picture here."

It was a picture, of course, of Father Solanus — dead since 1957. And there were no elderly friars nor bearded ones at the monastery.

The husband did get well.

Another story told to Brother Richard is about a young boy no more than six, who was in a coma for days. The family kept vigil by the hospital bedside. One day the grandmother arrived with a relic badge of Father Solanus. She placed this relic on the boy and sat quietly praying. Soon the boy came out of his coma. Noticing the relic, which had a picture of Solanus on it, the youngster exclaimed, "Hey, I was just talking to this man! He was in the real bright tunnel with me. He said I'm going to be okay."

Brother Richard thinks the boy's is not the only case where Father Solanus is turning up at sickbeds. But from what he hears, Brother Richard says Solanus is also making more low-key visits to encourage people. For instance, there is the one in 1994 to a woman who works at the Detroit monastery. Experiencing a difficult time, she woke in the night — is absolutely certain she was truly awake — to see Father Solanus standing quietly at the end of her bed. He did not speak. Just a reassuring wave of the hand and he vanished, leaving her comforted and encouraged.

ENDNOTES

[1] See my *Nothing Short of a Miracle* chapters on him.

[2] 1780 Mt. Elliot Avenue, Detroit, Michigan 48207-3496.

11 ❧ An Ikon of Divine Compassion

W e are Anglicans and my husband was to have an operation for cancer of the colon. This caused much worry … A Catholic friend advised me to write to Padre Pio the stigmatist and ask for his prayers. I told my friend I knew nothing about him and had never heard of him. She again advised me very strongly to write. I took her advice, posted the letter myself. I did not tell my husband or anyone. The letter was posted on a Saturday and the following Wednesday I visited my husband in the hospital and as soon as he saw me, he said, "Did anyone write to a Father Pio about me?" The suddenness of the question took me aback. I was very surprised he should speak of Padre Pio as he knew nothing about him. I said "Who is Padre Pio and why do you ask this question?" He said, "Because he was here in my room last night." I was stupefied. He then went on to say, "He stood by my bed and said very distinctly 'Padre Pio' as he brought his right hand up to his chest. This he did three times and then disappeared as suddenly as he came." I could no longer keep silent and told him what I had done. On relating this extraordinary happening to my devout Catholic daughter-in-law, she gave me books and photographs of Padre Pio. When my husband saw his photograph, he said, "This is the person who visited me last night."

This "visit" by the then-living Capuchin Franciscan monk, who never left his hilltop friary in southern Italy (a phenomenon called bilocation[1]), left an interesting change in the patient's condition. Until that night his cancer adhered to the back wall of his abdomen; now it no longer did so. This made a complete change in the surgical outlook: His surgeon was readily able to remove the entire malignancy and Rose Pieris' husband went back to leading a normal life.

Others visited during Padre Pio's lifetime through bilocation and even trilocation by the Catholic Church's best-known twentieth century miracle-worker, sometimes had only the odor of sanctity to announce his presence or a cure. Typical is the testimony of Catherine Green of Clonmel, Ireland, whose child, Ann, had distressing symptoms. Numerous doctors later, the diagnosis was "a leaking heart valve." After about seven doctors agreed on this, the physicians warned Mrs. Green that her child would only live to be about fourteen since, at that point, her body would get too large for her inadequate heart. A nun in a Presentation Convent suggested they write to "a very holy priest in Italy who can do marvelous things." This was Padre Pio.

Padre Pio got thousands of letters. This woman received an answer — after a very strange thing happened at her home. She witnesses, "I live in a side street with not even a blade of grass in sight, but the night before I received the letter our whole house was filled with the scent of roses."

Padre Pio's letter informed the mother her child would be all right without any operations on her heart. Somehow this occurred. Catherine Green writes her formal testimony thirty years later: Her thirty-eight-year-old healthy daughter has three children of her own.

During all this time that Padre Pio gallivanted around the world, he was almost crushed to death emotionally, spiritually, and sometimes physically by the throngs that found their way to his remote friary seven days a week, year after year, from all over the world — each person wanting a word, a moment, or much more.

At the same time (see page 34), he was involved in helping many dead people who clamored for his prayers. Even the old father of Padre Pio, spending a night in the friary, saw two dead Franciscans there who, Padre Pio explained to his dad, were working out their purgation from sin in the same place where they had erred. Two brief anecdotes of this phenomenon that has filled a book:

During WWI, an old man walked into the room of the friary where Padre Pio was absorbed in prayer. He said he was Pietro di Mauro and that he had died in the friary when it was a home for the elderly, on September 18, 1908. He died, he told the young friar, in room number four, having fallen asleep smoking a cigar that set the bed on fire. God, he said, had given him permission to come to Pio and ask his prayers, especially a Mass. Padre Pio, who was still young at the time, found this hard to take. He confided in Padre Paolino of Casacalenda, who had a few doubts of his own. Padre Paolino had the idea to go down to the town below the friary and check the death records, in which he discovered that this di Mauro, indeed, had died when and how he said. Padre Pio saw the old fellow again, when he had completed his spiritual growth and purification and was on his way to heaven.

In 1945, Brother Peter of the friary where Padre Pio lived went back to his room following the midnight prayers of the friars.

> To his great surprise and fear, he found seated at the desk a very young friar, his head covered by his hood and resting in the palms of his hands as if he were meditating. Even though he was scared, … (Brother Peter) had the courage to ask in a loud voice, "Who are you?" But the only answer he received was the young friar's disappearance into thin air. Very scared, Brother Peter cried out and ran to Padre Pio.…

Padre Pio, a dozen years Peter's senior and by now very used to such things, put his arm about his fellow Franciscan's shoulder with reassuring words. Pio knew this spirit well and explained that not yet purified enough to withstand the light of heaven, he needed prayer, but was no one to be afraid of.

While they did not upset Pio, the dead still added to the "impossible" burden carried by the mystic, taken note of by publications like the *New York Times* as well as "those tabloids." An ikon of divine compassion in a too-often pitiless century, Pio tried — like a variant on the mythical St. Christopher — to carry the world to God on his spiritual back. In two earlier books, I have written of his own weaknesses, spiritual struggles, and physical disabilities — as well as his joy and sense of humor — as he struggled to bring others to God, while existing, mysteriously, on amounts of sleep, food, and rest unable to sustain any human life, let alone one engaged in demanding, 'round the clock ministry.

After a lifetime given to the service of God and humanity, Padre Pio died September 23, 1968, in his armchair, a doctor present marveling at "the most peaceful and sweet (death) I have ever seen." Among the saint's last words as he looked toward a photo on his cell's wall of his mother: "I see two mothers." Most interpret this as meaning that the mother of Jesus was there, perhaps with Pio's own mother, to lead him to paradise.

Barely had he slipped so quietly into the next dimension then the dead saint reappeared and conversed with his old friend, physician Andrea Cardone in Pietrelcina near Benavento. It was only the start. During the thirty years from that day to this, Padre Pio has been busier than ever. I have written in detail elsewhere[2] of Kelly Wilkinson of the village of Clogherhead in County Louth, born with such a serious heart defect and liver problem that she was baptized on the spot. By prayer, she lived to be three, but always frail, always expected to die. Then, at three, when her heart condition had reached the crisis point, the tyke saw Padre Pio in her bedroom and was completely healed.

A second chapter on Padre Pio will give a detailed cure; here, I want to take the opposite tack and give short summations of many after-death appearances —concentrating on cures — to represent his work as a messenger of God, quoting testimonies archived at the friary where Padre Pio lived.[3] (As usual I am indebted to the kindness of Father Joseph Pius Martin.) My point: Like St. Therese before him, Padre Pio is a man who really gets around. In fact it can be said without exaggeration that the brown-robed Capuchin has appeared in the last thirty years just about everywhere in the world. Like Therese before him, God is using Padre Pio to cure, to redirect, to guide, to obtain great miracles, and to deliver everyday little favors, like the one to the elderly couple who told the dead saint they couldn't afford to replace their malfunctioning stove: they suddenly smelled "a beautiful perfume out of the blue" just at the hour a relative inquired of their son, "Did he know anyone who wanted a cooker?"

Padre Pio's own family had been poor — so poor that gentle Papa Forgione did manual labor (in the United States) far from his loved ones for years, to send home the money that not only fed the family, but enabled little Francisco, who loved God so, to quit the fields to study and one day be ordained as Padre Pio. Padre Alessio Parente quotes Padre Pio: "The immense pity I experience at the sight of a poor man gives rise deep down in my soul to a most vehement desire to help him...."

It is no wonder, then, that Padre Pio often carries God's blessings to poor working men. For example, on July 3, 1935, at his work site, Antonio Paladino was run over by a cart loaded with concrete. For *thirty-three years* he was pretty much immobilized as a result. In late September, 1968, Padre Pio died. On the 12th of December, the dead priest appeared to the invalid workman. Paladino felt Pio tap his left shoulder as the Capuchin — who could be seen clearly — told him to get up and walk without using his stick. Paladino obeyed. He found he could walk.

Similarly, on September 23, 1955, Antonio Di Pasquale of Pietranico, Pescara, Italy was lifting a sheet of marble when he felt an acute pain in his spine. He was paralyzed for fifteen years. Frequent hospitalizations left him feeling helpless and hopeless, especially as his hearing and sight faded to almost nil as well. His wife Lucia, upon Padre Pio's death, got hold of a handkerchief that had touched the dead saint. Very superstitious in some views. But the fact remains that God does not seem offended when people clutch at something belonging to His friends, the same way a desperate woman once grabbed Jesus' hem.[4] When Lucia begged Padre Pio's help, it appears he went to God and received a commission: On June 7, 1970, Antonio Di Pasquale saw Padre Pio. Deaf as Di Pasquale was, he heard Padre Pio order "Get up and walk." If he ignored that command, it was only because he had been, after all, completely paralyzed for fifteen years. But when Padre Pio repeated the order, something broke loose in the former workman's soul, or body, or both. He felt strength surge through him. He stood up. In that motion he not only regained movement, his sight returned, too. After a pilgrimage of thanks to San Giovanni Rotondo, he also pilgrimaged to the healing shrine at Lourdes. There, on August 6, his hearing came back.

Phyllis Capalbo's grandson Michael lost half his right toe when a thousand-pound cylinder fell on his foot. With his doctors not sure they could save the rest of the toe, Phyllis rushed to the hospital to give Michael a written novena requesting Padre Pio's prayers. As Michael read it, his father and sister arrived and, curious, looked on. Suddenly the room filled with the scent of flowers. No bouquets had been delivered or parked in the hall. Since the threesome knew nothing about Padre Pio, Michael's excited grandmother explained such perfumes often suggest the saint is making a visit. The toe was saved.

The cure may not always be physical: James Prior is also disabled in a work accident in March, 1984, when in his mid-fifties. He dreams of Padre Pio five years later and finds himself "more at ease with my disability." He begins saving money to visit San Giovanni Rotondo.

Of course, Padre Pio does not only turn up to help working men or those who are poor. The testimony of nurse Rita M. De Nitti:

> In 1974 I was the recipient of what my husband and I consider a miracle from Padre Pio. I was told in July 1974 I would be opened for major cancer. Since I was also a nurse at the hospital I knew the score. The surgeon told me very bluntly, "We are opening you up for major cancer, with the expectation of finding it, and praying we don't." The night before surgery my husband awakened about 2 A.M. to the scent of roses (a miracle in itself, since he was just out of the hospital from nose surgery and could smell nothing at all). He followed the scent to the living room where on the mantle was

a continuous candle burning in front of a statue of Padre Pio. Suddenly he heard a voice (no apparition) and it said, "Rudolph, don't worry; they won't find cancer: she'll be all right." My husband was stunned. The next morning I was in surgery six hours and the doctor came into my room smiling and said to me, "Do you know you had a miracle? There isn't a trace of cancer in your body anywhere. A large tumour was removed and it was benign."

The nurse made a thanksgiving pilgrimage to Padre Pio's grave.

Rosario Mendoza suffered for nineteen years from a bad heart. At the time of her experience, her condition had deteriorated until she had to use oxygen monthly and felt "my health was failing very badly." A friend gave her a card soliciting Padre Pio's prayers. On December 10, 1984, she fell asleep, weeping in great depression over her poor health and the lack of money for medical treatment. She dreamed "an old man" woke her up and asked her to get up and drink some water. He followed her and seemed to put medicine in the glass. The next morning she awoke feeling great. In a checkup, her doctor exclaimed "with joy and amazement 'a miracle! You are healed!' " Rosario's heart was perfectly normal. She was sure "the mysterious old man was Padre Pio."

Ethna Smyth writes to the friars:

> After two years of treatment I had lost the power of my right hand. I could use it very little and had to wear a support band as my wrist had dropped. I accepted the fact that I would be curtailed somewhat for the rest of my life. Then it happened. (I had been praying to Padre Pio. In fact, I brought a picture of him with me when attending doctors and hospitals, etc.). A friend of the family, a Holy Ghost brother, called at our house and just by chance had a relic of Padre Pio with him. I put the relic on my hand and we both said the prayer to Padre Pio [for his intercession]. I thought no more about it, but some hours later I thought I heard a voice in my own head saying, "You have not very much faith in me or you would not be wearing that old band." And I laughed and said, "Now Padre Pio, you know I cannot take it off." But the voice persisted and I felt Padre Pio was telling me I must have faith and take it off. After some more hours had lapsed the voice still kept on so I just pulled it off saying, "Now Padre Pio are you satisfied, but you know I cannot leave it off." But I did and I have never used it since

that day over a year ago. I am writing this letter with my cured hand. I can also drive a car and do all my housework.

Teresita Fearon sends a picture of a lovely young bride, born Rosemary Johnson, with her groom, from Australia. The accompanying testimony goes back to 1965, when Teresita's friend, who had six daughters, found herself pregnant at age forty-four. Her doctor advised an abortion, but Mona Johnson, a staunch Catholic, said "no." Still she worried plenty. Teresita gave her a scapular blessed by Padre Pio that Teresita had re-

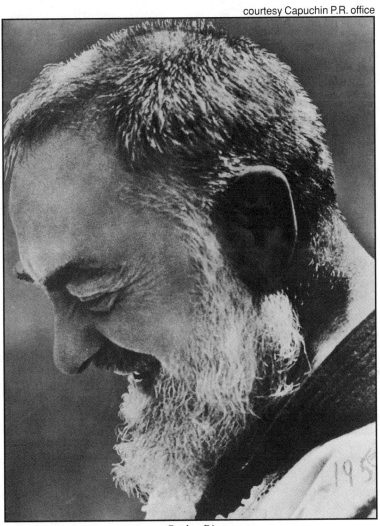

Padre Pio

ceived from Father Alessio Parente, a Franciscan close to Padre Pio. Every day from then on, the pregnant woman asked Padre Pio's prayers. On October 13, 1965, Rosemary Johnson was born. It appeared all that praying had been worthless, for the parents were told that "the baby did not stand a chance." Teresita writes that Rosemary "was born with a heart that was upside down, back to front, on the wrong side and it had extra tubes and valves. In both the upper and lower chambers the heart also had holes." Surgery was impossible: her mother was told by the delivery nurse that the infant, a pathetic little thing, would just get weaker and weaker and be dead in a few hours.

"No, she won't," Mona replied. "She's going to be all right."

"How do you know that?" the nurse asked, humoring her.

"God told me so," Mona answered. If she didn't believe the medical verdict, she felt she had a very good reason: Immediately after the birth, everyone's attention diverted to the very blue newborn, Mona was left alone in the delivery room. As she lay there, Padre Pio appeared and told the worried mother, "everything is going to be all right." Knowing the Australian medical people knew nothing of the Italian priest, she never mentioned him to them. But when the baby surprised the doctors by living long enough to go home, Mona pinned the scapular that Padre Pio had once blessed on her baby.

Teresita says, "she did look a very sick little baby. I remember seeing her so pale, so frail, with this lump on the right side where her heart is. I could see it beating very fast."

Mona, however, kept faith that God had not sent Padre Pio to lie to her. Faith well placed, as the picture of the lovely, healthy-looking young bride shows.

Marie Wallace's niece in April, 1987, was in such a serious traffic accident she almost lost her life. The doctors wished to amputate one leg, but her mother refused permission. Aunt and mother prayed hard and "a few nights later while staying in a house close by the hospital I woke up," reports Marie "and also woke up my sister with my shouting."

"Did you see him?"

"Who?"

"Padre Pio!"

"You're dreaming. Go back to sleep."

"I *wasn't* dreaming," Marie protested. In the end she at least half-convinced her sister she'd seen Padre Pio, who came with the message that Sharon would get better and walk again.

What makes this testimony interesting is that, at the very same hour, Sharon also woke up screaming, "Please stop pulling my leg."

"Who's pulling your leg, dear?" a nurse asked.

"The man in the brown habit. Don't you see him?" the injured girl cried.

The nurse was not surprised, Marie later discovered: The staff say Padre Pio appears to many people in their hospital, carrying God's healing. Sharon joined that group. When the testimony was added to the San Giovanni archives three years later in 1990, she walked without even a limp and had eighty-five to ninety percent movement in the leg that should have been amputated.

Mary Ryan's brother returned to Ireland from Nigeria and became very ill from malaria. Mary's mother sent a Padre Pio relic to the hospital. At 5:00 A.M. November 14, 1989, a noise woke Mrs. Ryan, who found the room filled with "very strong perfume which lasted fifteen to twenty minutes." Her husband *who had no sense of smell* [italics mine] smelled the luscious odor, too. Meanwhile, at the same time — exactly 5:00 A.M. — Mary's brother awoke in the hospital and knew he was well. Amazed at the change in his condition, the doctors ran more tests. No more malaria.

Georgina A. Lavandero wrote the friars in 1991 about a cure twelve years earlier:

> Back in 1979 my brother Carlos developed cancer in his larynx. Earlier he had been mistakenly diagnosed as having laryngitis for several years. Being a widower… (his wife had died of cancer), he had four children under his care aged five to twelve. He was immediately operated on. I started to pray to Padre Pio asking him (to obtain) my brother's health. I was desperate. I considered this a very pathetic case.… One night while I was praying and weeping asking Padre Pio for his intercession, a strong pleasant aroma of flowers surrounded my room. This perfume was too strong to be overlooked. Naturally I was frightened but I knew instantly that my prayers had been heard. I kept this secret to myself and waited for events to develop. And gracias Dios, after 12 years there is no sign of cancer.…

Gill Gleeson had a moving — and somewhat comical — experience with his dying father. Born a Catholic, the elder Mr. Gleeson lost his faith and all connection to the Church in his youth. I cannot be certain from Gil's testimony, but he may be a non-Catholic. Protestant or Catholic, certainly he is greatly enamored of Jesus. A loving son, Gil found a Catholic priest and took him to his father. To his relief the dying man was glad. However as Gil puts it:

> Dad had some huge blocks to faith; one of them was that God, if he existed was far too holy to be approached and another was that he thought he'd committed sins that were too serious to be forgiven....

Upset about his dad, Gil turned to Padre Pio, specifically begging the dead Franciscan "to do something to persuade Dad of the reality of Christ, where I had failed miserably." Gil writes:

> Next day I found Dad sitting up in bed looking so radiant that he reminded me of Moses after he'd been on the mountain. He told me that Jesus had come in the night and stood at the end of the bed. He'd opened his arms to Dad and said, "What are you afraid of?" They'd had a conversation in which his doubts had been resolved, his wrongs had been discussed and forgiven and he had developed a passionate attachment to Christ.

After awhile Gil's dad said to him, "This Jesus of yours — he's a funny looking bloke, isn't he?"

Gil wondered what he meant.

His dad described Jesus. As he listened to the description of the brown robe, the features, etc., the son realized it was Padre Pio who had appeared with open arms to Gil's father. He opted not to explain that to his dad, who died a few days later, reconciled to the Church, and assuring his son he'd give Jesus Gil's love.

A dying grandmother also found some relief — in her case not from spiritual problems, but plain old pain. Maeve Barry writes of her mother-in-law, who required larger and larger amounts of drugs to keep away the horrific pain. Until one day when she told the family that a man in a long brown dress had been there. Sitting on the end of her bed, he assured her "Your pain will soon be gone." Shown a picture of Padre Pio, she said her visitor looked like that. During the next several days of her life, she had no pain, "was in full command of herself," and died peacefully in her sleep.

Mrs. D.A. Morley writes about the shock she suffered when her husband went to work "a comparatively healthy man and came back that evening close to death" from meningitis and encephalitis. The family "bombarded heaven," as she puts it, with prayer. When after four days her unconscious husband woke up, she writes:

> He tried to tell me about a man he had seen standing in the door-
> way of his room, wearing a long robe and tied with a cord. He had
> a beard and was wearing a skull cap....

When doctors discharged Morley fifteen days after he entered the hospital unconscious, they called him "the miracle man." For his part, he couldn't forget the visitor in the robe and spoke of him frequently. Morley's wife thought her husband was a bit batty — undoubtedly reliving some hallucination brought on by his illness.

Then someone gave this Catholic woman a cassette and written material on Padre Pio of whom she had never heard. When she showed them to her husband, a convert, he exclaimed with amazement *"this is the man"* he'd seen standing in his hospital doorway. She was still uncertain, however: The bearded man in the brown habit her husband claimed to have seen, he also said, wore a skull cap. In Padre Pio's picture, he was bareheaded. But when she saw a video shot during the friar's lifetime, she saw he did, indeed, sometimes sport a skull cap.

A mother writes from Malaysia that her daughter left home for the first time to attend a university in America. Anxious as mothers are at such moments, the lady (who wishes her name withheld) sent her daughter out into the wide world armed with a rosary and Padre Pio medal and picture, asking the dead saint to watch over her precious child.

After a long flight, the daughter arrived in San Francisco, where her parents had made a hotel reservation so she could pass the night in safety and comfort before catching a second flight the next morning. But due to a mix-up the young woman was stranded at the airport and had to spend the whole night there with the mound of luggage young women tote.

It was a pleasant surprise when a very old porter appeared and took her and her luggage to a safe corner. This old man was always there, watching the bags when she had to use the restroom or stand in line to confirm her next flight. Unlike the usual porter, he refused to let her pay him for any of his services. The mother wept when she received her daughter's first letter detailing all this. Whatever anyone else thinks, she is certain that for one night God had Padre Pio play porter.

In July, 1986, J.G. Hilton and his wife pilgrimage to San Giovanni Rotondo. They have two things to thank God and Pio for. One is a cure.

Back on November 27, 1985, Hilton — who had angina problems — found himself having a bad night. The first dose of medication did nothing. The second let his pain subside enough that he slept for awhile. But then he woke and saw across the room "a priest dressed in his alb with his arms outstretched. In the background there were monks dressed in brown habits scrubbing and washing a refectory table." A lapsed Catholic who hadn't been to Mass for over thirty-five years, at the same time he had this strange vision, he realized he was suffering a stroke. His left side paralyzed, he woke his wife, who wanted to call for medical help.

"Wait a minute," Hilton said. Strangely, he could feel use returning to the paralyzed area.

Hilton confided in his Anglican wife about seeing the priest, expecting, he writes, she would laugh. Instead she said, "It's Padre Pio." Running for a book he didn't know she had, she showed her husband a picture of the saint. Hilton recognized him at once as the friar he had just seen.

He decided to return to the Church. Would his wife agree to have their civil marriage blessed? She not only agreed, some months later on June 24, 1986, she was received into the Catholic Church herself due to her great admiration for Padre Pio.

Shortly before this, as an aftereffect of his mild stroke, Hilton underwent a "risky" operation to clean out an artery leading to the brain. He says he felt no anxiety whatsoever — the implication being he felt God had Padre Pio on his case. And whether because he expected no trouble or because Padre Pio was indeed on the job, after surgery his was an "amazingly rapid" recovery.

An American, Bernadette Yaurren, writes Padre Pio's friars:

> Due to a car accident, I had an artificial plate in my mouth which did not fit due to an imbalance. I had to have my gums on the top of my mouth cut down to balance my mouth. I really suffered. After it healed and stitches were taken out, the doctor said it was not cut away enough. I asked Padre Pio to be with me and he did

give me strength all the way. Before I closed my eyes he stood over me and his sympathetic smile was for me not to be afraid. Later when they were taking out the stitches I was amazed to see Padre Pio standing in the corner of the room. He did not forget me when I had to go through more discomfort. I looked at the doctor and nurse but they did not see anyone, but the nurse got a beautiful floral scent and thought I was wearing perfume but I had no perfume of any kind on me....

A nun, Sister Alberic, writes the friary to express her thanks. It has been a year, she says, since she fell and broke her ankle, hip, elbow, and shoulder. The ankle and hip caused her the most suffering. But the surgeon said he could not do anymore for the foot. She'd "have to live with it." The nun did not throw in the towel, however: She attacked her problem both physically and spiritually, by going to physiotherapy and having another nun pray over her. A regular spiritual buddy of the dead Capuchin, she also daily asked his prayers. One morning as, still in bed, she was in the middle of saying a rosary and praying her usual novena prayer to Padre Pio, she heard a "gruff voice saying, 'Alberic, move your foot.'" She writes:

For a moment I was shaken. I pulled back the covers and moved my foot in every direction and found I could freely do so. I walked all round the bedroom and found I could easily do so without pain in my foot or hip. I believe it was the voice of Padre Pio that spoke to me. I am very well now.

ENDNOTES

1   For more information on bilocation in general, and Padre Pio's bilocations and trilocations, see my book *The Sanctified Body.*
2   In *Nothing Short of a Miracle.*
3   Most of these have been published in the English-language periodical of the friary *The Voice of Padre Pio.*
4   Similarly, others in need of healing sought handkerchiefs or any cloth that had touched the skin of the apostle Paul (Acts 19:12) or tried to position themselves so even the shadow of Peter might fall on them!

12 ✤ READY TO GO!

S aints do not all die the same way. Some long for death, like Therese
Valse-Pantellini, and die in ecstasy. Some, like Blessed Giuseppe
Moscati or Padre Pio, seem equally content to live or die as God
wills and slip into the next life at the divine call almost effortlessly. Others
— and I do *not* imply any way is holier — whether they long for God or
not, must endure long, painful illnesses and hard death agonies.

Among this group is St. Therese of Lisieux. Rather ironically, she who
would rescue so many on the battlefield or sickbed faced death adamant
that she wanted no miracle cures, no appearances of the saints, in short, no
"rescue" that might hinder God's designs in her.[1] She seemed to guess —
had she put Him up to it? — that the plan for the end of *her* life was to wring
her audacious confidence in God's goodness to its last drop. Therese felt no
mystical graces while dying a slow death of tuberculosis, deprived of pain
medication by a misguided Superior. Instead, she underwent months of temptation that her whole life — every legitimate pleasure she had willingly
given up as a sacrifice to bring about the Kingdom — was sheer stupidity,
because there was no Kingdom of God or afterlife at all. She said no one
should ever leave a means of self-destruction near someone seriously ill
and in pain: She understood how seductive suicide could be.

Yet, more valiant than any warrior, the French Carmelite never caved in
to despair but continued to stretch out the arms of her faith. In fact, it is
during this period when, without losing the peace deep in her heart, she *felt*
most abandoned, that she made astounding prophecies regarding her future. Statements like "In this world everything passes away, even little
Therese. But she will return!" And when another Carmelite piously said
that soon Sister Therese would look down on them from heaven, she found
the energy to retort "No! I will *come* down.

Since heaven is supposed to be a delightful place, some wondered why.

"I want to spend my heaven doing good on earth," she explained. And
elaborated that she wanted to do this to make God "loved by a multitude of
souls."

Tried until the end in the crucible of physical and spiritual suffering, moments before death Therese made a last effort to say, "My God I love thee." Only then did the veil part. She suddenly went into ecstasy, looked up at something that amazed and delighted her and entered the next life.

An old nun in the same Carmel, who habitually made biting remarks at Therese's expense, had even asked within her hearing, "what will we ever find to put in her obituary?" Now God let Therese, only moments after her death, indulge herself in the revenge of the saints: Feeling a sudden change of heart, the spiteful sister placed her head on dead Therese's feet and asked for forgiveness and to be cured of a long-standing physical problem. The cure was immediate. Astounded, it was this aged nun — not Therese's blood sisters — who began to tell everyone of the great sanctity of the dead twenty-four-year-old.

Such a cure is God's doing, not any saint's. But the standard interpretation in Catholicism is that the saint's prayers and lifetime of heroic goodness (acquired "merits," Catholics and Jews, among others, would say) are involved. The cure is attributed to God's response to the saint's prayers, and is also a "yes" nod to the Church that God wants the individual honored. Looking at it in this way (which is, of course, just our effort to understand that which is beyond human understanding)[2], you may ask yourself, as I have, how could Therese be at the work of prayer and intercession so quickly, having been in terrible suffering only minutes before?

Of course in God there is no time, only the eternal present. But I also surmise that saints are so ready to make the transition to the next world that they often need no "orientation" to the new life. For some of them, of course — people like Adrienne von Speyr and Padre Pio — this is, at least in part, because they have been living with a foot in both worlds for most of their lives, relating to and communing with the dead just as with the living through visions and other God-directed events.

One sees this experience of the lack of any boundary between life and death by the ability of some of the holy during their lives to see that others are dead before this is known. Four saints will serve as quick examples.

Although he lived in a remote Franciscan monastery in rural, southern Italy, one night when Padre Pio was in his room with a couple of friends, he asked them to kneel down and say a prayer with him for the soul of the king of England "because he has just died." Eventually, news reached the monastery that the father of Queen Elizabeth II had indeed died at the time Padre Pio pinpointed.

Similarly, in the diary kept under obedience to her spiritual advisor, Polish mystic Blessed Faustina Kowalska (1905-1938) writes in February, 1937:

"I learned today about the death of one of our sisters who died in Plock, but she visited me even before they told me about her death." This reference to a sister was not to one of the saint's siblings but to Sister Cornelia Trzaska, a member of the same religious order.

Shortly before the Spanish Civil War broke out in 1936, Sister Carmen Moreno was Superior of a small group of Daughters of Mary Help of Christians (Salesian Sisters) who ran a school and playground for young girls in the little Spanish town of Valverde. Among these nuns was Sister Eusebia Palomino. Much less educated than Carmen, Eusebia — who did menial work such as cooking and gardening for the community — was highly esteemed by the Superior for her exceptional holiness. After the deaths of Sisters Eusebia and Carmen (who, during the war, was dragged away and shot in the head by people who hated nuns when she stayed behind her fleeing Sisters to care for someone sick), a former pupil of the Sisters named Maria Gomez testified that in the pre-war period Sister Carmen saw how much Maria and her sister were suffering after the death of their father. Quietly she assured them, "I know you feel his loss very much; but you have the consolation of knowing that he is already in heaven."

"How do you know that?"

Sister Carmen hesitated, then explained that the night the man died, the Sisters, knowing nothing of it — because the death took place at midnight — were sleeping in their dormitory when Sister Eusebia screamed. That woke everyone up and she told them, "The father of the Gomez sisters died just now. He wants us to pray that he may soon go to heaven." Because Sister Carmen had experienced this sort of thing with Sister Eusebia many times (Eusebia was forbidden to talk about it beyond the nuns), and found such statements confirmed, she did not dismiss what Sister Eusebia said. In the morning, as Sister Carmen expected, news came that Mr. Gomez had indeed passed away. A few nights later he returned to thank Sister Eusebia and tell her he would need no more prayers.

Bavarian stigmatic and visionary Therese Neumann lived at home with her parents all her life, after she had to give up her dream of being a missionary nun. She led an active life of good works and had many friends among the devout of the area including priests and nuns. One of these was a young Jewish man named Bruno Rothschild of Vienna, who became a Catholic and then a priest after meeting Therese. Because he was unfortunately estranged from his family on account of the change in religions, the Neumann family invited Father Bruno to spend Christmas at their home in Konnersreuth. At the time he should have been on his way to Konnersreuth,

Therese had a vision that implied he was in heaven. A short time later word arrived that Father Bruno had died of a heart attack in the railway station. As this was just before the Nazis came to power, Therese rejoiced that her Jewish friend was safe with God.

Some saints, even those who, like Therese of Lisieux, don't habitually see into the next life, look forward to continuing to work after death: they are "primed" for it, one could say. Besides the well-known remarks of Therese, other saints have made lesser-known comments along these lines. His friends noticed how Blessed Andre Bessette (1845-1937), the feather-weight, French-Canadian miracle-worker, had absolutely no fear of death. The faster a car went the better because he could visit more of his beloved sick. And when he almost died on a trip, he remarked, "What difference if I die today or another time?" To those who complained they couldn't bear to think of losing his help, he explained that if he could help people now, he'd be able to do even more for them after death. St. Maximilian Kolbe also spoke enthusiastically of working for God more powerfully after death.

Not only have they no dread of death as they look forward (of course even a saint may have instinctive, animal-like fear during the actual process), saints often — not always — know almost to the minute when the event will take place, giving them a chance to be completely prepared for the transition. Take Flemish Benedictine Paul of Moll (Francis Luyckx), who died the year before Therese. When he recovered once from an illness, a friend who was a farmer joked, "You have entered upon a new lease (of life)."

"What's the usual term of a lease?" Father Paul responded with a smile.

"Why nine years," the farmer said, knowing Father Paul knew that.

"Well, my lease is for nine-and-a-half years," Father Paul said equably. The farmer kept this in mind and was awed to see that Father Paul died four days after nine-and-a-half years had passed.

For all saints there is one other obvious factor: unlike the average soul, who usually has work to do after death (the state called purgatory), saints have completed life's great task. They have achieved wholeness — or holiness, as we say from the spiritual perspective — by learning to love, to forgive, to trust God as a child trusts a good parent, to detach oneself from one's particular idols whether these be loved ones, certain projects, or whatever. They step into the next world "ready to go."

This, I theorize, may be why a dead saint can not only "pray" a miracle immediately after death, as Therese did, but even appear to someone so soon after death that news of the demise isn't even out yet. It is as if, as

Daisy Dryden (page 21) put it, there is no river to cross between the two dimensions for those pure enough. Dead, as alive, the saint — at least in some cases — without missing a perceptible beat simply goes right on working in, and for, God.

An extreme example of what I'm describing from "this side" is the case of Father Paul. Very feeble (his handwriting is the trembly scrawl of the dying) and confined to bed under a doctor's care in the abbey during his final illness, Father Paul still appeared in a city, in excellent health according to those he visited. These bilocations about which I wrote in *The Sanctified Body* included a visit to an innkeeper's wife who needed some spiritual guidance. He not only provided that, but brought with him some religious articles, medals and a scapular, which he left with her. Later these proved compelling physical evidence — to their recipient, anyway — that his presence was no hallucination. While there — the visit lasted about ten minutes at 11:00 A.M. on February 4, 1896 (he told her to note the day and hour) — he ordered this spiritual child *not* to attend his funeral, saying she would get too emotional. He mentioned he was in a hurry, as he had other errands. The witness recalled these included a group of religiously-vowed women known as Beguins (they are not nuns) and a notary. A member of the Beguins did have a visit that occurred about this day (she did not particularly pay attention to the date) from Father Paul, who told her she would not see him again.

After his death, when people saw Father Paul — I have given three instances in this book — it seems only a continuation of the work for God he was able to do via bilocation while on his deathbed.

In writing of saints appearing after their deaths on God's "business" before it is even known they are dead (something, it appears, that cannot occur in non-saints because they are not at that pinnacle of wholeness) the situation with the holy can be seen as a magnification of the lesser phenomenon of the non-holy dead who "stop to say good-bye" to loved ones just after their soul leaves the body. In the first chapter I wrote of the Jewish man who described himself as "a rationalist" whose sister came to him after she died, but before he knew she was dead.

In my own family, relatives have told of a strange experience during my twenty-seven-year-old mother's fight for her life in Spokane, Washington's Deaconess Hospital. My father took me to his in-laws' farm in Elk, where I was cared for by my Swedish grandmother. One gray, January day she was washing dishes while I, barely two, played on the floor with my blocks. After awhile I tugged on my grandmother's skirt and told her that there was someone looking in the window. "It was my mama," I said. My gentle grandmother went to the door with me to show me that no one was there, especially not my mother. Then she went back to her dishes and I to my play. But shortly I was tugging at her skirt, insisting "there *was* someone at the window and it *was* my mama." Again my grandmother tried patiently, but unsuccessfully, to convince me this could not be the case. However, she felt differently when she learned that my mother had died, calling my name, just before I insisted I saw her.

I, of course, with my usual spiritual flair, don't recall a thing about the episode. And naturally, I wonder if I was imagining what I must have desperately wanted. But the point here is that, assuming my mother, a lovely person but not holy, did stop to say good-bye to her only living child, her appearance, like that of the Jewish rationalist's caring sister, could only occur in this shadowy realm. Only the saints, it appears, can take this sort of thing further, making full-fledged appearances not just to loved ones, but on almost impersonal business matters immediately after death.

Blessed Dominic Barberi is the little-known, delightfully good-humored Italian Passionist priest who, as a missionary to England, received Anglican John Henry Newman into the Catholic Church.[3] Father Dominic — a mystic who, even in great sufferings and persecutions, was so in love with God he "often felt like singing for joy" — suffered a fatal heart seizure in 1849 on an English train. Shortly after:

> Dominic appeared to Father Vincent, the rector at Woodchester, and gave him certain vitally important information. The Superior (that is Father Vincent) was called away, and on his return Father Dominic was no longer there. It was later that day that the telegram giving news of Father Dominic's death at Reading was received. That afternoon three nuns, members of the Congregation of the Faithful Companions of Jesus, saw and spoke with Father Dominic as they were returning from school at St. Patrick's, Liverpool. Subsequently they learned that at the time he was already dead.

St. Julie Billiart (d. 1816) once hid in a load of hay while maddened French Revolutionists screamed, "The saint! The saint!" as they searched the area frenziedly, hoping to parade her head on a pike. Yet her French countrymen rightly call her "*la sainte qui sourit,*" the smiling saint. Joy-filled, Mother Julie still could be firm when it was necessary for the welfare of one of this foundress' many spiritual daughters:

> On the very night of her (Julie's) death, one of her best-beloved daughters, Sister St. Jean, Superior of the convent of St. Hubert, heard the curtains of her bed drawn swiftly back and saw Mere Julie standing at her bedside.
>
> "Daughter," she said in grave tones, "When did you do what I told you to do?"
>
> Recollecting that she had neglected to fulfill a commission laid upon her by her General, and never dreaming but that the latter had arrived, as she sometimes did without sending word beforehand that she was coming, Sister St. Jean sprang from her bed exclaiming, "Oh, ma mere! I beg your pardon," but saw to her astonishment that she was alone in the room.

The next morning this sister mentioned the strange "flying visit" of Mother Julie — hardly the norm, even for saints, in that pre-motorized era. Two days later it was learned Mother Julie was dead at the time she chided Sister St. Jean.

Some of these visits are in dreams. Here is the written testimony of a sister who lived in the same French convent of the Society of the Sacred Heart with Spanish-born visionary Josefa Menendez:

> The night she died, not knowing that she was worse, I saw her in a dream. She was most lovely, and lay on a bed adorned with flowers. She made me a sign to come near and said to me: "Oh Sister, do not be afraid of suffering, and do not lose the smallest particle that God may send you. If you could but understand what a privilege it is to suffer for Him … You must make a prayer of your work. Say to Him, as each occasion arises: "For Thee, dear Jesus, I offer it to Thee — so that He may see that you want to be with Him and to love Him. Oh if you only knew how much He wants to be loved! She spoke impressively, so that I was very much moved. All the more so when on coming down to Mass that Sunday morning I heard that she had died in the night.

St. Mary Mazzarello, a simple, Italian peasant woman who wanted to help young girls, founded the Daughters of Mary Help of Christians with St. John Bosco. Early in 1881 she went to the town of Turin to see a joint expedition of some of her nuns and Bosco's priests off to the missions. In Turin Mary was sleeping in the dormitory with two nuns when in the middle of the night she awoke one of them.

"Sister Arecco is dead!" she whispered. Then she said that the dead woman had just been there. They had spoken to each other. Sister Pacotto, the nun Mary woke up, just nodded and went back to sleep. She was sure Mary had just had an exceptionally vivid dream. Maybe she did. But in the morning a telegram was delivered: Sister Arecco had died "precisely at the time" when Mary saw her.

A quiet personality of true holiness, Mary herself died a short time later on May 14, 1881.

That evening, a priest in Sicily received a telegram with the news. His was the unpleasant duty of telling Mary's blood sister Felicina — stationed there as a nun in the same order — of her older sister's death. Knowing how much the two loved each other, the priest was nervous. But when he arrived at Felicina's residence before he could open his mouth, she blurted out, "Father, last night I had the most wonderful dream. Yet, somehow *it wasn't a dream*. It was so real. I really saw my sister. She was clothed in a splendid white light. She was radiant. She smiled at me and said, 'Goodbye, Felicina! Goodbye!'"

Felicina ended her account by saying to her visitor, "I wonder what all this means?" The suddenly relaxed priest, sighing happily, prepared to tell her, sure that God had sent Mother Mazzarello herself to pave the way for his announcement of her death.

St. Henry de Osso was canonized by Pope John Paul II in 1993. Father Henry (1840-96) loved to teach. In his native Spain, the founder of the Society of Saint Teresa of Jesus[4] is recalled as "a remarkable organizer of religious classes," who also educated through giving retreats, preaching, and writing, as well as teaching one on one by spiritual direction and hearing confessions. Founder of a series of associations to support the spiritual yearnings of various groups, author of many books, and editor of timely magazines, the Catalonia native led a brief, valiant life in a period when many forces in Spanish society derided the view that life cries out for a spiritual dimension to reach wholeness. If Father Henry differs from the sixty-some priests who founded religious orders in the nineteenth century in anything, it is probably the importance the Spanish priest gave to working with women. Thus he founded an order of educators (today spread far from Spain, including to the United States) primarily to work with girls because, he said, "educate a boy and you educate a man but educate a girl and you educate a family." It's fitting, then, that even after death Father Henry appears mostly to girls or women.

He died at only forty-six of a sudden cerebral hemorrhage, perhaps crushed (although he said only "this is coming against us from good people") by the perfidity of some ungrateful cloistered nuns. For them he had built a convent *gratis*; yet immediately upon accepting his gift, they brought legal action against him in the church's courts because they did not want him to

courtesy the Society of St. Teresa of Jesus

Father Henry de Osso

use some of the open land next to their new convent — given to him, not them — to build a school and a novitiate for his teaching nuns.

A person who dies in the middle of a big legal entanglement — especially one that is an unjust attack on oneself — can be expected to die with unresolved issues of anger, bitterness, etc. In St. Henry's case, he died during a month of spiritual retreat in a Franciscan monastery where he went as a stranger of unknown history. His spirit was so far above any bitterness or anger — to him it was certain God permitted all this only so a greater good should result in the end — that the friars raided his wastebasket for torn envelopes and even pencil shavings to save as relics, because it was obvious to them that an authentic saint had dropped into their midst.

Fray Francisco Domingo Paya, who heard Henry's confession on January 27, 1896, and venerated him as a saint, wrote that de Osso died that day sometime before midnight. That same night at just about that same time — she writes "sometime after eleven" — one of the nuns of the order founded by de Osso was at work faraway in a town called Taragona. This Sister Asuncion Mallol had the habit of staying up late to do certain work. Father Henry didn't like to see her missing her rest that way and admonished her, sometime before his death, about it. Glibly the sister promised she wouldn't stay up late any more. Father Henry responded he had no confidence in her promise. It's hard, he explained, when one has such a habit to give it up. Now she was proving him right, for she was up late working with two other sisters. Suddenly she noticed Father Henry in the room.

"Oh, our father!" she exclaimed with chagrin, caught in the act.

He said nothing in reply but, perhaps having made his point just by his presence, turned and walked into the next room. The three sisters followed, but did not find him. The next day they learned that he had died about the time they saw him. Of course, due to the "around midnight" and "after eleven," it is impossible to say whether he appeared by bilocation minutes before his death or immediately after it. Either way, as far as I'm concerned, shows a man in Padre Pio's words completely "attached to the thread of God's will."

Something interesting also happened in Toluca, Mexico, that same night. Young Concepcion Jimenez was one of the first boarders in the recently established school of the Teresian sisters, the order founded by Father Henry. At first she was terribly homesick, but gradually she was won over by one of the nuns who often talked a lot about Father Henry and the way he took such good care of his spiritual daughters, providing untiringly for their needs and giving them — in chaste fashion — the marks of affection women crave. Although she had never met this Father Henry, Concepcion began to feel he was her spiritual father, too, although she had no thought of becoming one of his nuns. Quoting directly the next part of her testimony:

> On the night of January 27, 1896, I was sleeping soundly. In a dream I saw our Father dead and laid out on a table, poor and wrapped in a sheet or some white material. As I was familiar with his picture, I recognized him clearly. Frightened, I approached the table. With awe I saw him open his eyes. He looked at me with affection and extending his right hand, laid it on my brow, saying "You will be one of mine."
>
> At the touch of that cold hand my brow froze and I awoke frightened and screaming, "Our father founder is dead."
>
> The sister (Maria Sarrio) who slept in our dormitory and the rest of the girls woke up in fright and, thinking that I was having a nightmare, tried to wake me up. But I continued screaming, "Our father founder is dead! My brow is still cold where he touched me!"
>
> The next day they told the story to the Superior who reproved me seriously and admonished me not to wake the girls up again nor to frighten them so. And to erase the impression that I still felt, she told me about the custom of laying priests out in ... vestments and not in a sheet as I assured them that I had seen our Father. I apologized for the scare that my dream had given them and promised sincerely not to perturb my companions' sleep again. The interview took place between eight and nine o'clock in the morning. On the afternoon of the same day a telegram arrived with the message, "Founder dead."
>
> ... Later it was confirmed that he had been laid out in the way that I had seen him and not in ... vestments. Three years later I became one of his.

The last instance that took place at this time is slightly different. It occurred in Montevideo, Uruguay, to a young maid named Carmen Gomez who was employed in the Teresian sister's school there at the time Father Henry died. Later Carmen Gomez became a Teresian lay sister. As her testimony, formally written up some years later when she had become a member of the community, is long, I will summarize it.

When word arrived that Father Henry had died in Spain, the Teresian sisters gathered to pray, their Superior handing Carmen the keys to the front door.

That evening she opened the parlor door and saw "a venerable priest sitting on the sofa." She wrote, "I thought that it was someone come to see the sisters and in my timidity did not dare address him, for he filled me with a certain respect that even now, after so many years, I still feel." Silently, she shut the door and scurried away.

But soon the shy, young housemaid felt an irresistible urge to open the door a little bit and peek in at the priest again. This time she watched him walking back and forth. Again Carmen was filled with awe to the point that years later she writes "I still seem to hear … the noise of his footsteps as he paced the room." Again, she was unable to step in and ask whom he wished to see. Finally, she once more wordlessly shut the door.

As she went on with her work outside the parlor, she decided she really must ask his name and inform the Superior of his being there. But when she opened the door the third time, the room was empty.

Remember ineffability, the certainty that something is real? Sister Carmen had that feeling. She had not imagined that the priest was there, she would swear. She knew that she had not let him in — remember, she had the keys to the locked convent door. And she knew for sure that she had not let him out. She says that the experience "made such an impression on me that never again did I dare go into that room alone."

Nor did she tell a soul of the strange event. Two years later she had joined the community and was sent to make her novitiate in Spain. There, she says, she saw a picture of Father Henry and "recognized the venerable priest who visited us in Montevideo on the same day that he passed to a better life."

Sister Carmen, then, had known Father Henry was dead: She just didn't know it was dead Father Henry she saw!

In an earlier chapter, I have written of visionary Maria Esperanza Bianchini at Betania, Venezuela. During the period in the 1950s when she lived in Italy, Maria Esperanza used to visit Padre Pio for spiritual direction. At first she made the long trip south from Rome to his remote monastery once a month. Then he told her to come every other month, then every third month. Finally he found her a spiritual director in Rome. After her marriage, Maria Esperanza returned to Venezuela, where she was when Padre Pio died on September 23, 1968.

At about 7:30 in the evening Maria Esperanza was attending Mass when she saw Padre Pio.

"Esperanza, I've come to say goodbye. My time has come," the priest stigmatist said. He also told her, "Now it's your turn," she claims, referring to the stigmata, which she also has (although not on a permanent basis like Padre Pio). Maria Esperanza says she "cried the whole evening and the next day I saw in the news that Padre Pio had died."

The holy Claretian priest — whom Cardinal McIntyre of Los Angeles dubbed "the Padre Pio of the West" for his extraordinary gifts — Father Aloysius Ellacuria had friends of every background. But two San Diego women, Melba Esparza and her daughter Lisa K., recalled in a 1991 video-taped interview[5] that Father Aloysius and Lisa's dad had an extra bond because they were both Basques.

Once a month Father Aloysius travelled from Los Angeles to San Diego to visit a group of spiritual children, including the Esparza family. He said the Mass of marriage for one of the Esparza daughters and baptized their oldest grandchildren. Lisa, a bridesmaid to the sister Father Aloysius married, saw him a number of times, at formal occasions like the wedding or some of those monthly gatherings.

Around the first of September, 1981, when she was twenty-four, Lisa got a call from her mom. "Rush to the hospital; your dad's taken a turn for the worst."

Lisa and her husband hurried to their car. They were soon at 5th and Washington Streets standing on the far side of a crosswalk from the hospital entrance. Suddenly Lisa said, "That's Father Aloysius. He must have gone to see daddy."

Only the length of the crosswalk from her, Father Aloysius had a slight smile, she recalls, while he "glowed" with a quality she stumbles trying to describe, searching her way from phrases like "emanating gentleness" to "peacefulness."

But emanating peace or no, seeing the Basque priest was not wholly consoling for Lisa. She knew her father must be really bad if her mom had summoned Father Aloysius, now close to eighty years old, from Los Angeles.

As she stood there at the light with her husband, who saw Father too, but did not know him (later his description seemed "right" to a priest of the order Ellacuria founded), Father Aloysius walked away from the door. Because the hospital had a lot of construction going on, there were the usual high board walls surrounding the site.

As he headed into that construction wall, there were no doors, *no place for him to go*, Lisa emphasizes. Yet when she looked away for a second and then back at the elderly priest, he was gone.

If she rushed into the hospital without focusing further on that peculiarity, it was only because of her anxiety over her father whom she found unconscious in the ICU.

When she saw her mom, Lisa mentioned, "Father Aloysius' been here."

"Don't be ridiculous, Lisa. Father Aloysius's dead."

"No, Mom, he was just here," Lisa protested.

When Melba Esparza told her daughter that Father Aloysius had died almost five months ago, Lisa questioned herself. But her conclusion didn't change. "I knew who it was," she says simply, fifteen years later. When another priest said he didn't think Father Aloysius would smile in such a situation, Lisa didn't argue. As far as she is concerned, people may think what they like. She knows what she saw. She even has definite convictions on why she saw her father's dead friend. Without hesitation she explains what she believes the apparition meant, first to her dad, and then to the family.

To her dad, Lisa explains, Father Aloysius was someone very special, so she is sure God sent Father Aloysius to guide his fellow Basque through a time of suffering and then lead him to heaven. As for the family, her sight of Father Aloysius, she feels, was a comforting reminder that there is a heaven and, in view of that, the family should not be afraid of the suffering and pain her greatly-loved father was enduring for a brief time. Nor should they run from their own pain and anguish at seeing him suffer. Lisa believes God's messenger helped the Esparza family accept and surrender the entire situation to God, looking beyond it to the eternal life beginning for her dad.

In the light of the gathering legislative momentum and strong opinions among some Americans that the dying should be spared all suffering through euthanasia, Lisa's statements are neither the mood of the time nor politically correct. But they are, I hope, thought-provoking.

ENDNOTES

[1] Not because she felt superior to those who seek a miracle, but because she somehow knew hers was another destiny.

[2] A saint has no will but God's will, so should never be pictured as begging a change of Divine plans. Nor does God "need" a saint to do any of God's works.

[3] Newman became a Cardinal and is a current candidate for beatification.

[4] Named for St. Teresa of Avila, sixteenth-century Spanish Doctor of the Church.

[5] By my friend Francis Levy, a close associate of Father Ellacuria's.

13 ✎ OF KID SAINTS AND MESSENGERS OF HEALING

Late July, 1959

Lourdes Hospital
Lafayette, Louisiana

A young, recently-ordained priest, whose duties include patients here, makes another visit to the twelve-year-old Cajun girl dying in room 411 of painful acute lymphatic leukemia.

To comfort the young Catholic, who has a deep devotion to Jesus' mother, he says, "Charlene, someday soon a beautiful lady is going to come and take you away with her."

For the rest of his life, Father Joseph Brennan will remember the simplicity and faith shining in Charlene Richard's (say REE-SHARD) brown eyes as she answers with a smile, "When the Blessed Mother comes, Father, I'll tell her you say 'hello.'"

Charlene, Father Brennan will claim years later, was no ordinary twelve-year-old. An opinion strongly seconded even in 1959 by nurse Sister Theresita Crowley O.S.F., head of the hospital's pediatric ward, who spends as much time as she can with this patient.

The second of ten kids born to Mary Alice and Joseph Richard, the small-town girl played baseball, was popular with her schoolmates, and captained a tournament-winning basketball team, but she had the spiritual maturity of a very special kind of adult, priest and nun believe.

"Her life was full in a short span," says Sister Theresita, adding humbly, "I learned a lot from Charlene, especially from her willingness to accept everything. She suffered a great deal but I remember her as a cheerful patient. She never complained." To Father Brennan, the Cajun child is a true saint.

The primary doctor who treated her, Dr. Daniel W. Voorhies, was interviewed by Louisiana Catholic-press reporter Barbara Lenox Guiterrez (to whose series of articles in the Lafayette diocesan paper, later combined with other material as the book *Charlene,* I owe most of this report). Ms. Guiterrez found the physician, predictably, did not want to talk publicly about his former patient, but the reporter noticed Charlene's framed photograph — the only patient he ever treated, Voorhies admitted, whose picture he had — occupying a prominent position on the medical man's uncluttered desk.[1]

Catholics are blessed in believing that anyone may choose to "offer up" life's sufferings (joys, too) as prayers for oneself or others; so when suffering hits, instead of succumbing to the "helpless and hopeless" syndrome, there is always the possibility of turning frustrations, pains, and difficulties into prayer energy. In her last weeks Father Brennan talked to Charlene about using what she was going through as prayers for others. Perhaps he sensed that Charlene — who asked her grandmother to teach her the rosary when she was five and confided several years later she wanted to be a saint like Therese of Lisieux — already did a lot of praying.

Charlene took readily to his suggestion and after it greeted the hospital chaplain each day with, "Okay, Father, who am I to suffer for today?"

Perhaps this unusual girl, who Sister Theresita flatly calls "a holy child," felt a special mission even in eternity to pray for those in need. At least after her death on August 11, 1959, Sister Theresita — who claimed "I felt she had gone into Life and ... was with me in a new way" — often found herself in room 411 asking Charlene's prayers for others. She went there, the Franciscan nun said, because the room may have been "the last dwelling place of a saint" and because "I have great confidence in her [prayers]." More than fifteen years later Sister Theresita still insisted "I feel her presence. I feel her smile."

Just a fancy of the sister's? Hardly. Every year thousands of people visit the grave of Charlene Richard to leave flowers, candles, photos, and notes, either thanking her for favors they believe they received through her prayers, or asking her to pray for them. In the book *Charlene*, several priests give instances of favors obtained, they believe, through this dead child, with whom they feel a bond reminiscent of the special feelings many priests have for St. Therese. Some of them know that Charlene offered some of her sufferings to have a brother who was a priest.

On August 11, 1989, when Harry J. Flynn, the local Bishop, celebrated Mass at St. Edward's Church in Charlene's small hometown to commemorate the thirtieth anniversary of her death, five thousand people showed up, forcing the Mass to be held outside on the grounds of the little church.

Bishop Flynn's diocesan archives hold hundreds of letters that testify to favors and cures granted through the young Cajun girl's prayers.

Among those who think a lot of Charlene Richard is the Price family of Morgan City, Louisiana. Parents and grandparents credit Charlene Richard with the cure of young Nicole Price from a rare cancer.

Nicole was diagnosed as a baby in 1987 with neuroblastoma. Surgeons took as much of a cancerous mass out of her stomach as possible. Then she was put on chemotherapy. One day her working mother received a phone call from Nicole's baby-sitter. Nicole was begging her to talk to "Charlene."

"I have no idea who she's talking about. We don't know anybody named Charlene," Mrs. Price told the sitter. When the blonde, blue-eyed tyke continued to ask for Charlene, the adults concluded Charlene was an imaginary friend. Still, they noted something odd: Nicole didn't talk about doing things with Charlene, as is usual with imaginary playmates, but begged to *see* Charlene, as if speaking of someone she knew who was now absent. Then the Price family had a phone call. A friend wanted them to know that she had made a special pilgrimage to pray for Nicole to the grave of a young girl — a girl named Charlene Richard.

Mrs. Price says her mouth dropped open.

She questioned Nicole carefully, "Where is Charlene?"

"In Heaven with baby Jesus," Nicole answered at once.

"Did she talk to you?"

"Uh huh."

"What'd she say?"

"Told me to be good."

After that dialogue, Nicole's mother went to see Father Floyd Calais. Father Calais is one of the priests who feel that Charlene, like a spiritual little sister, is always there to help him out. Father Calais did not tell Mrs. Price that her little one was imagining things. Instead he suggested the Prices take Nicole to Charlene's grave. He would accompany them.

The trip was made on Easter Sunday, 1988. In the cemetery, a permanently-displayed picture of Charlene was pointed out to Nicole who said, "That's Charlene!"

Of course, the toddler may have heard something from her parents or grandparents that predisposed that answer. Mrs. Price says sensibly, "I can't say that Charlene appeared to Nicole. But from the first night we heard from our friend about her, we've been praying to Charlene."

In October, 1991, a new tumor was found in Nicole's abdomen. Surgery was done immediately and the surgeon, while waiting for a preliminary biopsy before continuing the operation, came out to the waiting room to warn the Price family that lab tests would certainly show a malignancy. They did, and half Nicole's spleen was removed.

Between then and five days later when the full lab report came out, Father Calais got in his car and made the trip to Charlene's grave, asking her prayers for the toddler. And, of course, hundreds of other prayers — some invoking Charlene, others not — were going up for Nicole from other people. Only God can sort out the "credit" in such instances, but a funny thing happened: The full lab report found the tumor benign — no malignancy whatsoever.

As this is written, Father Calais tells me Nicole is a grammar school student who enjoys good health and "perfect medical reports."

If the idea of a holy child troubles you, I can only recommend you do more reading in the lives of the saints. While saints are grown more than born, and brats and neurotics have metamorphosed into saints, there are also children — I call them the Mozarts of sanctity — born with spiritual genius *and* the willingness to do the hard work of sanctity. For instance, Fatima child Jacinta Marto, who died at nine, was dubbed "heroically virtuous" after thorough investigation by the Congregation for the Causes of Saints.

But grace-filled babies? It's true that St. Therese of Lisieux claimed she obtained a great grace asking the prayers of her four dead siblings, who died from infancy to five years old. Still, the next subject I write about I can only offer sans commentary beyond the reminder of Blessed Katharine Drexel that "we live in the midst of innumerable mysteries which are solved by faith alone."

Many people are still alive who knew the Basque-born Claretian priest Father Aloysius Ellacuria who worked principally in Los Angeles, but also in Chicago, Phoenix, and San Antonio, Texas. Witnesses swear to have seen this simple, kindly mystic levitate; many have smelled delicious perfumes emanating from his body; and some found he read both their hearts and minds. They have seen him heal people physically and/or spiritually. In fact, as he once admitted quietly to very close friends, he had all the special gifts God gives to certain beloved friends meant to be magnets for souls.

Consider Joe and Connie Vorndran of West Los Angeles. A chief scientist at Hughes for thirty years before his death, brilliant, handsome, life-loving Joe was married to vibrant, warm Connie, a homemaker with cover-girl blonde beauty. Hardly flaky people. They met Father Aloysius in November, 1957. Their four-month old second child had been born that July, blind and with a hole in her heart, after Connie caught the measles from their firstborn.

Told on a Saturday about this very special priest, whose blessings sometimes brought physical healing and almost always great spiritual comfort, the distraught but devout young couple took little Maureen Elizabeth to the Claretian residence the very next day.

As always there was a large crowd lined up waiting for Father Aloysius to finish praying with his Claretian community. When he left the chapel, however, he walked straight to the young couple sitting with their fussy baby under a tree.

"Come, I've been waiting for you," he smiled.

At first they thought it a mistake. But no, this priest knew all about them before he ever saw them. Knew that they would become his spiritual children for the rest of his life.

Perhaps this will help the reader keep an open mind for the strange story of Maureen Elizabeth. Almost forty years later, Connie is still awed over the love Father Aloysius showed her "defective" baby, whom many today would say, with pity, "should never have been born." At first that love seemed understandable — a compassionate priest, he felt for the poor little thing. Later they would see more.

Telling Joe and Connie intimate things about their souls, he urged, regarding their baby, "Go home and be at peace. This child will not suffer another pain."

photo from the author's collection, courtesy Francis X. Levy

Father Aloysius Ellacuria

(In hindsight Connie is sure that, as he did with others, the priest arranged with God to carry Maureen Elizabeth's pain himself.) Then, rashly some would say, the Spanish Claretian promised the parents their blind baby would see on Christmas Day.

The feast of the Christ Child came and Maureen Elizabeth's previously unmoving eyes suddenly followed a little dog all around the room. She could see from then on.

Connie and Joe were visiting the kindly priest several times a week now for spiritual counsel and those precious blessings. At his request ("I know her heart is healed," he said) they took Maureen Elizabeth to a children's heart specialist. He told them, "This child's heart is perfect."

Yet their pediatrician on the next visit said, "No, it is defective."

Then in January, Maureen Elizabeth caught severe flu. She was rushed to Children's Hospital in downtown Los Angeles, where she was blessed with a Jewish physician so compassionate he wept when he had to cause her pain. This doctor sent Connie and Joe, who were keeping vigil at her hospital crib, home for a few hours rest somewhere around 4:00 or 5:00 A.M. They phoned Father Aloysius (he did not drive), who said "Pick me up at once." When the threesome arrived at the hospital, the doctor told them Maureen Elizabeth was gone.

Father Aloysius later said that as he stood over the very beautiful baby, he knew he could pray her back to life (no, not megalomania — saints have done it many times). But God showed him Maureen's destiny: At baptism she had received many more graces than the ordinary person — he used the term "infinite graces" — and was a very special, elect soul (remember those "different-size glasses," each filled to the brim) who was destined "to do her work from heaven." He told Connie and Joe that her special mission was "to young couples" and that she died in her total infant purity of soul in reparation for the sins of others.

For the rest of Father Aloysius' life he said Maureen Elizabeth never left his side.[2] She was his heavenly spiritual assistant, he claimed, to whom he gave many special commissions, which she fulfilled.

One has to ponder Father Aloysius' claims that Maureen Elizabeth was a special soul who helped him after her death. What better way, after all, for a great-hearted priest — if he didn't mind bending the truth a little — to comfort two devout young parents who lose a child tragically? One problem. Father would never bend the truth. Was he deluded? He wants to comfort so he believes this in good faith, even though objectively speaking it isn't true. Saints can be wrong about things. Pondering all this, I don't know what you will conclude. But I confess I believe Father Aloysius, *even though I don't understand.* My stance rests on the following two incidents involving two other holy priests.

A special Mass was always celebrated on Maureen Elizabeth's feast day — that is, the day she died and entered heaven. One year, Father Thomas Matin, another "canonizable-grade" Claretian who lived with Father Aloysius, said the Mass. Father Thomas was one of those with one foot in this life and the other in the next, a man who had the gift, people claim, known in the Cure d'Ars and other saints, of being able to see the status of souls in the world beyond.

After the Mass he came running up to Connie and Joe. "She's in heaven," he began.

"We know that, Father," Joe interrupted, bemused.

"No, I mean she's so *high* in heaven and (her soul) so beautiful!" Father Thomas clarified.

Those who knew them insist there were at least four saints in that group of Claretians. Besides Father Aloysius and Father Thomas in "the older generation," there were the younger Brother Salvatore Azzarello and Father Frank Ambrosi. The last two I had the unforgettable experience of meeting (separately) before anyone told me about them. For once I figured something out myself. Let me say simply, they were not like other good men but something much more, and I join many who will never forget them and who ask their prayers.

Father Frank Ambrosi, a spiritual son of Father Aloysius, met Connie and Joe some years after their second daughter's death. He had something to show them. He took a tattered and worn little card out of his breviary (the book containing the prayers, many of them psalms, which Catholic priests and others say daily). They recognized it at once. At Maureen Elizabeth's death, they had had the little card made, as Catholics traditionally do at a death. Such cards have Jesus, Mary, or a saint pictured on one side and a prayer on the other, with the deceased's name and the dates of the individual's life. The card serves as a reminder to pray for the dead person, as well as a souvenir. Without their thinking anything of it, in place of the usual saint's picture, the Vorndrans used a picture of Maureen herself as if — in some way I certainly can't explain or understand — this six-month-old child was holy herself. On the back, instead of the usual prayer, there is a poem about her eyesight miracle. Again, a kind of undeliberate "message" that this person requires not prayer, but recognition of God's goodness in her regard.

Father Ambrosi said to Connie and Joe, "You know I found this card at the Provincial House and I was so drawn to this child. I put the card in my breviary and whenever I say my Office (the Church's official daily prayer) she's always with me."

As far as I know, no one ever saw the dead infant make a visible after-death appearance, but the claims of "presence" lasted for years. Today all three priests are dead themselves. But Connie Vorndran says, too, that she feels the second of her four daughters "is always with me."

I mentioned that the Claretians, preaching evangelists, were founded by St. Anthony Maria Claret (1807-1870). As would be expected, Father Aloysius was devoted to his fellow Spaniard. I could stick my neck out and say he probably saw Claret just as he saw the Blessed Virgin (in one instance we know about, he was in the hospital in Santa Monica being readied for surgery for a brain tumor when she appeared as he said the rosary, touching him lovingly and instantly annihilating the tumor; the awed surgeon, finding the tumor gone in the last pre-op check, fell to his knees, asking Father Aloysius' blessing). But we must stick to things we have witnesses for.

Not long after God gave the Vorndrans their third daughter — named Antonia Maria for this saint — Connie was enduring a horribly painful though not life-threatening ailment. So she stayed home when Joe and oldest daughter Terry went to receive Father Aloysius' blessing on a Sunday afternoon. Those Sundays were exhausting for the priest, but he insisted to Joe, "when you get home, I want you to put Connie on the phone." So that evening the priest she regarded as a saint blessed Connie repeatedly over the phone, asking each time, "Are you better now?" Honest Connie could only reply "no." There was no lessening of her pain. So much for the placebo effect in her case! Finally Father Aloyisius told her to take the pain medication prescribed by her doctor and go to bed. He would continue to pray for her.

Connie says: "I went to bed with a relic of St. Anthony Mary Claret in my hand. It was the first time I could sleep since my problem began. My first sleep in days. I woke in the night and sat up. There at the foot of my bed St. Anthony Mary was standing. I've never had a vision in my life before and I've never had one since. But I did see St. Anthony Mary Claret. He was standing there and he was smiling. He never said anything. Just smiled. I turned to wake Joe up and tell him that St. Anthony Claret was there. When he woke and I turned back, St. Anthony Claret was gone. I realized then that the pain was completely gone too. Normally with what I had the pain could have gone on for another week, certainly for several more days.

"When I told Father Aloysius about this, he just put his head down modestly and smiled. But he never said anything."

Father Aloysius is dead today. But people like the Esparza family of San Diego (see page 178) claim he, too, is still doing God's work. And they are not the only ones to say this. Around Christmas 1994, for instance, he was apparently seen by a Mexican nun. Foundress of a flourishing new order, this woman of great spiritual ardor and down-to-earth common sense had an experience she is willing to share for publication as an aid to others' faith in supernatural realities — so long as I withhold her name and area so there can be no question of someone seeking personal publicity. "It was not a dream," she emphasizes in her excellent English. Beyond that she will only tell me that a "presence" made itself known — a priest from Heaven who have no name but said he would help her with the hard labor of creating the new community.

Then early in 1995 first-time visitors to her remote location, Americans Mary and Francis Levy, handed her a gift, a privately-printed memoir by Francis of Father Aloysius. In it the new foundress read with awe the exact words spoken to her by her dead visitor. She also learned that Father Aloysius founded the Missionaries of Perpetual Adoration, a men's order centered in Mexico with the same aims as her group — and discovered that only his death prevented his founding a companion women's order. Convinced that it was Father Aloysius God sent to pledge heavenly help, the Mexican foundress now hopes to affiliate her Order with the Missionaries.

Father Aloysius, I firmly believe, will be canonized one day. But many saints pass among us unknown. To represent them, fortunately, we have the first-person testimony of Jack O'Neil of Sewickley, Pennsylvania, a bedroom community ten miles down the Ohio River from Pittsburgh. A former writer in broadcasting and public relations, Jack masterfully boiled down his story to win a contest[3] on favors received from saints. With a little additional information from my November 1994 interview with him, here is Jack's story:

> After thirty years, my drinking had progressed to where it had
> devastated my marriage, my job, my friends, and most certainly

my health. Apparently I "hit bottom" when a police ambulance took me to St. Francis Hospital in 1963, unconscious and dying from bleeding ulcers.

My physician later explained the impasse — they couldn't operate until the bleeding stopped, but it didn't look as though I would stop bleeding.

Jack says once he was conscious again — with his finger being jabbed to check his blood every twenty minutes round the clock — he was so scared he was unable to sleep even though the nurses urged him to try. He continues:

> After three days, they scheduled emergency surgery for the next morning as a desperate "last resort."
>
> Still sleepless and only dozing between blood tests, I heard the sound of swishing skirts and clicking beads. I turned and saw an elderly white-robed nun enter the room. Wordlessly, she stood at the foot of the bed, crossing herself and barely moving her lips in prayer. She smoothed the sheets, plumping the pillow and pulling the covers around my shoulders.
>
> "And how are you, Mr. O'Neil?" she finally asked.
>
> "They tell me I'm probably dying," I answered.
>
> "Oh, no you're not," she said. "You have too much work to do."
>
> As she turned and left the room, I immediately experienced a feeling of peace sweep over me and I fell into a deep, restful sleep.
>
> The next morning, my doctor stood puzzling over my chart and said, "I don't know what happened, Jack, but your bleeding has stopped. You are completely stabilized and we have cancelled the surgery." He left the room, still shaking his head.
>
> The nurses were equally amazed, and one of them asked, "Where did you get this, Mr. O'Neil?" She showed me a green scapular pinned to the shoulder of my gown.
>
> "I guess that little old nun pinned it on me last night," I said.
>
> They asked, "What nun?" I described as best I could the elderly nun in the white habit and details of her late-night visit.
>
> The nurses, both veterans of many years at the hospital, told me that there once was an older nun who had visited patients in danger of death, praying over them and pinning green scapulars on their gowns. But that had been years ago.

"Well, I guess she is still sneaking past you and making her rounds during the late night," I shrugged.

"But you don't understand, Mr. O'Neil," they whispered fervently.

"The nun you described so perfectly passed away seven years ago."

One ESP expert I discussed it with maintains that Jack could have dreamed about a nun he'd never heard of through some kind of psychic transfer. Perhaps. Jack insists he was definitely awake. Dream or apparition, he has a green scapular to prove the old nun "came," one way or another. And some noteworthy aftereffects: while there was no instantaneous cure of his alcoholism, the dead nun's visit left behind her the incentive he needed to stop drinking. He had suddenly seen the possibility of an afterlife, he says, and wanted to clean up his act. After an up-and-down battle fought with the help of the original "Twelve Step" program, he reached complete sobriety on September 12, 1972. Twenty-two years sober in 1994, he is a member of St. James parish council in Sewickley, as well as a Eucharistic minister, lector, and hospital visitor — with a special ministry to alcoholics. In addition, he left his broadcasting career to counsel alcoholics, working first as a volunteer, then a paid staff member at St. John's Alcoholic and Drug Rehabilitation Center (later Mercy Center for Chemical Dependency Services) at Mercy Hospital in Pittsburgh, as well as with the Twelve Step Program.

Speaking to Jack O'Neil and his English-born, Anglican wife, Theo, today, it seems clear that the former drunk who claims to have seen a dead nun is neither a nut nor a con artist. Whether God sent the nun, or something else saved Jack, you will have to decide for yourself, of course. But something — or someone — certainly changed his destiny.

No matter how often they appear to people today, saints who died before 1800 are under strict orders not to appear in this book lest it become too thick to lift. But like the newsman Eddie Doherty, whose autobiographical writings relate a number of special favors from the Peruvian saint, I confess to a soft spot for St. Martin de Porres (1579-1639). The rejected, dark-skinned, illegitimate son of a Spanish knight and a freed black woman, Martin had every reason to be mad at the world. But his life is a St. Francis-like chant of joy — joy in God and joy in doing good, especially for the miserable of his day in Lima: The orphans, the slaves, the abandoned animals, the homeless, the sick, and the hungry. After his death the Dominican saint appeared over the years to a number of people, curing some, consoling others — according to the under-oath testimonies in the official investigation of Martin's sanctity. To not add such authenticated accounts to this book is hard.[4] So when Carmen Rivera of East Los Angeles shared a family experience concerning St. Martin with me, I weakened because this one you won't be able to find in print anywhere.

Carmen's Mexican-born father, Eusebio, prayed the rosary daily, went to confession monthly, and generally lived, as had his father before him, a devout life. Yet he proved to be very difficult for his daughter to care for in his last years. Clinging to his independence, he refused to call her when he had to use the bathroom — no matter how much the doctor told him that he must not try to navigate alone. Carmen worried about him as if he were a toddler — what would he do next, and would he hurt himself? Finally, when he was ninety-three she put him in a convalescent hospital in Maywood. This actually increased her responsibilities for Carmen visited daily, which meant a bus ride there and back.

On her arrival one day in May, 1980, her father complained. A molar tooth was aching uncomfortably. He wanted a dentist to pull the thing. Carmen informed the staff, who noted it on the chart. But the next day nothing had been done. The pain was worse. Again Carmen asked for a dentist. Another note on the chart. Again, no dentist.

This went on for four days, the callous staff ignoring the aged man's increasing pain.

Finally Carmen walked in and found her father happy and pain-free, the tooth in his hand.

"So they pulled it for you at last!" she exclaimed happily.

"No!" Eusebio Rivera shook his head. "Martin de Porres came in that door and *he* pulled it for me."

Carmen sat down slowly. She knew that, irascible and old as he was, her father's mind was alert and clear. She had never known him to tell a lie. And he was certainly too devout to joke about godly matters. Still, she checked with the staff to see if they had sent a dentist. They had not.

Carmen is a woman of faith. She knew that St. Martin de Porres in his lifetime served as a barber-doctor, first as a layman and then as a Dominican lay brother. In this job in those pre-dentistry days, the saint pulled a lot of teeth. For years Carmen, who is Hispanic and of modest means, has sent donations to a mission for poor blacks in Alabama like her mother before her. She finally concluded the black saint helped her father as a way to say "thanks." Since there is such a thing as holy anger, I add that the Lord and

Martin may have also gotten fed up with the staff of a certain convalescent hospital who heartlessly let an old man suffer.

Eusebio Rivera died at age ninety-four later in 1980, but Carmen still has the tooth — to her a relic because it was pulled, she believes, by a saint dead over three hundred and fifty years.

Since every diversion from our main topic should have a good reason, let this one remind us that no saint has "been dead too long" to be a messenger of God.

ENDNOTES

[1] Voorhies was a nonpracticing Catholic who returned to the Church and died in good standing in 1980 — a change some people credit to Charlene.

[2] See Caryll Houselander's more limited experience in chapter two.

[3] For readers of Catholic newspaper *Our Sunday Visitor* in 1994.

[4] You can find a number in *Saint Martin de Porres: Apostle of Charity*, an official biography written by Giuliana Cavallini at the request of the Dominican Order and the Postulator of St. Martin's Cause.

14   Lowering the Boom — Gently!

uida White was divorced, lonely, and depressed. Drinking seemed to anesthetize her pain. One morning her kids were fighting and she was too blue to handle them. The stack of greasy dishes in the sink seemed equally insurmountable. She made a wine cooler.

Then another ... and a third.

But this day even wine coolers couldn't dull her misery. At some point, something snapped. Grabbing her car keys, she rushed unsteadily out of the house. Abandoning her children, she gunned the motor and roared down the street, heading down the south hill into the downtown area of Spokane, the Washington city where she lives.

As she tipsily navigated one of the swooping curves on the hill, Guida lost control of the car, which spun crazily 'round and 'round like a top. She tried to grab the wheel, but it was moving so fast she had no chance.

Then, suddenly, seated next to her in the car's passenger seat she saw her dead grandmother, who more than one person has called "a saint."

"Grandma, what are you doing here?" she choked.

"Go home to your children," was the only reply.

A few seconds later the car stopped, tipped precariously, one side higher than the other, on a roadside bank of earth. Her grandmother was gone, but Guida noted that even in the car's tilted position it pointed back up the hill toward her home. In her spin, she had barely missed various pedestrians. Now these and other people clustered around the car, not screaming at her, but urging with concern that she be very careful how she extricate herself lest the tipped car go all the way over.

Because of her grandmother's guardian-angel-like appearance, Guida knew she was in no danger. She did not even try to climb out of the car. Carefully, frequently using her brake, she expertly eased the car onto a firm footing. Then, stone sober, she went home.

"I did the dishes," she told me. "I took care of my kids. And I didn't have anything to drink for a long time."

Freda Lindblad Sams, Guida's grandmother and my grandmother, too, is not beatified or canonized. The Swedish-born daughter of a lay preacher, my mother's mother was a Protestant. But the quiet one-liner spoken by this dead mother of nine not so long ago exemplifies what this chapter is about: The appearance of God's good friends as His messengers to "straighten out" someone who needs a gentle hint, a nudge, or even a forthright scolding to get them back on the road or keep them spiritually moving.

You will note that Freda did not abuse Guida about her wine coolers. God's messengers don't encourage self-hate or despair. (Appearances that sow either, however radiant the visitor, have their source in darkness.) Whether given through the Holy Spirit or delivered by a dead saint, God's messages always leave the recipient's dignity intact, as befits a creature that, called to the highest destiny, is free to tell even the Master of the Universe to "buzz off."

The telltale mark of a godly experience of this type, if I may be so bold, is the hovering sense of divine compassion, as when visionary Josefa Menendez, seeing Jesus after she had just disobeyed his explicit order, bewailed her failings, her miseries, and her fears, only to be told "If you are an abyss of miseries, I am an abyss of mercy and goodness" while he stretched out his arms, inviting "my heart is your refuge.... " Often the recipient of this sort of "corrective" visitation is not even told directly what they are doing wrong; thus when French St. Julie Billiart appears to a spiritual daughter before it is known she is dead, she does not say, "You didn't do what I told you!" Instead she tactfully asks, knowing full well the answer, "Daughter, when did you do what I told you to do?" And when St. Henry de Osso appears immediately following his death to a spiritual daughter who has broken a promise, his only reproach is — like Christ at Peter's denial — a wordless look.

To keep after-death appearances of saints in perspective, a reminder may be in order that when God wants to correct someone, dead saints are, by no means, the only divine resource. God speaks most often through the circumstances and people of our lives. Certainly the Lord speaks through scripture and other books. And sometimes the Holy Spirit speaks directly (called locutions) through a word of counsel heard interiorly or audibly. I believe I had an experience of that over a decade ago. I was engaged in some daily chore, when an interior voice said very distinctly, "If you don't give up self-pity you're going to get cancer." My circumstances didn't immediately change. But my attitude sure did!

People may *see* Jesus or His mother. And, of course, regarding saints, God does not tap only those from the nineteenth and twentieth centuries to carry His messages by any means. A few of these broader experiences will help keep our proper sense of the boundless horizon within which recent saints' appearances must be situated.

Twentieth-century miracle-worker Salesian Sister Eusebia Palomino y Yenes became so holy among the pots and pans of her Spanish convent kitchen that she is a candidate for beatification. Humble Sister Eusebia was not born some spiritual genius. She had to be nudged along just like the rest of us. Many of these nudges included visits from saints who lived long before even the nineteenth century.

Before she became a nun, the young peasant girl "with the timid yet luminous smile" was maid to the directress of a home for eighteen impoverished old people abandoned by their families. Most of her time ended up being spent helping these old people, who were for the most part sick, wretched, and quarrelsome. To her, however, caring for the difficult oldsters was living out one of her childhood's numinous dreams, so that in bathing their disgusting sores, for instance, she was tending the wounds of Christ. It was hard for the devout young girl, however, to see some of these old people die in such anxiety over the unhealed relationships and unmended hurts of what they considered "wasted lives."

In this period — roughly the era of the first world war — St. Teresa of Avila, who had died not far away in 1582, came to Eusebia in a dream. In it, Eusebia was a very, very small child again, playing with sand as she liked to do when little. St. Teresa, dressed in her Carmelite habit, walked up to her and said bluntly, "Little girl, do you want to die?"

Eusebia answered that if

courtesy The Daughters of Mary Help of Christians

Sister Eusebia Palomino

she knew she would go right to heaven, she'd like that; but as she wasn't sure she was pure enough yet, she was afraid.

"Come with me," the saint replied, taking the playing child by the hand. She led Eusebia through the local cemetery, speaking to her in such a way that Eusebia felt she should "consider myself like those corpses." Finally, they entered a beautiful garden, Eusebia thinking with relief, "Thank goodness, those graves were depressing!"

Suddenly she saw herself in the middle of the garden, dressed in pink and with blonde curls (extremely rare in the area, blondes were thought exceptionally beautiful).

"That's not possible," she cried. "I'm dark; my clothes are poor. Splendor like this has nothing to do with me!"

Then she heard an unknown voice say, "This is what you must become."

Turning to the saint, who still held her by the hand, Eusebia asked, "Is this heaven?"

"No, this is not. It is the antechamber. Paradise is much farther away." Then she led Eusebia in front of a beautifully embossed door made of crystal inlaid with diamonds. But the golden latch was firmly closed.

The saint said, "Until you become as small as you now see yourself (in this dream) you will never pass that door which opens into Paradise, because the Kingdom of Heaven is for little ones and those who resemble them."

A moment later Eusebia awoke. It was only midnight. This dream remained indelibly stamped on her soul, encouraging her to cultivate simplicity and humility.

Another experience of Eusebia's was not a dream, but a vision. This took place in 1923 on January 21 — the feast of an early Roman martyr, St. Agnes — while Eusebia was a novice nun. In church that evening, Sister Eusebia begged Jesus to tell her what about her was displeasing to Him. She explained later to her friend Sister Carmen Moreno that she did this because "I wanted to correct myself and become a saint."

As she made her brave request, the church around her disappeared and she found herself in a lovely garden. St. Agnes was walking there, radiant, even her hair looking like threads of gold. Jesus embraced Agnes and said, turning to Eusebia, "See how pure this soul is?" Then he indicated some of the garden blooms, "See how white these flowers are? Until my chosen ones reach this degree of purity, they cannot see me and speak intimately with me. Strive to acquire this virtue and you will be intimate with me, and I with you." At that moment, Eusebia saw herself clothed in a white garment that was spattered with mud.

In holy terror she asked if these spatters represented deadly sins. Gently Jesus said, "Not even small sins. But imperfections that prevent your coming to me." As they spoke He encouraged the Salesian novice to "have great purity of intention in all your actions" since this would permit Him to "treat you as an intimate: 'you with me, I with you.' "

From that day, Eusebia aspired to live this new directive.

Since, as with all Christian saints, it was with Jesus that Eusebia had her main relationship, as a reminder of this important reality, I summarize another guiding vision in which the Lord Himself gently prodded Eusebia toward greater holiness. In 1928 or 1929 she dreamed she was lifted up so that she could see some supernatural things, and vast groups of people below, who had no thought of supernatural realities but simply scurried to and fro "without any sense of direction." Many ran blindly into evil. While with sadness Eusebia observed this and three abandoned, broken crucifixes, she heard a voice say, "Ah, if you were better, if you prayed more, you could save and bring me all those souls ... Instead how little you love me."

Again, she immediately woke up. After that, offering her own daily chores, her prayers, *her very self* to bring others to God and wholeness became Eusebia's whole life. The devil, of course, loves to lay heavy guilt trips on people in any way possible, including, at times, with dreams or visions like this one of Eusebia's. That this was Jesus, not Lucifer, is clear because Eusebia became ever more content, loving, and joyfully alive.

Epileptics were not ordained in the first third of the nineteenth century. Studying for the priesthood in Paris, young Jacob Libermann — a German-born recent convert from Judaism — suffered a seizure reading a reproachful letter from his bitterly-sorrowing rabbi father (who certainly loved God as much as his son). When epilepsy was diagnosed, that was the end of Libermann's hopes to preside at a Catholic alter — but not the end of his movement toward sanctity. Kept on as a handyman out of pity at Saint-Sulpice seminary, Libermann was recognized by the seminarians as "a saint."

Even in that wretched era, when Jewish-Christian understanding was non-existent, Libermann — now known as Francis — burrowed into God's depths to that luminous place where the sad brokenness in our human family vanishes in a mysterious cloud of divine love. In these healing depths, epilepsy faded away. Libermann was ordained and went on to found the Holy Ghost Fathers, a group as notable for holiness as for missionary enterprises.

After his death in 1852, Francis appeared to the living a number of times. In the under-oath testimonies taken during the investigation that led to his being named Venerable, as one who "practiced heroic virtue," a nun testified that when she was sick — unfortunately no details are given as to the nature of her illness — the Servant of God Francis Libermann appeared to her in company with the Holy Family. She was instantly healed.

A married woman who revered this priest so much that — going a bit far with her veneration — she used to write her answers to his letters on her knees, also saw Libermann. He appeared to her in a static vision, his heart united to the heart of the mother of Jesus.

And once he turned up to very gently correct someone. A "correction" some readers will better grasp if I point out that for generations, Catholic men who want to be celibate (in order to put themselves at the service of God and the human family) have turned to Jesus' virgin mother for help. For some, Mary's help involves, at times, a material object called a scapular. No magic token, the scapular reminds the individual to ask Mary's prayers and also acts as a visible sign of the individual's reliance on her motherly assistance. Bizarre sounding, perhaps, but like a lot of things hard to explain in few words, a usage based on many generation's experience that "it works."

I mentioned the impression Francis made on the seminarians at the Saint-Sulpice Seminary in Paris. One of these individuals, who lived beside him during the years 1829 and 1830, went on to become a Carthusian monk at France's Grande Chartreuse monastery. On December 21, 1860, eight years after Libermann's death, Dom Salier wrote at length on how and why young Libermann so impressed him. Quoting just one brief segment, translating Dom Salier's original French from Volume I of *Notes and Documents Relating to the Life of Father Libermann:*

> My dear friend has served me not only when he was near, but also from afar. [That is, after death, according to Holy Ghost Father Michael Carroll] I recall several days after I had received the novice's habit — or maybe it was the same day — here at Grande Chartreuse, I lost my scapular of Our Lady of Carmel and I neglected to get another one. The following night, sleeping or waking, I really can't be sure — all I know is I found myself suddenly so sexually tempted that I can't recall ever having been in such cruel agony. I resisted the temptation but was so hardpressed I didn't think to pray. Thus the temptation grew ever stronger. In this state,

quite despairing, I saw Libermann, wearing a garment as white as snow with great sleeves like those we had at Saint-Sulpice. He had a completely heavenly air about him as he appeared before me carrying in his hand a scapular of Carmel in a way that definitely called my attention to it. The sight of the scapular at once delivered me from every temptation. At that same moment I saw behind Libermann several other seminarians of Saint-Sulpice whom I didn't know, but who also appeared like him to be favored with an angelic purity. They were wearing the same garment and carrying in their hands the same scapular, like warriors returning from battle carrying their triumphal palms. They made a neat line behind Libermann. After I had taken my time contemplating them, they walked several steps off and all disappeared. The next day I made certain to procure a Scapular and, thanks to God, I have never again given it up.

Sixty-two-year-old Sister Aimee of Jesus of the Lisieux Carmel recalled for the diocesan tribunal investigating Therese of Lisieux's possible sanctity about 1910-11 that she once saw the young saint slightly ruffled. Something humiliating had been done to Sister Genevieve, novice-director Therese's blood sister Celine (at that time one of Therese's novices[1]) by the imperious, if loveable, Mother Marie de Gonzague, Superior of the Lisieux Carmel.

Perhaps because Sister Aimee — who like Therese — was much less fond of Therese's three older Carmelite blood sisters, she protested, "Surely Mother de Gonzague has a right to test Sister Genevieve!"

"There are some ways in which people should not be tested and this is one of them," Therese retorted.

Sister Aimee dismissed the comment as someone just "being on the side of" her sister. Later Therese's critic felt the saint's criticism of Mother Marie had been a supernatural discernment that had nothing to do with family loyalty.

Mother Marie de Gonzague, their barely-reelected Superior, had her good qualities. And there is no doubt God used even her imperfections and honest mistakes to increase Therese's sanctity. Whether she always wielded her authority with discretion and benefit to the community or not, Mother Marie was treated with real respect and affection by Therese. The saint believed whatever happened to her — even the inadequate blankets or rancid food given to her because she didn't complain — was used for her good by God. But the fact remains that Mother Marie did not take proper care of her young nuns, so that a number of them — not only Therese — became tubercular.

After Therese's death, it appears God sent her back to make sure such neglect would cease. Sister Genevieve, the blood sister of Therese humiliated by Mother de Gonzague, held no grudge. She testified under oath after the Superior's death:

> (Mother Marie) told me of a favor she had received before a portrait of Therese as a child. It must have been a very vivid experience, because our poor Mother could not look at this picture without crying.
>
> I often saw her moved in this way, and she said to me: "Oh, the things she said to me! … How much she reproached me with! But how gently!"

The Carmelites found Mother de Gonzague much improved after God sent Therese to scold her. That Therese knew how to scold as well as how to encourage — and did it gently — came as no surprise to the small group of Carmelites for whom she had been novice mistress. Even one of the most difficult novices reported that Therese was "very sharp at seeing our defects and correcting us," but "she was kindness and charity itself.… "

To various of those novices, after her death Sister Therese came in one way or another, still urging — and if necessary scolding — them on to God.

Thus Sister Genevieve recounted a number of special "visits" under oath. I give two of these, quoting her tribunal testimony:

> … a sister took something from me that I needed, and I was just getting ready to recover it from her in a rather brusque manner when I distinctly heard the words "very humbly!" I recognized Therese's voice and my heart was immediately transformed and inclined toward humility.

To encourage these young nuns, Therese worked several physical miracles. One of them — in the mildest possible way — is a reproach.

Quoted is the under-oath testimony given the tribunal by Sister Marie of the Trinity:

For the sake of convenience, I had made a large pleat in my habit so that I would not have to adjust it every morning when I (dressed). It was firmly sewn with a lock stitch. I told the Servant of God about this a few days before she died, and she told me to unstitch it, that it was contrary to our [Carmelite] customs. I left it as it was, nevertheless, putting off the job of unstitching it till some other time. The day after her death I could not get this blessed pleat out of my mind. I said to myself: "She sees that I still have it, and maybe it grieves her." So I said this prayer to her: "Dear sister, if you find this pleat displeasing, undo it yourself, and I promise never to remake it." Imagine my amazement when on getting up the following morning, I found it was no longer there! My feelings were a mixture of terror and consolation. It was a warning to me to put all her counsels and recommendations into practice.

One wonders, did Therese prick those stitches out manually, or joyously order "In the name of God, undone!"

While few are so well-detailed as the one above, the testimonies of the nuns of the Lisieux Carmel[2] indicate that over the first dozen years after her death God apparently "deputized" Therese to raise that convent to a higher level of spirituality, through individual appearances, of one degree or another, to almost every nun. Engaged in such an effort, some appearances — like those just mentioned — were to reproach or even scold. In others, as when she had been novice mistress, Therese corrected or brought someone along by an encouraging word. Perhaps in the majority of cases where we don't know of a specific message, just that Therese somehow revealed herself to a nun, that by itself was a strong reminder to the individual that God and the afterlife exist and a Carmelite certainly should be among those shaping her life accordingly.

A few more of these instances, less detailed than those given so far, will buttress my contention that God was using the dead Carmelite to spiritually "shape up," that is, prepare, the Lisieux Carmel for the demands that have been placed on it ever since Therese's beatification and canonization.

In life Therese fancifully scattered rose petals around the statue of Jesus as a joyous visual representation of the love and sacrifices she offered Him. In the language of the poems she wrote, she remarked, "after my death I will let fall a shower of roses," meaning special favors. And she counseled her sisters to save those scattered rose petals because "they'll do a lot of good."[3] In a sort of cosmic play on those prophecies, Therese most often marked her presence in the Lisieux Carmel by scent — many times the scent of roses.

As mentioned in chapter two, such scents are called the odor of sanctity. The odor of sanctity, again, is simply a very pleasant odor — anything from incense to flowers to even "fine tobacco" or humanly-unknown scents — which speaks to someone's soul, has no possible human explanation, and leaves genuine spiritual aftereffects. It is sometimes — but not always — smelled by others besides the one for whom it signals some spiritual message or other favor.

In Therese's Carmel — probably so it wouldn't seem a "nest of nuts" and thus impede the saint's chances for canonization — the saint's "visits" were usually through this low-key approach, rather than Therese "walking in the door" or seen up high in glory, as occurred in many other places. While there were a few physical miracles and cures, the visits mostly left spiritual favors in their wake. Something much more valuable than either miracles or cures to women whose lives are meant to be a search mission for souls and God.

On these after-death appearances, I'm again quoting the official under-oath testimonies taken by the tribunal. Because with an enclosed group like this, someone may wonder about "mass hallucination," let me point out the appearances were basically individual, not group, events. It is also reassuring to have testimonies by Therese's natural sisters, because the Martin girls, reared by parents who are also candidates for formal sainthood, are neither suggestible nor "spiritual thrill seekers."

Under oath, Therese's sister Agnes of Jesus, who was at the time prioress, verifies that:

> All the nuns, except maybe one or two have from time to time, and in various parts of the convent, perceived various perfumes — incense, roses, violets, etc. — in ways that had no natural explanation…. The phenomena began as soon as Sister Therese was dead, and have continued intermittently ever since [Note: This would be thirteen or fourteen years after the saint's death]. They have been more frequent in the past two years.
>
> Asked if she had experienced these odours herself, she replied: "Yes, about ten times since the Servant of God's death."

Far from "pushing" the phenomena, Mother Agnes says:

> I had difficulty in believing in them myself at first. I was afraid
> of illusions, and, anyway, as prioress, I felt it my duty to pretend to
> pay little attention....

She also notes that the nuns, in general, "who experienced these sensa-
tions did not expect to do so, and most of them reacted skeptically." And
insists to the tribunal "I prefer interior graces," without even a hint, of course,
as to just what interior graces were signaled by those odors she experienced
"ten times."

Another of Therese's natural sisters, Sister Genevieve of St. Teresa (she
whom Therese had chided with the words "very humbly") also mixes a
kind of disdain with honest admission:

> ... One heard of perfumes by means of which she (Therese)
> made her presence felt. I don't know why I rebelled against this
> kind of manifestation; I suppose I thought it was rather vulgar be-
> cause of its appeal to the senses. Anyway, I decided I did not be-
> lieve in it. One evening in November I was returning to my cell,
> which is the one that Sister Therese used to occupy, when I smelled
> a strong scent of roses from the oratory next door. I was startled,
> but that passed and I remained still incredulous, saying to myself:
> "now people put perfume on everything; it could be a scented let-
> ter." I knew deep down there was no letter in that place, but I left
> the room without further investigation. Then near the stairs, and
> fairly far from the cell, I felt a little puff of rose-scented wind. That
> convinced me and I wanted to thank Therese, but it vanished im-
> mediately. This kind of thing has happened to me about fifteen
> times in the last two years.
>
> ... With two or three exceptions, when the fragrance lingered
> for some time, I noticed that the scent vanished as soon as I real-
> ized that it was Sister Therese. *They always underscored some
> particular fact or were sent as a consolation in time of trouble*
> [italics mine]. I also noticed that such phenomena never took place
> when I wanted them to; it always happened when such things were
> farthest from my mind, so that it always took a few moments for
> me to realize it was from Sister Therese.

Sister Genevieve testified that these perfumes began in 1908, eleven years
after her youngest sibling's death. But she obviously is speaking only for

herself. The third sibling of Therese who lived at the Carmel, her oldest sister, Marie of the Sacred Heart, witnessed:

> On the evening of Friday, October 1, the day after her (Therese's) death, Sister Mary of St. Joseph towards whom Sister Therese had exercised great charity during her lifetime, found her cell so scented with the perfume of violets that she thought someone had placed a bunch of them in her cell, and looked everywhere for it. In fact, nearly all the nuns in this community have smelt this mysterious perfume; I experienced it four or five times myself.... We all experienced it when we least expected it.

About those violets: There must have been a "card," that is, a spiritual message, in the "bouquet" (unless it was simply more "revenge" by the saint — doing good to one who caused her trouble). But Sister Marie either doesn't know the odor's meaning to Sister Mary of St. Joseph, or in the same way she withholds the spiritual meaning of her own "four or five" instances of the odor of sanctity, she thinks it unnecessary to reveal such personal material to the tribunal.

Even if "messageless," the violets are interesting because they show Therese working very early to help the spiritually underdeveloped sisters of the Carmel, in spite of the fact that it was often they who gave her trouble during her life. Besides this troublesome old soul who received the odor bouquet, there was the physical cure immediately following Therese's death of Sister St. Vincent, the cranky nun who specialized in biting remarks toward Therese. A cure that was accompanied by a total change in Sister St. Vincent's attitude.

Another individual who often gave Therese a hard time was Martha of Jesus, an orphan raised in circumstances that left her neurotic and — I borrow her own word — "difficult." Therese was Martha's novice mistress, and the mixed-up girl later admitted she deliberately tried to upset her spiritual mentor at times, learning something about genuine love from Therese's response that combined speaking the truth firmly with tact and compassion. Martha swore that four or five times Therese came to her after her death. She does not reveal the messages *but* other nuns have testified that "difficult" Sister Martha of the terrible childhood and rotten disposition ended her life as a spiritually-transformed woman, offering at least the *possibility* that God used Therese to help her by those "visits."

Another "difficult case" was Sister Marie-Madeleine. Today the Carmel says of her:

> The eighth of eleven children, already herding sheep at age five and put out to work as a servant at fourteen, [she was] illiterate, if intelligent [and] a gloomy, closed personality.

Faced by a novice director like Therese full of authentic joy, love, and insight, the withdrawn Marie-Madeleine clammed up even more. During Therese's life, all the young saint's patient devotion and disinterested love for this novice seemed to get nowhere, although when Therese was gravely ill, dour, taciturn Marie-Madeleine insisted on making a special soup "just for her."

While we don't know *how* Therese came to Marie-Madeleine after Therese's death — whether it was by a sense of presence, a voice, or something more — we do have the sworn testimony of this nun before the process tribunal. Somehow, after death Therese communicated effectively with the novice who had eluded her in life. Marie-Madeleine says:

> I wasn't in a state at that time [while Therese was alive] to profit from her counsels, but as soon as she was dead, I abandoned to her the care of my soul. And how she has changed me! It's unbelievable! I am completely peaceful and confident. I don't even recognize myself anymore."

Marie-Madeleine, too, died a holy death, the Carmel prioress of the day noted.

Another nun, Teresa of St. Augustine, is in still a different category. Not a bad egg, there was just something about her that Therese instinctively disliked; yet the young saint treated Teresa of St. Augustine with such kindness that Teresa of St. Augustine went to her grave believing — and in a sense she was completely correct — St. Therese had a special love for her. While even a saint may dislike a fine person and grow through struggling to treat the individual charitably, it is also possible this nun irritated Therese because of some personal trait — say pomposity or severeness — that actually needed changing. Whether Sister Teresa of St. Augustine had such faults or no, she says under oath that she twice experienced Therese's odor visit, too, adding "I have no desire to be favoured in this way; what I expect from Sister Therese are hidden graces that will benefit me spiritually."

One wishes her questioner had responded pointedly, "Well, did you get some? Details, please!" We don't know the fruits of these visits, but obviously God wasn't sending Therese back to Lisieux just for a lark. Most, if not all, of these odors of sanctity represent some spiritual gift to the individual involved, in spite of those bland statements to their questioners by the nuns. Of course they spoke as they did because Carmelite spirituality is a hidden way, where spiritual graces and progress toward holiness are covered under a veil of humility.

But there are hints. You recall that Therese's outspoken sister Celine (Sister Genevieve) refers to the hidden spiritual component of the odors when she says they "always underscored some particular fact or were sent as a consolation in time of trouble." And Marie of the Trinity, whose pleat was undone for her, mentioned experiencing Therese's odor of sanctity "one day just after I made an act of humility" and "on certain occasions when I was about to perform some service in connection with her."

What did all these visits — by odor or otherwise — accomplish at the Lisieux Carmel? We know from testimonies by Sister Genevieve and others that at least some, if not all, the nuns were raised to a higher level of spirituality. There was a general improvement as well: One of the holier nuns told the tribunal that since the young saint's death the Carmelite rule of life was better kept and the nuns treated each other with more love.

Still, not even shaping up an entire Carmel kept Therese too busy to deliver God's gentle scoldings elsewhere. One last example.

A missionary priest of the order of Oblates of Mary Immaculate — who wanted his name withheld for reasons you will soon probably sympathize with, as I do — shared with the Carmel an experience he had in Asia early in 1920. He'd yawned his way through the autobiography of Sister Therese. Very nice and all that, but not his cup of tea. Then he began hearing from other missionaries and through various publications that trickled into his distant outpost how powerful Therese's prayers were.

He began to feel like some teens I know, who heard that a new restaurant was serving complimentary hors d'oeuvres opening night. With no intention of ever becoming customers because the place was out of their price range, they threw on their best duds and rushed over for the free goodies. To the missionary, some similar kind of thought occurred. God seemed to be handing out favors right and left through this little dead nun. So just because he wasn't particularly one of her admirers, why shouldn't he get some, too?

A mission project — "very useful to the glory of God," he underlines, a trifle defensively — needed financing. To that end, he began "a fervent novena" for Therese's intercession. On the third day as he prayed, to his "surprise and emotion" — I read that last word "embarrassment" — he had barely made his "insistent request" for the desired funds when Therese suddenly appeared before him.

She said "in a tone of sweet reproach," as he puts it, "ask me for spiritual favors."

Then, tactfully — after all, he is facing her with spiritual egg on his face — she vanished.

That he wasn't really a spiritual slouch can be seen by the aftereffects: He went on with the novena — changing its purpose completely — and a few months later sent off a humble testimony of his experience for the Carmel archives. In this he comments that the nun whose prayers he turned to only for "free goodies," he now considers "his holy little sister," to whom he daily confides —I suppose he'd want it underlined — his "*spiritual* interests."

Over the years to come he must have heard many times of Therese helping other missionaries obtain needed funds. Probably he only smiled, knowing that God sends to each friend what he needs — whether it be cold cash or a gentle shaking up.

ENDNOTES

[1] Although older than Therese, Celine was a novice because she generously let her younger sister enter Carmel first. Then when their aged father became ill, Celine remained outside to care for him until his death, a matter of several years.

[2] Twenty-one is the usual maximum for a Carmel, but during Therese's life, by special permission, Lisieux had twenty-seven until some of the older Carmelites died.

[3] That proved an understatement. The rose petals, sewn into little sachet-type relics, are associated with some incredible cures. Relics are not magic; they are a visual aid to invoking the saint's prayers, just as when I hold the lock of hair of my dead mother, I think of and feel close to her.

15 ✤ FATHER KELLEY MEETS FATHER NEUMANN

Genial Father Thomas Kelley quotes his father, "Don't ever let them drop the "e" in Kelley, for we're descended from the Kings of Tipperary," adding his own view with a chuckle, "probably some guy who owned The Kings of Tipperary pub."

At seventy-one the good health of the full-of-life, retired Navy chaplain permits him a satisfying exercise of his priesthood at both the naval and civilian hospitals and various nursing homes in Beaufort, South Carolina. That's when he isn't standing in for priests who need a break from their parishes.

And yet in 1995 energetic Father Kelley should have been dead almost twenty years.

Back to 1975, the year the kindly-mannered, fifty-one-year-old celebrated twenty-five years as a priest of the Oblates of St. Francis de Sales: On leave before starting a new naval assignment in Taiwan, Father Kelley was at his brother Martin's, in their hometown of Philadelphia.

It had been a long time since they had had much time together so Martin and Tom, two of five siblings, were enjoying a good talk. But toward bedtime, Martin, an oral surgeon, remarked, "Tom, you don't look well."

The priest admitted he was awfully tired. He blamed the high humidity on Parris Island, his last post, coupled with long working days. But Martin's professional eye rested on him uneasily. The doctor persuaded his brother to come in the following day to Philadelphia's Holy Redeemer Hospital, where Martin was on staff. A quick checkup would make sure everything was okay.

Everything was not okay, the next day's blood analysis revealed. One reason for fatigue even a good night's sleep no longer mended, was internal bleeding. Father Kelley admitted he did feel some "uncomfortableness" in the appendix area and agreed to stay in the hospital overnight so a lower GI series could be run.

Dr. Martin Kelley went home that night afraid for his brother. Barely two weeks past, the family had buried their aunt and the previous year her sister — the Kelleys' mother — both dead of colon cancer.

Those fears proved warranted the next day, October 1. Clearly upset, Martin accompanied three other physicians into his brother's room to inform the naval chaplain that the GI series revealed a mass in the appendix area. From the symptoms, family history, and the patient's age, it was undoubtedly colon cancer.

Eventually, the stunned priest was left alone, except for his roommate, a non-Christian colitis patient, who did not intrude. Perched on the side of the hospital bed, the devout Oblate quickly came to terms with his situation, although with his hospital-chaplain experience, he knew exactly how bad colon cancer can get. What he was troubled over was whether to have surgery. He had seen surgery deplete patients like himself, who didn't seem all that sick until operated on, after which they lingered in hospital rooms in an unpleasant condition for months before death.

As he pondered, his thirty-five-year-old roommate suddenly interrogated, "Didn't you hear what the doctors said? If that was me, I would have fainted."

Father Kelley shrugged matter-of-factly, "What can I do about it?" and went back to his thoughts, which turned to reviewing his life and searching his soul in the face of the final hour suddenly soon to come.

He was interrupted again by another priest walking into the room. Gregarious Father Kelley was already on good terms with Holy Redeemer's chaplain. This was not he. Whoever the priest was, it was clearly Father Kelley he was here to see, for the visitor walked straight to his fellow priest.

Dressed in the standard clerical black suit with vest and white collar, the visiting padre was slightly built, a short man no older than late forties or early fifties. Gentle in manner, he seemed in no hurry, Father Kelley recalls.

Being experienced at visiting sick strangers, Father Kelley was struck that the priest didn't identify himself, something any priest making a hospital call of this type does right away.

But there was no time for queries, for the visitor started right in, "Father, I understand you have a tumor. I have a relic of Blessed John Neumann."

Father Kelley recalls "then he touched me around my appendix area and touched my lips with what I assumed was a relic of St. John Neumann." When Father Kelley says he "assumed" the visitor had a relic in his hand, it's because a Catholic chaplain with a saint's relic may offer it like this for a patient to kiss. Later Father Kelley would say thoughtfully, "When I look back on it, I could swear he had no relic because his fingers — nothing else

— touched my lips." Since any part of the body of a saint is a first-class relic, perhaps both the oblate priest's first and later impressions are right: If this priest was a dead saint, his finger was indeed a relic.

After blessing Father Kelley, the black-suited priest walked out. In spite of the fact that he did not act like a person in a hurry, he still had not identified himself.

Bothered by that, Father Kelley ran his visitor's description by all the nurses, since they knew all the local priests who dropped by the hospital to visit parishioners.

"Gee, Father, he doesn't sound like anyone we know," the nurses agreed. Nor had they seen anyone who fit the description.

Bishop John Neumann

He asked the chaplain, who also drew a complete blank.

And finally he asked his brother Martin, who had worked at Holy Redeemer for many years and could name any priest who regularly walked its halls.

"I thought I knew everybody here," Martin said, shaking his head.

Still Father Kelley knew better than most people how a priest may be called to see someone at a hospital he usually doesn't visit, or drop in at an additional room while on such a call. Although he could discover no one who had sent the relic-bearing priest to bless him, nor who the guy might have been, he put the mystery out of his thoughts.

That a priest in Philadelphia would have a relic of Neumann was not odd. Since Father Kelley was born in Philadelphia (on Christmas Eve, 1923, to a couple named Mary and Joseph, he chuckles, recalling his father's delight in telling the story), he was familiar from boyhood with local regard for the city's nineteenth-century Bishop.

If Neumann could help, great.

The ill chaplain went back to reviewing his life and thinking about what to do.

One decision was easy. Being in the Navy, he was obligated to transfer to

Philadelphia Naval Hospital, which he did the next day, taking his medical reports with him.

The Naval physicians were blunt: Surgery must be done immediately. On October 6, however reluctantly, he was on the operating table. The news after the operation was bad: What the doctors called a Dukes class B (A being better) tumor of the colon was in an advanced stage. It had eaten through the intestinal wall and erupted into his hip, releasing its deadly cells to create more tumors in other parts of the body.

Although the colon tumor was removed, the question was how to fight the cancer silently working in new areas. To try to trace the malignant enemy, his doctors used bone scans, liver scans, bone marrow biopsies, and other tests. Chemotherapy, they judged, would be no help. Instead, that December over a period of two weeks, four-thousand-five-hundred rads of radiation were pumped into the area around the chaplain's appendix — purely as a precaution, since the tumor was removed and all efforts had failed to pinpoint new cancer sites.

The radiation made him deathly sick. Vomiting and unable to eat for months, his normal weight of one hundred sixty pounds dropped to one hundred twenty-three before he decided to stop weighing.

As he had feared, after the surgery he remained hospitalized, weeks stretching into months. Still, ill as he was — from medical procedures like radiation as much as disease — he had no pain. And instead of dying — perhaps because so many people were asking God to help him, including families of "the couple hundred kids" he'd taught in religious education classes at his last assignment — he amazed everyone by getting better instead of worse. In fact, after five months of inactivity frustrating for such an active person, Father Kelley felt pretty good.

So good that by March, 1976, he was released from the hospital to undertake a limited assignment at the Chief of Navy Chaplain's Office in Washington, D.C. Certainly his new post was not as rigorous as his three tours of duty in Vietnam, his two sea duties on navy vessels, his assignments on Marine bases in San Diego and Parris Island, his postings at naval bases and hospitals in Florida and New York, or even his pre-chaplain work as coach, teacher and athletic director at Duffy High School in Niagara Falls, New York. Still, it was good to have work to do again — even if only until the new tumors doctors predicted showed up.

But at his frequent checkups, to his doctors' amazement, there were no new malignancies.

That May, however, as he moved — tumorless — toward once more resuming full duties, something hit the chaplain hard. Father Kelley still subscribed to Philadelphia's *Catholic Standard and Times* to keep up with the church in his hometown. When he picked up the paper that day, there was a picture of Bishop Neumann, who was to be canonized.

"Oh my Lord," he gasped, "it sure looks like that priest who came in to see me."

From that moment, he says, "I became very involved with Bishop Neumann." Struck once again by the oddity that the priest who had him kiss the "relic" hadn't identified himself, he began some personal research as to whether the unknown priest visitor could have been from one of the parishes around Holy Redeemer. He found no one who fit the bill.

Since then he carries a relic of the dead Bishop, with which he blesses others in his hospital calls or when he occasionally gives talks on the saint. He also prays a novena in Neumann's honor daily, asking the saint's prayers for those he ministers to as well as for himself.

Father Kelley believes John Neumann helps him help others. For instance, in August, 1991, he visited a longtime helper in the Parris Island Catholic educational programs, who was in the hospital. As usual he had with him his first-class relic of St. John Neumann. Mary Oenbrink, wife of a military dentist, had been diagnosed with a Dukes class C cancer of the colon that had spread into the lymph nodes. In other words, her cancer was even more advanced than Father Kelley's had been. After surgery, her doctors wanted to do both chemo and radiation, but Mary elected, she says, "to pursue no other treatment." Father says he did not know her diagnosis, for he did not ask what was wrong with her. ("Ask a woman and she may tell you in great detail," he grins, "so I learned years ago never to ask.") But he said a prayer for Mary and had her kiss the relic. Then he said a novena to St. John Neumann, asking the saint's prayers for her good health. Almost three-and-a-half years later — having taken no medication and having had none of the recommended treatments — Mary Oenbrink's tests all "register normal." Of course many people prayed for Mary's recovery, but Father Kelley thinks St. John Neumann's prayers are worth mentioning.

His brother, Martin, obviously can't say whether over the past twenty years his sibling has had no new tumors because he once kissed the finger of a dead saint; but Martin does have a firm opinion that — given the medical diagnosis and prognosis of his brother's case — something "miraculous" occurred.

Retired since 1986 only because the navy has a mandatory age sixty-two retirement for chaplains, and as busy as most working priests, Father Kelley still prudently makes time for check ups.

Recently he went in for his regular examination. The doctor looking him over was not a Catholic and knew nothing about Father Kelley's experience with the priest the retired chaplain believes was St. John Neumann. Shaking his head over his patient, the physician said, "you should have had many tumor recurrences."

Then he told the Catholic priest, "You know, you're a miracle."

16 ✇ A Sick Little Boy's Best Friend

December, 1982

The Intensive Care Unit
Children's Hospital, Philadelphia

Nancy and Chuck McGivern look at each other in shock. Surely this cold-as-death, plaster-white, motionless form with the Frankenstein-like, pressure-relieving bolt in its skull cannot be their healthy, seven-year-old son!

But in his tangle of I.V. lines and monitors, Charles Junior — Chucky, they call him — continues a mad free-fall, from being a kid home from school with chicken pox on Thursday, to a dying hospital patient with a dangerously-swelling brain by Sunday.

Aspirin, ordered by his doctor for fever, has triggered Reyes syndrome, which hits the central nervous system and attacks liver and kidneys. At least fifty percent of kids with Reyes die and survivors often are brain-damaged. Chucky's case is so severe that to move him from their local Philadelphia hospital to Children's has taken a nurse "breathing" for the comatose child by means of a pump.

Trying to "remain upbeat," Chuck Senior clings to hope, when the doctors go from giving Chucky a one-in-ten chance to live to saying, more and more firmly as three days pass, that there is *no* hope, since the kidneys are going and pneumonia has already collapsed one lung. Nancy, on the other hand, is so sure the youngest of her two sons is going to die that, to ease her agony with the knowledge other kids will have better lives, she has already agreed to give away Chucky's usable organs.

Visiting family speak of prayers being said all over, even by strangers, and in the McGivern's Catholic parish, St. Martin of Tours. But a fat lot of good those prayers are doing.

Then suddenly, what Chuck and Nancy call "weird things" start happening around their dying child. Things his parents try to ignore by mutual agreement. As Chuck says to Nancy in the hospital cafeteria — and Nancy wholeheartedly seconds — such things are scary.

First and easiest to explain away is the picture. Sunday afternoon, one of Chucky's team of twenty-five physicians enters the second-grader's room while Nancy and Chuck are standing by the bed. As the doctor repeats firmly that the medical team can give them no hope of Chucky's recovery, Nancy has to turn her eyes away. Her startled gaze meets that of the fourth Bishop of Philadelphia, who died in 1860. In an eight-by-ten on the wall across from the foot of Chucky's bed, the Bishop — St. John Neumann — stands with outstretched arms in front of that city's St. Peter's Church. On shiny paper, as if from a magazine, the picture, which reproduces an actual photograph, is blank on the back.

Neumann's likeness, which wasn't there before, seems to have been put up by a child, Nancy notices, because it is crooked and has been stuck up using some kind of white masking tape that is all wrinkled, as if inept little fingers have struggled with the tape.

"How did that get here?" Nancy wonders. Perhaps because its sudden appearance startles her, she asks everyone with access to Chucky's room — doctors, nurses, her relatives, Chuck's family — but no one knows anything about the eight-by-ten photo of the dead saint. Positioned to look down at Chucky, it has simply appeared out of nowhere. Of course, she tells herself, someone has to have put it up. Why don't they just admit it?

What happens next is harder to explain away.

A friend sends two relics. These happen to be relics of St. John Neumann, who so loved children he kept his pockets filled with candy and built the first American Catholic-school system for them. One relic is in cloth and the other is enclosed in a special relic case. The relic in the case Nancy puts over Chucky's head on top of one of the many machines he is hooked to. The relic in cloth she threads on a large safety pin with a Sacred Heart scapular and a St. Anne's medal other people have given — the Sacred Heart a visible reminder of the Savior's love, and the medal and relics representing the prayers for Chucky by God's saints in heaven joining prayers ascending from earth. This collection Nancy pins to her son's pillow to the right of his lifeless-looking little head.

On Monday when she enters the room, she notices the cloth relic of St. John Neumann is face down on the pillow, while the scapular and medal are face up as she left them. She takes the pin off and turns the Neumann relic face up like the others.

As Chucky's condition is now extremely critical, Chuck and Nancy are permitted in their son's room every fifteen or twenty minutes. After this short an interval, when Nancy returns to Chucky's bedside she finds the Neumann relic face down again. This jolts her, for in order for this to occur, the safety pin had to be unpinned, the other sacramentals taken off, the Neumann relic removed and physically turned over, then all of them rethreaded and the pin once more stuck through the pillow case and closed. Nancy does all this again without calling her husband's attention to it. She confesses years later, "I was afraid he'd think I'd lost it."

But when it happens a third time, she tells Chuck. And the next time they enter the room, he verifies that yes, something very bizarre is going on with that relic. When questioned, the nurses and other medical personnel are adamant: They have not touched it. Why would they?

Still, neither McGivern assigns any supernatural meaning to the relic's antics. Down-to-earth people, Chucky's mom and dad are praying for Chucky's life to be somehow spared, but they are not the sort to look for "signs."

That afternoon's visitors include Nancy's cousin, Jerry. After seeing Chucky, Jerry takes something out of his wallet. It is another relic: St. John Neumann again.

"This relic means a lot to me," he says, handing it to Nancy. "I really believe it helped me recover in my accident years ago in the service." Touched, Nancy has Jerry wait right there while she gets another safety pin from the nurse. She pins this relic of the Bohemian-born saint to the left side of her comatose son's head. So now Chucky has relics — all of St. John Neumann — to his right, to his left, and above his head.

Aware of how important the Neumann relic is to Jerry, Nancy assures him he will get the relic back. With a bravado she is far from feeling, she even promises Chucky himself will hand it back to Jerry. But the very next day this relic, too, calls attention to itself. Although pinned to the pillow, it disappears. Nurses join Nancy's frenzied search. Even the previous day's dirty bed linens are tracked down. All fruitless. Nancy feels terrible. But Jerry is less upset: he senses the relic has disappeared for a reason.

After that, there is the matter of the child. As Chuck and Nancy sit with other anxious parents in the waiting room on Tuesday, a ten- or eleven-year-old boy with dark, shaggy hair and dark-rimmed glasses steps in the door. The kid, Chuck says years later, is dressed "like he's going out to play baseball or something — kind of scruffy or poor." The boy looks around for a minute or two, glances at the ubiquitous hospital TV, meets Chuck's eye, and then walks out. Children's Hospital is built with so many interior walls of glass that even from the parents' waiting room outside the ICU, Nancy and Chuck can see Chucky's room. Chuck — until his thoughts wander elsewhere — idly watches the boy walking down the hall toward the intensive care rooms.

Not much later, a nurse enters the waiting room where the McGiverns are greeting Nancy's uncle.

"I think you should know we've had a little problem," she tells them.

While two doctors bent over Chucky, she explains, one looked up and saw, to his astonishment, a boy no more than three or four years older than Chucky in the doorway.

"What are you doing here?" the startled physician asks.

"I came to see my friend Chucky."

"How'd you get in?"

"I'll come back later with my mommy," the boy says, and runs out.

Children's Hospital of Philadelphia has tight security. No one just strolls in — and certainly not into its ICU. It takes a special pass to even get on the floor and there are security guards stationed by the elevators. Plus the child would have had to get past the nurses in the intensive care unit, where everything is designed for easy watching. Considering where Chucky's room is, it seems impossible that a child could arrive there undetected. So, eyeing Nancy's uncle suspiciously, the nurse wonders aloud if the child has come with an adult visitor of the McGiverns and — the implication "unwisely" hangs in the air — been sent unaccompanied down to Chucky's room.

The answer is a definite no.

But Chuck has seen the kid. "Remember, Nancy?" he asks.

Nancy doesn't remember. Although she was there, she saw no child in the waiting room. Then Chuck asks the other parents sitting there when the boy made his circuit of the room. None of them saw the child either.

"The old hairs went up on the back of my head," Chuck Senior recalls years later.

He compares his description of the boy he saw to Chucky's physician's description. They tally exactly. Alerted, security guards comb the hospital, but the shaggy-haired, scruffily-dressed child, who could not have gotten in unseen — and certainly not unaccompanied — is never found.

"You're sure he called Chucky by name?" the physician is asked.

The doctor is positive.

So matters stand when about four o'clock that afternoon Chucky is anointed by Father Robert Roncase of St. Martin's. The family has not asked him to come. He just shows up. A very special young priest, Nancy feels years later, Father Roncase has never given the sacrament of the sick to a dying child before. Showering at the time, Nancy misses seeing him and is sorry. Not the most regular Mass-goer, she has never met Father Roncase.

So shortly after Chucky is anointed that Nancy is still drying her hair from her shower, a nurse phones the parents' waiting room.

Excitedly she burbles, "Mrs. McGivern, come see your son: He's starting to *move*."

At that moment, the first stirring of hope moves in Nancy too.

Running towards Chucky's room, she bumps into her husband, tells him the great news, and they hurry to their son's side.

For about five minutes they stare as Chucky appears lifeless. Then a little, white hand twitches. A second later, Chucky's arm reaches up to finger the fearsome bolt in his skull.

I'll never forget this moment, Nancy thinks.

By eight o'clock that night their youngster's blue eyes even open a couple of times. His deathly-white body begins turning pink and warming up to their touch. Sleepy nods "yes" or "no" answer questions appropriately, putting to rest the specter of brain damage.

The next morning by 8:00 A.M. all tubes and machines are gone except the basic I.V. and the head bolt. And the bolt is taken out before noon.

Nancy will never forget one doctor who — grasping only too well the hospital's very limited role in Chucky's recovery — comes into their son's room, eyeing the various tangible signs of faith surrounding the little boy.

"Who did you pray to?" he asks Nancy.

"Why?"

"I've never seen anybody so gravely ill recover this quickly."

She tells him they asked St. John Neumann to join their prayers that God heal Chucky. That she can do. But the word "miracle" can't cross her lips.

When Chucky went upstairs to bed with chicken pox Thursday, December 9, 1982, he says years later, the next time he knew what was going on around him, it was December 14. But in between — while he was in a coma and expected to die by those twenty-five physicians handling his case — his mind was not a blank.

In what he terms a "long dream that just went on and on," he was in bed in a hospital — only weak, not deathly ill. He had no dealings with doctors. Nor were his parents there. But he was not alone. In and out of the room in a constant stream, dozens of Asian children made the seven-year-old happy by leaving him presents. Also there were a nurse and a boy a bit older than Chucky. Unlike the others, these two were his helpers, who supported the second-grader when he had to walk or took him for shots to make him better.

This older boy, a non-Asian kid with shaggy-cut, dark hair, wore dark-rimmed glasses. He was, Chucky recalls, "my right hand man" and "best friend." Whereas the other children came and went, leaving their gifts without really interacting with Chucky, Chucky and his special friend communicated well. A true blue pal, this boy had a gift for Chucky, too: A bow and arrow. More important, he "was always in the room."

"I was kind of scared in my dream being in the hospital like that," Chucky says, "and he was there to make me feel better."

That was comatose Chucky's reality: A little anxiety, but a comforting best friend and tons of gifts.

When Chucky "wakes up" from his long dream, he finds himself also in a hospital room. In the corner are a few presents from relatives and friends. But the piles of gifts left by the Asian youngsters are missing. "Where are all the gifts I had?" he asks his jubilant, but exhausted, parents on and off for the next three days. They pay little attention. Their son's coma dream is not a priority. And it's near Christmas — a season when all kids have presents on their minds.

Feeling fine, Chucky doesn't understand why people seem almost in awe around him. And no one is comfortable explaining that, medically speaking, he should be dead.

Before they diagnosed him as hopeless, doctors said that if he recovered, the best they could hope for would be to have him home for New Year's. Chucky touches the bolt in his head late Tuesday afternoon and — to his physicians' astonishment — goes home only three-and-a-half days later on December 18. He is at St. Martin's School for part of the last school day before Christmas vacation. His classmates — who also have no idea how sick he's been — throw him a "welcome back" party.

Then come the delights of Christmas.

Not long after that, Chucky finds himself with his parents at St. Peter's Church in Phildelphia. No one has said anything to the seven-year-old about St. John Neumann nor has there been any use of words like "miracle" that might give a kid ideas something unusual has happened to him.

Chucky says today that's because at the time his parents themselves hadn't yet "put all the pieces together. They realized," he adds, "some unusual things had gone on, but they thought maybe this was just what happened when you had a kid so sick and you lose so much sleep."

But somehow Chuck and Nancy are drawn to go to St. Peter's — where St. John Neumann's body is enshrined — to tell God thanks for Chucky's life, and see the shrine. The visit, Chucky emphasizes, is not especially about St. John Neumann.

They are shown around by a man named Harvey Gorman. Chucky doesn't know exactly what a saint is, but as Harvey talks about Neumann, he finds it interesting. Still, "basically," he says years later, "I was just with my parents and walking around with them." Then the adults go into the gift shop, Chucky tagging along.

Suddenly the second-grader comes across a photograph on the wall with some words under it he can't read.

"Mom and Dad," he points excitedly, "here's the kid in my dream — my best friend. He just doesn't have his glasses on." A second later the seven-year-old drifts away to look at something else.

But his parents and Harvey Gorman are stunned: The shaggy-haired boy in the photograph is St. John Neumann at about ten years old.

Suddenly, it seems there might be a very special reason why Chucky McGivern is alive and why his later follow-up tests for mental and physical capacities come out "perfect."

Remembering the unsolved mystery of the boy who appeared in the waiting room, Chuck Senior has to deal with the possibility he saw St. John Neumann too. A person who likes to keep his distance from "wonders," years later Chuck will only say carefully that the boy in the shrine photograph and the boy he saw are "similar." The face of the boy in the hospital seemed to him perhaps a bit less round and, as Chucky commented, minus the glasses.

Could the boy Chuck Senior saw in the hospital, Chuck and Nancy are asked years later, have simply been a friend of Chucky's — maybe a boy from their neighborhood?

"There were no kids in our neighborhood," Nancy explains "except a couple older girls across the street."

A classmate?

Hardly. Seven-year-olds don't pay hospital visits alone.

Could he have been an older friend from the school? Shy, Chucky had no known older friends. And the kids from the school did not know he was in the hospital. Because the prayers were asked that Sunday at St. Martin of Tours Church for Chuck McGivern, most people thought Chuck Senior was the hospital patient and that Chucky was just home with chicken pox. Even the parish priests were mixed up for some days.

All this points to the *possibility* — each must draw their own conclusions — that St. John Neumann, the Redemptorist Bishop of Philadelphia who died in 1860, came one-hundred-twenty-two years later to see Chucky McGivern in Chucky's coma "dream," leaving signs all over the place — from his photograph on a wall to his "misbehaving" relics and *perhaps* — as final confirmation? — also appeared in the halls of Children's Hospital.

If it was Neumann, some may wonder why he came as a child instead of in heavenly glory? Those familiar with the simple, unassuming Neumann chuckle that "heavenly glory" would hardly suit a Bishop who stands happily in the back of the church and lets a priest who loves the limelight preside on a major occasion. Coming as a child's "best friend" would be much more Neumann's speed. Even the cure being triggered through the young priest's anointing has the Philadelphia bishop's self-effacing style about it.

Obviously the McGiverns make no claims. But if God did give Chucky McGivern a miracle through St. John Neumann, we would expect a miracle's usual telltale trail of sweet "fruits" to follow the cure. Here are two aftereffects you may think qualify.

Before his illness, Chucky was an extremely shy child, often off in a world of his own. After the illness, his parents noticed a big change. Although he had been through the trauma of serious medical procedures — something so expected to jolt children psychologically that the Children's Hospital in my city routinely assigns mental health people to teams for many illnesses — Chucky was, if still quiet, much *less* withdrawn, more smiling and "tuned in." His grandmother crowed happily, "he just doesn't seem like the same child."

Nancy feels she and Chuck had new, better priorities, too. To mention just one, while Nancy had been a believer, her son's illness brought her faith alive: From being an irregular church-goer who attended sometimes from a sense that she "had to," she became a woman who went to Mass regularly because she "wanted to." She even went on a pilgrimage.

He has never dreamed of St. John Neumann again, Chucky says, adding cautiously "as far as I know." But the nineteen-year-old student at La Salle University is not cautious at all about saying that when he needs a friend to pray for him, the dead Bishop of Philadelphia always tops his list.

17 ❧ "I'll Find Someone to Help My Girl"

lice Topping, born February 10, 1932, was a much-loved, only child in the north England household of her parents and grandmother. An Anglican family, Alice went to Sunday school, attended church services, and participated in church youth activities in the city of St. Helen's (northeast of Liverpool) where the Toppings lived. Faith was not just for show, either. From a very early age, the child was especially aware that her grandmother — who frequently quoted the Bible — had a deep faith life.

Alice grew up, married registered nurse Frank Jones, had daughters Alison and Lesley, and by 1960 at age twenty-eight was happily making a career change from personnel work to primary-school teacher. She and Frank were now living in the smaller town of Haycock in a large Victorian house, but she remained very close to her family in nearby St. Helen's.

In 1968 her father died suddenly on September 23, the same day that the Catholic world mourned the death of Padre Pio. But Alice Jones, now a teacher at St. James Anglican school, knew nothing of Padre Pio. As the 1970s began — "always fit and well" — she loved her job and, in addition, recalls, "I was very active, looking after my family, and also my mother and grandmother."

As for church or a spiritual life, all that had sort of fallen to the side. Teaching at their school, she did attend services at St. James now and again, and saw that her daughters were confirmed there, but it was Frank, her husband, who was the more regular church-goer. Alice felt no lack. In her view, life for the four generations of the Jones-Topping extended family simply flowed along, busy and good, until what began as an ordinary day in March, 1973, suddenly changed everything forever. Let Alice tell it in her own words:

> My classroom was being renovated, and I moved with my class
> of thirty seven-year-olds into the parish room of the church, which
> was used as a dinner room for the children. On March 27 at 2:35

P.M. I was instructed by the head teacher to stack the tables in readiness for a meeting that evening. I was then to take the pupils into school for the music lesson. As I began to move the heavy tables, two boys began to fight, and one of them ran into me. I swung away from his face but fell on the central heating pipe, still clutching the table. I could not get up. There did not seem to be any power in my legs. I had a severe pain in my back and a member of staff took me home.

Frank came off duty and immediately called in my own doctor, who ordered bed rest and drugs for the pain. After a month I was referred to Dr. Heron, the Consultant Orthopaedic Surgeon. I was put into a corset, and was then seen at monthly intervals. I did try to resume my career, but each time I was defeated by extreme pain. In March 1974, it was agreed that I should have surgery, and I was admitted to Broad Green Hospital in Liverpool. At the operation, the surgeons found debris in the spinal canal, but much more serious was the discovery of a neurofibroma [a benign connective-tissue tumor of the nerve fiber] which had become trapped during my accident. They were unable to remove the tumor, so a hole was drilled in the base of the spine to allow a little more freedom within the canal.... I appeared to make a good recovery, although the pain was still there. I returned to my post in September, but found that I was unable to continue with my teaching career.

Whereas life had simply trundled along from one blessing to the next, suddenly troubles began to pile up with equal ease. Just when she needed their support, her ninety-three-year-old grandmother died and her mother, to whom she was very close, suffered a heart attack. Then in January of 1975, her trusted physician, Dr. Heron, died suddenly, a real blow to Alice, who relied on his medical judgments. Her new orthopedic man, she says:

... tried various treatments, epidural injections, and manipulations, but my condition continued to deteriorate. He suggested a spinal fusion operation to stabilize the spinal column. I was starting to fall, my left leg was very weak and there was no feeling in my foot. We talked it over with my family, and eventually I agreed to surgery.

In November 1976, I went into St. Helen's Hospital and had the operation. I was totally encased in plaster of Paris for 14 weeks. I spent Christmas and New Year in hospital, but we all believed that the operation would be a benefit to me. I was turned every 4 hours by a crane, the plaster cast was very heavy, and very uncomfortable.

In February 1977, I came home, still in pain. Any movement in my left leg had gone. I was totally devastated and began to lose hope. Five other patients also had the same spinal fusion and, like me, they all had problems.

In November 1977, I had to be re-admitted to hospital, with an infected donor area, where they had removed the bone from my right hip to transfer into my spine. Another operation followed, and the infected site was drained. The pain now was very acute and I had to rely on more powerful drugs. I used crutches to walk and wore a spinal brace.

I was re-admitted to hospital for traction in January 1978. It was from this time that I began to experience spinal spasms in the muscles, which used to contract, and I felt unable to breathe. I was sent home and felt totally useless.

In order for her to walk at all, she needed a metal contraption called a calliper on her left leg. This was a kind of support that went down one side of the leg, under the foot, and up the other. Springs around the ankle and knee lifted the foot as she moved, but the whole device was heavy and cumbersome. She writes:

I tripped easily and found that the safest place was on the floor. I developed a deep ulcer [from the calliper] in my left heel, which Frank dressed daily. I was embarrassed by the smell which accompanied the discharge. In a last attempt to regain some mobility, we paid for a consultation with a Neuro-Surgeon in Liverpool. He said that I had had too much surgery, and there was nothing he could do. He could only suggest further drugs. I gave up hope, and sank into despair. At this point, I really wanted to die. It was only the love of my family that really kept me going....

The use of the heavy drugs to ease her awful pain at times created dreadful mental confusion. As if all this was not enough, something else happened that seemed the last straw. Alice told me:

The first of April 1979 is a day that I will never forget. My mother, who was ill, came to visit. I was lying on the floor as usual. She said, "Alice, I feel that I have boarded the train for Heaven. I am only waiting for the Master to take me out of the station." I was angry and shouted, "You can't die," but she smiled at me and said, "I will find someone to help my girl."

We spoke no more about this, but the following Friday, April 6, Frank found my mother dead in bed. She was clutching a religious card. It said "Jesus Himself drew near and went with them."

Today Alice sees significance in this final message of her mother's — a woman who, like Alice's grandmother, had a deep love of God. But at the time, believing the bond between them snapped, Alice was devastated. "I cannot begin even now," she says, "to tell anyone how I felt: it was like a deep wound." She put no stock whatsoever in her mother's selfless promise to find and send help.

On the contrary, feeling abandoned, Alice says:

I went down hill rapidly. I was angry and turned against God, blaming him for all our misfortunes. I refused to attend church, and even refused Holy Communion on several occasions.

The birth of a grandson was "a spark of light," but basically, she says, the next year — the seventh since her 1973 accident — "passed in bitterness."

Not that she cared, but 1980 was the centennial of the Anglican Diocese of Liverpool, within which the Jones family lives. Every church made some special plans for the celebration. At St. James, the family's parish, where she had once taught in what now seemed to be a never-to-be-recaptured life, Alice recalls:

In May ... two priests were invited to speak to the congregation. One was Father Gabriel, from the Community of the Resurrection, at Mirfield, Yorkshire, and the other was Father Eric Fisher, from Buxton in Derbyshire. The latter was reputed to be a healer. Friends begged me to see Father Eric but I was adamant. I was bitterly opposed to any thought of faith healing.

On the evening of May 18, our parish priest phoned to say that Father Eric would visit the following morning. Frank accepted the offer, but I became quite angry, vowing not to see him. However, the following morning, he arrived on my doorstep, and I told him "no sermons" and raised my crutch to emphasize that I had no time for him. We began to talk and I was able to pour out my bitterness and pent-up emotions, laying the whole blame on God's shoulders. I really made a good confession.

For those who wonder, Alice clarifies she does not mean she received the sacrament of confession. She wasn't ready for that. But in her anger, she simply poured out her feelings, which Father Eric accepted, she recalls today, "with great gentleness." At the end of the bitter invalid's tirade, the Anglican healer gave her his blessing. That she had released so much anger was, of course, all to the good. While anger can be a help in illness when it motivates someone to struggle against a disability, the anger of despair can block healing. Not because God rejects the angry, but because those filled with despair's anger reject God and God's blessings. With all those festering feelings lanced, as it were, Alice remembers that the visiting priest:

> ... placed his hands on my back, and I felt heat and a radiating warmth. He left but the pain was still there and the disability. I treated the whole episode as a waste of time. The next morning I was surprised to find Father Eric on my doorstep again. He told me that during [his prayer for the sick] ... he had been told to come back to me. He then told me to remove my calliper, which I promptly refused to do, so he knelt down and began to undo the straps. I undid the strap at the top of my leg. Then he began to pray. And there was a sharp pain running the whole length of my leg and my foot felt like fire. I shouted for him to stop and, as I looked down, he seemed to change. There was an older face, almost like a negative photograph in front of the priest's face. I looked away. Then I was aware of another man in the room, standing by me. I presumed it was the other visiting priest, Father Gabriel.
>
> The man in the brown robe blessed me three times, saying "Jesu Maria!" Then he took my arm, and said "In the name of Jesus — walk!" I left my chair and walked across the room. Looking round, I noticed that my "visitor" had gone, but Father Fisher was still kneeling [in prayer]. I was so overcome with emotion that I passed no comment. I wept with joy and strangely I could only think that I had no shoes to put on. My shoe with the calliper would no longer fit my foot. So when Frank phoned me, I told him that I was walk-

ing and intended to go into town for shoes. He was very alarmed [fearing a drug induced hallucination or other medical problem] and begged me not to go out alone. When he came home later, I ran down the drive to meet him, and he almost passed me by. He did not recognize me until I called out to him.

Later that evening we went to a Healing Service at church. All the congregation were absolutely amazed. It was a time of great emotion. I looked around for my visitor, and then it gradually dawned on me that I had had some kind of mystic experience. When we arrived home, I told Frank that I had seen Moses!! He advised me to go to bed. I think he believed that I was hallucinating.

The next morning, Frank was going to dress my heel. I raised my leg and there was nothing. My ulcer had gone. The skin was completely clear. We both looked in astonishment. It was the first time that Frank used the word "miracle." We both wept.

Besides the completed physical cure, Alice Jones was still in the midst of receiving a cure of heart and spirit as well. She continues:

At 9:30 I went to church to receive Holy Communion. Everything looked different. Colours were clearer. And for the first time, I became aware of the true meaning of the Eucharist. I "saw" in my mind Christ's Suffering on Calvary. It was like being a witness to the Crucifixion. Heaven and earth became united in that moment. I stood in awe of the tremendous sacrifice for me.

How did this all happen to her — a bitter woman who had lost any faith she ever had in God's mercy and/or healing power? Today she feels that her mother when in heaven ran to the Savior, as she promised, to get help for her girl. And He sent a trusted friend. Alice writes:

On leaving church, Father Eric gave me a prayer card. And I instantly recognized my visitor — Padre Pio. I was content. I realized that he was a person and not someone I had dreamed up in my mind. I went home rejoicing.

Since one can — especially when taking heavy medication — as Alice feared, "dream up" things in the mind, I asked Alice what her previous experiences were with Padre Pio. She answered "none"; she had never heard of him until he appeared in her home to tell her, in Christ's name, to walk.

She didn't know about after-death appearances of saints, either. For when she learned the same day she received the prayer card that Padre Pio was dead, she got very upset. She says, "I truly believed I had become involved in Spiritualism and ran all the way back to church." Father Eric had gone back to his church in Buxton. But Canon Wilson, the St. James' priest, "a wise old man," she says, explained she had just had a vision in her moment of extreme joy — something that can happen, he soothed — and encouraged her not to worry about it.

The newly-alive woman went home determined to put that part of her cure "out of my mind." But "Padre Pio had other ideas," Alice says now. She found herself more and more curious about the dead mystic. Finally she and Frank went to visit Father Eric in Buxton, seeking information on one she today calls "my heavenly friend."

That November, on the advice of the Anglican priest, Alice and Frank journeyed to San Giovanni Rotondo. There a number of things took place: she found the answers to many spiritual questions. Her

courtesy Alice Topping

Her health restored, Alice Topping tries to bring hope to others suffering illness or in pain.

case became part of the archival material on Padre Pio. And the Anglican Englishwoman was enrolled as a spiritual child of the dead Italian Catholic who, she now believes, was sent by God to her at her mother's prompting.

What about medical verification of her cure? Her English doctors preferred not to go on record about "faith cures." Then, before her trip to San Giovanni Rotondo, she met Dr. Francis Mooney, "a highly respected forensic pathologist" from St. Helen's who was interested in taking an objective look at Alice's claim of having received a miracle. Dr. Mooney took her to Providence Hospital in 1980 for X-rays and other tests on her spine; then he prudently had all the test results — and Alice — examined by another physician, a Dr. McCarthy. The results, Alice says, left both men "dumbfounded." The open-minded medical men concluded, Alice jubilantly quoted to me, "that there had been supernatural intervention in the disease." They said this because with their own eyes, they saw two things: first, the X-rays reveal a badly-deformed spinal column[1] that made it clear the patient could only walk with the help of devices like crutches and callipers. The physicians also saw Alice not only walk unaided, but bend, stetch, run, and hop — things her X-rays "prove" she can't do.

Things she smilingly says, "I do, thanks to God and Padre Pio."

So when not running and hopping to startle medical men, how does Alice Jones spend her time today? For starters, the Anglican lady has an active spiritual life that includes Holy Communion, the rosary, and earnestly petitioning God for Padre Pio's official sainthood. Devoting her days to "making Padre Pio known in England," she talks to groups but prefers, Padre Pio relic in hand, to quietly visit the sick, especially "those with no hope." To such people and their families, she finds Padre Pio brings God's peace. And no one knows better than Alice, who once lived in despair, what that means.

ENDNOTES

[1] As for the neurofibroma, something interesting has happened there, too. Discovered in her first surgery and deemed impossible to remove surgically, the tumor, Alice told me when I asked about it in 1994, has not been mentioned in any X-rays taken since 1980. "It may seem strange," she says, "but I had not given much thought to its whereabouts, until you mentioned it."

18 ❧ THE PRIEST OF
THE GENTLE SMILE

B e sure the Lord gets the credit," Jolene Gil of Eunice, Louisiana, begs me anxiously at the start of our interview, a plea she repeats before we say good-bye. Not that she feels the prayers of Father Seelos' and others for her fourteen-year-old son, Brian Gil, are of no value — she herself has a prayer ministry — but because she wants to make certain no one becomes over-focused on those who pray and forgets the One prayed to.

God heals *all kinds* of people, I have learned in my researches. If I thought He only cared for "the devout," I could trot out the Gils as an example. As it is, I find their story a wornderful reminder that God is so responsive to those who steadfastly call on Him that sorting out who deserves "credit" for a healing becomes a reminder of how varied and many are the ways God showers His love and mercy on people — whether the person prayed for is to be healed or called home to Him.

Brian's story starts when Jolene and Nicholas Gil were considering adopting the little thirteen-month-old, the first of their four chosen children. The baby was pitifully sick at the time, suffering from bronchitis and pneumonia. Worse, the local doctor they asked to look him over heard ominous sounds in the baby's heart, which was beating way too fast.

The physician shook his head ruefully.

"Don't take this baby," he told the young couple. "You'll just end up with a lot of medical bills."

But Jolene said to God, "even if it's only for a few years and then we lose him, I still want him."

And the Gils adopted the sick baby anyway.

Only after the adoption went through did they take Brian to a heart specialist, who confirmed the first doctor's discouraging words: Brian did not have a healthy heart: In fact he had aortic stenosis, that is, a narrowing of the heart's aortic valve.

Surgery was not advised. Instead the new parents were urged to let their new son grow for as long as he could. At some point, probably as he entered his teens, the heart would demand medical attention. By then, hopefully, the boy would be more able to withstand the arduous surgery.

That was problematic at first, since the tyke suffered seizures so severe they lasted forty-five minutes — started, doctors thought, when he had a very high fever. But at the age of four, these ceased.

What he lacked in health, Brian made up for in personality. Bouts of ill health made him neither bad-tempered nor self-centered. Cheerful and very loving, the Gils' husky, brown-eyed, brown-haired child was easy to care for, although he could tease his siblings like any normal child.

By the time he was twelve the surgery doctors had foreseen when he was tiny could no longer be put off: Not only suffering a lot of chest pain, Brian was so short of breath he could take no more than four steps at a time. Doctors Terry Dean King and Myles Schiller, who saw the boy regularly in Opelousa, Louisiana, scheduled an operation at West Jefferson Medical Center in New Orleans to try to open his narrow heart valve.

Just before the Gils made the three-and-a-half-hour drive east to New Orleans, Jolene's mother, who lives in Opelousa, had a home Mass. Jolene was there, as was a friend known through the Cursillo movement. The friend took a relic of Father Francis Xavier Seelos (a Bavarian-born, Redemptorist candidate for beatification) off her own scapular and told Jolene to put it on Brian's. "Ask God to let Father Seelos pray for Brian's healing," the woman urged. And she gave them the phone number of the Seelos Center, next to St. Mary's Assumption Church in New Orleans, where Father Seelos was once pastor and where he is buried.

Jolene was asking *everyone* for prayer and already had Brian's name on prayer lists stretching from Texas to Florida — from those of the Carmelite nuns and the local Catholic charismatic group to the Protestant 700 Club and evangelist Benny Hinn's healing ministry. She laughed to her son that every time God turned around some angel must be telling him, "Here's

courtesy The Seelos Center, New Orleans, LA

Father Francis Xavier Seelos

some more prayers for Brian Gil." She gladly took the number and phoned the Seelos Center when they arrived in New Orleans.

The Center added a petition for Brian's healing to those in the basket kept on Father Seelos' grave in front of St. Mary's altar. Besides seeking Father Seelos' prayers in this fashion, the Center sent a volunteer, carrying the dead priest's mission cross, to the hospital to pray for Brian. Jolene found Mrs. Gerry Heigle a very sweet lady who really cared. Besides coming twice to pray for Brian, the Seelos Center volunteer kept in touch by phone to see how things were going.

They were going well. Jolene was amazed at how "the Lord took care of everything." She and Nickey arrived in New Orleans to find the free accommodations they'd been promised had fallen through and they didn't have the money for a hotel. But immediately they were called to the phone. Nickey's boss — who had no idea of any of this — was on the line: "I'd like to pay for your motel for five nights." During the next days, whenever money ran short for meals, someone would come along and press a fifty-dollar bill on Jolene. Even her clothes were taken home by a kind soul, washed, and returned. And when they left the hospital, money from friends and family had come in to the exact amount of Brian's entire bill, which they gratefully took away marked "paid."

The actual operation and its aftermath were less smooth. After surgery opened the aortic valve — which was only the size of a pen-point — Brian began hemorrhaging. It turns out he is a "free bleeder," as Jolene puts it; that is, he has a blood disorder that makes surgery very life-threatening. His doctors had to reopen their young patient's chest and pour scalding hot water inside him to try to stop the hemorrhage.

During that emergency, Jolene recalls being half-crazed in the waiting room, where many members from both Jolene's and her husband's extended families had joined them. Suddenly she saw a flash of light that she felt was supernatural. Angry at that moment, she groused at God interiorly, "I've done everything you wanted me to do. Don't come here. It's my child who needs you." Immediately the light disappeared.

Moments later, a relieved doctor came out and announced the bleeding had stopped.

The hospital priest, Father Prescott, also proved to be a great support during such times. "He even helped us to laugh," Jolene recalls with gratitude. But Father Prescott did get a little upset about one thing. Hospitals don't allow just anyone, even in a Roman collar, to disturb their patients. In charge of such matters, Father Prescott permitted other priests to visit if they were closely connected to a patient, such as an individual's parish priest. Two priests the Gils knew hoped to get over to New Orleans to see them. Neither made it.

But a smiling priest did come striding into the intensive care unit where Brian, as he recuperated from surgery, was enjoying a game of Nintendo with another kid.

This priest carried a crucifix that Brian noticed looked just like the one Mrs. Gerry had blessed him with, only bigger. The visitor asked the boys if they wanted to receive Jesus in Communion. They said "yes," so he fed them the wafer that Catholics believe is truly Jesus present. Then he prayed for both boys, touching the cross, Brian remembers, to the young, heart patient's head. Having finished the prayer — of which Brian can't recall a single word — the smiling priest turned and strode out again. He had not given his name.

The Gils thought Father Prescott had sent an assistant. But Father not only has no assistant, he was unhappy about this incident — the sort of thing that shouldn't happen in a well-run hospital.

Driving home in their van after the hospital released him, Brian, who was wide awake, became frightened because he saw the Virgin Mary.

"Mama, am I dying? Has she come to get me?" he asked Jolene.

His mom, who has visions herself, reassured him. Later when they were at home and Jolene had to insist, to Brian's disappointment, that he follow his doctors' instructions to rest when he wanted to play, he saw Mary again, this time splendidly crowned.

They did not know that while they faced the dangerous surgery in New Orleans, Father Joe Alexander back in Eunice, was asking the Virgin's intercession, promising if Brian came back alive the priest would consecrate this boy — who from his earliest years has spoken of being a priest — to Jesus' Mother. Which Father Joe did shortly afterwards.

But at that time, Jolene had a shock. For while they were in the church, Brian saw a picture of a priest and said, "Mama, that's the priest who prayed for me in the hospital."

"Why, Brian," Jolene sputtered, "that's Father Seelos."

His mother says Brian is an innocent, honest child, and the now-fourteen-year-old is firm about what he saw.

With so many prayers and so much supernatural support, one would think that Brian's heart would be strong as an ox. But God's ways are not always so simple. Brian is an unusual child, who once sent even his devout mother into a tizzy by confiding "I'd like to be crucified like Jesus." Not that he isn't also an ordinary boy. The nurses at West Jefferson loved the cheerful, brown-eyed kid who was so undemanding; but he cried once, complaining to his mom, "I'm so hungry and they won't feed me!"

Not long after the surgery, in December, 1992, Dr. Schiller gave the Gils bad news: Brian's valve had closed again. More surgery would have to be attempted — even with the bleeding problem that could kill him — because with the valve's tiny opening, the ever-more oversized heart's muscles, severely thickened from having to pump so hard, were creating new problems. This time there could be no simple effort to open the valve. It would have to be completely replaced — an undertaking with its own possibilities for complications.

"I'd like to operate in January," the doctor said.

"If it won't be bad for Brian, could you wait until February?" Jolene asked.

The doctor thought he could.

In her testimony submitted to the Seelos Center, Jolene wrote:

> We came back home and I told my family that I was tired of trusting the doctors, that I was putting my trust in God.

She and the family had sometimes watched Protestant evangelist Benny Hinn's healing crusades on television. When Jolene saw people apparently healed of physical problems by God through this man's prayers, she'd say to her oldest child, "See, Brian, it's possible." Then she read Hinn's book *Good Morning, Holy Spirit* with profit. "It opened my eyes," she says, "to the presence of the Holy Spirit I felt in and around me but which, until then, I couldn't identify." While she didn't agree with everything the evangelist had to say, and she worried that people would put their faith in Hinn rather than God, she was still happy to learn the healer was to come to Houston, Texas, in January, 1993. She would take Brian, Jolene decided, to Hinn's healing crusade.

While the decision brought criticism from some of her Catholic friends, it turned out to be a growth experience for Jolene. The Lord revealed to this cradle Catholic, she says, that she did not have to be either prejudiced toward, or afraid of, mixing with Protestants lest "they pull me into something cultish." God loved all people, she realized, no matter which religion they belong to.

Jolene worried that Brian needed faith to be healed.[1] But how to give a young boy who has just been through a harrowing experience that almost killed him this kind of faith? His mother tried varied ways. One was home prayer: The family prayed over their oldest child each night after saying the rosary and Brian often felt heat — many times a sign of healing — around his heart. One night Jolene recalls "I asked the Blessed Mother to come in and carry God's healing to Brian. 'Touch his foot, please,' I said to her — not out loud but inside. Although we all had our eyes closed, Brian and I both saw a flash of light just after that. Then Brian said, 'I feel somebody touching my foot and the warmth is going up to my heart.'"

Besides continuing to ask the Blessed Virgin Mary, Father Seelos, and "all the saints" to pray for Brian's healing — in order to build faith that healing miracles were *possible* — Jolene nightly read aloud to the family Bible passages on Jesus' healings. The four children, who are stairsteps each only a year apart — at this time, nine, ten, eleven, and Brian just turned thirteen — sometimes protested mildly, "Oh mama!" But Jolene was adamant, "sit down, hush up and listen." Nickey Gil is a man of serious faith but even he — a *cursillista*[2] — wondered if his wife was pushing things too hard.

For Jolene was putting God on the line. She knew, she says, you shouldn't put Him to the test. But on the other hand, His scripture says that faith can achieve healing. "I'm either going to look like a fool or your promises are going to come true," she goaded God. To use my less genteel words, the serious Southern homemaker was asking the Lord to put His money where His mouth was.

(In this, Jolene was acting in one genuine Catholic tradition. Twentieth-century beatification candidate Father Solanus Casey, for a recent example, used to encourage people to feel free to put God "on the spot" so long as they got out of His way by giving up worry and anxiety. "How wonderful are all God's designs for all who have confidence in Him," Solanus encouraged — and the American healer-saint meant this equally whether one was to be healed or enter the next life. Similarly, Franciscan James McCurry counsels it is always right to pray for healing, with the understanding that leaving this life for heaven can be a healing, too. Of course equally-holy people may decide to simply pray, "Thy will be done.")

During this intense period one of Jolene's close friends mentioned a book she had just borrowed called *Nothing Short of a Miracle*. Jolene writes in her testimony "the minute she mentioned the book to me, I could feel the Holy Spirit's anointing all over me; I knew the Lord wanted me to see something in this book." She asked to borrow it, but the friend was reluctant to loan something she had borrowed herself.

"Well, just bring it over before the crusade," Jolene asked.

About 5:00 P.M. the day before they were to leave for Houston to attend Hinn's healing service, Jolene was feeling the stress; if a miracle didn't occur, more surgery could not be postponed. Suddenly she had that same sense of the Holy Spirit. She looked out the window and saw a familiar car pulling into the driveway.

Her friend rushed in just long enough to hand Jolene the book and say, "I'll leave it with you until after the crusade."

"Let's go in the living room and see what the Lord wants to tell us," Jolene said to her kids.

"Gosh, the Holy Spirit's so strong," she exclaimed.

"I feel Him," Brian agreed. From the stress she felt and her great need, Jolene began to weep. She began flipping through the pages, reading a word here and there. Then she came to a chapter about a miracle.

She slapped her leg. "That's us! That's what we need!"

Brian grabbed her arm.

"I think you're going to be healed, baby," she crowed.

"I'm starting to believe you," her son replied.

Jolene began to read the story. Suddenly Father Seelos — whom she recognized from his picture on the relic given them — appeared to her, giving the homemaker his characteristic gentle little smile.[3] A second later he was gone. Shocked, she looked down at the book and realized the chapter was on cures given through the prayers of Father Seelos.

While they had asked God to permit Father Seelos to pray for Brian, and Brian believed Father Seelos had come himself to pray for him in West Jefferson Hospital, Jolene still was not particularly focused on Father Seelos. Given a prayer card asking this saint's intercession while they'd been in New Orleans, she had prayed that prayer no more than twice. But she could see now, that it was Father Seelos the book was meant to remind her of.

That night about midnight, she woke suddenly, as often happens to her, feeling the familiar presence of the Holy Spirit. At the foot of her bed, again with "a soft smile" stood Father Seelos. "He didn't say anything," she recalls, "he just looked at me with that gentle smile and then disappeared. I knew the Lord was trying to let me know that Father Seelos was praying for us."

The next day they took off for Houston and were among many at Benny Hinn's service. Jolene writes:

During the Our Father (we were singing) I had my arm around my son with my hand resting on his chest. His heart started beating very rapidly. It felt like it was going to jump out of his chest. And then all of a sudden his valve popped open. I felt it hit against my hand. And Brian felt it open up in his chest.

God had put some money down on those biblical promises of His.

When they returned to Eunice and prepared for the trip to New Orleans, Jolene stuck her spiritual neck further out. She told everybody that, yes, Brian was going to the hospital but he would not need surgery. They'd only be there three days, in fact.

"They all thought I had lost it," she laughs. Let her tell it:

> We went to the hospital and the doctor ran the tube up Brian's leg and into his valve to check it. Then he came out white like a ghost. He kept telling us he was sorry — that he must have mis-read Brian's x-rays. That the valve was open now. On the third day we came home with no surgery. Everyone was in shock. No one believes in miracles anymore.

She phoned the Seelos Center and left a thank-you message on their machine. Then she promptly forgot about Father Seelos again, until a day when she was on the phone with her cousin. Father Seelos' name came up and Jolene said, "If I mention Father Seelos, I get chills all over me and I feel the Holy Spirit." Her cousin said, "I'm getting the same thing." They began trying to figure out what God wanted to get through to Jolene. Suddenly she saw Father Seelos for a third time. Standing before her in the long, black cassock the genial Redemptorist wore during his missionary endeavors until his death in 1867 caring for yellow fever victims — a death he casually foretold in its precise details a year before it happened — the dead priest gave the Louisiana mother his usual gentle smile, but said nothing.

After that, Jolene felt she should contact Mrs. Gerry Heigle for a little cross touched to Father Seelos' relic that the volunteer had spoken about bringing Brian, then forgotten. The Seelos Center volunteer sent it at once. Today the cross — a smaller version, Brian says, of the one the priest he believes was Father Seelos blessed him with in the hospital — is kept in Brian's room, but Jolene takes it with her many times when, her kids in tow, she makes hospital calls to pray for the sick.

She also felt she should let the Seelos Center know in writing the role that the dead priest's prayers played in Brian's heart valve reopening. Her seven-page letter appeared in the Seelos Center bulletin in May, 1994, just in time for me to include the warm, compassionate Father Seelos in this new book.

As I write this, Brian still has a bum ticker, but his heart valve remains open. Without any further surgery, he can run and ride his bike — if not so far or long as his peers. At an age when many teens are hard for their parents to handle, he remains a cheerful, loving kid whose mom both laughs "I know everyone says their kids are special," and seriously insists Brian is "a special person through whom God works."

Prayers continue for the health of Brian's heart. But in the ways that matter most, Brian Gil may already be a very well young man.

ENDNOTES

[1] Actually, people either too young (infants) for faith or in deep comas have been healed, as have atheists who would not pray for themselves, but had someone else praying for them.

[2] One who has attended a retreat called a Cursillo, an intense, life-changing encounter with God.

[3] Asked whether he appeared in front of her or within her mind, Jolene says she and her spiritual director have tried to figure this out in regard to a number of visions she has had, but while she knows what she sees, she doesn't know how she sees it — whether interiorly or exteriorly.

19 ❧ "That Little Man Put His Hand on My Forehead"

The same issue of the *Father Seelos and Sanctity* bulletin that featured the Gils' experiences with Father Seelos asked prayer for two-year-old Rochelle Freeman, who had "an inoperable tumor." Rochelle, the daughter of David and Elaine (Abadie) Freeman of Marrero, Louisiana, it turns out, may also have seen Father Seelos.

In the summer of 1993, Elaine — barely home from delivering her third child — took Rochelle to the doctor, concerned that her middle child was lethargic — wanting just to lie around and watch TV, without appetite, and gradually losing weight.

What Rochelle's regular doctor found made the tiny girl a patient in Children's Hospital of New Orleans just two weeks later — that is, in August, 1993.

Children's Dr. Schorin was attempting to treat a firm malignant tumor called a neuroblastoma that was the size of a grapefruit and wrapped about the two-year-old's aorta. Pressing against it, in fact, so hard that the aorta was pushed out of its rightful position. Smaller tumors, common sidekicks to this sort of major mass, lurked in the child's bone marrow and behind her eyes, so that one eye slightly protruded. Staging cancer by how far it has progressed from a mild situation at stage one to "final" stage four, Rochelle's tumor was a four.

Dr. Schorin was blunt with the toddler's parents. "She will die of this."

But he assured them time could be bought with chemotherapy.

To start the particular chemo recommended by the hospital's tumor board, Rochelle was admitted for three weeks. Her little sister Kyla was just eight weeks old and her mom, who also had seven-year-old Jeffrey at home, was a working mother.

One day Elaine's mother-in-law, Mabel Freeman, was sitting with Rochelle at the hospital. When she stepped inside the bathroom attached to the child's room, Mabel could still hear clearly if someone came into the room or if anyone was talking to her granddaughter.

All was well, for she heard nothing in the few minutes she could not actually see the child.

But when she came out, Rochelle told her, "That little man put his hand on my forehead. He told me I was sweating. Then he put his hand on my belly."

Perplexed, the grandmother stuck her head out in the hall. She saw some nurses at their station, but no men. The doctors making rounds had been by long before and none were visible on the floor.

Yet Rochelle was adamant.

Later, when Mabel Freeman told her daughter-in-law about it, Elaine wondered if it could have been one of the saints they were praying to. These were principally Father Seelos, St. Jude, and St. Peregrine, the patron saint for cancer.

She decided to show Rochelle some pictures of different saints and ask, "Did any of these look like the man who visited you?"

Rochelle pointed to the picture of Father Seelos. Elaine had some other pictures of Father Seelos, different enough that a two-year-old might not recognize them as the same man. She mixed these in. Unerringly, Rochelle picked out every Seelos representation.

Maybe I just led her in some way, Elaine began thinking. Chagrined at the thought and tired after a long day at her job, she said, "You didn't really see anyone, did you?"

Rochelle was also weary — and she was getting tired of being pestered by her mother with all these pictures.

courtesy the Freeman family

"Mama," she said indignantly, "*this* is the man I saw." Then she went through the array of sacramentals pinned to her hospital gown, little relics and scapulars that had been put there by Elaine with no explanation to the child whatsoever, until she found a tiny relic of Father Seelos with his picture on it.

"*This* is the man," and again she whipped through the sacramentals until she found another Seelos relic. The two-year-old continued until she had pointed out each of the Father Seelos items and no others.

Elaine was moved, for she knew that no

Rochelle Freeman

one had named these tiny pictures to Rochelle. That same evening the doctor making rounds — a young resident — came in. He put his hand on the little girl's abdomen where the very firm, grapefruit-sized tumor was easily felt. He frowned. "I don't feel anything here. It is on the right side, isn't it?" he questioned Elaine, checking his chart.

The next scan showed the tumor was indeed still there. But beginning on the night when Rochelle insisted she was visited by Father Seelos, the hard mass had turned very soft. This, said Dr. Schorin, meant that the chemo was changing a thriving tumor into a sick one, whose cells were now disorganized and "on the run."

Elaine did credit the chemo. But she also credited prayer.

Among the many seeking Father Seelos' intercession with God for Rochelle was Seelos' fellow Redemptorist, Elaine's great uncle, Father Alphonse Abadie. Father Alphonse, who died in 1994 after a long period of suffering, including kidney dialysis, confided to the young priest who gave him the last rites that he was offering all his suffering for this little niece's cure through Father Seelos. Elaine is sure Rochelle now has two Redemptorists praying for her in heaven.

By February 1994, the main tumor had shrunk by a third, so it was now the size of a large orange. The tumors behind her eyes were gone. The malignancy in the bone marrow had been gone, but was now coming back. As this recurrence signaled that the bone marrow cancer might be resistant to the combination of drugs, these were changed.

That August, after a year's chemotherapy, the main tumor was reduced to the size of a large egg while the smaller tumors were all gone. The aorta was also back in its normal position.

The doctor reiterated that the chemo was doing its work.

"I believe it's prayers and chemo," Elaine said boldly.

In December Rochelle's doctors decided they could try to remove at least part of the shrunken tumor CAT scans had repeatedly shown wound about the child's aorta. During surgery the doctors were cheered — a minor miracle? — to discover the tumor and aorta were no longer attached. It was "child's play" to remove a malignancy that floated on abdominal viscera instead of melding into the aorta. They "got it all," although they could not guarantee no malignant cell was left behind.

To deal with that possibility, several severe measures were taken even though Rochelle was "in remission" following the surgery. First beginning in late January, 1995, small doses of radiation were given to the eye and abdominal areas where tumors had once been. Then as February came to a close, the child was hospitalized anew for chemo so intense it endangered every organ in her body. Other intravenous medications attempted to shield the nonmalignant parts of her body, while deadly chemicals coursed through it on a search and destroy mission for hidden neuroblastoma cells.

Because there had also been cancer in Rochelle's bone marrow, some marrow was harvested before it was completely killed off by radiation and the intense chemo. From previous treatment, what was harvested was only one percent malignant. That one percent was purged, then the marrow frozen. On March 1, 1995, Rochelle underwent a marrow transplant, receiving back her own, once-more-healthy bone marrow.

Surviving the critical one hundred days following these radical treatments, as summer arrived Rochelle smilingly took off the mask she had to wear against the germs and rejoined her siblings in a normal child's life. If she makes it past the one-year anniversary of her bone marrow transplant, her doctors agree she may be cured.

But even as they enrolled her to start school in the fall of 1995, her parents understood Rochelle's doctors did not expect that outcome. Considering she was in its "final stage" when her illness revealed itself, the medical men look for the neuroblastoma to return. Then there will be nothing more they can do.

A woman of spiritual depth, Rochelle's mother accepts that "God is in charge now" and He may know it best for a family or for an individual child to go to Heaven as a little innocent. Elaine Freeman notes, too, that "God uses these things to teach people." She can see that Rochelle's illness is mysteriously being used by God to change a lot of people. Still like any mother, Elaine is praying ardently for her child's healing. No longer accepting the medical prognosis of inescapable death, she follows the counsel of those like healer Sister Briege McKenna (who has prayed over Rochelle) to trust God and persevere in prayer.

And she hopes, as do many, that God sent Father Seelos to put a cure in motion when the dead Redemptorist dropped in, Rochelle believes, to soothe her brow and reassuringly pat her sick tummy.

20 ✑ DIVINE LOVE

Some saints so frequently see those from the next life that when they themselves turn up as God's messengers after death, it only continues a life lived in both worlds.

But there are equally genuine saints of a different ilk. Ones I jokingly imagine saying to God, "You're kidding, right?" if asked to make an after-death appearance. Take St. Madeleine Sophie Barat, for instance. In Burgundy, where Sophie Barat was born December 12, 1779, people traditionally distrust imagination or fantasy. The very look of the area's ordered rows of staked vines marching in perfect conformity across their land — less than a hundred miles, but a lifestyle world's away from Paris — is earthy, anti-mystical. So was the Barats' financially-comfortable lifestyle — the father a barrel maker, that most down-to-earth, essential trade in wine-making country. Sophie, the youngest of three children, inherited her father's practicality and steady good nature as much as her mother's fine intelligence and capacity for love. No one in the Barat family was prone to visions or supernatural experiences.

Had vivacious Sophie shown any mystical tendency, it would have been squelched at once by her severe, utterly humorless, eleven-years-older brother. Louis, who became a Jesuit and an educator, saw that his youngest sister — an obviously gifted child — could end up spoiled rotten by their mother, one of those women who, disappointed in marriage, look to their children for what is missing in their lives. Was Louis an instrument of the Holy Spirit? Perhaps. At any rate, when he was no more than eighteen, he exercised his prerogative as only son, seminarian, and Sophie's godfather, to elbow his mother aside.

Louis sat seven-year-old Sophie down and shoved a "boy's" schoolbook under her nose. While other little girls played and acquired a much less rigorous "woman's education," the littlest Barat grappled with French history, Bible history, grammar, arithmetic (including geometry), and physics. She mastered Latin and Greek, memorizing long passages from ancient authors like Virgil and Homer. Louis' idea of recreation — even as a child he never liked games — was to give the little girl lessons in modern languages like Italian and Spanish.

When Sophie was ten the French Revolution swept away this ordered, if demanding, world of her childhood. As a Jesuit, Louis was imprisoned and sentenced to die.

Although he was no longer hovering, Sophie never abandoned her studies, so much had her brother's iron will penetrated her soul; but she did add literature, delighting in novels like *Don Quixote*. When Louis unexpectedly returned alive[1] — and more determined than ever to serve an "iron God" cast in his own image — he was not pleased. He knew Sophie wanted to be a nun, preferably in the Carmelite contemplative order, rather than a housewife, but here she was reveling in books full of adventure and romance. Worse — with the family's older daughter now married — Sophie and her mother were once more so close that, with their tender natures, Louis feared neither would ever let go of the other.

Louis strongly suggested that sixteen-year-old Sophie return with him to Paris to continue her studies. She balked. Their mother wept. But implacable Louis bore his sister away. In Paris he soon destroyed any new leaning toward sentimentality or romance in Sophie's warm nature with stiff courses in scripture, theology, and the Fathers and the Doctors of the Church.

Intellectually, by the time she was twenty, her brother's protegee was a virile woman. Not that she was severe like Louis, prim or lifeless. The pupils of her own she had by this time adored her. A nephew later recalled a ramble along a river with his young, attractive aunt Sophie, who charmed the little boy with stories, memorized verses, and something in her personality that enveloped him in warmth and concern. All her life not only children, but adults of every type — from royalty to coachmen — would find in Sophie Barat this same genius for relationships. Hard on herself because Louis had ingrained that characteristic into her very soul, she lavished on others the thoughtfulness and tenderness basic to her being.

That she kept her winning liveliness and charm is a minor miracle. For Louis — who loved her, but was congenitally unable to do anything with a light hand — treated his sister's minor faults as grave sins and wanted her to pore over her every deed in search of impure motives, if not outright wrongdoing. At times he had Sophie so frightened she dared not go to Communion.

It is said everything works together for good for those who love God. Louis' carping did keep an extremely gifted young woman from becoming proud. But if he kept his sister from preening herself on her fine intellect, winning personality, and superior accomplishments, he also made her timid and insecure.

Perhaps because of the excellent mothering she received in Joigny, Sophie maintained her equilibrium anyway during four years under Louis' thumb in Paris by learning to laugh both at herself and — without unkindness — at his severity. A well-meant severity that perhaps also forced his sister into God's arms for comfort. At any rate, somehow Sophie learned God was not like Louis: God does not carp on our imperfections and sins, but reaches out to us with love and forgiveness.

Sophie as an educator would want children taught the horror of sin and a healthy fear of offending God, something missing from today's unbalanced teachings; but the major focus of her spirituality was God's love. All God's commands, for Sophie, are loving designs to make peoples's lives smoother.

The way of divine love became her official spiritual path in 1800, when she was inducted into a new post-Revolutionary religious order, The Society of the Sacred Heart. The order was not contemplative like Carmel, of which she had dreamed. Instead it would use her intellectual and spiritual training to educate and spiritually form upper-class girls,[2] hoping that if you molded them into upright souls, they would do the same for their sons and daughters to the benefit of their societies.

The priest who set Sophie to this work permitted her to give up those piercing self-examinations so dear to Louis. Thinking less of herself, her gaze turned more to Jesus. In this way, she was set afire with His love — a much better way, she found, to destroy one's sins.

Not patterning herself on Louis in educational theory, either, Sophie saw herself and all the Sacred Heart nuns not as taskmasters, but

courtesy the Society of the Sacred Heart

St. Madeleine Sophie Barat

as mothers who must bring up their pupils as their spiritual children. Named Superior of the new order when she was only twenty-three, for the next nearly sixty-three years, hers were the burdens of not just educator, but of foundress and administrator in a Europe racked by political turmoil. Houses would be established — she opened a hundred in her life — and then another revolution would put the nuns on the run.[3]

Her time in charge should have been brief, since she was found to have terminal cancer at age twenty-five.[4] Two years later she was instantly cured. Her daughters' prayers probably were responsible. Above all, she was a spiritual mother to this big group, 1,368 preceding her in death and 3,500 alive at her passing.

Some of those dead nuns had been very holy. There was one, for instance, at whose death miracles began. Sophie asked God to "knock it off." God obliged. But God — whose sense of humor is well-known to His friends — had His revenge: When Sophie died on the Feast of the Ascension in 1865 at age eighty-six, He started working miracles through *her* and sending her to counsel the living. Due to the miracle cures atop her Church-verified heroic virtue, the dead Burgundian became a canonized saint in 1925.

Later in this book, I detail the great cure of a spiritual daughter's deformed spine. Mentioned earlier was the 1907 after-death visit Sophie made in Madrid to the mother of visionary Josefa Menendez (1890-1923) which resulted in the cure of the dying woman. In the early 1920s the Lord sent down-to-earth "don't-give-me-any-of-this-miracle-nonsense!" Sophie to Josefa, a humble, much less educated woman who was so mystical she could hardly keep *one* foot in this world. This celestial "odd couple" met not once but many times, primarily at the monastery of the Sacred Heart (called *Les Feuillants*) at Poitiers, France, where Mother Barat spent many happy hours during her life. Visits that helped Josefa — who didn't *want* supernatural experiences that made her "different" and "suspect," but had no way to turn them off — keep her equilibrium. And which, through dead Sophie's counsels recorded in Josefa's diary, help the rest of us grasp divine mercy.

Josefa was ordered to keep the diary because of her experiences, which included very frequent visions of Jesus Christ, many of His mother, and a few of His saints — primarily Sophie and St. John, the beloved disciple. The order came from leaders in Sophie's Society of the Sacred Heart, in which Josefa, who had been a seamstress in Madrid, was now a lay sister. Her role: Backing up the order's teachers and administrators by humble tasks such as sewing the uniforms and First Communion dresses for the students.

Because of this diary, which helped her Superiors determine that she was a true mystic, rather than a fraud or a nut, I can report the visits of Mother Barat in Josefa's own words (translated into English):

> Today, the feast of our Blessed Mother [she refers to the feast day of Sophie who was then beatified — thus called "Blessed"], I went into her cell many times to whisper a little prayer to her, and once (I was in my blue working apron) I just stood for a moment and said "O Mother, once more I ask you to make me very humble, that I may be your true daughter."
>
> There was no one in the room and this little invocation escaped me out loud. Suddenly I became aware of the presence of an unknown nun. She took my head in her two hands, and pressed it lovingly, saying "My child, commit all your frailties to the Heart of Jesus and be faithful to the Heart of Jesus."
>
> I took her hand to kiss it, then with two fingers she made the sign of the Cross in blessing on my forehead, and disappeared.

This first meeting on May 25, 1921, was followed by many others up and down the cloisters of the old Cistercian monastery whose monks, driven out at the Revolution, had been replaced years later by Barat's nuns. Dead Sophie Barat acted as a spiritual mother to Josefa, counseling her just as her living Superiors did. Had this sort of thing happened to Sophie during *her* life, she would have found it very hard to deal with. Josefa, who had trouble accepting that Jesus Christ should take note of her, accepted her dead foundress' visits gratefully.

On March 14, 1922 alone in her cell Josefa fretted that she had been less than generous with Jesus, who both passionately attracted and terrified her, because she had to report every one of His frequent appearances to Superiors, who were not looking for "visionaries," but simple, devout nuns. As she was torturing herself that due to her latest "misdeed" based on this terror, she'd never see Jesus again, Mother Barat came to comfort her.

"Remember, daughter," she said, "that nothing happens unless it is in God's designs."[5] Josefa moaned that there was no way she could repair the consequences created by her weaknesses, most specifically that fervent desire to be safely ordinary while the Lord toyed with her in extraordinary ways.

"But my child, you can repair your fault(s)" Sophie insisted, "if from your fall you draw great humility and generosity."

Josefa writes, "I asked her whether Jesus would ever return again...."

"But you must expect His return, my child," interrupted her visitor. "The longing and expectation of the bride are the glory of the Bridegroom."

Only a couple of Poitiers' Superiors knew of Josefa's visions and the mystical phenomena that took so much of her psychic energy, but — a sign of the genuinely supernatural — never interfered with her daily chores or spiritual obligations. Convinced in part by the embarrassed lay sister's mistrust of her experiences[6] that Josefa was a true mystic they transferred her temporarily in May, 1923, to the monastery of Marmoutier so the Superiors there could observe her as well. Jesus assured the anxious mystic he would go with her.

Sister Josefa Menendez

Still "at a loss how to act in between (His) visits," as she noted in her diary, Josefa at the new, strange monastery asked Blessed Madeleine Sophie to help "and suddenly she came herself."

"So my child, you are here!" Sophie said, her face warm with love and concern.

In response, Josefa poured out all her anxieties to the dead woman as easily as a child to its mother. And later recorded her dead foundress' advice:

> "I have but one word to say to you, and you must turn it over all day, my child: "Love meets with no difficulties that it does not change into food for the flame of love." Later I will explain this to you, but while you are here just love — love — love...."

That year Mother Barat's feast was moved to May 28. When that day came, the Spanish nun was naturally thinking of her French foundress. Blessed with loving parents, Josefa was basically a well-balanced person; but the closer she came to God's radiant perfection the more her imperfections — that's right, even saints aren't perfect — loomed forbiddingly, marring the total gift of self she longed to make. As Josefa begged the dead saint's intercession for her "unworthiness and wretchedness," Mother Barat appeared to guide her in how to use even personal inadequacies to make spiritual progress — including Josefa's tendencies to worry and anxiety, to lack of confidence, to imperfect humility, and wavering trust.

"My own dear child!" Sophie exclaimed with her usual vivaciousness, making the sign of the Cross on Josefa's forehead. "I love you just as you are, little and miserable.... I too was just the same and as little as you, but I found means to utilize my nothingness by giving it totally to Jesus who is so great! I abandoned myself to His holy will and sought the glory of His Heart only. I tried to live in the knowledge of my lowliness and nothingness, and He took charge of everything. So, child, live in peace and confidence. Be very humble, ... deliver(ing) yourself over wholly to the Heart that is all love."

About seven o'clock that July 16, the first anniversary of Josefa's vows in the society, Josefa went into the little cell that had once been Mother Barat's and was now a little prayer room. In the diary she notes:

> ... Suddenly I saw her there, simple and humble as ever.... She said to me: "So, my child, it is already a year since you made ... [your vows]."

Josefa's diary records her joy at having vowed herself to Jesus forever, but that she was also worried, as usual, over what she saw as "my ingratitude." Sophie reproached her:

> "But my child, surely you know that His Heart is a blazing furnace, and its fire exists only to consume our miseries. As soon as you have owned them to Jesus, He remembers them no more. And if, in exchange, He has already granted you so many graces, He is prepared to grant you others greater still. His Heart is an inexhaustible Fountain: the more He gives, the more He desires to give. The more He forgives, the more He wants to pardon."

Josefa told Sophie of her promises, written in her diary, to be faithful to whatever Jesus asked until her death, a death she knew was near. Mother Barat encouraged her:

> Believe me, child, Jesus has forgiven and forgotten all your failings and all your strivings against His will, but He never forgets

your good resolutions and He takes pleasure in them. His Heart is an abyss of mercy, and it will never fail you. It is, too, an abyss of riches which will never diminish, however largely distributed. Love Him as much as you can. He cares for nothing else....

There is more, including a reminder not to fall into pride — which is always a temptation of those led on extraordinary paths like Josefa's. Finally, Josefa writes, Sophie "gave me her blessing, I kissed her hand, and she was gone."

That fall Josefa went to Rome, ostensibly accompanying the Mother Superior of the Poitier monastery to help with the extra housework at a gathering of all the order's Superiors. In fact, she was being given the once-over by the head of the society herself. During Josefa's days in Rome, Jesus asked the lowly lay sister to deliver a message to this woman, who, however kind, was formidable in Josefa's eyes. Quite happy to do housework, Josefa experienced terror at the thought of saying to the head of her order, "Jesus Christ told me to tell you...."

Some days after the message was delivered, on October 15, Josefa was passing a little prayer room where Sophie had once stayed. She heard the well-known voice of the dead saint call her. Still unnerved and fearful, Josefa feared an illusion.

Sophie dragged her in.

During their conversation this day Sophie confided, "during my life I sought nothing but the glory of the Divine Heart. And now that I live in Him and by Him, my only desire is to see His Kingdom come."

At Sophie's next visit that same month, just before Josefa left Rome, the dead saint comforted her:

> You must not be afraid or worried when light is not granted you [regarding what to do], as Jesus will give it to you when you need it and will do everything to bring about the full accomplishment of His wishes. Your part is to obey and surrender your will to His. True, there are moments when all is dark; the Cross rises stark before us and prevents our seeing Jesus Himself. But then it is that He says to us, "Fear not, it is I." Yes indeed it is His very self and He will guide and finish the work He has begun. Have no fear, be faithful and remain in peace.

That December was the last month and the last Advent season of Josefa's life. Sophie appeared to her several times, once humbly announcing herself as "your mother, the poor creature whom God chose to be the foundation stone of this little Society." This time she urged Josefa to pass on to other members of the society not only Jesus' special love for them, of which she had spoken to Josefa a number of times, but to urge these women — who by the nature of their mission associate with the rich and powerful — to never lose their humility.

On December 20, as thirty-three-year-old Josefa lay in her final illness, she was attacked by terrible pain; alone, she felt herself dying, but had no voice to call for the last rites. Suddenly St. Madeleine Sophie stood by her side and took her spiritual daughter in her arms, comforting and supporting her until the crisis passed. Two days later as Josefa received the last rites, she saw — others did not — Sophie there with Jesus and His Mother (both of whom, I remind the reader, had appeared many more times to Josefa in the past three years than had her foundress).

During all these "visits," of course, the incorrupt earthly body of Blessed Madeleine was at Jette, Belgium. Its incorruption, too, one of those laughing "revenges" of God on His down-to-earth saint.

The Church has not yet completed its investigation of the heroic sanctity of Josefa Menendez, who died to her own desire to be "safely ordinary" to let God work His will in her. But the Society of the Sacred Heart believes time will prove that sanctity genuine. They point to various signs (see page 37 for example), including one on the night of Josefa's death. The nuns went to clothe the corpse in its religious habit and discovered something strange: Their monastery is hardly open to the public; still someone had been there ahead of them.

> Under the blankets which were tucked in to the very top ... Josefa was lying, her arms by her sides, clothed in her gray petticoat which was carefully tied at the waist and covered her down to her feet. When? How? Who had done it? No one had entered the room since her death, as her next-door neighbor in the infirmary testified, and the little sister (Josefa), who had been incapable of the slightest movement, could not have done it, nor did she even know where the petticoat had been put away.

Jesus had told Josefa that she would die alone. She had, expiring during a sliver of time when, at the sick woman's urging, her nun attendant had rushed down to community prayers and the infirmarian, away for a few minutes, had not quite returned. But His mother and Sophie had promised Josefa they would be there to lead her to paradise. They knew, too, the little Spaniard's extreme modesty.

The schoolmistresses of the Sacred Heart, who have taught the children of prime ministers, royalty, and even an American president, are well-educated women not given to credulity. But they suggest the hands that clothed Josefa, who so dreaded "being handled after death," were those of one — or maybe two — who were long finished with this life.

ENDNOTES

[1] For several years in various Paris prisons, he waited his turn to mount the carts that carried men and women to their death by the guillotine. His name was never read. One of Louis' former schoolmasters, whose grisly job was to write out the names of the day's condemned, kept "forgetting" his.

[2] This was their main mission. Mother Barat also tried to open day schools for much poorer girls wherever she could.

[3] After her death, even her body had to be spirited out of France to Belgium during one such upheaval.

[4] Due, her priest cofounder felt, to her brother's encouraging her to treat her body so badly.

[5] That is, either desired or permitted to occur by God in deference to free will.

[6] Throughout her three brief years as a nun, far from making her proud, Josefa's extraordinary experiences left her afraid they might be delusions, and worried she'd be expelled from the society as a "mystical poser" or outright nut.

21 ∞ "MY MOTHER FELT A HAND ..."

No saint has turned up more often in this century to bring God's healing to ordinary people than St. Therese of Lisieux. And that says nothing of the even larger number of cures through her intercession that take place with no sign of her presence. Ignoring healings in mission lands since these have had their own chapter, here is a sampling of cures where Therese, in some way or another, "shows up."

For immediacy I have sprinkled events from recent years throughout this chapter. Some reader may wonder why I give far more from the pre-beatification period. It is not, I assure you, that no one ever writes Carmel these days saying they have seen Therese, although with Europe a post-Christian society, there are certainly fewer letters. In my files are at least fifty names and addresses of people I could contact regarding recent "favors" from Therese, some including appearances. But I would have to try to authenticate these myself, for the cloistered Carmelites no longer feel the need to require testimonies come with corroboration. The investigation into her sanctity is over. There is no longer any need to "prove" anything. If someone today sends a letter of testimony, the nuns simply add it to the archives without any judgment as to its authenticity. In a sense, letters today are almost surely sincere, for there is absolutely nothing to gain from sending a testimony. But, as you know, sincere can be sincerely wrong!

It is the older cures, then, with their statements of corroborating witnesses and testimonials from competent sources as to the reliability of the person making the claim that I rely on. Most of these individuals now dead, they can no longer be pestered by TV or tabloid emissaries, so I will sometimes give names and even addresses. It's fun if you're in the area to go see the house where a miracle took place (assuming the street hasn't been renumbered, as I found on one quest!). On the other hand, to protect the recent recipients of Therese's attentions (many of whom are French, the race that values privacy perhaps above all others), while I assure you I have held the original letters in my own hands in those chilly archives, I will use neither names nor addresses. While I realize this may cause some reader to conclude St. Therese never helped anyone after 1915 and, in my shame over that, I am inventing "new" cures, let me simply refer doubters to the Lisieux Carmel, where every letter quoted or summarized (usually in my translation) may readily be found.

You may have read of one important early cure in John Beever's excellent, authenticated biography of Therese, *Storm of Glory*. Fortunately, at the Carmel archives in an old publication of the nuns I found the full medical statements by the original, attending Protestant doctor; other Protestant medical men who treated the patient; and the doctor brought in by the Church to investigate the cure, who also called in his own medical experts. Due to all this, I can offer you more details of this well-authenticated cure, which took place in Glasgow, Scotland, in 1909, before Therese was an official saint.

A Scotch Catholic widow in her early fifties, Mrs. Dorans of 9 Stanley Street entered the Western Infirmary in Glasgow for the third time on April 28. Suffering for years from various nasty symptoms centered on the left side of her abdomen, her medical chart shows that, when admitted this time, she complained of great pain in that area, sickness, and vomiting. Her doctor of eight years, Daniel George Carmichael, who had sent her to the hospital, notes in his formal testimony that she was extremely weak and emaciated with a distended abdomen, dropsical legs — especially the left — and a tumor about the size of an orange that was very easy to feel. His hope in admitting her was that surgery could be done.

But the conclusion of the hospital surgeons was that her tumor, which they diagnosed as *carcinoma of the sigmoid flexure of the colon* (that is, a cancer of the intestines) was inoperable. Because she preferred to die at home, she was released on May 8, having had as treatment only some enemas (which found the area nearly blocked), pain medication, and a "careful diet" in hopes of the patient's keeping some nourishment down.

For ten weeks at home, still nauseous and vomiting, the Glasgow woman grew weaker and weaker, able to take only a few liquids. Finally even liquids were not retained. All this in spite of the fact that her family, friends, and various priests were making novenas of varied kinds, including directly to Jesus, begging God's cure of the cancer. By August 22, conscientious Dr. Carmichael making a Sunday house call, warned her children that she could not live much longer.

That same day, a Sister of Mercy visited, too, and, aware of the dying woman's great faith and desire to live, suggested a novena to "this young French nun people say is so holy." With no time to lose, they began the novena on the spot. For four days it seemed any healing granted through the prayer intercession of this Sister Therese was going to be the final one of entrance into the next life, for Mrs. Dorans' decline simply accelerated.

Thursday, Dr. Carmichael said she would die that night.

At eleven o'clock the widow sucked on a little ice to moisten her dry mouth. Even those few drops of water made her retch violently. Exhausted from pain and vomiting, finally she slept. According to the experienced doctor's expectations she should have slipped into a coma, followed by death before dawn. Instead, about 5:30 the next morning the Scotswoman wakened from "the best sleep she had had in years." What made her eyes open was a gentle pressure on each shoulder as if someone were leaning solicitously over her. She looked up. Her daughter slept soundly in a chair across the way. Otherwise the room was empty. Yet surely someone had just bent over the bed and gently touched her.

With a sudden start, she realized another oddity: Her constant pain was gone. Her hand moved at once to her abdomen. Her searching fingers could detect no trace of the orange-sized mass, not even a little bulge. The formerly distended abdomen, in fact, was flat.

Waking her daughter, she asked for something to drink. While just sucking a chip of ice had brought on violent vomiting six hours earlier, now she relished a glass of soda water, then moved on to tea and a roll for breakfast. When Dr. Carmichael dropped by to sign the death certificate, he found a healthy, if emaciated, woman who had only a marble-sized lump where an inoperable tumor had been the night before. (The "lump" was no tumor either, as the Church's medical experts later verified by X-rays, which showed only perfectly normal abdominal contents.) Mrs. Dorans' Protestant doctor, in his formal testimony, says what was most impressive to him was the suddenness of his patient's change from the final stage of terminal illness to health.

Mrs. Dorans was an honest woman. She said she hadn't seen Therese. She hadn't heard her say anything. She didn't dream of her. But she remained certain nonetheless that early that Friday morning God sent the young French saint to touch her and make her whole.

Why didn't Jesus respond to the earlier prayers to Him? Apparently, as in Galilee where He could have healed everyone in the whole country, but preferred to send out seventy-two disciples to cure in His name, He wanted this healing to come through His later disciple, Therese.

July 9, 1913, is the date on a testimony from Le Champ near Thouarce in France, signed by both parents, their parish priest, Abbe Gustav Hautreaux, and a "bystander," that is, a person with no connections to church or family. The foursome certify the cure of Bazile Horeau, Jr. in the pre-antibiotic era when many children died of childhood diseases or simple infections. Quoting my translation:

> In March four-year-old Bazile became gravely ill. He had a high fever and suffered from a terrible headache. The doctor, who was coming daily, declared he had meningitis in a tubercular form and was frank with the parents that there was no hope for their child.
>
> Having learned this sad news, Louise Gazeau loaned the parents a relic of Sister Therese of the Child Jesus. They placed it near the head of the little one and commenced a novena. During the novena he improved visibly. They made a second and from that time their child was in great shape. *In fact he was stronger than he had been before he fell ill* [italics mine].
>
> He had no convalescent period at all, only a little weakness in his legs the first few days after his recovery. As to his intellectual faculties, there was no brain damage — he showed simply no trace of the terrible malady but was simply a very intelligent, very nice child.
>
> One morning after his cure, while his mother was dressing him, he said, "See, Mama, she passed her hand like this on my head and then I was cured and [after that] I've never been sick!"
>
> The mother, very surprised, replied, "But who do you mean passed her hand on your head?"
>
> "Why Sister Therese. I was in my bed. Papa was there. He saw her!"
>
> How to judge this naive tale from a child of four? The adults, that is parents and the friend who loaned the relic, decided that Sister Therese *had* come and caressed the child, because when his mother questioned him about it, he always said, "Papa knows all about it: he saw her." The father no doubt had been keeping watch by the sickbed when the child saw Therese [so the child assumes his father saw whatever he did].
>
> Another day, more recently, Madame Horeau was talking to little

Bazile of his guardian angel and the child had a bunch of questions "Oh so do you have a guardian angel too? Where is he then? When we sleep is it around us?" Then, raising his short arms up as high as he could, the little boy questioned "Is it like that — like Sister Therese was?" indicating that Therese showed herself raised up before him.

Another French child — this one a little girl whose family wanted the names withheld — also had an impressive cure. Born April 17, 1903, she was only one year old when she became ill with deadly influenza, with such a high fever she went into convulsions. The toddler lived, but was "stone deaf." Obviously this made learning to talk very difficult. Mostly the child made her wants known by signs while saying a few more or less unintelligible words.

Her parents had sadly decided to send her to what at the time was called "a deaf and dumb school" where she could hopefully get some sort of education. Then the warmhearted mother of a family the parents were very friendly with learned of their decision. She urged they let her first make a novena to Sister Therese of the Child Jesus, begging the child's cure.

The friend, identified only as Madame C., must have been a woman of great faith, for she did not make this novena quietly. Instead she began the audacious undertaking with the totally deaf little girl kneeling with her for the prayer each day, as if saying, "See this youngster they plan to send away. I've told her you can help. You certainly aren't going to disappoint her now, are you?" And she applied further pressure on the heavenly throne by beginning the novena on September 30, the anniversary of Therese's death.

They say God just can't resist people with faith like that — especially when it is expended so unselfishly for someone else. The child remained deaf as a stone on days one, two, and three of the novena — but on the fourth day, the child's mother suddenly noticed her little girl could hear.

Once her hearing returned her speech was at the level of the one-year-old she had been when she became deaf, using only the simplest, usually single, words. Madame C. at once began working with her, teaching her short prayers and new words. The child seemed quite intellectually gifted, the family's motherly friend noted happily, and made good progress.

Although the deafness was gone, Madame C. joyously continued the novena in thanksgiving and had the healed child kiss a relic of the Carmelite saint each day.

On October 6, the seventh day of the novena, the little girl became frustrated with her limited vocabulary and reverted to some pantomime to try to explain that the day before, she first received a lovely odor from the relic, and then, going to bed, saw Sister Therese "very beautiful and surrounded by a heavenly light." The saint, the child managed to communicate, extended her hands as if to bless the little girl, then disappeared.

As a test of whether this was perhaps a case of an overexcited imagination, Madame C. gave the child a piece of brown material of the color worn by Carmelites. Immediately she ran to a picture of the saint and placed the piece of brown cloth against the robe that Therese wore. This was verification to Madame C. If only the account said the picture was not in color, it could be equally important to us!

But Madame C. offered other "evidence," as well. She pointed out that over a period of many months, whenever the little girl saw a picture of Sister Therese, "her face brightens" with obvious joy. Madame C. also noted that "when she sees the sun shining on anything bright, she says joyously … pointing to its rays, 'Little Therese.' " A mother herself, Madame C. observed "to my mind the best proof of the vision is the enthusiasm she shows after so many months have elapsed; for as a rule, children forget so easily and tire so quickly of any one thing." Eight years old when the formal report was made in January, 1912, the little girl often happily prayed near the saint's relic.

The report sent to Carmel contained not only statements from members of the child's and Madame C.'s families, but also the medical reports and references as to these people's stability, all in the form of legal documents, certified at the Town Hall and the respective parishes of the two families.

There are many cures of children from late in this century as well, some with apparitions of Therese, such as the tiny French boy cured in 1984 when he sees her. In 1991, in their French-language magazine, the Carmelites published a letter written by a mother of two who did not see Therese, but felt her presence all the time during a pregnancy where she had toxemia, and both lab and medical men advised her "the risks were too grave to the child" to continue the pregnancy. While she had never had any particular devotion to Therese, she felt inspired to ask her help in carrying this threatened baby. For nine months she read and reread Therese's biography, feeling her heavenly mentor near. Her second child is well, born completely normal.

Since they can be nebulous, I report few nonphysical cures. But two can be mentioned here, since most people can relate to the fear of death or grief over a death. In the archives I read a touching letter sent to the nuns in 1980 by a woman whose nineteen-year-old daughter had died. A few days after this devastating event, the woman went to her daughter's grave to pray. As she knelt there, she looked up and saw in the sky the Virgin Mary and St. Therese *with her daughter*, who used to say, "St. Therese is the one I love best of all the saints."

A Provincial Superior of the Catholic order the Little Sisters of the Poor testified around 1910 that Therese "has obtained the conversion of many old men" in the sister's homes in Scotland and Ireland. To help elderly men was fitting, since Therese was just crazy about her father — whose heroic virtue is recognized by the Church — and Louis Martin spent a period toward the end of his life in a "home" for mentally incurables after some strokes left him incapacitated with a condition rather like Alzheimer's.

Remember the old man cared for by the Little Sisters of the Poor who grew a new tongue? I want to spotlight here another old fellow with a terrible fear of death. Since she seemed so willing to help their old men, the Sisters gave this old man a picture of Sister Therese, asking her to reconcile him to dying. Shortly thereafter, according to the Sisters' report:

> Therese appeared to him in a dream, in which he saw himself all laid out and ready for burial... Taking him by the hand, she assured him that the moment of death had not yet come. From that time onward, he became very fervent.

During his final hours, he asked, "Don't you see that beautiful lady?" Therese? Or someone else giving him comfort and support? In any case, all his fear was gone: The report closes "he died like a saint."

That cure occurred early in the century. In 1992, at "The Hermitage" in Trosly-Breuil, France (one of the "Arks" scattered around the world where families are formed by mingling mentally handicapped and so-called "normal" folks), a sixty-two-year-old retarded man suffered from advanced Alzheimer's. Rene no longer responded to things such as photographs, could not eat or drink without help, and was only a month away from his death on December 18. But two individuals who lived at the Hermitage reported to Carmel[1] that on November 14, when they brought Rene into the kitchen, where one of the two had hung above the stove a photograph of Therese costumed not as a nun but as Joan of Arc, something quite "impossible" took place for one in Rene's advanced state of the disease. I translate a brief portion of their long account:

> ... to our great stupefaction, we heard him say "There! There! Look! Look! Look!... and we saw him completely radiant, all "illumined" pointing his finger toward the photograph. His whole body was stretched upwards and his eyes raised....
>
> One has to understand that in such an advanced state of Alzheimer's for him to take such an attitude and speak like this was, for us, a true "miracle."
>
> It was visible that something was taking place between him and her.... We were bowled over.... We felt that Therese manifested her presence and said to us "I am here and I am going to help you."
>
> ... And that day on his own initiative Rene ate and drank on his own, something that had not happened for a long time and which never happened again.

courtesy the Lisieux Carmel

Sister Therese took off her Carmelite habit to portray St. Joan of Arc for a play staged within the cloister in 1895.

The writer of this long testimony gives other indications of how Therese kept manifesting her relationship with the mentally-disabled old man. Assuring the readers he is writing of only those things that he personally witnessed, his account includes his frequent experience that if Rene suffered a coughing spell or had trouble breathing, showing him a picture of Therese found in his room brought obvious physical relief. Rene also intelligibly said, "Come! Come!" several times when shown this picture. And yet this was a prayer-card likeness of the saint, a stylized interpretation of her in nun's garb, not anything like the photograph of Therese he had reacted to in the kitchen.

Just two nights before his death, unable to move, not only did looking at this picture stop a coughing spell, but the advanced-Alzheimer's patient stared fixedly at the photo, indicating mental attention, and tried to kiss it. By his grimace when it was withdrawn, he made clear he wanted it back.

When Rene died very peacefully, the witness, who was rubbing his feet at the time, says one could feel a "presence" — the implication is that this was Therese — near him.

Lest someone worry God reserves Therese's visits for old men, here from Havana, Cuba, is a letter dated January 11, 1913, signed by an E. Daura:

> My mother who is 65 years old, was bedridden, suffering from great problems [paralyzed] which made it impossible for her to move; her mind was also affected: she could hardly articulate a few words.
>
> A friend, who felt for us in this trial, sent us *The Story of a Soul.* Full of hope after reading it, I proposed to my mother that we make a novena to the Child Jesus in order to ask her cure through the intercession of Sister Therese.
>
> During the novena, nothing changed: but the day after it ended, at dawn, we suddenly saw our dear patient get up, walk, and go out of the house.
>
> We were stupefied. My mother said simply, "I saw Sister Therese. She put her hands on my shoulders and she's the one who helped me get up and walk."
>
> May this testimony, which is sent out of gratitude to the dear saint, serve to encourage and console all who suffer.

There is a postscript to the effect that after six months of walking, the mother fell and had to take to her bed again; but this accident had no mental repercussions. The aged mind, cleared by Therese's visit, "remained perfect."

Another cure of the elderly was received by an aged Dutch nun, Sister St. Peter of Limbourg, Holland, whose rheumatism-riddled hands became more and more crippled the older she grew. St. Therese's own sisters, Marie and Celine, suffered similar problems as aged nuns. When the pain of her hands got so bad that sleep became a problem, Sister St. Peter turned to "little Therese," as she called her, wrapping the worst hand with a picture of then-unbeatified Therese in the wrapping. One night when the infirmarian was unable to massage Sister St. Peter's hands to lessen the pain before the rheumatic Sister tried to get some rest, Sister St. Peter called with greater earnestness than ever on Therese. In the depths of that night she felt someone take her swollen, crippled hand and gently rub it. Without seeing Therese, the old nun was sure the young one was at her bedside. Eventually Sister St. Peter sensed that Therese slowly withdrew. From what the testimony writer calls "that happy night" the rheumatism was gone. With normal hands, Sister St. Peter could do any work, even things like laundering in cold water, without discomfort. The Dutch nuns end their testimony, "May God be praised for the favours bestowed through the intercession of Sister Therese of the Child Jesus!"

From Scotland, dated April 13, 1913, a packet came to the Lisieux Carmel containing the testimony of Charles Campbell of 3 North Woodside Road in Glasgow; medical photographs; an accompanying attestation by the family's confessor, Jesuit Bernard Blake; and a long, detailed testimony by nuns of a Glasgow convent who visited Charles Campbell's mother for several years while she endured great sufferings. While Charles' statement is clear, the nuns' more detailed contribution shows that the situation was even more serious and the cure more wonderful than the son's testimony might indicate. This is a good reminder that many times the full extent of a miracle never is known — or known only by a few. Rather than giving these long testimonies separately, I combine pertinent details from each and report what took place in my own words.

In 1913, it had been almost twenty-one years since Charles' mother injured her leg as she entered a horse-drawn tram. The wound did not ever heal, causing her now more, now less suffering. Eight years after the accident, much of the leg was affected. She had by this time consulted several doctors, but the only recommendation they had for her was to try three months of bedrest, something impossible for this busy mother. Still at times the pain became so acute she did have to take to her bed until it eased up. Various salves and other healing remedies were tried, but the leg seemed incurable.

By the winter of 1912-13, the pain was nearly unbearable. Sores covered her leg from ankle to the knee, with two deep, large wounds above the ankle and another gross swelling above the knee.

In January, 1913, that is over twenty years since the original injury, she had just spent a month in bed, her leg swollen to double its normal size and full of these open sores that in places had eaten away the flesh to the bone.

With abundant matter oozing out, the doctor the family summoned believed that blood poisoning was setting in. He ordered an ambulance to transport Mrs. Campbell to the hospital. Her son's and the nuns' accounts agree that death seemed inevitable [remember, this is before antibiotics could challenge such an infection] and the son believed it only a matter of "hours."

When the ambulance arrived, the Scotswoman stubbornly refused to get in it. Her daughter-in-law had obtained a relic of this "little French flower," as some Scots called Therese. Feeling that two decades of medical help had been decidedly ineffectual in regard to her leg, Mrs. Campbell insisted her family join her in praying for a cure.

Giving up all medical remedies — never a recommended thing to do, of course — they began a novena for Therese's prayer intercession.

Somehow the dying woman hung onto life for the nine days. Then the final night of the novena period, she heard a voice say, "your leg is cured."

The next morning when it was time to change the bandages, they were full of corrupt flesh, as if it had all suddenly sloughed off. As for the leg, it had new, perfect, and healthy flesh. Where the wounds had once been there were well-healed scars.

This woman, too, did not see anyone, only heard a voice. But her family and the nuns agreed with the healed woman's opinion that words accompanied by a cure like this could only come from one of God's messengers. To them that messenger was obviously the young French saint.

From that day, seventy-one-year-old Mrs. Campbell resumed an active life — even traveling a lot — without ever having another problem with her leg. A year later, as the formal testimony was put together, she said her more than twenty years of sufferings seemed hardly real — more like some barely-recalled nightmare.

The seamen of Nice are hardly an otherworldly lot, but the captain of a frigate whose home port was this Riviera city contributed the following:

> My wife had a terrible influenza that infected her whole body: pains in arms and legs, no appetite, night sweats, continual fever, a frequent cough, ... The doctor had an air of little confidence.
>
> The nun nursing [my wife] spoke to us of Sister Therese of the Child Jesus. We began a novena. Nothing came of it — the troubles just worsened: my wife began to have a lot of pain in her heart and neck.

> But the 14th of December [1912] we started another novena and as soon as my wife received a relic of Sister Therese from Carmel, she claims to have very distinctly heard a voice say to her "You are cured!"

Note the husband's wary use of "she claims." No one can mistrust a woman's sanity in such moments like her husband! However the seaman goes on to note "from that moment she became greatly improved." Then he carefully lists all the symptoms and how each went away, and reports his wife — after two months in bed — is already again doing light housework without any fatigue. Both doubting and faith-filled, the marine office says, warily, "she has all the appearances of health," then goes for broke and states that as a seaman he has had occasion during a long career to experience God's protection, but through Therese's intercession "this time God has intervened in our favor in a miraculous way."

In 1979 a woman writes the Carmelites about her husband's two, very serious, open-heart surgeries. A blood clot from the first surgery formed a thrombosis in the body's largest vein, near his kidneys. During the second surgery the clot, which was the length of a cigar, got away and went through the heart to a lung, causing a pulmonary embolism. In the middle of it all, she remained calm, the wife says, because before the surgeries St. Therese had "manifested herself" through a strong, unaccountable odor of roses, giving the woman the certainty that her prayers for her husband would be heard. She ends that her husband not only survived, although he is still under medical treatment for his kidneys damaged by the thrombosis, but his state keeps improving. "At the hospital," she happily tells the nuns, "my husband is surnamed 'the miracle.' "

From Ireland, Sister Mary John of the Convent of Our Lady of Mercy at St. Michaels in Athy wrote on behalf of a man who apparently didn't want to deal with this sort of "supernatural stuff" himself. Sister Mary John had sent her account to a French priest, Pere A. Roche, stationed in Liverpool, who sent it on to Carmel, vouching for the nun's integrity and sanity. I translate from a 1913 Carmel publication what is probably a Carmelite's translation of original English!

> A man from Kilkenny was attacked by a leg problem which rapidly got worse. It was a wound of a very nasty aspect that gave him

a lot of suffering. Soon he had to give up all work and take to his bed, which desolated him, especially since his chances of cure were doubtful.

One of our sisters having spoken to him of Sister Therese of the Child Jesus, he got the idea to start a novena, persuaded somehow that only through her [prayers] would a cure come to him.

The second night of the novena, he woke suddenly, feeling several strokes by a mysterious hand on his bad leg. He looked all around and saw no one....

The cure didn't happen at that second; but the morning of the last day [of the novena] to the astonishment of the poor man when his bandages were lifted off, the leg was perfectly cured to the point that the wound had disappeared without leaving a scar or a trace of any sort.

In 1982, an Englishwoman suffered a brain hemorrhage and was in a semiconscious state for an entire month. She had no particular devotion to St. Therese, she says frankly, when she writes the Lisieux Carmelites after her recovery. But she wants them to know that at the point she felt she was dying "into my line of vision came a pair of praying hands and then St. Therese followed. She came across and put her hand on my head." The woman put her own hand up and felt the crisp mantle of a Carmelite, which seemed for that moment to be on her own head. An illness-induced hallucination? Or a saint's presence? The woman feels a need to write the nuns....

No one is more sophisticated, they say, than a resident of Paris, so one hardly expects testimonies from Parisians about a saint known for the Little Way of simple, childlike confidence in God. But in 1985, the Carmelites receive a letter from a woman in Paris who wants to tell them what happened back on April 15, 1938. A little slow with the report, perhaps, the family has still never forgotten what St. Therese did for them. On that spring day in 1938, the writer's mother was trying to eat her lamb chop while her young son and daughter — proving even in Paris children are the same — were driving their mother literally to distraction by their squabbling. In her agitation, she swallowed a bone, which lodged in her throat. It would neither come up nor go down. The doctor immediately summoned (this is long before the Heimlich maneuver) said the sufferer was going to die from asphyxiation. That they had been tormenting her moments before, of course, did not at all mean the children didn't love their mother. Seeing her menaced, the girl immediately began to talk to St. Therese of Lisieux on her parent's behalf. Wanting to cut a deal, the child promised to donate her First Communion outfit to a little girl who couldn't afford a new dress for that important occasion, if only God would let St. Therese come help her mother.

Years later, one can still sense the joy of that moment when she writes "the miracle took place. My mother felt a hand which turned the bone so that she was able to get it out. She was saved." To the family, there is no question that the hand was Therese's.

ENDNOTES

[1] Their witness is found in the periodical *Therese of Lisieux* June, 1993, issue.

22 ❧ A SAINT'S REVENGE

If any work is most important to saints — living or dead — it is conversion in its literal meaning, "a turning around," or change of heart. If this type of conversion is rarely written of anymore, it's probably because society has temporarily forgotten that healthy guilt for misdeeds is a blessed thing. Like pain in the body, it alerts to the need for healing, prodding an individual to take whatever actions will put him in better psycho-spiritual health. Results are greatest, of course, when non-neurotic guilt is recognized as a gift of God, who loves each of us no matter what. Divine love accepted — in the case you're about to read, from the hands of a dead saint — heals inner wounds, letting guilt act as a reliable guide toward wholeness. And you already know saints desire to "do good" to enemies. With these two thoughts, here is a modern saint's story that has already become part of the enduring wealth of the Church.

Born October 16, 1890, Maria was the third child and oldest daughter of Luigi and Assunta Goretti, impoverished Italian peasants rich in their love for each other, their family unity, and their understanding of eternal realities and moral necessities. Because their postage-size plot of land near Ancona would not feed the six children remaining after their eldest boy died, the Gorettis were forced to move. They ended up near Anzio. As tenant farmers in an unhealthy marsh area, they shared even the wretched house on the property with a second tenant, Serenelli. Having signed the lease with the property owner, Serenelli had the Gorettis — as junior partners — under what proved a pitiless thumb.

Luigi Goretti was dead almost immediately, victim of the malaria rampant in the marshy fields. His "partner" — whose family consisted of a silent, cynical, teenaged son — now had the Gorettis even more enslaved, forcing Assunta and her oldest boy to labor like men in those deadly fields. In the house day after day, nine-year-old Maria cooked, washed, and cleaned, while minding the three younger children and baby.

Serenelli kept both families' food locked in a cupboard, doling it out to Maria to prepare in amounts never enough to nourish all seven Gorettis after he and his son dished up ample portions first. Maria went hungry often, sacrificing her food to the two Goretti field laborers or the younger children.

After a year of this slavery and an excellent harvest, Assunta's underfed children watched silently as she and Serenelli settled accounts. The result: The Gorettis owed fifteen lire to the company store where the food was purchased.

Assunta might have despaired, except for Maria, who encouraged her over and over, "Don't worry, Mama; we're all getting bigger. Things will get better."

"Maria Goretti's a saint," those who knew the child agreed. Certainly Maria knew, as only saints do, the distance — stretching into eternal reaches, they say — between right and wrong. When Serenelli's nineteen-year-old son, Alessandro, who like his father scoffed at religion and morality, began trying to seduce the tall, pretty eleven-year-old, she didn't tell her mother. The twisted young man threatened to kill Assunta if Maria did. And it was Maria's constant desire to spare — not worry — her mother.

But the child-housekeeper kept studiously away from Alessandro as much as possible. In spite of the fear in her dark eyes, when he harassed her and (as he testified later) she tried to discourage him, two things were even more obvious: her resolve to avoid what she believed with all her heart wrong, and her concern lest Alessandro wound his own soul.

As the days passed, the junior tyrant got hold of a dagger. With this to persuade her, he cornered Maria in July, 1902, as she sat mending a shirt in the kitchen while his father took a siesta on the outdoor stairs, and the youngest Goretti, Teresa, age two, napped in plain sight on a blanket. The other children were off playing while Maria's mother and brother slaved away in the fields with their hoes.

Knife in hand, Alessandro swaggeringly gave Maria a pitiless choice: He would have her sexually or she would die.

"No! It's a sin, Alessandro," she cried. "God does not want this! You'll send yourself to hell!"

With the knife to give him courage, he attempted to take the eleven-year-old by force. When the slim child proved inexplicably able to ward off the nineteen-year-old, he exploded in fury, stabbing her repeatedly. When she staggered and fell, he sank the blade deep into her back.

Taken to the district hospital, Maria lived twenty agonizing hours, was operated on without anesthesia, denied a drop of water in torturing thirst — all fruitless efforts to save her.

She had a few words for her terrorist. Unexpected words. "I forgive him for the love of Jesus and I want him to be with me in Paradise," she said firmly, adding, "May God forgive him because I already have."

That this declaration was a heroic act of the will, not of any hidden feelings for her brutal killer, became clear in her delirium after peritonitis set in. As she relieved the attack she screamed repeatedly in horror, begging those at her bedside to "keep Serenelli away!"

A martyr to the virtue of purity at the dawn of a century that mocks the word, Maria Goretti would prove she meant what she said about wanting Alessandro Serenelli to make it to heaven.

When the police broke down the door and dragged him out of the dirty bedroom where lewd and violent photographs plastered every wall, Alessandro Serenelli was remorseless. If Maria hadn't wanted to die, she could have given in, he seemed to say. And at his trial the swaggering youth cynically asserted he took a child's life so he could be cared for in prison the rest of his without having to work. Given thirty years, the maximum sentence for a minor, as a prisoner he remained sullen and withdrawn, as sick a personality as in the Anzio farmhouse.

Until the "mysterious, surprising dream":

He was in a garden and Maria came to him carrying lilies. "Take them," she urged. As he did so they turned to flames in his arms. He felt something he called "grace" melt and remake his malformed heart.

That was the whole dream, vision, or whatever it was. Two words and a matter of moments in the span of a life. But it was the end of Alessandro Serenelli's cynicism; his bitterness against life, God, and society; his brutality; and his sexual per-

OSV file photo

There are no photos of Maria but her mother found this painting a reasonable likeness. She is carrying lilies as Alessandro Serenelli saw her.

versions. He was released after twenty-seven years — three years early — because of long years of model behavior that began the morning after his "dream."

Some may be interested in his life after prison. In 1930 — about a year after his release — two women hesitantly sought out the ex-con. Interested in Maria's possible beatification, they were relieved when Serenelli did not snarlingly send them away.

Instead he willingly told them of his disturbed past, speaking without bitterness of the morally impoverished upbringing that led him to pornography, then to acting out sick fantasies of domination and sexual conquest against an eleven-year-old girl. He described his crime and the years in prison without self-hate or self-excuse, neither seeking sympathy nor engaging in self-exhibition.

When the women cried "Poveretto!" at his life story, he shook his head and reminded them that even twenty-seven years in prison do not make up for a life one has taken. He preferred to talk about Maria, whom the once-brutal killer described as "an angel of a girl — innocent as water, kind, good, so helpful to her mother and the other children — really a model...."

The pair wondered timidly if it weren't an exaggeration, though, that Maria was more concerned with her assailant's soul and her own modesty than saving herself from the dagger. But he told them solemnly those two attestations "were only too true."

After the women reported the totally unexpected attitude of Serenelli, a Passionist priest, Padre Aurelio, dared knock at his door and cautiously broach the subject of whether her murderer might consider giving a formal testimony for the investigation into Maria's possible sanctity.

"It is my duty to testify," the middle-aged, gray-haired man declared. At the priest's obvious surprise, the ex-con explained, "I must do everything in my power to make reparation."

He told Padre Aurelio of Maria's goodness and innocence, as he had the women. And he confided to the priest, "Maria Goretti is certainly a saint. She is a true martyr. Many times in prison at night when I could not sleep, I began to think, 'if there are martyrs in heaven, she is the first among them ... with all that I have done to her!' "

The ardent testimony of her murderer was crucial to Maria's rapid beatification, especially since it was seconded by an outpouring of miracles — supernatural signs favoring her Cause. Between 1945 and her 1947 beatification alone, there were roughly one hundred, mostly healings, some including appearances. In the official under-oath investigation of her sanctity, for instance, is the witness of a stonemason saved by Maria as a roof fell in on him, and the testimony of Maria's niece Isolina Goretti — who became a nun after the experience — that Maria came "tall, beautiful, strong, [and] dressed in white," to save Isolina from a bolt of lightning.

In addition to his public testimony, Alessandro also faced Assunta Goretti and begged her pardon for killing her daughter. Mother of a saint, Assunta was a formidable woman herself. But how do you forgive your daughter's murderer? More and more in today's press, I see the answer: You don't; you do your best to get him fried. Assunta had another view, that of the Man on the cross. A view that can demand anguish and self-violence, but leads to peace. With her own hands, Maria's mother cooked dinner for her daughter's murderer. Did she remember how often he ate his fill while her children looked on hungrily? Maybe. But she did not bring it up and that night — it was Christmas Eve, 1936 — Assunta Goretti and Alessandro Serenelli knelt side by side in her parish church. The reminder that, in the Christ they were worshipping, there is no "unforgivable" held her up. It reduced those who knew who the pair were to tears.

They knelt again in St. Peter's in Rome in 1950, as Pius XII canonized Maria Goretti before the biggest crowd ever assembled to that date for the public proclamation of a saint.

Faded from public notice, Alessandro now was a member of the Third Order of St. Francis, lay people affiliated with the Franciscans to strive for personal holiness. Feeling a need to be close to God in the most literal sense, he worked quietly at a Capuchin monastery as a gardener.

Undoubtedly he continued to think frequently of Maria Goretti, a young girl who cooperated with God to do good to her worst enemy, and saved a poor wretch from himself.

OSV file photo

Alessandro Serenelli

23 ❧ CURES OF THE HOLY

Mother Madeleine Sophie Barat (1779-1865), whose whole life sings of divine mercy, has returned to guide and to deliver God's healing even though the miraculous was definitely not the Frenchwoman's style in life. While she would probably have modestly preferred God send someone else, it was dauntless Sophie whom the Lord chose as His associate for a first-class miracle to one of her spiritual daughters — a cure accepted for Sophie's canonization.

This spiritual daughter was Marie de Salm-Salm, born at Anholt in Westphalia (Germany), February 20, 1874. Marie was a healthy child until age eleven. Then her spinal column began to twist. Doctors put her in a so-called orthopedic appliance which — like the baby boards of some Indians or the foot bindings of the Chinese — was supposed to force a body part into the desired shape. And she spent several periods in an institution where specialists labored to unkink backs like hers. None of this straightened the child's spine. While not the sort to talk of her own suffering, no doubt the young girl also had her share of the cruelties afflicted children face from other kids.

Suffering can make or break. In Marie's case, it drove her to God. At the age of twenty-one, on July 2, 1895, just thirty years after Mother Barat's death, the young Westphalian entered the Society of the Sacred Heart founded by Sophie.

As you recall, this is an order devoted to education. Although following the tightly-scheduled life of a teaching nun was harder for Marie than for her fellow aspirants, she did not flunk out. In fact, her Order recalls her steadfastly carrying on her work assignments "with great courage," in spite of constant suffering from terrible headaches and pain in her deformed bones. Admitted to first vows in 1897, in February, 1903, she was allowed to make permanent ones. She was in Austria by then, teaching at Riedenburg.

Sister Marie did not complain about her physical problems, even on those days when healthy teachers would feel overwhelmed. What caused this holy soul suffering was having to be dispensed from fully keeping the Society's relatively mild rules due to her rotten health.

In 1912 during the summer vacation, she was sent to her order's place in Jette, Belgium, for some rest. In Jette also rested the "exiled," incorrupt body of Mother Barat — spirited out of France during one of those anti-Church uprisings that periodically send these influential and intelligent nuns fleeing Sophie Barat's homeland.

Marie began a novena by the tomb of the dead saint. She was not asking to be cured. No, Marie's modest — some might say foolish — request was simply to be strong enough to "keep the rule." Particularly she wanted to be able to function with less sleep and get up at 5:00 A.M. daily to join her community in prayer.

Those who think God very strict warn that one must be careful in prayer: you will receive no more than you pray for, they insist. But one of the special gifts of Sophie Barat was to grasp how lavish God can be, how readily — even "wastefully" — He showers goodness and blessings on those who approach Him with confidence or love. Undoubtedly when she took the request to God then, Sophie plumped it up a bit.

Making her daily prayer by the tomb, Marie felt inspired one day to help herself to some of the oil from the lamp that burned before the reliquary holding the foundress' intact body. She dabbed this on her forehead and at once her dreadful headache stopped. Given heart by this wonderful event, the next day she took some of this oil back to her room and smeared it on her chest before she slept.

When she awoke her pain and suffering had vanished. Much more incredibly, while she slept God had untwisted her spine. Her back was suddenly so strong the German nun could kneel and adore God with her arms extended sideways, shaping her very body into a symbol of her faith. Apparently that is what she was doing in ecstatic thanksgiving when Mother Barat appeared to her.

We must forgive Marie that she doesn't say what they talked about as they conversed for a short while. Her reticence only shows we're once again dealing with the genuinely holy. Was the deformity that vanished overnight very small? I think not. Once her spine became straight, the official account says Marie's clothes had to be lengthened because she was "much taller."

X-rays, taken as part of the formal investigation of the miracle, showed a beautifully normal spine. Mother Marie de Salm served the rest of her long life in Austria, except for a period as Superior of the society's members in Rome. She died straight-spined at the age of ninety-two on August 18, 1966, at Riedenburg — the spot where sixty-three years earlier as a determined young nun she ignored constant pain to dedicate herself to loving and serving God in others.

During her lifetime Mother Barat, as head of nuns working with the "upper class," had to graciously interact with the cream of European society, while on her frequent business journeys making friends with coachmen and people of every class. She took it all in stride, although she would have preferred to live a hidden, contemplative life. St. Therese of Lisieux lived that hidden life, but exploded into action after death. While Sophie probably blissfully enjoyed the hidden prayer chambers of heaven, Therese was joyously flitting all over the world on God's errands, including carrying healing to those aspiring to holiness.

Among these was an Ohio woman named Rhoda Wise. In 1932, at the age of forty-four, the Canton housewife had a thirty-nine-pound tumor removed without any complications. Four years later, in December, 1936, while walking down a dark street she was less lucky: Stepping off the curb, she plunged into a drain-opening whose iron cover had broken. One leg and foot were seriously injured. After medical treatment had done its best with plaster casts and other techniques, the foot remained bent inward, and putting her weight on it caused pain so severe that she could walk only with crutches. A number of doctors advised the problem was permanent.

Determined to seek health whatever some doctors said, in June, 1938, she returned to Mercy Hospital in Canton to get still another cast. A nurse noticed an abscess on her six-year-old abdominal incision. Doctors found the abscess was caused by adhesions formed on the bowel underneath the surgical incision, where the big tumor had been removed. To try to deal with the adhesions and cure the abscess, Rhoda endured surgeries in July and August that year and again in January of 1939. Far from mending matters, the last incision from these surgeries refused to heal. Shortly after the third surgery the bowel underneath the wound perforated and intestinal contents began to come through the unhealed incision.

During her various stays in the Catholic hospital, Rhoda became interested in Catholic prayer. By 1938, she was saying the rosary and making novenas to St. Therese of Lisieux. About the time the bowel perforated she was received into the Church by Monsignor G.N. Habig of Canton's St. Peter's Church. With her medical problems she was unable to attend Mass, however, and was even confirmed in bed at the hospital.

February 12, 1939, her doctor told her there was no hope of curing the abdominal wound. Still they kept her in the hospital where it could be dressed daily until May 8, when she was discharged as "incurable."

To her relatives the doctor explained that Rhoda was now suffering from cancer, something that sometimes occurs in old surgical scars or adhesions. From that time, a visiting nurse came daily to her home to dress the middle-aged woman's wound. There was little to be done for the state of the patient's abdomen, which was raw-skinned and terribly sore.

Then on May 28, 1939, at 2:45 A.M, her bedroom suddenly became bright and Jesus appeared to Rhoda. He sat on a chair by her bed, robed in gold and gloriously beautiful, with the marks on His forehead where thorns had once pierced His brow.

"Have you come to get me?" Rhoda asked, thinking she was dying. But the Lord told her it was not yet her time. They discussed some things, including Jesus assuring Rhoda that her dead mother was in heaven, then He disappeared, telling Rhoda He would be back in thirty-one days.

On June 28, 1939, at the same time of the night, He returned in an effulgence of light clothed in white. With Him was St. Therese. Therese walked over to the invalid's bed and motioned to her to pull back the coverings and remove the dressing from the wound. The saint placed her hand on that malignant ugliness and said, "I'm the Little Flower [Rhoda's usual way of referring to Therese]. You've been tried in the fire and not found wanting. Faith cures all things."

Rhoda made a movement to replace the dressing. Therese forestalled her. The saint then walked back to Jesus' side. He said He would come again, then both vanished.

As so often occurs after such apparitions, Rhoda immediately fell into a deep, healing sleep. She awoke at 5:00 A.M. to find the wound closed. The raw skin extending over her whole abdomen was also gone, healthy, apparently new skin in its place.

With this cure, Rhoda found new impetus to deal with her inability to walk. On July 14th she returned to Mercy Hospital for a new cast on her leg. When this fairly-light cast did not keep the foot from turning inward, on August 11 the frustrated doctor decided to go all out. He encased her leg in the-cast-to-end-all-casts, which he intended to leave on for three months.

The only problem with this (pardon the pun) heavy-handed approach: because it was so heavy and tight, the new cast was very painful. On the night of August 15, Rhoda was sitting up in bed awake, weeping from the pain. Suddenly the room lit up and St. Therese was there again, standing by the Ohio housewife's bed.

"That's a very little thing," the saint smiled. "Stand up and walk."

Obediently Rhoda placed her feet on the floor and stood up. As she did this, the cast, which was over a foot long, split open from top to bottom. (Having once watched a doctor struggle to remove a similar cast, I regard this as at least slight evidence that Rhoda was not imagining or making up this visit.)

"Go to church now," Therese said and disappeared.

Rhoda looked down at her foot. It was straight. She could place her weight on it without pain for the first time in two-and-a-half years. Joyfully, she walked freely around the house until 6:00 A.M., when she went to Mass at the chapel of Mercy Hospital.

Rhoda Wise was to see Jesus and St. Therese on a number of other occasions, and herself become, Monsignor Habig believed, a genuine mystic and stigmatic before her death in Canton on July 7, 1948.

God's sense of humor is the only reason I can find for why the "straightest" dead saints are often sent as messengers to the "flakiest." Thus learned, practical Sophie Barat to visionary Josefa Menendez and simple, uncomplicated Therese to stigmatic visionaries like Rhoda Wise and Therese Neumann, the controversial inedic, whose Cause is underway in spite of her many Catholic critics.

Before Therese Neumann became a stigmatic, it was Therese of Lisieux who appeared to prepare the extremely-devout Bavarian for her rare apostolate by words of guidance, accompanied by major physical cures. (A word to those who may be tempted to apply personally words directed to individuals like Therese Neumann: The vocation of the "reparatory sufferer," that is, one who is called

Therese Neumann

to carry others' burdens in a tangible, physical way, is extremely unusual. If you feel called to it, you probably aren't. Every individual I've studied who genuinely falls in this category fought tooth and nail to get out of it. The few saints of this extremely rare vocation should never be taken as models in this regard without much guidance by spiritual directors of great wisdom.)

At the same time I have written in another book[1] of the universal phenomenon whereby some — certainly not all — people must become very ill before they can, often once again in excellent health, become holy. In the same book, I looked at some of the stranger bodily phenomena associated with Therese Neumann and her early health problems which — like those of Rhoda Wise or Alice Jones — began with an accident that eventually turned her into an invalid for some years. Here I can only sum up that the strong Bavarian girl, employed in her twentieth year as a farm worker but hoping to become a missionary nun, attempted to "play the man" while the village's men were off fighting WWI. Hoisting heavy buckets of water above her head while clinging to a ladder, on March 10, 1918, she seriously injured her spine in an effort to put out a fire on her employer's farm. With repeated serious falls — down things like cellar stairs — because she tried to "keep going" in the ensuing months, she eventually lost movement and sight — the blindness from repeated head injuries and consequent hemorrhages, both affecting the optic nerves, including a final hemorrhage at the base of the skull when she slipped out of a wheelchair.

As often happens with those who are paralyzed, in spite of her parents and younger sibling's efforts to give the family's oldest child devoted care at home, Therese Neumann suffered from terrible ulcerated bed sores. She, too, is one of those such sufferings only carried deeper into prayer and compassion for others. After several years in this state, God cured her completely — but not all at once. Instead her healing took place over a couple years in various ways, all related to Therese of Lisieux. While this book is only about after-death appearances, Therese Neumann's cure from all the accident-caused disabilities is one healing, in stages, it seems to me, so I am going to give a few details of even those portions of the cure where St. Therese was involved, but made no discernible appearance.

The resurrection of the extremely devout invalid began in a rather low-key fashion on April 25, 1923, when a relic of Sister Therese of Lisieux was touched — with a prayer — to a stomach abscess on Therese Neumann, which was causing the invalid severe suffering. The stubborn "ulcer" immediately broke up and healed.

Four days later, on Sunday, April 29, Therese was beatified in Rome. Therese Neumann's father had brought back a couple pictures of Sister Therese from a nearby town before leaving in 1914 for compulsory military service against the French. During the war the German family asked the "enemy" saint's prayers for their soldier and, at some time, Therese Neumann appropriated one of Therese's pictures. In honor of the beatification, the German invalid had it adorned with flowers in her room, although she herself was blind. In this period she used to say daily a prayer to the child Jesus that was written by St. Therese, and also planned — but apparently hadn't gotten around to starting — a novena of prayers in honor of the new official saint, not asking for anything but, just, she said later, "to add a little to the beatification" of God's friend. At the moment Therese was beatified, miracles occurred in many places and Therese Neumann suddenly found that she could see again after four years of blindness. Her mother and sisters gathered around the invalid's bed and wept with her for joy.

But as May began that year, Therese Neumann's mother was very upset that her oldest child's left foot would have to be amputated due to "unceasing festering" of terrible sores that laid the foot open from ankle to toes. Wanting to bring "a little comfort to my worried mother," Therese Neumann prayed [for] "at least a lessening of this evil." When her sister bandaged the bad foot, they placed some rose petals from Therese of Lisieux's grave between the windings. Almost at once the foot stopped hurting and began itching, as healing flesh may do. Intrigued, Therese Neumann asked her sister to unwrap the bandage but the sister begged off.

"You can wait until I bandage it again tomorrow," she chided. When the next morning came and the bandage was changed, the usual festered matter and blood were in it; but the ulcerated area now had, Therese reported, "a new though tender skin." That was the end of trouble with that foot, although she still had bedsores in many other areas.

Two years later, on May 17, 1925, Blessed Therese of Lisieux was to be canonized in Rome. Therese Neumann was saying her rosary. Quoting her words:

> Suddenly there was a light before me. At first I was frightened at it. The light was before my eyes over the bed. It was good for my eyes. In the first excitement, I let out a cry that my parents heard downstairs.

Therese Neumann — whose family called her Resl — did not see anyone, just the light. But an unknown woman's voice talked with her familiarly in German, as follows:

> Voice: Resl, do you wish to be cured?
>
> Resl: It's all the same to me. To be cured, to be sick, to die — whatever the Good Lord wants.
>
> Voice: Resl, would it not please you if you had a lessening of your suffering, if you could at least sit up and walk?
>
> Resl: Whatever the good God sends pleases me.
>
> Voice: You'll still have plenty to suffer; but don't be afraid. I've helped you up to now and I'll help you in the future.... It is precisely through suffering that many souls will be saved. I wrote before that through suffering more souls will be saved than through the most brilliant sermons.[2]

"You can have a little joy," the voice urged the paralyzed women. "You can sit up; go on, try it: I'll help you." To the mother and father of Therese Neumann who had run upstairs at her daughter's cry, Therese now seemed to reach her arm up to air. Therese experienced being pulled up in her bed.

The voice gave Therese Neumann more guidance as to how she was to serve God — without mentioning the stigmata she would receive the following year — and then added "you can walk too." At the most painful spot of her spine, Therese Neumann felt pain and a click, as if something snapped into place. The to-that-moment paralyzed woman got up and walked around the room with the help of her father. In those same moments all the terrible bedsores — some open to the bone — disappeared as well.

How does anyone know the unseen "visitor" was St. Therese? Setting aside that it was her canonization day — a day when God often works miracles out of joy, it appears, at the honor to one of His friends — the voice referred, not only to having helped Therese Neumann before, but to the visitor's writing a specific phrase. Carefully Therese Neumann — who jumped to no conclusion that it was Therese — repeated that phrase to her pastor. Therese Neumann had no writings of the new saint. Nor did the pastor. But he borrowed some and, sure enough, found the precise words written (in a letter, one source says) years earlier by Therese.

That September 30 the cure was completed. The same voice — again no one seen — told Resl that she would now be able to walk without any help and that problems she still had with her eyes "would be lessened." The rest of this "visit" was devoted to spiritual guidance.

As October began Therese Neumann was once again a well young woman. However, she received two other cures that year. Early in November, a doctor who specialized in appendicitis was summoned to the Neumann home, where Resl had suffered horrible pain for three days. He said surgery must be done immediately and raced off to prepare the operating facilities in Waldsassen, five miles away from the Neumann's village of Konnersreuth. As this Dr. Seidl sped away, Therese Neumann, with her pastor's concurrence, asked St. Therese of the Child Jesus to "help me." She heard once again the same voice, saying, "so that the world may know there is a higher intervention [than surgical], you will not have to be operated on now," and was cured again. Again, the voice also offered spiritual guidance.

The acutely infected appendix harmlessly emptied itself, Dr. Seidl noted with awe. He explained later to Therese and her pastor that this does occur spontaneously in rare instances. But in such cases, the patient takes longer to recuperate than if surgery were done. Therese Neumann had no convalescent period.

During one of the curing visits (I can't specify which one, as some authorities disagree) Therese Neumann actually saw "a slender white arm" reach toward her, out of the light. That is as close as she came to *seeing* Therese in all these instances. Odd, since during her lifetime the Bavarian visionary saw other saints and Jesus at the drop of a hat!

Before 1925 ended Therese Neumann contracted pneumonia, almost died, and was cured "miraculously" again. Why all this? It appears God was "kneading" her, as one works bread dough. By 1926, the rather strong-minded young woman was pliable enough in the divine hands to begin her very rare and long ministry — it would last until her death in 1962 — as an inedic and stigmatist, whose hospital-verified ability to survive on no food or drink except the Eucharist, and periodic crucifixion wounds, brought a materialist century face-to-face with spiritual realities it longed to ignore.

Even before she was canonized Therese of Lisieux, of course, helped many who aspired to holiness who would never be candidates for beatification as is Therese Neumann. And perhaps because the young Carmelite herself had died after so much suffering from her lungs, God used her time and again as the agent of divine healing to illnesses centered in the lungs.

In Holland in 1922, a young German nun, a schoolteacher, wrote up her experience from four years earlier for one Father Caenen, a Jesuit, who sent it to the Lisieux Carmel archivist with a letter and addendum of his own. As it is very long, I sum up some of the less important statements (indicating this by brackets) as I translate from the French:

It was in April, 1915 (I was 23) that I came down with tuberculosis in my lungs. I began to bring up blood, then to cough, and I got weaker and weaker. The doctor judged my situation a grave one: already both lungs were affected and from that winter, I was bedridden. In spite of all the cares my Superiors surrounded me with, this bad state just kept getting worse until August 1917 when, having tried without any success all possible treatments, the physicians had to declare they could do nothing for me.

My hemorrhages were frequent and my feebleness extreme: I was given the Last Sacraments. I had made the sacrifice of my life yet I could not think I was going to die: at the bottom of my heart I conserved an unbreakable confidence in Sister Therese of the Child Jesus. From the day, when studying with the Ursulines in Holland, I had read the *Story of a Soul*, Therese was my celestial friend who helped me in every circumstance. From the beginning of this illness, I had charged her with asking God to cure me if it was His wish; I carried her relic and I keep her picture near my bed, pleasing myself by repeating a prayer I had taught sometimes to my little students. Here it is....

Little Therese, soul so pure

Remember me at the side of the Child Jesus

And help me become like you.

However my fever kept going up. In the first months of 1918 it was 40 Celsius in the morning. [She tells how her Superior also was seeking Therese's prayers, having all the Sisters and students make novenas and promising God that if the young Sister were cured, the Mother Superior would see to it that everyone under her knew and loved Therese. Yet during two novenas] the danger to my life just increased.

Holy Thursday I could no longer take nourishment. My neck was edemous, my tongue had turned black, and so swollen that it adhered to my palate. By Monday April 8, my life seemed to have run its course. My chaplain told me the end was near, which was also the doctors' opinion. I could no longer recognize and hardly hear the Sisters who prayed by my bed. [She gives details of their prayers].… Having brought up more blood, I rested so spent that I couldn't even open my mouth.

I heard Sister Superior affirm that I would die either in the evening or during the night. [After that the dying nun lost her ability to follow the conversation between the infirmarian and Superior over the next six hours or so while they prayed and vigiled at her bedside but she gathered that the Superior was very disappointed that Therese hadn't helped them. She did understand when the Mother Superior said to her directly] "Therese could have saved you, but she undoubtedly didn't want to because she's French and you're German and there's a war on between us."

As she said these words, my eyes wandered to the image of Therese which I could see clearly and I heard at that moment this word: "Don't fear anything; you'll be cured."

Sister Superior had barely left when I felt suddenly so happy Oh so happy with a happiness unknown. Then the same mysterious voice of which I can't find words for its sweetness said "You're cured." And all my illness disappeared: I could see, hear, speak, get up — I was truly well. Impossible to express the sentiment I experienced in that unforgettable hour.

The Sister watching over me was stupefied. She couldn't believe her eyes.

Later I learned my Superior had left me to hurry to the chapel. There on her knees before the tabernacle, she begged God to prove that the prayers of St. Therese were powerful before Him. His response was immediate. In curing me, the Lord glorified Therese. I never suffered any more: my neck, tongue and lips all were normal again and I was very hungry. At ten p.m. that night I was eating a rich tart.

There is another page of aftereffects, which I sum up: The next day the "dying" teacher was up. The doctor, of course, was flabbergasted, but in spite of being a non-Catholic materialist, was willing to declare that her lungs were completely healthy. She went back to teaching and four years later, as she writes in her testimony, enjoys good health. Her readers will understand, she is certain, that she likes to tell children about her very powerful little heavenly friend!

The Jesuit's addendum is interesting, too. He points out that the funeral Mass was all arranged and the nuns' chaplain had deferred a trip to attend;

there was no doubt of imminent death because the doctor, the day before the inexplicable cure, found one lung destroyed — "eaten away" — and the other so far gone that it had no more than a day or two left.

The Lisieux Carmel received a testimony in June, 1913, from a group of Notre-Dame nuns in Torokbalint, Hungary:

> Around the month of April 1912 one of our postulants became gravely ill with pneumonia. Her fever was 41.3 and she was gasping for breath. Her cough was tearing and she expectorated dark-red, rusty-colored matter. All of this augured as badly as could be. The evening of the 3rd day of this the doctor left us very concerned, fearing some complication [was developing]. The night began badly.
>
> Then our Reverend Mother gave the sick one a relic of the dear saint of Lisieux, as well as her picture, telling her to have confidence and Therese would obtain her cure. At once the postulant began to pray [for Therese's help]. A Sister stayed by her side.
>
> Toward one o'clock in the morning, the sick girl sat up a bit in her bed and exclaimed in low tones, "How beautiful you are. I beg you to cure me!"
>
> The Sister on duty was very moved and said. "You see the little Therese?"
>
> "But of course. There — above my bed. Don't you see her? Her clothes are so marvelously white and there are beautiful angels all around her."
>
> The Sister, although she did not have the happiness of contemplating this apparition, still felt herself penetrated by the supernatural to the point that she shed sweet tears.
>
> An instant after she had seen Therese, the postulant fell asleep.
>
> When she woke up, she told everyone joyfully that "the little saint" had come to cure her. And in effect the fever while it had never been lower than 40 degrees in the preceding days was 37. All the danger was past and a few days later, the privileged one was back at work.

Seeing Therese, of course, could have been some sort of fever-driven hallucination. But the nuns who were on the spot thought not, due to the sudden cure. The report is signed by the Superior, the two Sisters in charge of the infirmary, and a fourth Sister who acts as assistant to the nuns' physician. As I mentioned, God must have sent Therese on so many lung cures because He knew how satisfying they would be to one who had died of TB. Whether she *appears* or not, such healings are found frequently in Lisieux's archives and publications. Several TB cures, in fact, are among the formally-ratified beatification and canonization miracles. Still, not every TB case "turned over" to Therese was cured.

Here is the last portion of the report of a Mother Superior, who requested anonymity:

> … We made several novenas to our Seraph [Sister Therese] but Sister Teresa of Saint Augustine only laughed saying, "She will not cure me; she is coming to fetch me."
>
> … "Little Therese," I cried sadly, "you work miracles everywhere, and yet in spite of all my supplications, you do not cure our daughter."
>
> All that evening I was heartbroken.… Sleep came to me and with it this beautiful dream: The bells sounded loudly and the community intoned the *Latatus sum.* Soon the harmonium in the Church sent forth the most beautiful music and a multitude of voices were heard singing; one voice louder and more distinct than the others brought these words to me which I believe awakened me. "She has always desired heaven. The gates are opened and I will lead her there without delay."
>
> On awakening my soul was filled with mixed feelings of joy and sadness. I was unable to account for the supernatural atmosphere with which I was surrounded.
>
> When I related this dream to Sister Teresa of St. Augustine she cried joyfully, "It is I, Mother; little Therese is coming to fetch me."
>
> On the eve of her death, being with the invalid and wishing to give her a drink, I suddenly found the room filled with an exquisite perfume which gave me a sweet consolation.
>
> Assuring myself that there was nothing in the Infirmary which could give such an odour, I said to myself: "It is Sister Therese who is near the bed of our sick daughter." On August 30th, our dear Sister asked all those near her to look at the beautiful roses strewn upon her sheet. She alone saw the beautiful heavenly flowers which Sister Therese had doubtless caused to rain on her.

Holy Viaticum was then brought to her. Immediately after receiving it, she opened her eyes which were of a heavenly brightness. She seemed for some time to be beholding something of ineffable beauty and, in this ecstasy of love, she expired.

All these holy women thinking they see Therese and being cured — or carried off to heaven in ecstasy — may seem just too nebulous and otherworldly to some. Let me end the chapter then with a cure testimony that arrived at the Lisieux Carmel in August, 1913, from the Sisters of St. Joseph in Chambery at the Savoy region of France, because this time Therese left physical evidence of her visit behind her. Once again, translating from the original French:

> One of their postulants named Delphine Miege on August 15th met one of the Sisters in a narrow corridor. Trying to draw back so the other could pass, Delphine hit her elbow against the door of a wall cupboard with unusual force.
>
> For the next quarter of an hour, the poor young thing endured indescribable pain. But not wanting to say anything, she carried on. It did not pass away, however. The next day toward the end of the morning, she had to reveal her condition. The night was very painful and the following morning she could not dress herself nor even make the sign of the cross.
>
> All the usual measures for such an injury were taken but in vain. Everything tried only aggravated her sufferings and increased the swelling.
>
> Sunday the 17th of August, the Superiors asked the Infirmarian to take Delphine to a surgeon who also proved unable to help her.
>
> That same evening, moved by the pain the poor thing was enduring and her concern that due to this health problem she would be sent away, (not being yet a formal part of the community, since as a postulant she had yet to take any vows), the Sisters commenced a novena to Sister Therese to ask Delphine's cure. At the same time a relic of Therese was placed over the painful area.
>
> That night and the next day the suffering only augmented. However the evening of August 18th, around 9 o'clock the postulant fell asleep, weeping. As she slept during that night — she could not tell at what hour — she saw a religious who touched her injured arm which was completely bandaged even to the hand.

Deeply asleep, because for several nights she hadn't slept, she believed it was the infirmarian and just let her do what she would without coming out of her drowsy state.

The next morning, when she woke up, she realized she felt no more pain. Astonished, she moved her arm. It was perfectly supple. Then she looked at it. The bandage had been removed and the arm no longer was the least bit swollen — all trace of any injury was gone.

She noticed next that the bandage had been carefully rolled up and placed on the chair by her bed. This didn't surprise her in itself because she still thought the Sister infirmarian had visited her in the night. What seemed strange to her was just the so sudden [and] so radical cure.

[She went to] the Mistress of Novices who was also astonished and who sent her to find the infirmarian.

The infirmarian was stupefied. And she said she had *not* returned to the injured girl since the previous evening. Then they asked all the Sisters: none had touched Delphine's arm nor the bandage.

After all these undertakings, the Sisters were obliged to conclude that Sister Therese of Jesus had "descended," as they put it, "on our humble convent to save a vocation and give us a sign of her heavenly protection."

The testimony was signed by the cured girl, the Mistress of Novices, and the Superior.

ENDNOTES

[1] In *The Sanctified Body.*

[2] This dialogue will be found in many English-language biographies. One which also gives the precise German words Therese Neumann heard is Adelbert Albert Vogl's *Therese Neumann: Mystic and Stigmatist*, Tan, 1987.

24 ❧ Of Buddhists, Sufis, and Black Elk

When devout Japanese Buddhists retrace the footsteps of the holy Kobo Daishi[1] (774-835) — the words mean "great Buddist teacher" — on Shikoku (Japan's smallest major island), they begin at the saint's tomb, asking "his blessing, his guidance and protection, *his company* on the pilgrimage.… "

Scholar Oliver Statler, who lived on Shikoku for years beginning in 1969, made the centuries-old pilgrimage many times. He writes:

> The pilgrim believes … [he has] the Daishi at his side … [because] it is a fundamental tenet of the pilgrimage that the pilgrim walks with the Daishi — to some quite literally; to others, in spirit. The motto of the pilgrimage is "We Two — Pilgrims Together," the Daishi and I.

Sometimes, it is said, the holy man appears. For instance at temple number two on the pilgrimage route, a statue of the Daishi celebrates a legend regarding a woman from Osaka. She suffered miscarriage after miscarriage, never bearing a child. Becoming pregnant again, she gave up trying to take care of her body and set out afoot on the arduous pilgrimage that usually takes two months. Beginning at temple eighty-eight, where most pilgrims end, by the time she reached number two she was almost finished with her spiritual trek. There labor pains set in and the Daishi himself appeared and helped deliver a healthy child.

Long after the Japanese saint helped bring Buddhism from China to Japan and was laid in his tomb, the Daishi appeared to a reigning emperor in a dream. The dead saint had a modest request: A new robe. In answer, the emperor "hastily dispatched to Koya an imperial minister accompanied by a high priest."

When the tomb was opened so the body could be re-clothed in its new garment, a thick mist arose that hid the Daishi from their eyes. The high priest took the supernatural fog as a personal rebuke, throwing himself on the ground and weeping that he had been found unworthy to see the dead saint's body. Then the mist cleared and the Daishi appeared, permitting them — the priest now weeping from joy — to clothe him in the new robe and to shave his hair "which had grown very long." While both men saw the Daishi, a young acolyte who accompanied them saw nothing. To console him, the high priest "took his hand and placed it upon the knee of the Daishi and ever after, this hand had a fragrant odor...."

To devout followers of the Daishi's Shingon sect of Buddhism, such stories of supernatural wonders hearten them to live with moral uprightness, compassion, and other spiritual virtues taught by the Daishi. But other Buddhists, even whole sects such as Zen, believe visions and all mystical phenomena are "a bunch of hooey" — a distraction from the true path of virtue and enlightenment. Many Buddhists, in fact, claim to believe in neither saints nor souls. Others speak of "Bodhisattvas" (enlightened individuals with the heroic virtue summed up by the word "saint") who may appear, like the Daishi, after death for holy purposes.

As I see it, the major religions — Buddhism, Hinduism, Christianity, Judaism, and Islam — are each divided into two camps: *thinkers,* who find God more readily through reasoning, reflection, and virtuous "rational" models like St. Thomas More, and *feelers,* who see God more easily in signs, wonders, and mystic models like Padre Pio. Every religion, I believe, needs both types, just as every person is fully developed only when both tendencies are in balance.[2]

Why do I mention this? Because in reporting after-death appearances from the non-Christian branches of our human family, I know some members of those groups — individuals who simply don't believe in after-death appearances — are going to clutch their heads and moan at being represented by such "crazy" anecdotes as those about the Daishi.

So my apologies to those of non-Christian traditions who read this book and groan over how I have "missed the whole meat" of your faith and offered only a colorful, but hardly sustaining, sprig of parsley. Take comfort, if you can, in knowing some of my co-religionists will see this whole book the same way.

And to Christians, a word on why non-Christian examples of after-death appearances. Certain "basics" in spirituality — such as a belief in life after death — turn up wherever men and women of goodwill search for God. Seeing after-death experiences universally acknowledged I hope will buttress your faith in the reality of life after life.

In addition I want to say frankly that I write not just for my fellow Catholics, or even Christians, but for the human family. Like it or not, we are in this world together, formed by the same God and bound for the same eternity. In an age where the existence of God and moral realities is denied by so many, I believe all the great faiths would do well to stand together in support of our common values. Respectfully recognizing our theological differences, we can — even while we try to convert each other through love, not the sword — join hands as God's children to pray for our world and each other.

As one who has chosen the Catholic tradition for my own, I am convinced Jesus Christ is the Savior of all peoples, those who know Him and those "baptized by the desire to serve God however they conceive the divinity," who know Him not. Thus, in complete accord with the teachings of my Church,[3] I see the Holy Spirit working, to varying degrees, in and through all faiths and present in all people of *good will*.

The Three Wise Men, for instance, were not Christians and no line in the Bible suggests they ever became Christians. Yet God favored them with mystical graces and spiritual wisdom. John the Baptist was a pre-Christian whose holiness was extolled by Christ Himself. On the Mount of Transfiguration Jesus saw two dead Jewish men who, all readers of the Bible agree, are "great friends of God," that is, saints.

Obviously then there are not only Christian saints, but holy people in every tradition where people have discovered a God of light, love, and justice (I exempt religions that serve darkness, such as the Aztec cult that ripped out human hearts from living victims).

When I speak of saints like Buddha, Mohammed, the Torah's holy men and women, holy Hindus, and certain shamanistic sages, I do so comfortably with the hope of hastening the day when all of us who believe in supranatural realities and moral imperatives change our world through our love for each other and for God Who, as Hindu priest Narasimha Bhattar of the Southern California Hindu Temple says, is " 'One' even if our mode of praying and religious beliefs are different.' "

This does not mean the dogma of each of these saints' faiths is "the same" or that "it doesn't matter what you believe" at all (consider the Aztecs or those who sacrifice animals in voodoo rites today, if you are tempted to think a faith's beliefs unimportant). It means that God accepts the heart even when dogma is imperfect, even as He accepts you and me in spite of our incomplete understanding of — and far from perfect adherence to — His teachings.

So let us proceed.

The only Moslems willing to discuss mystical events like after-death appearances are those of the Sufi sect — known as the mystical branch of Islam. Susan Fine of Rochester, Michigan has found in Sufi Islam "wonders" which cement her relationship with God and encourage her drive for spiritual "wholeness." After consultation with leaders of the Naqshibandi Sufi order, Susan — who lives in a Detroit suburb and is married to a Jew — gives me instances of after-death appearances among Sufis.

For starters, she points out that her own mentor, Sheikh[4] Hisham (his last name withheld since, like most Sufi masters, he is not eager for publicity) says "all saints are 'ever-living' " and able to appear to someone in dreams or by other means, even if dead. Hisham speaks of the scent of holy perfumes noted when the spirits of dead "Moslem saints are present and wish to send greetings and blessings." Termed *the odor of sanctity*[5] in regard to Catholic saints, such perfumes marking the presence of holy dead are also known to Buddhists (see the acolyte above). Susan, who has smelled such odors in regard to dead holy Sufis, says they most often take the scent of rose fragrances or of sandalwood, odors also associated with Catholic saints like Padre Pio.

In most major traditions, saints' followers visit their tombs to seek spiritual graces and other favors through the saint's intercession. Sufis, too, visit the graves of their dead saints, Susan says, and believe the saint knows they are there because God lets the saint be somehow actually alive in the grave, not just "present in spirit."

When meditating or dreaming, the Michigan woman at times has heard one of the Naqshibandi sect's dead leaders speaking to her — someone she never met while he lived. She says, "I thought it was my imagination until recently when someone who knew [this leader] before he died ten years ago imitated his s-l-o-w, ... commanding and precise voice. And it was identical to what I had heard...."

Susan also relates Sufi tradition — pointing out Hasidic Jews believe the same[6] — of saints and prophets, dead hundreds or thousands of years, who appear to help people in trouble or test them — "like the beggar," she says, "who accosts you in a test of charity."

"How do you know the beggar isn't simply a homeless person or a con artist?" I ask. The type of visitor Susan refers to, she replies, "seems real but vanishes" when his or her purpose is completed. Susan speaks of once being awakened at night by a beautiful "angel," who turned out to be such a test. The visitor offered Susan many worldly "rewards," but turned into a demon and vanished, when she asked only to trust, love, obey, and serve God.

In his book *Mercy Oceans: Pearl and Coral: Secrets of the Sufi Way*, Sheikh Hisham writes of his own spiritual mentor, Sufi Shaikh Nazim:

> I was walking with my Sheikh on the street in Damascus one day. He always kept change in his pocket. He said: "Never reject a poor man who asks. Always keep change in your pocket. You don't know when a saint comes in the guise of a poor person to test you: are you generous or not?" That day we met many beggars on the way. He kept taking from his pocket and giving, taking and giving. On our way back, someone came and my Sheikh had no more change in his pocket. That beggar asked something. Mawlana Sheikh Nazim took his watch — it was very important for him because it came from his Sheikh — and gave it away. What to do. He only had the watch to give. After he gave it, we walked away and he said to me: "Look behind you." I looked and that person had disappeared. He said: "He is one of them. If I had not given the watch, I would have failed the test."

courtesy Susan Fine

Hashim adds, "You don't know when Allah [God] comes to you through his saints," in such ways.

In a talk given on February 22, 1992, Hisham told of a Sufi saint named Ibn 'Arabi, ordered hung as a heretic by his fellow Muslims (a fate that has met Christian saints as well). Told by a supporter that as a saint he had the power and should "change his destiny," Ibn 'Arabi refused, saying, "I am going to Him," explaining, "this is what He wants for me ... "

The saint's body was thrown in a garbage dump as a final expression of his society's rejection.

Two hundred years later, the area

Sufi Shaikh Nazim, who gave his watch to a beggar, lest he fail the "test."

was conquered by the Ottoman Empire and a sultan named Salim entered Sham, the place where the saint had been executed and his body left to rot.

This sultan Salim was an interesting figure. Upon arriving in Sham, he did not loot the city's riches. Nor did he call for choice delicacies to eat, or dancing girls. No, this conquering hero — I picture him affectionately as a portly, peace-and-quiet-loving man — climbing down from his camel or horse, dreamed of a nice relaxing soak.

Easy enough, it seemed. The sultan simply commandeered the city's best Turkish bath, ordering the place emptied at once. As he waited impatiently, he could almost feel his body relaxed and limp in the soothing mineral waters that rose, nicely-heated and buoyant, from the depths of the bath's natural spring. As the last hastily-clad, moist citizen scurried out, the mount-sore sultan hurried in, calling back strict instructions that he be left completely alone in the huge, dim space. No attendants, not even a masseuse, were to disturb his peace.

He was furious when he discovered an old man still soaking peacefully in the warm waters. He began to mutter and then shout about hanging people. But the old gent was not intimidated in the least. Rather than groveling and prostrating himself with proper Middle-Eastern addresses before the city's conqueror, the elderly soaker barked, "Salim, come here! Rub my back!"

The sultan was so taken aback that someone would dare speak to him that way he was speechless. Then he sensed something supernatural was going on. Strangely afraid and awed, he went over and rubbed the old man's back. Insatiably, the cheeky old man let him rub for a full hour. Unhappy as this made the sultan, somehow he dared not stop.

Finally, the old man said, "Salim, I am Muhyi-d-din Ibn 'Arabi, who passed away more than two hundred years ago."

He had a mission for the sultan: Salim was to go to the highest point in the city. There, said Ibn 'Arabi, "you are going to find a light coming from the place where they threw this body. Go there," he ordered, "and you will find me."

Sultan Salim — I see him muttering over his missed soak, "Just my luck: I order the living away and the dead turn up to harass me" — did as he was told. From the city height, he saw the light, brought men to its source, and set them to digging. Soon they uncovered an immense treasure of gold and diamonds.[7] Digging further in the old garbage dump where two hundred years earlier the saint's body was thrown, from the upturned earth a beautiful smell began to rise. It came from the saint's incorrupt body, which soon was uncovered, looking as if he had just died that day.[8]

Is this Sufi story the literal truth? I can only assure you Ibn 'Arabi, who died in 1240, was a real person. A great lover of God, he has written of how he once became so enraptured from the sight of the angel Gabriel he could eat or drink nothing for days. But no Islamic scholar, I can't offer proof of his after-death appearance. Its value, to me, is its assurance that the concept of God sending dead saints to the living is also found in Islam.

Under the term "shamanism" are hundreds of belief systems, ranging from sophisticated to extremely simple, from benign to horrific. But all shamanistic peoples are open to the other world and its inhabitants as they conceive them — often as positive spirits, which may take human, animal, or other forms, and/or "demons," which also take varied forms.

Some shamanistic peoples have been dominated by dark spirits — often seen as dead ancestors — who are feared and placated; but that is not our topic. Other shamanistic groups *their elders believe* experienced after-death appearances which prepared them for Christianity. For instance, the Oglala band of the High Plains Lakota (part of the larger group dubbed Sioux by white explorers) were visited "many generations ago" by young, beneficent and beautiful Buffalo Cow Woman "bearing what appeared to be a child." Her gift to them — aiding their communication with a caring fatherly Almighty — was a ritual pipe. Years later when they were introduced to Christianity, Lakota wise woman Lucy Looks Twice (daughter of the widely known Sioux visionary Black Elk) says their Jesuit priest accepted that it was the Blessed Virgin who had come as Buffalo Cow Woman, adding *"and that was what we* [Lakota] *always thought."*

Her father Black Elk, Lucy says [her testimony is found in Michael F. Steltenkamp's *Black Elk: Holy Man of the Oglala*],[9] saw "all [Sioux] Indian ceremonies" — including the purifying Sun Dance where men fast for three days from food and water, some even shedding blood — as "connected to Christianity." He claimed, his daughter remembers, that from the foundation laid by the Virgin's appearance as Buffalo Cow Woman, the Lakota "knew, somehow, that in the future our Lord Jesus Christ would come one day to his people" and in the Sun Dance "they somehow already practiced the faith they would later know fully."

Farfetched as it sounds that the Lakota had some pre-knowledge of Christ and were visited, perhaps, by the Virgin Mary, there is a similar, if more mysterious, story told among the Toltec, a very different religious group found in the Vera Cruz area of Mexico. Scholar Janet Barber, IHM, tells me that Toltec priest, culture hero, teacher, and political leader from around 900 A.D., Quetzalcoatl (literally either "precious" or "feathered" serpent), "many seriously believe was St. Thomas the Apostle," which would, of course, have to mean this saint made a prolonged after-death appearance. Barber agrees that could be, or it could also have been the still-living St. Thomas, if he brought his ideas to an earlier people, the Olmec, and those ideas percolated down into Toltec culture.

In either case, Quetzalcoatl definitely, "planted the seeds of the gospel," as Catholic documents put such things,[10] including forbidding human sacrifice as practiced by the Toltec's neighbors, the Aztecs.

Seemingly defeated by evil, Quetzalcoatl had to leave the area, but prophesied he would return in a certain year, which in western reckoning is 1519, the precise year when missionaries appeared accompanying Cortez. They were puzzled, Barber says, by the many seemingly Christian aspects of the areas' religions, such as baptism and confession.

Of course, these possible appearances of Jesus' mother and His apostle Thomas are shadowy events from the mysterious realms of legend and myth whose truths cannot be validated — or maybe grasped — by twentieth century research methods.

Someone we know more about because he lived until 1950 — the era of fast cars, milk shakes, and post WWII consumerism — is visionary Black Elk. Born in the era of tepees, horse and foot transportation, buffalo hunts — and sometimes famines — under leaders like Red Cloud, Crazy Horse, and Sitting Bull, Black Elk as a young teenager scalped one of Custer's dead soldiers at the Little Big Horn battle in 1876. He was there, on the fringe of the slaughter, at the massacre of his people at Wounded Knee in December, 1890. Between these events, during the years 1886-1889 he traveled in Europe in Buffalo Bill's Wild West Show.

An innately spiritual individual, he had visions from the time he was about five. These were often of spirits in the form of animals but he also saw venerable people, such as spiritual "Grandfathers," who may have been dead elders of his people. Such experiences opened Black Elk to God's gift of curing the sick and cheering the downhearted as a Lakota medicine man and were the foundation, he said, for his later work as a Christian leader.

With intellectual dishonesty all too common where Catholicism is concerned, poet John G. Neihardt (probably because he favored Hindu Vedanta and American Indian spiritualities over Christianity),[11] in the book *Black Elk Speaks* wrote of Nick Black Elk's early life and Lakota spirituality without so much as a footnote to acknowledge that this saintly man chose to live the last fifty to sixty years of his life — carrying out duties like those of today's deacons — as a Christian leader of his people.

One his fellow Indians even today recall as a very special man of prayer who always had a rosary within hand's reach. The Oglala Sioux's children, trained by their father, were faith-filled, too. Once, for instance, son Nick, Jr., had a hemorrhage, bleeding from the nose. His sister, Lucy, recalled years later "he was dying." The family knelt and prayed the rosary and appealed to the compassionate heart of Jesus.

Suddenly the dying boy asked they seek the prayers of St. Therese. This was done.

The boy not only recovered, but confided to Lucy he had seen Therese, insisting "I know it was her."

Like Father Aloysius Ellacuria later claiming a dead Los Angeles baby helped him in his ministry, Black Elk spoke of his "little helpers" and "guides" — dying babies he had baptized on the reservation when no priest was available.

When Black Elk himself (his age cannot be precisely determined, but he was somewhere in his mid-eighties, his daughter thought) sensed his life was over, he told Lucy not to mourn because "you know I will be happy." While asking that Lucy and her husband Leo never let a single day pass after his death without praying for him (which shows the holy man's humility, that he thought he might still need further purification), he also reassured Lucy:

> "Do not worry. There is a man who comes to see me everyday at three o'clock. He is from overseas, and he comes in to pray with me. So I pray with him. He is a sacred man."

Lucy explained to Michigan anthropology professor Michael F. Steltenkamp [from whose book cited earlier I take all quotes on Black Elk in this chapter] that "when he was living my father always used the phrase *wicasa wakan* when speaking about a Blackrobe [Jesuit] priest. And that's the phrase he used in talking about that visitor — *wicasa wakan*. So he might have been a Blackrobe who visited him."

Nick Black Elk was staying at the time with his son Ben. Was this a local, foreign-born priest who somehow found time to visit Nick every afternoon on the reservation, where homes are scattered and drives between them often long, or was it some dead Jesuit saint? While I wonder if some after-death appearances are hallucinatory, if it was St. Ignatius himself who turned up to pray with Black Elk daily, it wouldn't surprise me. I think Black Elk that holy.

And so do the Sioux.

Before he died on August 17, 1950, Black Elk remarked quietly to Lucy, probably to comfort her, "I have a feeling that when I die, some sign will be seen.... God will show something. He will be merciful to me and have something shown which will tell of his mercy."

To someone else, he was much more explicit. Like Neihardt, Joseph Epes Brown had also interviewed Black Elk and written a book (*The Sacred Pipe*, 1953) on Black Elk's early spiritual tradition. Brown was in Europe when Black Elk died. But before Brown sailed, the holy Lakota Sioux told him, "You will know when I am dying, because there will be a great display of some sort in the sky."

What took place is not exactly an after-death appearance, but it is the sort of phenomena that has accompanied the deaths of saints and later been dismissed as "legend." So let me give a few details here to show that such things do happen. William Siehr, a Jesuit brother who attended the wake for the old catechist, gave Steltenkamp a long, detailed recollection of the phenomena that got his — and everyone's — attention that night. Excerpted here are only some of the more striking comments.

> ... When we left the place [of the wake], we noticed ... the sky was just one bright illumination ... something like a display on a fountain of water where you see light reflecting on the water as it's being sprayed up.... But it was all in every direction ... coming up from the east and the south, the north and the west. And they'd all converge ... rising up into the sky ... It was a tremendous sight.
>
> [Acknowledging that the Aurora Borealis is seen there, he still maintains this was greater].... That's the first and only time I ever saw anything like it.... It was something I rather associated with the old man....

Nick Black Elk
holding rosary beads

Some sort of heavenly display, a celestial presentation — that's
the way I looked at it. It was sort of a celebration....

In talking to Indians on the Pine Ridge about it after he returned from
Europe, Joseph Epes Brown said they claimed the "sky was filled with
falling stars" when Black Elk died.

One of those Indians, John One Goose, told Steltenkamp:

"I remember that night very well, and those bright stars. Everything looked miracle-like.... I was scared a little bit — but I knew
it was God's will. I know God sent those beautiful objects to shine
on that old missionary ... because he was such a holy man....

That was not quite the end of Nick Black Elk. His daughter told
Steltenkamp that after her father's death, people did not quickly forget him.
Individuals would get up and speak of Black Elk either at church or in other
gatherings as a man of God whose prayerfulness and example should be
imitated. Lucy also reported "people would feel *that he was present in our
chapel or meeting house*" [italics mine]. She herself and her family, she
confided, often experienced her father's help. As an example, she spoke of
something that had happened very recently. Her brother Ben had died and a
memorial gathering was planned for him, when suddenly Lucy's son was
taken to the hospital close to death. She wondered what to do: Cancel or
postpone her brother's memorial or go on with it? "All of a sudden, something came to me," she said "like a flash — like somebody speaking to me
clearly." She was told to go on with the gathering since it was for a good
purpose, people gathering to pray and express their regard for their Catholic faith and Lord. And suddenly Lucy recalled vividly the time her father
"had two coffins in church and still preached, even though those two coffins held his own children." She says, "I know it was my father speaking to
me ...

ENDNOTES

[1] As a Buddhist priest who founded a major Buddhist sect — the Shingon
— the Kobo Daishi was named "Kukai." After his death, Japan's Imperial
Court titled him "Kobo Daishi," the first word meaning "to spread widely
Buddhist teachings," and the second "great teacher," or spiritual master.

Others have been "canonized," so to speak, by the title "Daishi," but if the word is heard by itself, it refers to this individual.

2 Without *thinkers*, proper awe at the numinous can degenerate into literal "non-sense," where phenomena-seekers become religious groupies who have no time to feed the hungry, comfort the sorrowing, or the other "works" God's followers do in this world — let alone pray — because they are too busy chasing apparitions and seers. The credulity of such extremists gives spiritual things a bad rap, reducing whatever religions they follow, in the eyes of onlookers, to play-time for the brainless.

Without *feelers*, on the other hand, those who think about God and carefully follow His rules can become legalistic. They, too, can end up with no time for good works — or do them without the charity that alone, St. Paul reminds, gives them value — because they are so busy arguing over interpretations of minor points of minor dogmas, or whether the least important observances of God's laws are being precisely kept. These people can degenerate into sponsoring witch hunts, stake burnings, and religious crusades against other faiths — "in God's name," of course — again giving religion a bad rap, as meant only for self-righteous fanatics.

3 See, for instance, the encyclical *Redemptoris Missio* and other recent statements of Pope John Paul II.

4 Sheikh (also spelled shaikh) means saint or "enlightened spiritual leader," but it is sometimes used merely as a term of respect. It should never be confused with "sheik," which is not a spiritual term.

5 I have written about the odor of sanctity related to Catholic saints at length in *The Sanctified Body*.

6 Although it is often forgotten in the face of political conflicts, Jews and Islamics share many beliefs. On his passage through India after participating in a Tibetan Buddhist-Jewish dialogue, poet Rodger Kamenetz writes in his book, *The Jew in the Lotus*, of finding a Jewish Muslim saint Hazrat Sarmad (d. 1650), whose grave is visited to this day.

7 The saint had been hung for saying "your god is beneath my feet," a "blasphemous" phrase that actually meant that what these materialists worshipped — riches — was buried beneath the ground.

8 Sheikh Hashim commented the saint's body did not decompose because it was "not full of sins" like ordinary bodies.

9 Published by University of Oklahoma Press, 1993.

10 See *Ad Gentes* and *Nostra Aetate*, as well as the more recent (1990) *Redemptoris Missio*.

11 It has been suggested that Neihardt dishonestly "reshaped" Black Elk's

early memories and, above all, the Lakota Sioux's attitude to them (Black Elk understood no English so could never read Neihardt's depiction of him) due to Neihardt's personal anti-Christian bias. In this vein, I note that at age sixteen, Neihardt had already published a long poem based on Hindu Vedanta philosophy. Christians of that era (1897) would have been aghast at this spiritual leaning which might have further alienated the young poet from traditional western religions. Further support for the supposition that Neihardt wrote *Black Elk*, not only with an avowed preference for shamanistic over Christian practices but with a bias *against* Christianity, turned up as I wrote this book. A reporter for a major newspaper (who wishes anonymity) wrote me after reading a newspaper article I had written on Black Elk's Catholicism. My informant reported that around 1975, she attended seances started in the early- to mid-1960s by Neihardt on his midwestern farm. Born in 1881, Neihardt was almost eighty in 1960 so his involvement in groups antithetical to Christianity had been lifelong. He had died by 1975 but his daughter, having inherited both the farm and her father's unconventional spiritual allegiances (the group was also "into" flying saucers), was continuing her father's Spiritualist sessions. Black Elk was spoken of at these meetings (as Neihardt had portrayed him, that is, without even a whisper regarding the Indian's Christianity). And allegedly the Lakota Sioux was among the visiting spirits summoned up by the seance leader. All these spirits communicated by "knocks" so nothing was seen, no voice heard, nor any other evidence offered — beyond this easily fraudulent or suggestion-induced phenomenon — to indicate a true after-death appearance. That the saintly Black Elk could have been summoned up at a seance is, to this writer, extremely improbable. Holy people — living or dead — respond only to God's call. Both holy Protestants like minister John G. Lake and Catholics like St. John Bosco have attended seances to uncover the truth and found no real after-death appearances. Lake found the "spirit" of a dead member of his flock was willing to discuss many trivial things but not her fervent faith in Jesus Christ. A spirit was present all right, the holy Protestant concluded, but not the dead girl's. Instead, Lake was certain, a dark spirit was posing as the dead child. Why? To lead her grieving parents away from God, in whom alone is found true consolation and peace. Asked by a bishop to attend a highly "successful" seance, St. John Bosco's mere holy presence totally disabled the "spirits," so that nothing could take place, the medium complained, again indicating that — whether simple foolishness, fraud, or "of darkness" — there was nothing there of God.

25 ❧ Some Top-Ranking (Hasidic) Generals in God Almighty's Army

The Bratzlav sect of Hasidic Jews believe in "concrete personal guidance through the teachings of a rebbe." In their case, a dead leader, believing (to quote Rabbi Rosenfeld speaking in Herbert Weiner's *9 1/2 Mystics*) "better a dead rebbe who is alive, than a live rebbe who is dead."

Odd thinking to some (and one does have to wonder — I am only half-joking — about ease of everyday communication). But an idea in perfect accord with Christian saints like Auschwitz martyr of charity Maximilian Kolbe, who taught "while we are alive we can only work (for God) with one hand, lest we fall ourselves; after our death, we can work with two." Or as Weiner puts it, once safely with God the holy person "no longer has the limitations of the human condition" and is completely at God's disposal to help others.

Jewish groups who accept this — some Reform Jews even question whether there is life after death — point to evidence like the very rational Joseph Karo from the seventeenth-century, "author of a legal work which still guides the Orthodox world of our day." Karo was "regularly visited by a preacher from the higher world."

Jews of this kind — mostly Orthodox — also believe, as do some Moslems and Christians, that through their "merits" the holy dead — both those whose holiness is recognized and those whose sanctity is known to God alone — can intercede with God to win favors such as "protection" for the living. Furthermore Hasidic Jews believe God may send the holy dead to rescue the living at times — whether the holy person knew those helped personally or not.

In 1814 in Poland, the book *In Praise of the Baal Shem Tov* was published in Hebrew. The Baal Shem Tov — literally "the spiritual Master of the Good Name" — is the eighteenth-century holy man considered the founder of modern Hasidic Judaism. (A reaction to the academic formalism of rabbinical Judaism of the day, the Baal Shem Tov's movement emphasized the mercy of God and encouraged a joyous response through music and dance.) This very important book for Hasidic Jews and those of us interested in saints and mysticism was put together by the son-in-law of the man who had been scribe to the Baal Shem Tov and consists of anecdotes collected from the scribe and others close to the Hasidic holy man, who'd been dead only some fifty years.

In these days available in English, the book is rich with anecdotes that most people dismiss as pious legends, but which those familiar with authenticated lives of even some recent saints find worth careful consideration. Among the stories of the Besht (as the Baal Shem Tov is sometimes called) and his holy circle is one of his brother-in-law, Rabbi Gershon.

In brief: Rabbi Gershon was caught in the water when the ship he was traveling on resumed sail. A fine swimmer who once rescued a drowning man, he swam after the vessel and caught up to it, but those aboard did not hear his cries while the ship's high side, coated in pitch, was too slippery for him to climb. Finally he began to drown and, no longer able to speak, anguished that he was unable to properly make a last confession. As he agonized that he would be denied heaven for this failure — the Besht might have rebuked such a lack of faith in God's mercy! — he is quoted as saying:

> Immediately someone appeared on the ship and saw me. He put out a small boat. He pulled me out of the water, brought me to the ship, and threw me into it. I went down to the stern of the boat and lay there for about two hours. I was vomiting because of all the water that I had swallowed. I lay there until I rested a little, and then I put on my clothes.

However when he went to look for his rescuer whom he calls an Ishmaelite (probably meaning an Arab), he found no such person on the boat. Finally he concluded that "probably it was Elijah the Prophet."

No one can insist you believe the dead Jewish prophet rescued the Polish rabbi. If you point out that in those two hours while the rabbi was vomiting, his rescuer might have jumped in his little boat and rowed away, who can argue with you? But from the fact that Rabbi Gershon even thought of being rescued by Elijah, it is clear that Hasidic Judaism has a living belief in the after-death appearance of holy "rescuers."

As for the great Baal Shem Tov himself, let me say he simply had all the gifts you ever found in a great mystic, whatever your faith background: simplicity, purity, compassion, humility, humor, holy wisdom that reads minds and hearts, and spiritual vision that saw things happening afar. Naturally he worked miracles and healed the sick. He also bilocated into people's dreams, was luminous in prayer, a near-inedic at times, and used to see the dead "in droves" coming for his prayers. Centered around this figure are other early Hasidic holy men, such as Rabbi Abraham — called "the Angel" for his great piety — who died at age thirty-six in 1776.

Another rabbi asked Rabbi Abraham if he ever saw his dead father, also a holy rabbi named Rabbi Dov Ber of Mezhirich, but known even before his death in 1772 simply as "The Great Maggid" — that is, Great Preacher and Spiritual Storyteller:

"Yes."

"In dreams? Or are you awake."

"He comes in my dreams. We talk and then when I wake up, he talks to me while I'm awake."

This dialogue provides the background to an interesting story. A wealthy man caused Rabbi Abraham a lot of grief. So this friend of God complained to his dead father. The Great Maggid said he would summon the man to his son's house of study (part of a synagogue).

The dead man sent a living messenger to the wealthy man. When he said, "The Great Maggid summons you," the wealthy man snorted, "What do you mean 'summons me'? He's dead!"

"Nevertheless he's calling you," his visitor (perhaps holy himself?) said calmly.

When the pair arrived at the house of study, there was the dead rabbi sitting at the head of the table, dressed just as he had been when alive.

The rich man got a scolding but — apparently a person with true gall — continued to protest and excuse himself. Finally the Great Maggid snorted, "Take him home!"

Home they went. Only then did it hit the wealthy man that he had been summoned by a holy dead man to whom he had given nothing but lip. He fainted.

Revived, he was taken to Rabbi Abraham, who smiled and said, "Probably my father summoned him."

"How do you know?"

"Oh he told me he would."

World War I brought many people to God (as seen in chapter three), but spawned a postwar culture in which influential writers and thinkers no longer found faith relevant. The next generation, shaped by those thinkers, touched off the much more barbarous World War II, which ripped the mask of "civilization" from the face of Europe. After the Holocaust of the Jews; the attempted genocide of that ancient people from India, the gypsies; and plans to wipe out the Slavic races through sterilization and forced labor; when the war ended with the great fireballs over Nagasaki and Hiroshima, it seemed only "mature" to many to set "childish" ideas of a loving God aside.

Where was God when the people of Israel fed Hitler's chimneys, Jews asked in anguish and/or anger in books like Andre Schwarz-Bart's *The Last of the Just* and Elie Wiesel's *Night*? Evil seemed stronger than love or goodness to those who wrote and read such works. Many influential Christians, too, anguished over the Holocaust and Hiroshima. Strident voices announced "God is dead."

Softer voices, sometimes half-embarrassed whispers, maintaining that God was there — weeping over victim and perpetrator alike — during all the horrors men of free will created and visited on others, were drowned out or shouted down. But they have persisted and occasionally been recognized.[1] For instance in 1982 a book by Holocaust survivor Yaffa Eliach won the Catholic *Christopher Award* given to books that "light a candle" in human darkness. Dr. Eliach, professor of history and literature in the Department of Judaic Studies at Brooklyn College and founding director of the Center for Holocaust Studies, experienced the horrors of the Holocaust firsthand. When the slaughter of Jews of her Polish town began in 1941, Yaffa, then a little girl, would have died with 236 relatives had she not been plucked to safety by a non-Jewish woman. In 1944 Yaffa's mother returned alive only to be murdered with her infant by another Polish neighbor, who screamed "This is for Jesus Christ" as he fired. Turning "despair into hope and death into life" — what she has called "the burden of survival" — the pages of Dr. Eliach's book *Hasidic Tales of the Holocaust* are permeated with a healing sense of God's presence although telling the Holocaust stories of Hasidic Jews. God's interventions in their lives during those terrible days included appearances by the dead. Here three examples from Dr. Eliach's highly-recommended book, beginning with the rescue (slightly condensed) of two holy rabbis:

> The rabbi of Belz, Rabbi Aaron Rokeach, and his brother Mordechai, the Rabbi of Bielgory, were smuggled out of the Bochnia ghetto in May 1943. In charge of the rescue operation was a brave Hungarian officer who was handsomely rewarded for his bold plan.
>
> According to his plan, the high-ranking Hungarian officer would be traveling in the service of the Hungarian Army. His "mission" would be to bring back to Hungary from Poland for interrogation two prominent generals captured on the eastern front. The two captured generals would be none other than the Grand Rabbi of Belz and his brother.
>
> The Hungarian officer made all the necessary arrangements at the various border checkpoints both in Poland and Hungary. All the forged documents were in perfect order, as were the various license plates he prepared for his car. The only possible problem was the fact that he had forgotten to bring along two sets of Russian uniforms. When he realized his error, it was too late to go back. However, the Hungarian officer had confidence in his plan....
>
> With the two "generals" in his back seat, both clean-shaven and dressed in civilian clothing, the brave Hungarian officer successfully passed the first checkpoint. As he passed each additional checkpoint, his confidence grew and he merrily sang Hungarian songs.... He even left his two illustrious passengers alone in the parked car while he entered a bar to have a few drinks.
>
> When he returned he could not find the car ... only to discover that the car was parked in precisely the same spot where he had left it. But it was shrouded in a heavy mist as if to conceal it ... He crossed himself for now he was sure that all he had been told about his two passengers was indeed true.
>
> ... At the first major checkpoint in Hungary, the officer did not foresee any mishaps. As they stopped at the barrier, he presented all the necessary papers.... The guard ... checked their names against a list in his possession. "Sorry, I can't let you pass. I have no order by my superiors to expect the arrival of two captive generals,"...
>
> "Check with your superior," the Hungarian officer suggested in

a commanding voice. The superior appeared moments later. He apologized for the inconvenience, but he confirmed the young soldier's statement. He had no instructions to allow the passage of two captured Russian generals. "Where are your uniforms?" he asked the gentlemen in the back seat. They remained silent.

"They are under strict orders to speak to no one except at head-quarters. How long do you expect us to wait at this godforsaken place?" The Hungarian officer continued speaking in a confident tone while he tried to figure out what had gone wrong and work out an alternative plan.

Just then out of the mist appeared three Hungarian generals mounted on beautiful horses. They ordered the border guards, both the junior officer and his superior, to let the captive generals through. As the car crossed the border, the three mounted Hungarian gener-als saluted the two "generals" in the car. Once more the car was on its way to freedom....

The Hungarian officer was bewildered. "I know all the high of-ficers in the Hungarian Army, but I must frankly admit to you I did not recognize the three high-ranking military men who came to our rescue at the border."

"We did," responded the Rabbi of Bielgory. "They were our fa-ther, Rabbi Issacher Dov Baer (1859-1927), our grandfather, Rabbi Joshua (1825-1894) and our great-grandfather, Rabbi Shalom the Seraph (1799-1855), all top-ranking generals in God Almighty's Army!"

Yaffa Eliach Shtetl Collection

On the left, Rabbi Aaron Rokeach; right, his brother Mordechai (unknown man in center).

Another case chronicled by Dr. Eliach where dead holy family mem-bers saved the living took place in a concentration camp near Vienna. Ignac Grunsweig was a teenage, Czechoslo-vakian Jew who had already lived through a number of these hells-on-earth when he arrived at Mauthausen in the winter of 1945, a survivor of one of those end-of-war death-marches where camp prisoners were driven like cattle ahead of the advancing Allied forces. When a "selection" was made upon arrival, picking out living skeletons for transport later that day to the gas chamber, Ignac — a bundle of bones — was among the doomed, but saved his life by giving a false I.D number from a previous camp.

When the death trucks had left with the condemned, back in his barrack that night Ignac dreamed of prewar days. In his dream:

> He was a young yeshiva student, going to visit his grandfather, the Dolha Rabbi, Rabbi Asher Zelig Grunsweig [of Carpathian Russia]. It was Sabbath afternoon at dusk. The little house was filled with twilight shadows and the special tranquil Sabbath spirit permeated each corner.... It was time to eat the third Sabbath meal. While Grandmother set the table, he and Grandfather washed their hands from the special big copper cup with two huge handles. Grandfather made the blessing over the two loaves of hallah. It was warm [in the house].... They were singing zemirot, traditional Sabbath songs. Grandfather was stressing the importance of the third meal, telling him that it is the most spiritual and mystical of the Sabbath meals. He who becomes imbued with its spirit will be spared the battles of Gog and Magog. "Remember what our sages say, 'Whoever observes the three Sabbath meals will be saved from the suffering to precede the coming of the Messiah, the rule of Purgatory.' Grandfather was caressing Ignac's head while he spoke to him in his good and gentle voice. "You will grow up, my child, and will survive the suffering that precedes the coming of the Messiah and the rule of ... Purgatory. But you must always attempt to observe the third Sabbath meal, for its merit will protect you."

This dream was so real that when Ignac woke, he could still feel his holy grandfather's hands on his head and even smell his grandmother's good bread. The day's nightmare began at once. But night after night the same dream refreshed his soul. To live its meaning, he disciplined himself each day to hide one crumb of bread from his starvation-level rations. With these seven crumbs, week after week on the Sabbath he celebrated the third "meal."

The prophecy of his grandfather — who was known during his life for his scholarship and holiness — came true months later on May 6, when the camp was liberated by Allied forces. That this was a true after-death appearance is at least possible, for the holy rabbi had perished, with others of the family, at Auschwitz.

Another holy rabbi memorialized in *Hasidic Tales of the Holocaust,* the grand Rabbi of Bobov, Rabbi Ben-Zion Halberstam, had a special love for young people. Each Sabbath at the rabbi's house in the Ukraine many men and boys congregated to welcome the Lord's day with singing and dancing.

Then the Nazis arrived.

On July 25, 1941, the rabbi and his family were among two thousand Jews arrested. Four days later, the rabbi, dressed in his tall fur hat, was striding toward the open pits in the forest where the Nazis and Ukrainian collaborators were waiting to kill the entire group.

Urged to escape, the holy man said calmly, "One does not run away from the sounds of the Messiah's footsteps."

A short time later he was with God.

He was not a "survivor," but something greater: One who faces the worst that evil can devise and triumphs in spirit, entering the next life with the palm of victory.

Fourteen-year-old Moshe, one of those young boys who, in another world, had gathered at the rabbi's to worship God with joyous prayer and music, did not know of the rabbi's death as he himself — sole survivor of his large family — struggled to stay alive during the next four years as a slave laborer, first at Auschwitz and then, in 1944, at Mauthausen. He felt certain though that the rabbi:

> … was guiding him and watching over him even amidst the intolerably harsh realities of the camp. The image of the rabbi as he had seen him on many Friday night visits to the rabbi's house was constantly before Moshe's eyes. In the bleakest moments in camp, in spite of physical exhaustion from his slave labor at the granite quarry or at the subterranean aircraft factory, in moments of despair and hunger, he felt the presence of the rabbi next to him. The rabbi's soothing voice comforted him and commanded him to live.
>
> Wherever Moshe went, he felt the Bobover Rabbi guiding his steps, almost as if the rabbi were pulling him and pushing him, often in directions opposite those he would have chosen to follow.

In prewar days, Moshe's favorite melody of the rabbi's songs was the one to which the rabbi chanted the holy Zohar, the mystical *Book of Splen-*

dor. Any time life in the camps ground the teenager down to where his humanity began to slip away, he would concentrate on the rabbi's Zohar melody. Unfailingly this would produce "warm, human tears" that rekindled his spiritual fire.

Then a bitterly cold winter decimated the ranks of the camp inmates through exposure, starvation, and disease. The growing fourteen-year-old was simply a bag of bones by December, 1944, when the prisoners were stripped of their filthy, thin clothes and sent into showers as part of a de-lousing regimen. Suddenly the naked men were ordered out on the parade ground, into what Eliach calls "a howling December wind." To reconcile a difference of one between the overseer's list and the number of actual bod-ies he had counted entering the showers, naked, starving men stood in this weather over an hour while frost formed on their bodies. People collapsed and died. But the diabolical "count" continued.

Moshe felt himself freezing into a pillar of ice that was about to topple over.

> Suddenly he felt the Rabbi of Bobov, Rabbi Ben-Zion Halberstam, supporting him. The rabbi's reassuring voice rang in his ears: "Don't fall, my young friend, don't stumble! You must survive! A Hasid must sing, a Hasid must dance; it is the secret of our survival!" The rabbi's melody was burning in his head ... but his frozen lips could not utter a single sound. Then slowly his lips began to move. A note forced its way through the colorless lips. It was followed by another and another, individual notes strung to-gether into the ... melody. Like burning coals, the tune scorched his lips and set his body aflame. One foot began to move, to free itself from its chains of frost. The ice crackled; one foot began to dance. The other foot tore itself away from the clinging ice. The snow became red as skin from the sole of Moshe's foot remained grafted to the ice. Bones, muscles, and sinews began to step in the snow, to dance to the rabbi's [tune]....

When that period of horror was over, many lay dead on the ground. Young Moshe walked away.

Years later, a rabbi himself in Monsey, New York, when he told this story of the Bobov rabbi's care from beyond the death pit, Moshe's eyes glittered with tears.

In Dr. Eliach's book there are a number of other moving stories of people rescued through after-death appearances. I leave them for you to read in that book but summarize a "miracle," as she calls it, where one of the holy dead played matchmaker.

Rabbi Israel Perlow (1869-1922) was one of the greatest Hasidic rabbis of Lithuania. Known as the Babe of Karlin-Stolin because he was a spiritual leader at the age of four, the holy rabbi died (during one of his many trips) in Frankfurt, Germany and was buried there. During the Nazi period, many Jewish cemeteries were vandalized, but his grave was never touched.

After the war a handful of Hasidic survivors from the rabbi's Karlin-Stolin area ended up in Frankfurt on their way to new lives in Israel or America. Some found comfort in prayer visits to their holy leader's grave. One day a Hasid, who had a surviving son of marriageable age, said a few Psalms at the grave.

> Then he poured out his heart before the holy grave, begging the … [rabbi] that his holiness would intercede with the Almighty so that his son would find a proper mate, befitting a pious young man. As is also customary, he wrote his son's name and his request on a piece of paper.

This scrap he folded and placed in a crevice of the tombstone. He left with renewed joy and hope that his prayer would be answered. It was. For shortly afterward, a Hasid with a surviving daughter of marriageable age came to ask the holy rabbi's intercession for the same need. Unfortunately he had no paper with him. As he realized his lack, a soft breeze blew a blank scrap to his feet. He wrote his prayer request, then noticed there was writing on the other side. He read it.

A few days later the two young people were married in a displaced persons camp.

ENDNOTES

[1] Christian examples include concentration camp survivor, Protestant Corrie ten Boom's *The Hiding Place* about her holy family's experiences, Michel Carrouge's *Le Pere Jacques: "Au Revoir Les Enfants,"* Buchenwald survivor Jacques Lusseyran's *And There Was Light,* and my own *A Man for Others* on Fr. Maximilian Kolbe.

26 ❧ It Happens to Hindus, Too

H oly rabbis are becoming a staple in mainstream Catholic publications, long-overdue recognition that Jews are, as Pope John Paul II puts it, every Christian's "spiritual elder brothers." The founders of Buddhism and Islam, too, do not raise many Christian eyebrows these days. After all, Buddha, the devout Indian spiritual-seeker who found "enlightenment" under the Bodhi tree, never claimed to be more than a man. And Islam is adamant that Mohammed is no god, but God's prophet. Such individuals may be comfortably accepted by Christians as holy. Shamanism, too, is today understood as reflecting the natural human instinct to worship and seek contact with God. In books like *The Cross and The Pipe: A Christian-Sioux Dialogue*, Catholics write of the Holy Spirit at work in shamanistic cultures — in some, clouded under rituals which insult human dignity; in others, like that of the Sioux, shaping people of noble character through devotion to a supreme being associated with light and goodness.

Formalized by recent papal writings,[1] this new understanding insists all men and women — of whatever tradition — who in life were genuine servants of God also belong to the great human communion crossing this life into the next. Still, Hindus give the average follower of Jesus pause. Odd in a way, since Hindu saints are almost interchangeable with Christian ones in their moral commands, their virtues, their devotion to prayer, and other marks of the holy. Those orange-robed Hindu monks (called swamis), for instance — when they are the genuine article[2] — follow the way of celibacy, poverty, and obedience. Even the Hindu theory of reincarnation, which Catholics do not accept, can be seen as a different conceptual way of trying to deal with a truth Catholics have long recognized: That nothing impure can withstand the light of God, and so many who die — choosing light and goodness — are still not ready for heaven.

Here I'm going to tell you about a saint from the Vedanta, or Ramakrishna, Society (both names have been used), a legitimate organization whose "tests" for holiness and moral guidelines could slip into those of Christianity — or other faiths too, for that matter — without a ripple. Their founder, Ramakrishna, has every sign of holiness of a certain contemplative type from his joy in God, his magnanimity of spirit, his horror lest he be tainted by money, his sexual renunciation and purity that regarded all women as mothers, his belief in doing penance for others' sins, and even his habit of falling — during his twenties particularly — into ecstasies that made many dismiss him as "a nut." A great ecumenist — within his theological understanding — in a country where a high caste Brahmin like himself would be "contaminated" by even touching a Moslem, Ramakrishna went so far as to try to worship for periods as a Moslem, a Christian, and in other traditions, so he might "encompass God in all His aspects."

While I am certainly not encouraging Christians to reduce the Savior to "one aspect of God," I hope you can see that, given his background that led him to interpret Christianity in quite a different way than Christians do, Ramakrishna was a wonderfully large-hearted man willing to follow God beyond his society's rigid caste system.

used by permission of the Vedanta Society of Southern California

Serada Devi

After the death of Ramakrishna, many of his younger, unmarried male disciples renounced the world to become monks in a new order called by his name (just as in Catholicism we have Dominicans and Franciscans, among others, named after their founders). Two branches grew up, one contemplative and the other active, running schools and other institutions. As did *not* happen with Dominic or Francis, but certainly did with Buddha, more and more of his followers began to worship the dead saint as a "divine incarnation." They point out that he, himself, claimed at times to either be one with, or *be*, depending upon interpretation, various deities.

Whatever Ramakrishna *meant* by his remarks (Christian mystics also speak of union with God in terms such as sanctity "has in itself the power of transforming ... man into God" [Padre Pio in a 1915 letter] [3]) obviously I don't see Ramakrishna as a god. But it seems clear he was a man whose heart's cry was "God alone!" from the "fruit" of his life: The number of his close followers who became holy monks or lay people. In his life I find no evidence the dead appeared to him, although he had many visions of God. However Sri Ramakrishna appeared many times after his death to one of his closest disciples.

While she was given a longer name at birth, this disciple was known as Serada Devi. [4] Born December 22, 1853 in Bengal, in her later years she was often affectionately called "holy mother" (a title of veneration such as Josefa Menendez's reference to her mentor Sophie Barat as "blessed mother"). Because men of her era were often against education for women, she never learned to write even her name. But this woman of great intelligence and, later, wisdom did manage to learn to read, more or less on the sly.

At the age of five, at his family's instigation (and her mother's later intense regret, then final satisfaction), she was married to Ramakrishna, who was in his early twenties. Her bridegroom, irrevocably committed to chastity and celibacy, returned soon after the ceremony to a faraway temple. There he lived, plunged into long ecstasies and other contemplative practices, giving rise to the opinion in their Bengal countryside that poor little Serada had been given in marriage by her family to a man who was insane. Perhaps in part because Ramakrishna didn't live at his parents' home, the little girl wasn't reared by her mother-in-law, as was traditional for child-brides, but by her own family.

When she was eighteen, Serada persuaded her father to deliver her to her bridegroom, who was then thirty-six. To her relief, Ramakrishna accepted her cheerfully, only asking that she not try to turn him from God.

In answer, the young woman assured her husband that she wanted him to lead her, too, to the Divine.

In a sense they lived as husband and wife, Serada caring for him when he was sick and handling various household matters, and Ramakrishna, so much older, teaching the young bride various practical skills, such as how to entertain guests tactfully, and how to season food for his highly-sensitive digestive system. In another sense, the celibate pair were fully-spiritual master and disciple, Ramakrishna teaching Serada how to meditate and find God through practices such as constant repetition of the Divine Name, while not hesitating to pour water under her door to soak her bedroll if she wasn't up by 3:00 A.M. for prayer, something a disciple will put up with, but no real wife!

Serada Devi came to her husband as a strikingly beautiful virgin of great innocence and purity (he once remarked that when they were married he prayed she would never know lust so as not to tempt him). They lived in close proximity, maintaining complete celibacy until his death in 1886 at age fifty from a painful throat cancer. Serada — a very nurturing person — would have liked children, without which an Indian woman was thought a tragic failure. She died having seen her husband's prophecy fulfilled that, if he had given her no children by blood, through him many would consider her their spiritual "mother."

In spite of that important role and her great natural abilities she became neither the spiritual leader nor practical administrator of the new sect that formed around the dead man (probably because she was a woman). Her early role instead was as maternal guide and inspiration.

When not meditating or worshipping, most of this simple woman's life passed in heroic charity and service. Up at three to pray during the earliest hours of the day — regarded by many as the best time for prayer — she retired usually at 11:00 P.M. after a day full of plain, old work — shopping, cooking, laundering — much of it done in primitive conditions (such as washing her many guests' bed linens by hand in an open water tank). Her work was not only for the disciples Ramakrishna left but — as the oldest child and only living girl — also for her family: Widowed mother, brothers, sisters-in-law, nieces, and nephews. Anyone familiar with Catholic Blessed Anna Maria Taigi (d. 1837) will recognize Serada Devi as one of that tribe of saints called to holiness by patiently bearing with nasty relatives!

In the holy Hindu's life, she was first led to God by the way of joy, through service to a spiritual teacher who treated her with great respect. In the second part of her life she won sanctity by her loving and forbearing response to brothers who hounded her for money; an insanely jealous, mentally deranged sister-in-law whom a dying brother "left" to her care; and this sister-in-law's daughter who — a few screws of her own loose —on occasion physically attacked the holy aunt who brought her up with only kindness.

While Serada Devi is also "divine" to her followers, I leave such distinctions for theologians to unravel and present this beautiful soul simply as a

Hindu saint who had many after-death experiences with her dead spiritual leader/husband.

The first appearance took place just after Ramakrishna's body was cremated the day following his death. Hindu widows, of her day at least, were not allowed to remarry no matter how young. Instead, they were supposed to turn their thoughts Godward, signing this by cutting off their long hair, no longer wearing a bright stripe on their saris, and taking off for good their earrings, bracelets, and other jewelry.

Even though she was married to a holy man, Serada Devi had not renounced jewelry. Sadly now she took off her gold earrings, her nose ring, and her necklace. All that was left were her bracelets. As she felt for the clasp of the first one, her dead husband suddenly was next to her.

Gone were the ravages of the cancer: The hand that pressed hers lovingly to prevent her undoing the clasp was vigorous and unemaciated.

"Am I dead, that you're acting like a widow?" he chided. "I've just moved from one room to another."

While she gave up the other jewelry, the bracelets — in spite of much criticism — stayed on the rest of Serada's life.

That did not mean she was frivolous. Her grief at the loss of one who was both a beloved husband and spiritual master was intense. Sometimes when she went to religious services immediately after his death, she became disoriented from the depth of her prayer mixed with an utter disinterest in life now that Ramakrishna was gone. In this period, she later said, in one of those times of disorientation, "It was the Master who brought me home, holding me by the hand."

Does she mean literally? Perhaps, for during this period the dead husband appeared to his living wife numerous times. Many of these visits seemed to be no more than husbandly solicitude — occasionally veering into bossiness — toward his much-younger wife. For instance, while traveling on a pilgrimage with some of her husband's other disciples, according to her offical biography,[5] she saw him in a visionary way:

> She was in the habit of wearing on one of her arms Sri Ramakrishna's gold amulet, which had been given him to allay the burning sensation of his body when he practised intense spiritual discipline.... In the train she lay down with her arm on the window sill, leaving the amulet exposed. The Master suddenly appeared and looking at her through the window, said "Why are you keeping the amulet that way? You may lose it." After that

vision, she took it off and kept it in a tin box with the Master's photograph.

Other times he came directly to comfort her, as she was still prone to weep for him. For instance, one time he appeared....

> ... and said: "Why are you crying so much? Here I am. Where have I gone? It is just a change from one room to another — isn't that so?"

Similar, repeated incidents of this type finally led her to accept her loss. At that point her own holiness began to blossom, as she prayed, for instance, "that she might not see other people's blemishes." From then on, when those around her tore others down, she excused herself, saying that through Ramakrishna's intercession she had gotten rid of this habit of seeing others' defects. On her deathbed many years later, she repeated "If you want peace, then do not look into anybody's faults. Look into your own...." In the same period, ecstatic prayer experiences further changed her sorrow to joy.

Even when young, Serada Devi had been noticeably patient and compassionate. But after this period — she was in her mid-thirties — these virtues of hers became magnified. Thus she welcomed, not just into her home but as her beloved spiritual children, untouchables, criminals, Moslems, and others who by the tenets of her society made her impure by their very touch.

To a limited degree she now became a spiritual leader.

> One day Sri Ramakrishna appeared before her and asked her to give Swami Yogananda[6] formal initiation [i.e. spiritual instruction in Ramakrishna's mode of meditation].... [She] thought it was a freak of her mind. She even felt embarrassed to think that people might criticize her action and say: "See, she has already started to make disciples." But the vision was repeated on each of the two days following. On the third day, she said to the Master: "I do not even speak to Yogen. How can I initiate him?"

Her dead visitor told her to take one of the women disciples who lived with her. Shy and self-effacing as she was, she still might not have done it. But Swami Yogananda also saw their dead spiritual leader, who told him he was to seek instruction from Mother. This began a new chapter in her life, and that year she experienced many visions and ecstasies, finally realizing that "the purpose of her own life" was to help "awaken people's spirituality."

Did the visits of Ramakrishna gradually peter out once his shy widow was on the road, so to speak? Perhaps. Or maybe she simply became more quiet about her spiritual life. For instance, one day she was sitting in her house with some of her nieces when she suddenly said the word "Master," which referred to her dead husband, and went into ecstasy.

After her eyes and face were sprinkled with water to bring her out of it …

> … she regained normal consciousness. [A niece] Nalini asked: "Aunt, what happened to you?" "Oh, nothing," the Mother replied. "I felt a little dizzy when I was threading your needle." Years later, referring to the incident, she said: "I was physically weak at that time and was seated on the porch at noon. Nalini and the other girls were sewing near by. It was a very hot day and the sun was bright. I suddenly noticed that Sri Ramakrishna came in through the main gate.…"

As for the ecstasy, she said modestly, even in this confidential account, "I became dizzy."

In Hinduism, too, saints' lives often intersect those of other saints. For instance, Paramahansa Yogananda[7] (1893-1952), the well-known Hindu founder of Self-Realization Fellowship in the United States and author of *Autobiography of a Yogi*, had an early spiritual guide who was a disciple of Sri Ramakrishna. Young Yogananda thought a lot of this individual, but the holy man told him that not he, but another, would be his guru.

Not too much later, after graduating by the skin of his teeth from high school — because he rarely made it to class, spending his days instead looking for God — Yogananda became a full-time disciple of another holy man called Sri Yukteswar (born May 10, 1855, in Serampore, Bengal). During the first four of his ten years with Yukteswar, Yogananda was also — at his guru's behest — an unenthusiastic college student, since the saint had already foreseen that his young disciple would travel to the west and would need a college degree for credibility.

Yukteswar was a disciple of Lahiri Mahasaya, the guru of Yogananda's devout parents. As an eight-year-old child, dying of Asiatic cholera,

Yogananda was inexplicably and instantaneously healed when his mother encouraged him to seek the intercession of her dead guru and from his photograph on the wall came "a blinding light" that enveloped the sick boy.

Lahiri (b. 1828) had, at that time, been dead about six years, having died September 26, 1895, just a few days before his sixty-seventh birthday. After his death, he appeared to several close associates, according to their reports to Yogananda [contained in Yoganandu's *Autobiography*]. If he appeared to Sri Yukteswar, the saint did not confide that fact.

One disciple, Swami Keshabananda, told Yogananda that several days before Lahiri died, Lahiri bilocated before him at the swami's distant hermitage, as he had done a number of times.

"Come at once to Banaras," he said, then vanished.

Keshabananda got up and went to his guru's home, where he was present as the Hindu saint died in an ecstatic state.

Since he was a married man, the holy Hindu was cremated (Hindu monks are usually buried). Keshabananda told Yogananda:

> The following day, at 10 o'clock in the morning, while I was still in Banaras, my room was suffused with a great light. Lo! before me stood the flesh and blood form of Lahiri Mahasaya. It looked exactly like his old body, except that it appeared younger and more radiant.

He had some words for his disciple, including that he would not leave the earth entirely, blessed him and left, leaving his disciple filled with "wondrous inspiration" and "uplifted in spirit." Years later, Keshabananda said the dead man had visited his Himilayan hermitage "many times."

Those who recall Padre Pio's trilocations — when he apparently appeared to two different people in two places at the same time — will appreciate what I am about to report next, purely as having been reported to Yogananda by the speaker. Another disciple of Lahiri Mahasaya, whom Yogananda describes as "the saintly Panchanon Bhattacharya," said:

> Here in Calcutta … at ten o'clock of the morning that followed his cremation, Lahiri Mahasaya appeared before me in living glory.

There is one more. Also about ten o'clock, but I cannot be sure this is not the day before or day after the two instances cited above, Swami Pranabananda, who was a bilocator himself, later told Yogananda:

A few days before Lahiri Mahasaya left his body, I received from him a letter that requested me to come at once to Banaras. I was unavoidably delayed, however, and could not leave at once. Just as I was preparing to leave for Banaras, about ten o'clock in the morning, I was suddenly overwhelmed with joy to see in my room the shining figure of my guru.

"Why hurry to Banaras?" Lahiri Mahasaya said smiling, "You shall find me there no longer."

As the full import of his words dawned on me, I cried out brokenheartedly, believing that I was seeing him only in a vision.

The master approached me comfortingly, "Here touch my flesh," he said. "I am living as always. Do not lament; am I not with you forever?"

In 1920, Yogananda came to the United States as a Hindu missionary, something very unusual for this many-sected religion that generally does not proselytize in this way. In 1936, like Pranabananda or Bishop Cagliero in South America (next chapter), Yogananda heard a voice summoning him to see his guru again before the latter's death. He made the trip back to India and saw Sri Yukteswar at least twice before the saint died that March. Following the funeral rites, the dead man appeared to his spiritual son various times. The first time, Yogananda prophetically knew he was dying, but did not know he was dead for sure. On a train on his way to his spiritual father, the Hindu missionary saw "a vision of Sri Yukteswar.... He was sitting very grave of countenance, with a light on each side.

" 'Is it all over?' I lifted my arms beseechingly," Yogananda writes.

"He nodded, then slowly vanished."

Yogananda arrived to find Sri Yukteswar dead. After the burial, about a month later he continues in his *Autobiography*:

I was roused from my meditation by a beatific light. Before my open and astonished eyes, the whole room was transformed into a strange world, the sunlight transmuted into supernal splendor.

Waves of rapture engulfed me as I beheld the flesh and blood form of Sri Yukteswar.

"My son," the Master spoke tenderly, on his face an angel-bewitching smile.

For the first time in my life I did not kneel at his feet in greeting [proper for one's guru], but instantly advanced to gather him hungrily in my arms. Moment of moments!

Yogananda says he poured out his regret at not having been there for the moment of his spiritual father's death. Sri Yukteswar reassured him. Some of the conversation regarding the nature of the body Yogananda clasped — ethereal to the dead saint, tangible to the live one — I have reported in chapter two. It will interest some readers that, just as St. John Bosco in the after-death visits he experienced could at times smell things, Yogananda reports, "I could detect the same faint, fragrant natural odor which had been characteristic of his body before."

The twenty-page instruction on the nature of the afterlife given by the dead saint to Yogananda during this appearance is naturally in terms of Hindu theology and will be of interest only to Hindus or those who like to compare faith views of the afterlife.

Having in the course of my research brushed against Hasidic, Islamic, Hindu, and various shamanistic reports of the afterlife, I am happy to leave scholars to sort out the differences and note contentedly to myself, "all these groups say we are created to find and end with God." Even the smallest of His "many mansions" — a Catholic one, please, but where I can wave at my friends of other persuasions — will be good enough for me.

ENDNOTES

[1] Such as John Paul II's encyclical *Redemptoris Missio*, or pp. 80-83 in his 1994 publication *Crossing the Threshold of Hope*.

[2] The West has been invaded in recent years by some orange-robed opportunists looking for money, power, and easy sexual access. These predators, some of whom have been deported, are about as truly "Hindu" as Jim Jones of Guyana massacre fame was truly "Christian."

[3] Catholic mystics also speak of Christ becoming human so that humans may become divinized or as St. Paul puts it in his famous cry "No longer Paul lives but Christ lives in me!"

[4] Devi, which literally means "goddess," is a generic title for high-caste Hindu women.

[5] Swami Nikhilandanda, *Holy Mother*, distributed by Vedanta Press, 1962.

[6] Not to be confused with Paramahansa Yogananda, the founder of the Self-Realization Fellowship.

[7] Born Mukunda Lal Ghosh, when he became a monk (a swami), he took the name Yogananda, which means "bliss (ananda) through divine union (yoga)." Paramahansa is a title of spiritual distinction, which was latter bestowed on Swami Yogananda.

27 ❧ THAT BOSCO BUNCH

Saints are like grapes. Hindu, Hasidic, or whatever, they grow in bunches — the first group of Christian saints forming out of the motley crew around Jesus Christ. Shaping up those fellows required the Savior to make any number of after-death appearances and finally drench them in His own Holy Spirit.

Thereafter, the apostles went out and formed bunches of saints of their own. If the early Church were our topic, I could write of many groups who carried each other to heaven. There is, for instance, the legend of forty Roman soldiers martyred by exposure on a frozen lake because, while loyal to the emperor, they would not *worship* him. Taunted by comrades-in-arms, who watched by enticing fires on the lake's edge, the fighting men held firm. Then one bolted for the life-giving warmth of the nearest bonfire. His weakness could have triggered a flood of others. But when the half-frozen Christian stumbled, shivering and blue-faced, to the fire, one of the soldiers there strode out upon the ice and took his place.

Was he a naturally-righteous soul, indignant at the cheap jeers toward men sentenced to die for something everyone knew had no real bearing on soldierly loyalty? Or did Christ whisper in his ear?

We know only, if such an old tradition is correct, that forty Christian soldiers marched singing onto the ice and forty bodies — perhaps including one non-Christian — were carried off. With God's help they had seen each other through.

Families make up other holy clusters. St. Bernard of Clairvaux led thirty-one friends and relatives — including his uncle and four brothers, all of them battle-tested knights — to the first Cistercian monstery[1] in 1112. Among that group and those who stayed home — but were influenced by and influenced Bernard in turn — the saint's father is today known as Venerable Tescelin, his mother as Blessed Alice, his older brother as Blessed Guy, other brothers as Blessed Gerard, Blessed Andrew, Blessed Bartholomew and Blessed Nivard, his sister as Blessed Humbeline. And these are only Bernard's blood relatives! Other saints such as, to mention only one, the English-born abbot who received the troupe, St. Stephen Harding, are also part of the same holy bunch.

More recently, the parents of St. Therese of Lisieux, Zelie (Guerin) and Louis Martin, have been named Venerable for their heroic virtue. Not only Therese, but all the Martin children, including Helene who died at five, and various extended family members, from Zelie's sister, a Visitation nun, to cousins "caught the holy contagion of virtue" (chapter nine). Less known is the Zhu family of China, persecuted — and some martyred — in the 1950s for holding out against the same old idolatry the Romans dangled before the forty soldiers — worship the state, not God. Or the recent Ledochowska family of Poland and Austria. Their uncle Miecislaus a Cardinal, three children, at least, of Count Antony Ledochowska were special souls: Vladimer, who became superior general of the Jesuits; Blessed Mary Theresa, who founded the Sisters of St. Peter Claver; and Blessed Julia, who founded an order of Ursulines.

Cities experience outbreaks of holiness. Lima, Peru, from the late 1500s through the first half of the 1600s, for instance, was known as the "city of saints." Those officially named saints by the Church from Lima in that era include St. Martin de Porres, St. Rose of Lima, St. Francis Solanus, Blessed John Massias and even the archbishop, St. Turibus. Religious orders can experience such outbreaks, too: In Los Angeles, a city little associated in most minds with heroic virtue, three Claretian priests and a Brother spurred each other to holiness, while leading many others in that direction. Effects from the lives of Father Aloysius Ellacuria, Father Thomas Matin, Father Frank Ambrosi, and Brother Salvatore Azzarello — the last two dying in the early 1990s — can still be seen in the western states where these men worked, as well as in a new men's religious order in Mexico founded by Father Aloysius.

Groups have found holiness around some Christian ideal — whether through sheer longing for a holy life, or a particular way of getting there — as St. Ignatius Loyola, who attracted six fellow students at the University of Paris. These companions introduced Ignatius' "Spiritual Exercises" to their church and began what is today the Jesuits. Three of those first seven "official" saints, members of this vibrant group, drew in others such as Peter Canisius and Francis Borgia, both also today canonized.

In the case of nineteenth and twentieth century women's orders mentioned in this book, it is usually the foundress who is singled out for beatification and/or canonization; but in every case I know, these officially-recognized saints are merely the most notable in a cluster. For instance, among the first women who joined St. Madeleine Sophie Barat in founding the Society of the Sacred Heart, pioneer missionary to the U.S. Philippine

Duchesne (1769-1852) is beatified, but a dozen others are equally holy. The same can be said of Mother Cabrini's spiritual daughters. Or the companions of St. Mary Mazzarello.

Some official saints, others never given this kind of public recognition, members of any of these groups guide and encourage each other to holiness in life. And go right on, with God's permission, doing the same after some of them are dead.

Let's look at after-death appearances in one representative bunch — or spiritual family, if you want to be more dignified. I put before you the Salesians[2] and their women's branch, the Daughters of Mary Help of Christians, co-founded by Mother Mazzarello, for a simple reason: the Salesians, unlike, say, Mother Cabrini's maddeningly reticent daughters, see a value — probably because their work is with the young, who need models — to publicizing Salesian holiness.

courtesy the Salesians

In this family everything radiates from central figure, John Bosco — the fellow who strolled, dead, into the infirmary (see the prologue), encouraging one nun and healing another. "He was a spiritual magnet," explains Blessed Louis Guanella, who as a young priest lived with Bosco for almost three years, in order to imbibe the older priest's spirit and methods before founding another religious order. "I didn't suffer as much when my parents died as I did on leaving Don Bosco," Guanella claimed, citing how much he benefited from Bosco's "example of so much virtue," as well as from the saint's direct spiritual guidance.

St. John Bosco

Guanella is echoed by thousands — yes, thousands. Don Bosco's is a huge bunch, a veritable spiritual army comprising in its largest cluster all those educated by him, or by his spiritual sons and daughters, according to his prevention system.[3] Among this group, roughly a hundred are "Servants of God;" that is, they lived such holy lives that they are under study for beatification; at least six are Venerables; several have been beatified, including past pupils Michael Rua and Philip Rinaldi, and spiritual sons Louis Orione and Guanella, and some pupils of Bosco's spiritual sons and daughters. Bosco's spiritual daughter and co-foundress, Mother Mazzarello, is canonized; as is his spiritual son, Dominic Savio; confessor, St. John Cafasso; several helpers in the saint's work for young people, such as St. Leonard Murialdo (who directed one of the saint's playground-catechetical centers for a time); and, on the fringe of this bunch, various Turin priests who joined Bosco in mutually supporting each other's apostolates, such as St. John Cottolengo, whom Bosco helped financially.[4] Enough! It's a BIG bunch — the Bosco family. Now a sampling of its after-death appearances.

Back in John Bosco's seminary days, he formed a deep spiritual friendship with classmate Louis Comollo. Louis was quite different from John: Much more introverted, mild, and otherworldly. Brawnier, earthier, great-hearted John tended to be aggressive — even somewhat of an exhibitionist — as when he challenged a professional gymnast to feats of daring in a public contest and beat him. True, John's motive was to stop the gymnast's luring people away from church services, but Louis would have tried to accomplish this solely by prayer and example! A natural leader, John gave good example, but was still struggling against a tendency to occasionally encourage certain followers to greater virtue by banging their heads together. In short, he was only on his way to becoming a saint, a robust young man who (probably unlike less vital Louis) had the capacity to enjoy fully all the good things of life; yet whose goal was to sacrifice everything else to be a father in God to young people.

John and Louis liked to spend their free hours in long, intimate conversations, while walking in the Piedmont countryside. In one of those talks John was startled when Louis confided he thought he would not live much longer.

"But are you ill?" John's handsome face was all concern.

"No, not yet." Louis explained that he felt his love for God "carrying me away" and found himself unable to resist.

John did not consider Louis a nut. Maybe from his reading on the saints he knew that some have literally died of love. At any rate, he took Louis' confidence seriously. So seriously that they did something that Bosco learned the hard way was most unwise. In their youthful enthusiasm, they agreed Louis should try to get God to send him back to tell John if he went straight to heaven.

Not long after this Louis Comollo caught some trifling illness and died, to the surprise of everyone except John. Picking up Bosco's own account:

> It was the night between April 3 and 4, the night after his burial. I was sleeping with twenty other theology students in the south dormitory facing the courtyard. I was in bed but not asleep, and I was thinking about our promise. Almost as though I had a premonition of what was about to take place, I was strangely afraid.
>
> At the stroke of midnight, I heard a dull sound at the end of the corridor. As it drew nearer, it became sharper, more lugubrious and louder. It sounded [successively] like the rumble of a heavy cart drawn by many horses, a railroad train, or like the boom of a cannon. I cannot adequately describe it except as a composite crashing sound so vibrant[5] and, somehow, so violent that it terrified and rendered me speechless. As it drew closer to our dormitory door, the very walls, ceiling and floor of the corridor re-echoed as with the roar of crashing steel slabs being shaken with great force. And yet the rumble gave no clue as to where it came from. It was like trying to pinpoint the position of a locomotive by the trail of smoke it leaves in the air.
>
> All in the dormitory were startled but nobody dared say a word. I was petrified. The din was getting closer and ever more frightening, but still it sounded outside the dormitory. Then the door was flung open, the roar grew in intensity, and a slim, flickering multicolored light, which seemed to modulate with the sound, pierced the darkness. Abruptly all noise ceased, the light flared more brilliantly and Comollo's voice was clearly heard. It was more frail than it had been when he was alive. Three times in succession he called out: "Bosco! Bosco! Bosco! I'm saved!"
>
> At that very moment a light flooded the entire dormitory and the sounds which had ceased were again heard ever louder. It was almost as though a thunderbolt had struck the house and it was collapsing. Immediately again all noise ceased and the light vanished. My fellow seminarians leaped out of bed and fled wildly in all

directions. A number huddled together in a corner of the room to boost their courage. Others grouped themselves around the dormitory prefect, Father Joseph Fiorito of Rivoli. They spent the night this way, eagerly awaiting dawn. All had heard the noise; several heard the voice, but not the words themselves. They kept asking one other what the noise and the voice could have meant. Sitting on my bed, I told them to calm down, assuring them that I had clearly heard the words, "I am saved." A number had heard the voice directly above my head and this became the accepted version at the seminary for a long time afterward.

I was so shaken and frightened that, at the moment, I would rather have died. As far as I can remember, this was the first time that I really was afraid. This too was the beginning of an illness that brought me to the edge of the grave and left me in such weak health that I did not fully recover until many years later....

Bosco later wrote a biography of Louis Comollo which he had read and corrected regarding this unforgettable event by those there that night; so the account rests not just on his say-so. That is certainly important, since John seems to have suffered a mild nervous breakdown, which could suggest that the experience was a momentary psychotic episode, rather than objective reality. With these other witnesses, that "explanation" must be set aside. Why did Comollo's return shake Bosco so? The saint's own comment was "whenever we attempt to breach the supernatural, especially when it is unnecessary for our eternal salvation, we are bound to suffer ... [unpleasant] consequences." In that view, we can theorize — obviously no one reads God's mind! — that one reason God let Louis return was to scare the pants off his friend, so he'd realize that such visits are to be initiated by God, not by "pacts" between buddies.

Years later, as a full-fledged saint, Bosco frequently spoke to the dead who came to his slum room to guide and encourage his backbreaking labors as "the friend of poor kids." For instance, as a young priest living — with his widowed mother to protect his reputation — in rented rooms next to a brothel and tavern, John received another visit from Louis Comollo.

We know this because his mother just had to tell someone about a very strange experience, and bent the ear of a kid named James Bellia. Mama Margaret, as the boys called her with affection, confided to James that she woke once an hour or two before dawn, and heard her son talking to someone in his room. At times he seemed to reply to questions. At other times he asked them. She strained to listen but could catch no words. The front door, she knew, was secured. Nor would John bring visitors traipsing through their small quarters in the middle of the night. Eventually the conversation ceased. When her son opened his door sometime later, his mother peeked in and observed that the closet-less room had no one else in it. Margaret, like her son's slum kids, felt an awe about that almost bare bedroom-study with its plain iron bedstead, sensing that extraordinary things went on in there. The boys knew if they asked for particulars, their big buddy would detour the conversation with a joke or pleasantry. Margaret tried not to be inquisitive too. But this morning she could not contain herself. Looking her son squarely in the face, she said, "Who did I hear you talking to last night?"

Saints keep a low profile in a world only too quick to credit them for God's work. Still it was Margaret — widowed when this youngest son was only two — who set John firmly on the path to God and taught him most of his wise educational system.

To her he said simply, "That was Louis Comollo."

"But he's dead," she protested. "He's been dead for *years*!"

"Yes," her son admitted, "but I was still talking to him."

End conversation. But her mother's eye observed that, however matter-of-factly her son spoke, his face was flushed, his eyes glittering. For the next few days, he was somewhat abstracted, almost "distraught," with emotion he kept to himself.

As the years went on, for their spiritual benefit, Don Bosco began to narrate to his youngsters and his first crop of homegrown adult spiritual sons what he called "dreams," but which he privately admitted to some of the older group were "much more." Even to the boys at times he made offhand, equivocal remarks such as "as you know, dreams come in one's sleep. So during the night hours ... while I was in my room — whether reading or pacing back and forth or resting in bed, I am not sure — I began dreaming." These experiences which often, but not always, took place in symbolic images and language like certain Biblical parables, always had a guide. Sometimes this was Jesus or His mother. Those instances Bosco would humbly cover up by saying something like "a distinguished man" instead of "Jesus."

But many guides were dead people he had known well. Louis Colle, for instance, was the saintly young son of a family that was very generous to Don Bosco's works. After dying a holy death, this youth, Bosco's intimates testified, "used to appear to Don Bosco to reveal secret things to him." It was Louis Colle and angels who guided Don Bosco through one of his great prophetic visions (narrated by the saint in 1885 to encourage some of his closest associates). That night, Louis and the angels showed Bosco the future of his little band of Salesians, revealing they would work — as they do — in places such as Australia, the center of Africa, and the Middle East. In another visit in 1883, Louis Colle took Don Bosco on a mystical visit to all the South American tribes his sons would serve, the "travelers" sitting peacefully under a tree with cannibals. Such visits assisted Don Bosco in planning for the future.

At other times Louis Colle's visits, it appears, were much more personal matters, such as to encourage his parents, who as "Cooperators" — lay people involved in the Salesians' ministries — were also part of Bosco's spiritual family. For instance on the day Louis died in 1881, while Don Bosco was hearing confessions he had what he called "a distraction." Actually a momentary vision, he saw Louis "in a very beautiful garden" enjoying himself with other boys. With this image came the ineffable assurance that Louis was happily in heaven, a consolation he passed on to the young man's family.

On May 27, 1881, as Don Bosco was saying Mass for the Colles, Louis appeared to the priest at the Consecration and later again, "bathed in light, beautiful ... (radiating) joy and well-being." Following the service, the dead youth appeared a third time in the sacristy where Don Bosco was saying some prayers of thanksgiving. With him this time were several other of Bosco's dead boys. The dialogue between the holy priest and his boys is unknown, but we do know Don Bosco asked Louis' advice on how to console the Colle family.

Among Louis' answers was to encourage them to "make friends with the Blessed," that is, I take it, with the saints in heaven. When Louis appeared a month later on June 21, he spoke of how St. Aloysius — a Catholic patron of youth — "has been a good friend" to him. Whether he meant in life or in heaven is unclear from the context.

Because in other visits the dead boy says how much he loves his parents and how he prays for and is "waiting" for them, one day Bosco groused, "Why don't you let your parents see you? They love you so much."

"Yes, I know they love me," the dead boy answered, "but the permission of God is needed for them to see me. If I spoke to them, my words would not have the same efficacy as when they are relayed through you." Does he mean they might become troubled about whether they were hallucinating? Possibly. People who know their grief makes them vulnerable might well trust a saint's experiences more than their own.

Bosco did not accept seeing Louis credulously. He pondered and undoubtedly sought guidance. Finally he wrote to the boy's mother:

> When I reflect upon these appearances and *study them through and through* [italics mine], I feel that they are not at all tricks of the imagination, but real. All that I see in them is clearly in conformity with the Spirit of God. Undoubtedly, Louis is in heaven. As far as the frequency of these visions [Note: they were occurring often] I do not know what God has in mind. I only know that Louis advises me and teaches me things I did not know about Theology and science.

Some of Louis' teachings the saint jotted down (always from memory, naturally, since he did not write while the experience unfolded) and some were recorded by spiritual sons to whom he narrated what took place. Too long to give in full, I extract a bit of dialogue from one example:

> "Are you happy, Louis?"
> "Very!"
> "Are you dead or alive?"
> "My body is dead, but I am alive!"
> "Isn't it your body that I see?"
> "No."
> "Your soul, then?"
> "No."
> "Your spirit?"
> "No."
> "Then what am I looking at?"
> "Just an apparition."
> "How can an apparition speak?"
> "Through God's power."
> "Where is your soul, then?"
> "It stands before God and in Him. Your eyes cannot see it."
> "How do you see us?"
> "We see all things in God — the past, the present, the future — as though in a mirror."
> "What do you do in heaven?"
> "I give thanks always to God — to Him who created me; to Him who is master of life and death; to Him who is the beginning and end of all. Thanks! Praises! Alleluia!"

(Contrast Louis' role to that of St. Therese of Lisieux, who seems to have a different role than continual praise; the reader may find new meaning in the term "many mansions" — or Catholic, Jewish, and Hindu saints' references to "levels" of Heaven.)

Louis taught the saint science, Bosco said. Quoting again from *Dreams, Visions, & Prophecies of Don Bosco*:

> During Don Bosco's journey to France in 1883, Louis appeared to him many times. On March 4 ... he accompanied Don Bosco by train from Cannes to Toulon and discoursed in Latin on the wonderful works of God. He even turned his attention to the skies and gave him some facts of astronomy that the saint never knew before. He told Don Bosco: "If you were to go by express from earth to the sun, you would reach it after 350 years! And to cross the sun's face you would need just as long a time. Each nebula out there is 50 million times larger than our sun, and its light needs 10 million years to reach us."
>
> When Louis kept giving him these astronomical figures, Don Bosco cried: "Enough, Louis, enough! My poor mind cannot keep up with you."

"And yet this is only the beginning of God's greatness," Louis replied.

Louis showed up in people's homes, too, like the time Don Bosco was invited to a fancy dinner in the luxurious home of a benefactor. Aware of how those who start out to help others can be corrupted by acquiring the tastes of the rich who want to help them, Don Bosco was extremely abstemious in a quiet way. So I find it surprising that at this banquet, when Bosco met Louis in a hallway, the boy complained, "Such rich foods! Too much money is spent (on this sort of thing), when there are so many hungry people in the world. You must fight excess in eating and drinking." It seems impossible that Louis was admonishing Bosco for himself. And I can't imagine the charitable priest passing on this message to his hosts! I conclude it was for Bosco's Salesians-in-training, whom the saint later warned, citing Louis, against becoming attached to fine foods or drink, since this seemingly harmless indulgence, he believed, would erode their vow of poverty.

While generally Don Bosco *saw* Louis Colle, at least once he came to Bosco only as a "felt presence" I quote:

One day while preparing a sermon, Don Bosco felt as if someone was standing near him. He looked to the left, but the presence
seemed to pass to the right; he looked to the right, but the presence
passed to the left. It all took place in an instant. He demanded to
know who was there, and heard the reply: "You do not know me?"
"Oh Louis!" exclaimed Don Bosco....

Margaret Bosco guided her fatherless son toward becoming a saint primarily by her example. Among the thousands of youngsters he befriended
in his boarding facilities, trade schools, workshops, and playgrounds, John
found a number of spiritual sons, who in turn modeled on the priest who
cooked for them, tailored clothes for them, played with them, tutored them,
and formed their souls. Thousands of "Bosco's boys" became devout priests
— in the Salesians, in other orders, and at least twenty-five-hundred in the
diocesan priesthood. Many more thousands grew into good family men.
And some of those he helped in one way or another died as boys or teenag-
ers. From this latter group, God also sent various individuals to show the
saint what he should do next, what the future held for him, and the precise
state of soul of each youth under his charge (so he could help those ame-
nable to change). In one vision, two boys — the saint later identified one as
a past pupil named Valfre — were his guides. And in another six boys, now
in heaven, returned in celestially-white garments to enlighten Bosco as to
the spiritual condition of his charges of the moment.

Among Bosco's boarding-school boys who returned after death is St.
Dominic Savio (1842-1857). His goal "to become a saint," under Don
Bosco's tutelage, when Savio died at fifteen, there was no difficulty establishing the teenager's virtues were heroic. In 1876 in a "visit" lasting much
of the night, Dominic let his onetime mentor see that the next decade would
be a tough one for Bosco, predicted developments in the Salesian order,
and revealed the future of some individuals. Odd as it may sound, the dead
saint even showed Bosco lists of all the boys in his care — and some the
youth apostle didn't know yet, but would meet later — divided into three
groups on the basis of their spiritual condition. When this moving experience with his dead spiritual son was over, Don Bosco immediately grabbed
his pen and wrote down as many as he could recall of the predictions made
during that long night so he could see, as time passed, if these things really
occurred. Everything proved accurate, even to the dates of eight boys' deaths,
none of whom were anywhere near dying at that date.

Dominic's blood father, a country blacksmith brimming with goodness, also had a profound influence on his son. Even though he had many children, in his last years Charles Savio chose to live with Don Bosco, and thus is part of the extended Salesian family. It was to his dad that Dominic made his first after-death appearance:

> About a month after Dominic's death, Charles Savio lay in bed one night unable to sleep. The memory of his son for some reason or other, was particularly vivid to him that night. As he stared at the gray ceiling, he gradually grew aware of something odd. The ceiling above him began to glow, dimly at first, and then brightly. Finally it became a circle of light and in the center of the light appeared Dominic, radiant and smiling.
>
> "Dominic! Dominic!" cried Charles. "Where are you? Where are you? Are you in heaven?"
>
> "Yes, Dad, I'm in heaven."
>
> Immediately Charles Savio begged Dominic to pray for his brothers and sisters that they might go to heaven too. Dominic said he would. Charles asked his dead son to pray for his parents. Again Dominic said he would. Then the radiant teenager disappeared, the light faded, and the ceiling went back to its ordinary gray.

Years later when the elder Savio was living with Don Bosco, the saint many times questioned Dominic's father about this, as did others. Always the devout blacksmith maintained that he was not asleep when Dominic came to him; furthermore, he insisted he was so stirred that he was unable to fall asleep "for a long while afterward." He had never had any experience like that before — asleep or awake — and even though he would have loved to see Dominic again, it never happened.

In 1935, when Don Bosco and Charles Savio were long dead, a Salesian nun, Eusebia Palomino (chapter fourteen), lay near death in Valverde del Camino, a village in the mountains of Spain's southern Andalusia region. Unknown to the world, she was venerated by those who had contact with her as a holy woman with extraordinary charisms. Now, after those at her bedside thought her dead, Sister Eusebia revived unexpectedly. She said she had seen Dominic Savio. Dominic at this time, you understand, was dead almost eighty years in another country, and neither beatified nor canonized. More about Sister Eusebia later.

The following year, also in Spain, Consuela Adelantado, a little girl studying with Salesian sisters, double-fractured her left elbow, with dislocated bone splinters, as the translated report rather awkwardly puts it. Twenty-one days after the accident the elbow still showed no signs of healing.

Then she had a dream.

A priest she did not know came to her and told her to make a novena for the prayers of Dominic Savio. If she had Dominic praying for her, the priest assured her, she would be playing the piano again by the following Friday.

Consuela's family, not overly religious, were quite skeptical. But when she told the dream to her Salesian teachers, they were interested. Curious as to who this priest that appeared in the child's dream might have been, the nuns showed her a picture of St. John Bosco.

Consuela shook her head, "No, not him."

Scurrying about, the nuns dug up photos of other Salesian priests. Consuela kept nodding "no." Finally someone showed the school girl a picture of Don Bosco's onetime pupil, and Dominic Savio's boarding-school pal, John Cagliero.

"That's him!"

This caused a mild hubbub among the sisters, for dead Cagliero, a missionary leader and the first Salesian Cardinal, had been very closely associated during his lifetime with the Salesians' women's branch. He had also worked hard to push along the beatification of his old school chum, Dominic, but died with that task still unaccomplished.

Quite excited, sisters and student began the novena.

The dead Salesian Cardinal had promised that Consuela would play the piano Friday. Thursday night — seven days into the novena — the Salesian infirmarian looking after the little girl began trying to "push" the miracle. (Maybe she felt Consuela would lose faith in God if not healed "on time.")

If you've ever been to a healing service you may have seen this sort of thing — someone so determined that another be healed immediately that, unable to leave it to God, they get into the act themselves, ripping away crutches and ordering someone to walk, only to usually cause the individual to crumple to the floor. It's sad, but also comical because of the implication one can order God around this way.

In this case the infirmarian was still working on Consuela — who was equally fired up — at three o'clock Friday morning. A Salesian writing from original testimonies says, "the only result of their labors was a red and dangerously swollen arm, and great pain."

At 4:00 A.M., worn out and sobbing in her pain, Consuela pleaded with Dominic Savio to do what the Cardinal said he would do. In answer a huge invisible weight seemed to fall from her arm. She raised it. No pain. She examined it under light: no more wound, no swelling, — nothing but a perfectly normal arm.

In her joy the school girl kept swinging and moving her elbow until 6:30, when she went to Mass. That same day she was indeed — no thanks to the poor, frenzied infirmarian — playing the piano.

Comparing before and after x-ray photos of her arm, medical men agreed the healing was "instantaneous, complete and perfect," a cure accepted by the Church for Dominic's beatification. So what Cardinal Cagliero could not accomplish for his fellow Salesian and boyhood friend as a prince of the Church, he managed to pull off as a humble messenger from heaven.

With Don Bosco my starting point, I have worked down three generations. But Bosco was helped along by those before him as well. A number of those individuals, too, God sent back to guide or encourage the youth worker. We know, for instance, that six years after her death, Bosco's saintly mother, Margaret, was part of a guiding vision he had one night. Another time — in August, 1860 — Margaret came to her son in a more personal way. In this dream or vision, he seemed to be walking near the shrine of Our Lady of Consolation in Turin, the North Italian city which was his headquarters. Suddenly he met his mother, who looked beautiful.

"But aren't you dead?" he gasped.

"I died but I'm alive."

The son asked if she were happy and was assured she was very happy. After asking her questions about various boys who had died and herself, Don Bosco begged, "Tell me what it is you enjoy in heaven."

The dead woman protested that she could not explain, a statement similar to that of many saints. (The revived Sister Eusebia Palomino, pressed to explain her experience of heaven, said in exasperation, "If St. Paul couldn't do it, how can I?")

"Well just give me an idea of it — a glimmer," Margaret Bosco's middle-aged son wheedled his mother.

In life, every time John found a few bucks, with which Mama Margaret could replace her threadbare dress, she took it willingly, *promised* she would get herself "something nice" — and promptly spent the money on some needy boy. Now she appeared in heavenly glory garbed in magnificent robes no money can buy.

> ... She began to sing a song of love to God that was indescribably sweet and went straight to the heart, filling it and carrying it away with love. It sounded as if a thousand voices and a thousand tones — from the deepest bass to the highest soprano — had all been blended together masterfully, delicately, and harmoniously to form one single voice, notwithstanding the variety of tones and the pitch of the voices ranging from loud to the barely perceptible. Don Bosco was so enchanted ... he was out of his senses and ... no longer able to tell or ask his mother anything.
>
> When Mama Margaret (ended her song) ... she turned to him and said: "I'll be waiting for you. You and I must always be together."[6]

Then she was gone.

Can an after-death appearance mix with a real dream? If it can, St. John Cafasso, Turin's apostle to condemned prisoners and Bosco's confessor, may have appeared to the saint in December, 1860, after Cafasso's death on June 23. At least Bosco is clear he saw Father Cafasso in one of his "dreams," but two others were also there — one dead and the other a living nobleman, who later died as a holy Salesian priest. All I can say is that thinking of this, and all after-death appearances involving dreams — even with saints as extraordinary as Bosco — it is safest not to make overmuch of what may well be, after all, merely a striking, but normal, dream.

To further keep Bosco's visitations from the after-world in context, I add that, in addition to visits from members of the extended Salesian family, Don Bosco received many visits from Jesus and/or Mary, and a few from non-Salesian saints, such as Peter and Paul. For instance: Three Roman soldiers named Solutor, Adventor, and Octavius came to him in what was either a dream or a vision early in Bosco's Turin ministry, when the young priest with his boisterous troupes of slum kids was regarded as a troublemaker or a nut. The three dead saints pointed out the field on the city outskirts where they had been martyred under the Romans. There the Virgin Mary joined them, indicating that on this site Bosco would build a church, and offering encouraging details of the future. All came true, although those few people the penniless, harassed Bosco confided in at the time shook their heads and murmured "poor Don Bosco — he's gone round the bend."

"Come to heaven with me," Bosco whispered in many a tough slum-boy's ear. Even gang leaders proved open to that invitation because of the genuine love in the words as much as because he could outrun them, out-play them, outwit them, and smilingly hammer a nail into the wall with his bare hand to impress even the dimmest that here was a *man*. In his lifetime Bosco turned thousands of lives in new directions, at the cost of great opposition, attack, and labor so arduous that occasionally he simply fell asleep standing up. "We'll rest in heaven," he often encouraged his over-tasked helpers. And Bosco certainly has not made the number of after-death appearances of someone like Therese, who wanted to "work 'till the end of time." But Don Bosco has at times interrupted his heroically-earned rest to come as God's messenger to members of his spiritual family. Betania, Venezuela visionary Maria Esperanza says it was he who told her when she'd meet her husband. I'm guessing Don Bosco also appeared to his "right hand" man and first successor, Blessed Michael Rua. But in Rua we have a saint so self-effacing he wouldn't even sleep in Don Bosco's bed after he inherited his mentor's room, but bedded down on a kind of couch instead. No use looking to Rua for any testimonies. A good reminder, actually, that all the after-death appearances to saints we know about are only "the tip of an iceberg" hidden in God's depths.

Fortunately there are cures. People who are cured will almost always give you most of the details. From the healing of Sister Giovanna, we know of Bosco's two visits to Sister Teresa Valse-Pantellini. In addition Don Bosco appeared twice in numinous dreams to a nun, unquestionably dying in 1938 of a duodenal ulcer, announcing her cure. Those bending over her bed shook their heads, since even as she gasped out Don Bosco's promise of a cure, she was in the throes of death. But cured she was, with a sudden great shudder, as if her body were hit by lightning.

As Spain in the middle 1930s edged toward civil war, the Salesians' fourth successor to Don Bosco, Blessed Philip Rinaldi, recalled what Don Bosco had told him fifty years earlier: Much blood would be shed in that country after Bosco's death — some of it Salesian. Was it the dead Bosco who told Sister Eusebia? No one knows. But she knew all about the horrors to come — even that her close friend, Sister Carmen, would be martyred, and that Valverde, where they worked, would be attacked. When the Salesian sisters quaked as they hid out the first time, Sister Eusebia soothed them "nothing will happen *this* time." But seeing what was coming, with her confessor's permission, she quietly offered God her life[7] for the country.

When she made her sacrificial vow, Don Bosco (who apparently appeared to Eusebia at least one other time), came to her one night accompanied by Michael Rua. Rua — the reticent miracle worker with the wry little smile — had a paper in his hand, which he presented to Don Bosco. This was probably the offering of Eusebia. Then the two dead leaders of her order discussed in front of the humble little cook whether what she was doing was in keeping with the Salesian spirit. In the end they concluded that Sister Eusebia was doing "the will of God," comforting the nun that she was on the right path.[8]

When Eusebia died on February 10, 1935, having seen Dominic Savio, the Virgin Mary, and Jesus during her final days, her death left her mother, Juana Yenes — whose entire family was now dead — alone and penniless, with a young grandson to rear. Eusebia, who as a child used to wander begging with her father at certain periods in order to leave what little there was to eat at home for her mother and sisters, always felt great compassion for the sufferings of her mother's bare-bones poverty. The Salesians tried to help Juana, but for a period they themselves fled the country, hid, or were slaughtered.

In the early 1940s the Civil War was over but not Juana Yenes' troubles. A cancerous growth on the left side of her neck, for three years just a lump, now became an oozing wound with ugly black spots and rootlike branches. With it came acute pain and "unbearable" nausea. Medical men said they could operate, but the cancer

courtesy the Salesians

Blessed Michael Rua

would still never heal — she would suffer from it the rest of her life. Juana turned to her dead daughter's prayers. Eusebia must have been just waiting to be asked, for her mother's growth disappeared so suddenly and so completely that her physician, Dr. Luis Escalda Gutierrez of Eusebia's native Cantalpino, offered to certify a medically-inexplicable cure.

After another ten or eleven years Juana died. The elderly peasant's emaciated, work-drained body was laid out by neighbors in the black dress and apron of Spanish village women. There was no coffin. The body of the impoverished old woman simply lay on the floor of her miserable quarters and the neighbors knelt around it to say the rosary. When dark came they closed Juana's rickety door and went home. In the morning they came again before the funeral. Someone else had been there. The pleats of the threadbare dress were now perfect, the apron spread more widely, and beautiful red roses — like those the rich send each other — were arranged all around the old woman's body.

Some Salesians believe Sister Eusebia, who loved red roses, had been there. Maybe not. But in little Cantalpino no one has ever discovered who decked out the dead saint's mother.

courtesy The Daughters of Mary Help of Christians

Back in 1887 in South America, missionary Bishop John Cagliero lay recuperating from broken ribs when a supernatural voice told him to get up and go assist Don Bosco on his deathbed. The young Bishop painfully straddled a mule to the coast, hobbled aboard a ship and traveled to Turin in time to comfort his spiritual father, as Bosco had so often comforted impetuous John. With Cagliero came thirty-four-year-old Sister Angela Vallese. Angela had been only twenty-three on No-

Mother Mary Mazzarello

vember 14, 1877, when, at the command of St. Mary Mazzarello, she led the first group of six Salesian nuns to Uruquay, then into Patagonia. Don Bosco died on January 31, 1888. That November Angela headed the third Salesian women's expedition to Tierra del Fuego, a bleak, lawless area at the remote southernmost tip of Chile. Another twenty-five hard years and in 1913 Sister Angela made the arduous trip to Italy again to attend a council of Salesian leaders. To her disappointment, her superiors cancelled her return to Chile. She proved their assessment of her condition correct by dying the next August 17. Angela Vallese, too, then appeared to a number of people. I can mention here only the experience of Salesian Monsignor Joseph Fagnano.

> While he was on board ship in the latter half of February, 1916 on his way from Ushuaia, the southernmost city in the world, to Punta Arenas, he saw before him a vision of Angela surrounded by a great light. She made several predictions to him about the Mission and when she had finished, she exclaimed, "Oh blessed Tierra del Fuego!"

Less holy than Angela, but still a noteworthy individual in the generation that clustered around St. John Bosco and St. Mary Mazzarello, was Sister Louise Arecco of Mornese, Italy. Remember how Louise at her death came to Mother Mazzarello before it was known that Louise was dead. The "visit" was reciprocal — that is, via bilocation, although in another town, Mary Mazzarello appeared to Sister Louise when the younger nun cried out during her last illness for her spiritual mother.[9]

Louise also made a second after-death appearance to Mary. On this occasion Mary was traveling with Father Cagliero in Italy. Not feeling well, she lay down for a rest, only to hear someone groan. Thinking it was a another sister who was also ill, she drew back the curtain that gave her bed some privacy, only to see Sister Louise.

Carefully she explained later that Louise was not exactly "in the flesh," but that there was no doubt it was she. Like the true mother she had always been to Louise (who came from a messy background), Mary immediately questioned her spiritual daughter as to whether she was saved, how much spiritual work she had left to do before she could enter heaven, etc. Satisfied that Louise would be done with her purgation by the coming Easter, the foundress of the Salesian sisters quizzed Louise, "Tell me what in me works against the glory of God?"

Dead she may have been but Louise squirmed in front of her mentor and refused.

Mary cajoled.

Insisted.

Finally Louise told her.

Emboldened, Mary wanted to know what should be corrected in their community?

Louise was not hesitant on that one. She pointed out something that didn't seem so harmful, but was a wedge opening the nuns to worse things.

When she left, there was no more rest for Mary. Wide-awake and energized, she headed for the chapel to help Louise's after-death work with some prayers.

On the morning of February 24, 1910, Michael Rua, who first met Don Bosco when he was seven and had now for many years been head of the Salesians, confided to his associates a curious dream. Although fifty-seven years dead, Rua's saintly brother Louis — claimed by Don Bosco to be equal in sanctity to the canonized Aloysius Gonzaga — had come to Michael. Louis told his Salesian Brother that he was going to die and he had come to take him to heaven. The dream was off by six weeks — Blessed Michael Rua lived until April 6. Did Louis Rua come *that* day? If so, tight-mouthed Rua kept it to himself.

courtesy the Salesians

Rua's right-hand man, Philip Rinaldi, a late vocation gently nudged into the priesthood by Bosco — who seems to have known Philip, too, would one day head the Salesians — was a fatherly man very much like his beloved Don Bosco. A troubled young nun once told him she would not mind dying young, in order to have the much older Father Rinaldi still alive and able to help her in her last moments.

Blessed Philip Rinaldi

"Well," he smiled, "if you die before me, count on my being there. Should I go before you, then I will ask the Lord to let me come assist you just the same." And in 1925 while giving a talk, Father Rinaldi said of St. Therese's desire to spend her heaven doing good, "I, too, would like such a grace from the Lord: To do good upon earth while also in heaven. Wouldn't you?" Affable, great-hearted Father Rinaldi died December 5, 1931. He did indeed do good from heaven, obtaining during WW II what Church authorities call "a great miracle" for a nun machine-gunned in the face by enemy planes. Such favors have led to Rinaldi's beatification. As to the nun who wanted his help at her death, I can't find out what happened.

But this I do know. Where the bonds between people are woven in God — whether the dead return visibly or not — there is no breaking the life-giving connection between those in heaven and those on earth.

ENDNOTES

1. An offshoot of the Benedictines, it was more rigorous.

2. Official title of this group, which even they rarely use, is the Society of St. Francis de Sales. Bosco named his group after a saint known for his affability, kindness, and success in evangelizing those in his sphere.

3. Based on reason — rather than physical force, coercion, or manipulation — religion (especially the guidance of a loving confessor, and frequent reception of the sacraments) and, above all, kindness, particularly the rock-solid conviction by the young person that he or she is loved by those in charge, the Preventive system takes a genial approach with kids that "anything goes but sin," and fills their spare time with sports, music, and other wholesome activities in which the educators participate fully, rather than act as spectators or referees. Wholistic — holy, I could also write — the Preventive system educates children intellectually, spiritually, emotionally, and physically. It was ahead of Bosco's time, when corporal punishment was overused, and it is ahead of our own, when children receive, generally speaking, no genuine spiritual education and little assurance that their teachers — or sometimes even parents — have their best interests at heart, let alone will sacrifice themselves for them.

4. Cottolengo kept afloat a huge hostel for the sick, the aged, the retarded, and other "refuse of society."

5 This sound is also described relating to supernatural events in some Hindu sources, so it is apparently a universal phenomenon — which will add credibility to Bosco's dramatic description to some.

6 Since some readers may wonder by that last remark if Margaret was a possessive mother, I add that she was living very contentedly with another son and his family in her peaceful country village when John asked her to resettle in the grimy Turin slum to protect his reputation due to the prostitutes next door. Margaret said openly this was a great sacrifice, but she did it willingly, feeling it "God's will." Once there she gave herself up to the slum kids, mothering them as she had her own two and the stepson inherited when she married a young widower.

7 Such acts, traditional in the Church all the way back to Paul in scripture, are always done in union with Christ's sacrifice since this, Catholics believe, is what gives them their value.

8 Another night, a dead blood sister, Antonia, and their dead father, Agostino, appeared to warn the thirty-six-year-old nun that she still had a long time to suffer, a prophecy that proved true. But after her death, Valverde was saved in a way that, witnesses insist, was both "miraculous" and had Sister Eusebia's stamp on it. And until the present, Valverdeans — including members of the Salesian spiritual family — have experienced miracles attributed to the meek, smiling little nun who said on her deathbed, "I will come back and take my little walks here!"

9 Mary Mazzarello herself appeared in a dream before the telegram arrived that announced her death to her blood sister Sister Felicina (pages 172-173).

Epilogue

In writing these pages, I have dipped my pail in a mere hundred seventy-five years of the stream of time. Its living waters rush on, filled with the universe's abundant life — including after-death appearances of saints and mystics. May such visits remind us not only that there is a greater life after life but that it is God's love which makes this so and sends us His messengers.

INDEX

OF SAINTS AND MYSTICS

Mohammed 27, 289, 310
More, St. Thomas 288
Moscati, Blessed Dr. Giuseppe 79, 166
Mother Anne of Jesus, Venerable 139

N

Nazim, Shaikh 291
Neumann, St. John 28, 34, 208-213, 214-221
Neumann, Therese 33, 37, 58, 132-133, 148, 168-169, 276-280

P

Padre Pio 21-22, 28, 30, 34, 36, 39, 113-114, 131, 153-165, 166, 167, 177-178, 227-229, 288, 312, 317
Palm, Father John Baptist S.J. 114-117
Palomino, Sister Eusebia 168, 195-197, 331-332, 333, 335-337
Perlow, Rabbi Israel 309
Pius X, St. (Pope) 74-75, 149
Pochet, Robert 57
Possenti, St. Gabriel 126-128
Pranabananda, Swaimi 317-319

Q

Quetzalcoatl 294

R

Ramakrishna, Sri 310-316
Rinaldi, Blessed Philip 323, 335, 339-340
Rua, Blessed Michael 323, 335, 336, 339

S

Savio, St. Dominic 38, 323, 330-331, 336
Schervier, Blessed Mother Frances 62-67
Seelos, Father Francis Xavier 230-238, 239-242
Serenelli, Alessandro 267-271
Shalom the Seraph, Rabbi 305
St. Ambrose 118
St. Augustine 118
St. Benedict 118
St. Bernard of Clairvaux 320

Y